THE OXFORD BOOK OF

PRAYER

THE LATE George Appleton, whose ministry in the Anglican Church was wide and varied, is the author of many books, including *The Quiet Heart, The Practice of Prayer, In His Name,* and *Jerusalem Prayers.*

THE OXFORD BOOK OF PRAYER

GENERAL EDITOR
GEORGE APPLETON

OXFORD
UNIVERSITY PRESS

OXFORD
UNIVERSITY PRESS

Great Clarendon Street, Oxford OX2 6DP

Oxford University Press is a department of the University of Oxford.
It furthers the University's objective of excellence in research, scholarship,
and education by publishing worldwide in

Oxford New York

Auckland Cape Town Dar es Salaam Hong Kong Karachi
Kuala Lumpur Madrid Melbourne Mexico City Nairobi
New Delhi Shanghai Taipei Toronto

With offices in

Argentina Austria Brazil Chile Czech Republic France Greece
Guatemala Hungary Italy Japan Poland Portugal Singapore
South Korea Switzerland Thailand Turkey Ukraine Vietnam

Oxford is a registered trade mark of Oxford University Press
in the UK and in certain other countries

Published in the United States
by Oxford University Press Inc., New York

First published by Oxford University Press 1985
First issued as an Oxford University Press paperback 1968
Reissued 2002, 2009

British Library Cataloguing in Publication Data
Data available

Library of Congress Cataloging in Publication Data
Data available

Printed in Great Britain
on acid-free paper by
Clays Ltd, Elcograf S.p.A.

ISBN 978–0–19–956123–0

Preface

THE idea of producing an *Oxford Book of Prayer* in their series of 'Oxford Books' came from the Oxford University Press. An approach was made to the contemplative Community of the Sisters of the Love of God at Fairacres, Oxford, and Bishop George Appleton agreed to act as General Editor. With his wide contacts, he gathered a group of about a dozen people, representing the main Christian traditions and some from other traditions of faith. It seemed right to include some prayers from the latter, as prayer is everywhere the expression of man's basic attitude of dependence and humility towards his Creator (in whatever terms he thinks of the Power behind the universe).

The climate of today seemed favourable for such a venture: the widespread interest in meditation; the reprinting of early English mystics; the turmoil of liturgical renewal following Vatican II, and the presence in our midst of considerable numbers of people of other races and religions—all these witness to a general interest in things of the spirit.

Many hundreds of prayers were assembled, and the task of selecting and arranging was undertaken by a small group of six. An anthology is necessarily selective, and limits to the length have to be set. The result, therefore, is not comprehensive, though it is hoped that in the various sections of the book a reasonably representative selection will be found.

Generous collaborators have been: The Sisters of the Love of God; The Sisters of Stanbrook Abbey; Bishop Kallistos Ware and Fr Simeon Lash of the Orthodox Church; Canon Hugh Wybrew, for guidance in liturgical matters; Dr Sebastian Brock, Fellow of Wolfson College and University Lecturer in Syriac and Aramaic; Mrs Diana Spencer, to whom we are grateful for translating the lovely prayer to Our Lady from the Ethiopian; Mrs Freda Wint for her selection of Buddhist devotion; Dr Joseph Needham for the selection, translation, and editing of Taoist acts of devotion; Bishop Kenneth Cragg, for most generous help in the selection and translation of Muslim prayers; Rabbi Hugo Gryn, for equally generous help in the selection of Jewish prayers; Mrs Murray Rogers for advice about prayers from Raimundo Pannikar's book *The Vedic Experience*; Sister Binney of the Society of the Sacred Heart for help with the rich treasures of devotion from the Roman Catholic Church; Dr John Huxtable, for valued help and advice in prayers of the Reformers; the Revd Gordon Wakefield for his wide knowledge of Methodist devotion; Dr Horton Davies of the Department of Religion,

Princeton University, for generous advice about the Liturgies of the Free Churches; the Revd Caryl Micklem for guidance in the Church of Scotland tradition, and for prayers of his own praying; the Revd Martin Reith for suggesting Gaelic prayers; the Revd Anthony de Vere for his helpful interest; Dr A. J. Krailsheimer for valuable advice; Dr Carmen Blacker and Canon Raymond Hammer, for the selection of Japanese prayers; the Revd John Carden, for prayers of overseas Churches and from his own collection *Morning, Noon and Night*; the Revd Peter Cobb for help with the prayers of Dr Pusey; the Revd John Mbiti for his book of prayers from African religion; Mr Harmindar Singh for help with Sikh prayers; Mr Philip Hainsworth for advice about Baha'i prayers; the High Priest of the Zoroastrian Community in Great Britain.

Special gratitude is due to Mrs Diana Hanmer, the secretary of the editorial group, who has not only carried out those duties but has been a valued co-worker, untiring in the long and exacting task of producing this anthology.

Contents

CONTENTS

General Editor's Introduction

PEOPLE who study the religious life of mankind are aware of two interesting, even exciting, phenomena in this second half of the twentieth century. The first is a widespread interest in the practice of prayer and in different methods of meditation. This is not confined to Christian circles or the Western world, but is taking place in other world religions, and can be observed in the growing number of teachers of meditation from Indian, Buddhist, and Sufi traditions who have come to the West and attract many people eager for a deeper spiritual life. Here in the West the increasing list of books of prayers or books on prayer is evidence of this phenomenon, as well as the discovery of a whole tradition of contemplative prayer going back to that earliest classic of English spirituality *The Cloud of Unknowing*, and the writings of mystics like St John of the Cross and St Theresa.

Further evidence of this widespread movement can be seen in the new forms of liturgical worship that have been drawn up by the various Churches since Vatican II. It should be remembered that this liturgical movement and experiment is still in process, so that new forms and prayers have not finally proved themselves.

The second phenomenon is the revival and confident spirit of religions other than Christian. World religions are in contact with one another more than ever before, so that it is possible to learn from their faith, experience, central affirmations, ways of worship, and formal prayers. This anthology includes prayers from other faiths; in fact it might have been entitled 'Prayers of Mankind'.

The anthology was gathered together by a group of Christians of different denominations, so, understandably, the majority of the prayers included come from Christian sources. However, we have had the advantage of consultation with people of other traditions, who are practitioners of prayer and meditation. We recognize that it is as outsiders that we have chosen prayers from these other traditions. That we have not given them equal space is not because we did not desire to do so, but because we had not the experience or knowledge.

The *first* concern of those occupied with compiling the anthology has been recognition of spiritual quality. Next, on the level of human competence, was the consideration of literary quality—man's art in the service of divine gift—ranging as it does from colloquial simplicity to eloquent elaboration. Thirdly, it was asked of each prayer, Is it live for anyone who would pray? Or, at least, has it validity with allowance for differences of period and circumstance, although the idiom is no longer current? In short, does that prayer still ring true? Answers to such questions cannot but be subjective. They were answers made corporately and in sincerity.

Those who risk compiling anthologies are surely most vulnerable. Perils of collection (or omission); perils of selection (or prejudice); perils of arrangement (dullness or fanciful ingenuity), are only too obvious. And even then when all is said and done the 'unprofitable servants' know that the result can amount to no more than an attempt to bring together things old and new, treasures to be assembled with the hope of recovery, preservation, and extension of knowledge. An anthology of prayers represents an endeavour not to lose whatever seems humble, reverent, urgent, or penetrating in the effort to speak to the longings of human beings in moments of spiritual insight and so to minister to their needs.

Two special considerations are perhaps worth mention. Though saints are, by definition, people of prayer, not all spirituality leads to the composition and transmission of prayers: the correspondence is not exact. Equally, many who have been able to enrich the tradition would lay no claim to sanctity, yet for a moment each has felt the touch of the holy and hopes to touch others in turn.

Some prayers, not unlike ballads, have grown with handling and may be the better for the usage and deepened meaning of several generations. Where there was no unquestioned author or original the choice was made of the version that was judged most seemly and telling.

The compilation has taken over five years to complete, during which time more than twice as many prayers were collected as it was possible to include. The standards by which selection was made were determined by guidelines accepted in the early stages of the work: the prayers would need to be addressed to God by whatever name he might be called; they would need to be humble, creaturely, and worshipping, and warm with the spirit of love: prayers which will help other people to pray and lead them into the prayer of their own hearts and direct communion with God.

In the Free Churches devotion is expressed notably in spontaneous prayer, and obviously this cannot be dealt with in any anthology. Hymns, too, are prayers expressed in poetry and melody, and a small number of 'sung prayers' has been included from early office hymns and from Charles Wesley's prolific collection.

Prayer is essentially man standing before his God in wonder, awe, and humility; man, made in the image of God, responding to his maker. In Christian terms, this is the Holy Spirit acting within man. But God can and does break in upon a man at any moment and in any circumstances.

It is man's attitude of openness—looking, listening, and waiting—which prepares him to receive whatever God may give, and to obey. 'Morning by morning he wakens, he wakens my ear to hear as those who are taught . . . and I was not rebellious' (Isaiah 50: 4, 5).

In section V an attempt is made to collect from the Scriptures and from the lives of saintly people words which the writers in question believed to be messages from God and which speak to people today. This particular section, though short, makes the point that prayer is a relationship in which God speaks and man is ready to hear because he listens.

As the prayers included are studied and prayed some examples of cross-fertilization may be observed in areas where more than one tradition has been at work which sometimes reflect the prevailing culture and so make the prayer more relevant to life. As people of different faiths become aware of others, this tendency may grow, and prayers be adopted and adapted. For example, some of the lovely prayers of Muslim mystics may be used by Christians, or some of the devotional prayers of a modern Hindu poet, like Rabindranath Tagore. On the other hand an influence from the Hebrew Bible may be seen in some prayers from African religion, while the three Sioux Indian prayers (nos. 1069–71) show how Christians can pray in the spirit of their indigenous culture. A Christian influence may perhaps be seen in the contemporary prayers of Zoroastrian worshippers.

The compilers of this anthology recognize the debt owed to religious communities down the centuries, who have made prayer in all its aspects the priority of their lives, not desiring to escape from the world but to engage in spiritual struggle for its deepest happiness, and for the establishment of God's Kingdom and the doing of God's Will on earth as in heaven. Nor should the Ashrams in India be forgotten or the monasteries in Buddhist countries and the communities of Muslim Sufis, or our Jewish elder brothers and sisters, from whom Christians have learned to worship and pray.

When this anthology was conceived the compilers hardly realized the immensity of the task they had undertaken. After five years of labour they are almost moved to pray with the prophet Jeremiah, 'Lord, thou hast deceived me', you did not make clear the travail and labour which would be needed! With the completion of the task, all realize how imperfectly it has been done, yet they offer it to God and to their fellow men, in the hope that it will witness to the reality of God, to the spiritual nature with which he has endowed man, and will deepen the interior life of those into whose hands the book may come.

A problem was apparent in our consideration of acts of devotion from Theravāda Buddhism, whose adherents do not think in theistic or personal terms. It was agreed that any collection of world prayers should include a section on Buddhist devotion, both as a glad acknowledgement of the spiritual genius of the Buddha and also as a recognition that there is a sense of Transcendence in the concept of Dharma (Truth) as well as in the thought of Nirvana as the sphere of final blessedness, which Buddhists regard as ineffable and indescribable, much in the way that Christians regard with awe and reticence any attempt to speak of the Godhead. A similar question arose about Taoism, where the Tao (Way) is often regarded as transcendent and to some extent personal. Therefore sections of Buddhist and Tao devotion have been included, in the belief that the Transcendent Reality which Christians call God may in his wisdom and mercy have other ways of revealing himself to people of different experience, religion, and culture.

The version of the Bible from which most quotations are made is the Revised Standard Version; only in exceptional cases where the meaning seems clearer is another translation used. In the section dealing with prayers from the Psalmists, we have relied on the version used in the 1662 Book of Common Prayer, as that version seems to be the one best known in English-speaking circles and to have been accepted in literature as well as in devotion. Only the future can tell if this will continue to be so.

The inner group at the heart of this collection of prayers owes much to Peter Spicer, formerly of the Oxford University Press, for its inception, to the Reverend Mother Jane of the Sisters of the Love of God for her inspiring confidence, for her nomination of Sister Ruth and Sister Isabel Mary to be active partners in the enterprise, and for generous hospitality of welcome and refreshment during our many meetings. A further member of the editorial group has been Kathleen M. Lea, formerly Vice-Principal of Lady Margaret Hall, whose wide knowledge, critical judgement, and meticulous scholarship have been invaluable.

In conclusion, may I as General Editor express my personal gratitude to this editorial group, and also to the collaborators mentioned in the preface. A feeling of spiritual fellowship and mutual affection has developed in the course of the many consultations and appeals for information, clarification and advice. Together we offer this *Oxford Book of Prayer* to all who value the religious experience of mankind, and are seeking the Eternal Mystery and Transcendence, and who believe with us that man has a spiritual nature which is constantly seeking its Source and the creation of human society purposed by the Creator for this world and the world beyond.

Easter 1985

+ GEORGE APPLETON
GENERAL EDITOR

I

PRAYERS OF ADORATION

Introduction

Worship is the submission of all our nature to God. It is the quickening of conscience by his holiness; the nourishment of mind with his truth; the purifying of the imagination by his beauty; the opening of the heart to his love; the surrender of will to his purpose—and all of this gathered up in adoration, the most selfless emotion of which our nature is capable and therefore the chief remedy of that self-centredness which is our original sin and the source of all actual sin.

William Temple, 1881–1944

To adore . . . That means to lose oneself in the unfathomable, to plunge into the inexhaustible, to find peace in the incorruptible, to be absorbed in defined immensity, to offer oneself to the fire and the transparency, to annihilate oneself in proportion as one becomes more deliberately conscious of oneself, and to give of one's deepest to that whose depth has no end.

Teilhard de Chardin, SJ, 1881–1955

We praise thee, O God: we acknowledge thee to be the Lord. 1
All the earth doth worship thee: the Father everlasting.
To thee all Angels cry aloud: the Heavens, and all the Powers therein.
To thee Cherubim and Seraphim: continually do cry,
Holy, Holy, Holy: Lord God of Sabaoth;
Heaven and earth are full of the Majesty: of thy Glory.
The glorious company of the Apostles: praise thee.
The goodly fellowship of the Prophets: praise thee.
The noble army of Martyrs: praise thee.
The holy Church throughout all the world: doth acknowledge thee;
The Father: of an infinite Majesty;
Thine honourable, true: and only Son;
Also the Holy Ghost: the Comforter . . .

Te Deum Laudamus, BCP

O Thou Supreme! most secret and most present, most beautiful and strong! What shall I say, my God, my Life, my Holy Joy? What shall any man say when he speaks of Thee? 2

St Augustine, 354–430

3 God is what thought cannot better; God is whom thought cannot reach; God no thinking can even conceive. Without God, man can have no being, no reason, no knowledge, no good desire, naught. Thou, O God, art what thou art, transcending all.

Eric Milner-White, 1884–1964

4 O Lord my God, I behold thee in the entrance of paradise and I know not what I see, for I see naught visible. This alone, I know, that I know not what I see and can never know . . . Thou, God, who art Infinity, canst only be approached by him whose intellect is in ignorance; to wit, by him who knows himself to be ignorant of thee.

Nicolas of Cusa, 1410–64

5 Come, my Light, and illumine my darkness.
Come, my Life, and revive me from death.
Come, my Physician, and heal my wounds.
Come, Flame of divine love, and burn up the thorns of my sins, kindling
my heart with the flame of thy love.
Come, my King, sit upon the throne of my heart and reign there.
For thou alone art my King and my Lord.

St Dimitrii of Rostov, 17th century

6 O God, your immensity fills the earth and the whole universe, but the universe itself cannot contain you, much less the earth, and still less the world of my thoughts.

Yves Raguin, SJ

7 May none of God's wonderful works keep silence, night or morning. Bright stars, high mountains, the depths of the seas, sources of rushing rivers: may all these break into song as we sing to Father, Son and Holy Spirit. May all the angels in the heavens reply: Amen, Amen, Amen. Power, praise, honour, eternal glory to God, the only Giver of grace, Amen, Amen, Amen.

Anon., 3rd–6th centuries

8 O burning mountain, O chosen sun,
O perfect moon, O fathomless well,
O unattainable height, O clearness beyond measure,

O wisdom without end, O mercy without limit,
O strength beyond resistance, O crown of all majesty,
The humblest you created sings your praise.

Mechtild of Magdeburg, 1207–94

O most glorious and exalted Lord, you are glorified in the heights above 9
by ministers of fire and spirit in most holy fashion, yet in your love you wished to be glorified by mankind on earth as well, so that you might exalt our mortal race and make us like supernal beings and brothers in your dominion. Free us, Lord, in your compassion from whatever cares hinder the worship of you, and teach us to seek the kingdom and its righteousness in accordance with your holy commandments that bring life; and may we become worthy of that kingdom along with all the saints who have done your will, and may we sing your praises.

Maronite Shehimto
Syrian Orthodox Daily Office Book

King of Glorie, King of Peace, 10
I will love thee;
And that love may never cease,
I will move thee.
Thou hast granted my request,
Thou hast heard me;
Thou didst note my working breast,
Thou hast spar'd me.

Wherefore with my utmost art
I will sing thee,
And the cream of all my heart
I will bring thee.

. . . . .

Small it is, in this poor sort
To enrol thee:
E'en eternitie's too short
To extol thee.

George Herbert, 1593–1663

Glory to you, O my Lord, who created us even though there was no cause 11
for you to do so at any time; glory to you, O my Lord, who called us your living image and likeness; glory to you, my Lord, who nurtured us in

freedom as rational beings; glory to you, O just Father, whose love was pleased to fashion us; glory to you, O holy Son, who put on our flesh and saved us; glory to you, O living Spirit, who enriched us with your gifts; glory to you, O hidden nature, who revealed yourself in our manhood; glory to you, O my Lord, who brought us to the knowledge of your Godhead; glory to you, O my Lord, who made us rational instruments for your service; glory to you, O my Lord, who invited us to the exalted habitation of heaven; glory to you, O my Lord, who taught us the ordering of the heavenly beings; glory to you, O my Lord, who held us worthy to glorify you together with the angels; glory to you from every mouth, Father, Son and Holy Spirit, from those above and those below; glory to your Trinity; in both worlds glory to you, from both spiritual beings and from those in the body, from everlasting unto everlasting.

Syrian Orthodox

12 Glorious Lord Christ: the divine influence secretly diffused and active in the depths of matter, and the dazzling centre where all the innumerable fibres of the manifold meet; power as implacable as the world and as warm as life; you whose forehead is of the whiteness of snow, whose eyes are of fire, and whose feet are brighter than molten gold; you whose hands imprison the stars; you who are the first and the last, the living and the dead and the risen again; you who gather into your exuberant unity every mode of existence; it is you to whom my being cries out with a desire as vast as the universe, 'In truth you are my Lord and my God'.

Teilhard de Chardin, SJ, 1881–1955

13 Praise and glory be to the omnipotence of the eternal Father, who in his providence created the world out of nothing. Praise and glory be to the wisdom of his only-begotten Son, who redeemed the world with his blood. Praise and glory be to the loving kindness of the Holy Spirit, who enlightened the world in faith. Praise and glory be to the holy and undivided Trinity, who formed us without our deserving it in their image. We give praise and glory to you, most blessed Trinity, for the blessing of our creation, by which you granted us bodies and souls, you adorned us with your image and likeness, and added us to your Christian flock, making us sound and whole in our senses and in our members, above all the creatures who are beneath the heavens, and gave us your holy angels as our guides and ministers. For all this be pleased that we may praise you, world without end.

Latin, 15th century

O Father, give the spirit power to climb 14
To the fountain of all light, and be purified.
Break through the mists of earth, the weight of the clod,
Shine forth in splendour, Thou that art calm weather,
And quiet resting place for faithful souls.
To see Thee is the end and the beginning,
Thou carriest us, and Thou dost go before,
Thou art the journey, and the journey's end.

Boethius, *c.* 480–524

Come, my Way, my Truth, my Life: 15
Such a Way as gives us breath:
Such a Truth as ends all strife:
Such a Life as killeth death.

Come, my Light, my Feast, my Strength:
Such a Light, as shows a feast:
Such a Feast, as mends in length:
Such a Strength, as makes his guest.

Come, my Joy, my Love, my Heart:
Such a Joy, as none can move:
Such a Love, as none can part:
Such a Heart, as joys in love.

George Herbert, 1593–1633

We worship and adore you, the living Christ, 16
most fully man and fully God,
who art the fulness of all that is created . . .
We worship and adore you, the living Christ,
that in the high place of the spirit's sphere
you have manifested in flesh the Spirit's truth
that all things are created to acknowledge God . . .
We worship and adore you, the living Christ,
that you have known the fulness of the devil's power
and you have given men the grace
that in you they may be sustained
in temptation's darkest hour.

Fr Gilbert Shaw, 1886–1967

17 O God, let me rise to the edges of time and
open my life to your eternity;
let me run to the edges of space and
gaze into your immensity;
let me climb through the barriers of sound
and pass into your silence;
And then, in stillness and silence
let me adore You,
Who are Life—Light–Love—
without beginning and without end,
the Source–the Sustainer—the Restorer—
the Purifier—of all that is;
the Lover who has bound earth to heaven
by the beams of a cross;
the Healer who has renewed a dying race
by the blood of a chalice;
the God who has taken man into your glory
by the wounds of sacrifice;
God . . . God . . . God . . . Blessed be God
Let me adore you.

Sister Ruth, SLG

18 Grant to me, O Lord, to worship thee
in spirit and in truth;
to submit all my nature to thee,
that my conscience may be quickened by thy holiness,
my mind nourished by thy truth,
my imagination purified by thy beauty.
Help me to open my heart to thy love
and to surrender my will to thy purpose.
So may I lift up my heart to thee
in selfless adoration and love.
Through Jesus Christ my Lord.

G.A.

19 For ADORATION seasons change,
And order, truth, and beauty range,
Adjust, attract, and fill:
The grass the polyanthus cheques;
And polish'd porphyry reflects,
By the descending rill.

PRAYERS OF ADORATION

Rich almonds colour to the prime
For ADORATION; tendrils climb,
  And fruit-trees pledge their gems;
And Ivis, with her gorgeous vest,
Builds for her eggs her cunning nest,
  And bell-flowers bow their stems.

Now labour his reward receives,
For ADORATION counts his sheaves,
  To peace, her bounteous prince;
The nectarine his strong tint imbibes,
And apples of ten thousand tribes,
  And quick peculiar quince.

Christopher Smart, 1722–71

You, O Christ, are the kingdom of Heaven; You the land promised to the gentle; You the grazing-lands of paradise; You the hall of the celestial banquet; You the ineffable marriage-chamber; You the table set for all; You the bread of life; You the unheard-of drink; You both the urn for the water and the life-giving water; You moreover the inextinguishable lamp for each of the saints; You the garment and the crown and the One who distributes the crowns; You the joy and the rest; You the delight and the glory; You the gaiety and the mirth; and Your grace, grace of the Spirit of all sanctity, will shine like the sun in all the saints; and You, inaccessible sun, will shine in their midst and all will shine brightly to the degree of their faith, their asceticism, their hope and their love, their purification and their illumination by Your Spirit. 20

St Symeon the New Theologian, 949–1022

Praise to the Holiest in the height, 21
  And in the depth be praise;
In all his words most wonderful,
  Most sure in all his ways.

O loving wisdom of our God!
  When all was sin and shame,
A second Adam to the fight
  And to the rescue came.

O wisest love! that flesh and blood,
  Which did in Adam fail,
Should strive afresh against the foe,
  Should strive and should prevail;

And that a higher gift than grace
  Should flesh and blood refine,
God's presence and his very self,
  And essence all-divine.

O generous love! that he who smote
  In Man, for man, the foe,
The double agony in Man,
  For man, should undergo;

And in the garden secretly,
  And on the cross on high,
Should teach his brethren, and inspire
  To suffer and to die.

Praise to the Holiest in the height,
  And in the depth be praise;
In all his words most wonderful,
  Most sure in all his ways.

John Henry Newman, 1801–90

22 Blessed, praised and glorified,
Exalted, extolled and honoured,
Magnified and lauded
Be the name of the Holy One, blessed be he;
Though he be high above all the blessings and hymns,
Praises and consolations,
Which are uttered in the world;
And say ye, Amen.

Authorized Daily Prayer Book (Jewish)

23 Blessed are You, Lord our God, and God of our fathers, God of Abraham, God of Isaac, and God of Jacob, the great, the mighty, and the awesome God, God beyond, generous in love and kindness, and possessing all. He remembers the good deeds of our fathers, and therefore in love brings rescue to the generations, for such is his being. The king who helps and saves and shields. Blessed are You Lord, the shield of Abraham.

You, O Lord, are the endless power that renews life beyond death; You are the greatness that saves. You care for the living with love. You renew life beyond death with unending mercy. You support the falling, and heal the sick. You free prisoners, and keep faith with those who sleep in the dust. Who can perform such mighty deeds, and who can compare with

PRAYERS OF ADORATION

You, a king who brings death and life, and renews salvation. You are faithful to renew life beyond death. Blessed are You, Lord, who renews life beyond death.

Forms of Prayer (Jewish), 1977

Blessed are You, Lord our God, king of the universe. By his word He brings on the evening twilight; in wisdom He opens the gates of dawn, and with foresight makes times pass and seasons change. He sets the stars in their courses in the sky according to his plan. He creates day and night, turning light into darkness and darkness into light. He makes the day fade away and brings on the night, and separates day and night, for He is the Lord of the hosts of heaven. Blessed are You, Lord, who brings on the evening twilight. 24

Forms of Prayer (Jewish), 1977

Great and holy is the Lord, 25
  the holiest of holy ones for every generation.
Majesty precedes him,
  and following him is the rush of many waters.
Grace and truth surround his presence;
  truth and justice and righteousness are the foundation of his throne.
Separating light from deep darkness,
  by the knowledge of his mind he established the dawn.
When all his angels had witnessed it they sang aloud;
  for he showed them what they had not known;
Crowning the hills with fruit,
  good food for every living being.
Blessed be he who makes the earth by his power
  establishing the world in his wisdom.
In his understanding he stretched out the heavens,
  and brought forth wind from his storehouses.
He made lightning for the rain,
  and caused mists to rise from the end of the earth.

Dead Sea Scrolls

To God belongs the praise, Lord of the heavens and Lord of the earth, the Lord of all being. His is the dominion in the heavens and in the earth: He is the Almighty, the ever-wise. 26

Qur'an, Surah 45: 35

27 He is God. There is no god but He. He is the King, the holy One, the Peace, the Trustworthy, the Preserver, the Almighty, the ever-powerful, the exalted.

Glory be to God beyond all that idolaters conceive. He is God, Creator, Fashioner, Maker. His are the most excellent Names. All that is in the heavens and in the earth magnifies Him, the Almighty, the ever-wise.

Qur'an, Surah 59: 23–4

28 Praise be to God, ever unmatched in power and greatness, from and to eternity. His is the glory that excels, He the One, the only, the ever-living, the all-sufficient, the disposer who brings into being and makes to pass away, the arbiter of will who decrees and decides and determines, in whose power resides all lapsing and receding and approaching in the world of things.

He is the listener, the observer, who hides us in His grace, who surveys all that we conceal or that we disclose, the King who bestows and withholds, who brings together and who puts apart, who enriches and makes poor. He is the One who speaks the eternal word from of old which never perishes and never fades.

The thunder, the rain, the stars and the trees speak His praise, with jinn and men, with sun and moon.

In everything there is a sign of Him and in every utterance a meaning to open out the mysteries to those who apprehend, that they may hear the chorus of all created things and behold in every artefact a goodness that spurs us to take knowledge of His being and makes us zealous for His righteousness and glory, that the hearts of those who love Him should not fail of longing to encounter Him and their inner being be seized with wonder and pathos, in awe of how awesome He is.

Tahārat al-Qulūb

29 TAO

There is a Spirit which was before the heavens and the earth were.
It is the One dwelling in silence, beyond earthly forms, never changing, omnipresent, inexhaustible.
I do not know its name: but if I have to give it a name, I call it Tao, I call it the Supreme.
To go to the Supreme is a wandering, a wandering afar, and this wandering is a returning.
Man on earth is under the law of the earth. The earth is under the law of heaven. Heaven is under the law of Tao. Tao is under its own law.

BRAHMAN 30

There is a light that shines beyond all things on earth, beyond us all, beyond the heavens, beyond the highest, the very highest heavens . . . This is the light that shines in our heart.

All the universe is in truth Brahman. He is the beginning and end and life of all. As such, in silence, give unto Him adoration.

There is a spirit that is mind and life, light and truth and vast spaces. He enfolds the whole universe and in silence is loving all.

This is the Spirit that is in my heart, smaller than a grain of mustard seed, greater than the earth, greater than the heavens, greater than all these worlds.

He contains all work and desires, all perfumes and tastes.

This is the Spirit in my heart, this is Brahman.

To Him I shall come when I go beyond this life.

And to Him will come he who has faith and doubts not.

Chandogya Upanishad, 800 BC

AN EGYPTIAN KING'S HYMN TO ATON (THE SUN) 31

Creator of the germ in woman,
Maker of seed in man,
Giving life to the son in the body of his mother,
Soothing him that he may not weep,
Nurse (even) in the womb,
Giver of breath to animate every one that he maketh!
When he cometh forth from the womb . . . on the day of his birth,
Thou openest his mouth in speech,
Thou suppliest his necessities.
When the fledgling in the egg chirps in the shell
Thou givest him breath therein to preserve him alive . . .
He goeth about upon his two feet
When he hath come forth therefrom.
How manifold are thy works!
They are hidden from before us
O sole God, whose powers no other possesseth.
Thou didst create the earth according to thy heart.

Iknaton. 14th century BC

PRAYERS OF ADORATION

32 **IN PRAISE OF AHURA MAZDA**

I address myself to Thee, Ahura Mazda, to Whom all worship is due. With outstretched arms and open mind and my whole heart, I greet Thee in spirit. Turn Thy countenance towards me, dear Lord, and make my face happy and radiant.

My heart yearns for Thee with a yearning which is never stilled. Thou art my most precious possession, greater and grander, lovelier and dearer by far than the life of my body and the life of my spirit. My joy is in Thee, my refuge is in Thee, my peace is in Thee. Let me live before Thee and with Thee and in Thy sight, I humbly pray.

Zoroastrian

33 In the beginning was God,
Today is God,
Tomorrow will be God.
Who can make an image of God?
He has no body.
He is the word which comes out of your mouth.
That word! It is no more,
It is past, and still it lives!
So is God.

A Pygmy hymn

34 All you *big* things, bless the Lord
Mount Kilimanjaro and Lake Victoria
The Rift Valley and the Serengeti Plain
Fat baobabs and shady mango trees
All eucalyptus and tamarind trees
Bless the Lord
Praise and extol Him for ever and ever.

All you *tiny* things, bless the Lord
Busy black ants and hopping fleas
Wriggling tadpoles and mosquito larvae
Flying locusts and water drops
Pollen dust and tsetse flies
Millet seeds and dried dagaa
Bless the Lord
Praise and extol Him for ever and ever.

An African canticle

PRAYERS OF ADORATION

My God, Whom I worship and adore! I bear witness unto Thy unity and Thy oneness, and acknowledge Thy gifts, both in the past and in the present. Thou art the All-bountiful, the overflowing showers of Whose mercy have rained down upon high and low alike, and the splendours of Whose grace have been shed over both the obedient and the rebellious. 35

O God of mercy, before Whose door the quintessence of mercy hath bowed down, and round the sanctuary of Whose cause loving-kindness, in its inmost spirit, hath circled, we beseech Thee, entreating Thine ancient grace, and seeking Thy present favour, that Thou mayest have mercy upon all who are the manifestations of the world of being, and to deny them not the outpourings of Thy grace in Thy days.

All are but poor and needy, and Thou, verily, art the All-Possessing, the All-Subduing, the All-Powerful.

A Baha'i prayer

Day after day, O lord of my life, shall I stand before thee face to face? 36
With folded hands, O Lord of all worlds, shall I stand before thee face to face?

Under thy great sky in solitude and silence, with humble heart shall I stand before thee face to face?

In this laborious world of thine, tumultuous with toil and with struggle, among hurrying crowds shall I stand before thee face to face?

And when my work shall be done in this world, O King of kings, alone and speechless shall I stand before thee face to face?

Rabindranath Tagore

Bless the Lord, O my soul! 37
O Lord my God, thou art very great!
Thou art clothed with honour and majesty,
who coverest thyself with light as with a garment,
who hast stretched out the heavens like a tent,
who hast laid the beams of thy chambers on the waters,
who makest the clouds thy chariot,
who ridest on the wings of the wind,
who makest the winds thy messengers,
fire and flame thy ministers.

Thou didst set the earth on its foundations,
so that it should never be shaken.

Thou didst cover it with the deep as with a garment;
the waters stood above the mountains.
At thy rebuke they fled;
at the sound of thy thunder they took to flight.
The mountains rose, the valleys sank down
to the place which thou didst appoint for them.
Thou didst set a bound which they should not pass,
so that they might not again cover the earth.

Thou makest springs gush forth in the valleys;
they flow between the hills,
they give drink to every beast of the field;
the wild asses quench their thirst.
By them the birds of the air have their habitation;
they sing among the branches.
From thy lofty abode thou waterest the mountains;
the earth is satisfied with the fruit of thy work.

Thou dost cause the grass to grow for the cattle,
and plants for man to cultivate,
that he may bring forth food from the earth,
and wine to gladden the heart of man,
oil to make his face shine,
and bread to strengthen man's heart.
The trees of the Lord are watered abundantly,
the cedars of Lebanon which he planted.
In them the birds build their nests;
the stork has her home in the fir trees.
The high mountains are for the wild goats;
the rocks are a refuge for the badgers.
Thou hast made the moon to mark the seasons;
the sun knows its time for setting.
Thou makest darkness, and it is night,
when all the beasts of the forest creep forth.
The young lions roar for their prey,
seeking their food from God.
When the sun rises, they get them away
and lie down in their dens.
Man goes forth to his work
and to his labour until the evening.

Lord, how manifold are thy works!
In wisdom hast thou made them all;
the earth is full of thy creatures.

Yonder is the sea, great and wide,
which teems with things innumerable,
living things both small and great.
There go the ships,
and Leviathan which thou didst form to sport in it.

These all look to thee,
to give them their food in due season.
When thou givest to them, they gather it up;
when thou openest thy hand, they are filled with good things,
when thou hidest thy face, they are dismayed;
when thou takest away their breath, they die
and return to their dust.
When thou sendest forth thy Spirit they are created;
and thou renewest the face of the ground.

May the glory of the Lord endure for ever,
may the Lord rejoice in his works,
who looks on the earth and it trembles,
who touches the mountains and they smoke!
I will sing to the Lord as long as I live;
I will sing praise to my God while I have being.
May my meditation be pleasing to him,
for I rejoice in the Lord.
. . .
Bless the Lord, O my soul!
Praise the Lord!

Psalm 104

For the Trumpet of God is a blessed Intelligence and so are all the instruments in Heaven. 38
For God the father Almighty plays upon the Harp of stupendous magnitude and melody.
For innumerable Angels fly out at every touch and his tune is a work of creation.
For at that time malignity ceases and the devils themselves are at peace.
For this time is perceptible to man by a remarkable stillness and serenity of soul.

Christopher Smart, 1722–71

O Praise God in his holiness: praise him in the firmament of his power. 39
Praise him in his noble acts: praise him according to his excellent greatness.

PRAYERS OF ADORATION

Praise him in the sound of the trumpet: praise him upon the lute and harp.
Praise him in the cymbals and dances: praise him upon the strings and pipe.
Praise him upon the well-tuned cymbals: praise him upon the loud cymbals.
Let everything that hath breath: praise the Lord.

Psalm 150

II

PRAYERS FROM THE SCRIPTURES

Prayers of Patriarchs, Kings, and Prophets

Prayers of Abraham

FOR SODOM 40

'Wilt thou indeed destroy the righteous with the wicked? Suppose there are fifty righteous within the city; wilt thou then destroy the place and not spare it for the fifty righteous who are in it? Far be it from thee to do such a thing, to slay the righteous with the wicked, so that the righteous fare as the wicked! Far be that from thee! Shall not the Judge of all the earth do right?'

Genesis 18: 23b–25

ABOUT HIS SONS 41

Then Abraham fell on his face and laughed, and said to himself, 'Shall a child be born to a man who is a hundred years old? Shall Sarah, who is ninety years old, bear a child?' And Abraham said to God, 'O that Ishmael might live in thy sight!' God said, 'No, but Sarah your wife shall bear you a son, and you shall call his name Isaac. I will establish my covenant with him as an everlasting covenant for his descendants after him. As for Ishmael, I have heard you; behold, I will bless him and make him fruitful and multiply him exceedingly; he shall be the father of twelve princes, and I will make him a great nation. But I will establish my covenant with Isaac, whom Sarah shall bear to you at this season next year.'

Genesis 17: 17–21

GOD'S PROMISE TO ABRAHAM 42

But God said to Abraham, 'Be not displeased because of the lad and because of your slave woman; whatever Sarah says to you, do as she tells you, for through Isaac shall your descendants be named. And I will make a nation of the son of the slave woman also, because he is your offspring.'

Genesis 21: 12–13

43 *Prayers of Moses*

'See, thou sayest to me, "Bring up this people"; but thou hast not let me know whom thou wilt send with me. Yet thou hast said, "I know you by name, and you have also found favour in my sight." Now, therefore, I pray thee, if I have found favour in thy sight, show me now thy ways, that I may know thee and find favour in thy sight. Consider too that this nation is thy people.'

Exodus 33: 12–13

44 'I will sing to the Lord, for he has triumphed gloriously;
the horse and his rider he has thrown into the sea.
The Lord is my strength and my song,
and he has become my salvation;
this is my God, and I will praise him,
my father's God, and I will exalt him . . .
'Who is like thee, O Lord, among the gods?
Who is like thee, majestic in holiness,
terrible in glorious deeds, doing wonders?'

Exodus 15: 1–2, 11

45 'Alas, this people have sinned a great sin; they have made for themselves gods of gold. But now, if thou wilt, forgive their sin—and if not, blot me, I pray thee, out of thy book which thou hast written.'

Exodus 32: 31b–32

46 'If thy presence will not go with me, do not carry us up from here. For how shall it be known that I have found favour in thy sight, I and thy people? Is it not in thy going with us, so that we are distinct, I and thy people, from all other people that are upon the face of the earth?'

Exodus 33: 15–16

Israel's Prayer at Sinai

47 'All that the Lord has spoken, we will do.'

Exodus 19: 8

Two Prayers of David

'Blessed art thou, O Lord, the God of Israel our father, for ever and ever. 48
Thine, O Lord, is the greatness, and the power, and the glory, and the victory, and the majesty; for all that is in the heavens and in the earth is thine; thine is the kingdom, O Lord, and thou art exalted as head above all. Both riches and honour come from thee, and thou rulest over all. In thy hand are power and might; and in thy hand it is to make great and to give strength to all. And now we thank thee, our God, and praise thy glorious name.

'But who am I, and what is my people, that we should be able thus to offer willingly? For all things come from thee, and of thy own have we given thee.'

1 Chronicles 29: 10b–14

'The Spirit of the Lord speaks by me, 49
his word is upon my tongue.
The God of Israel has spoken,
the Rock of Israel has said to me:
When one rules justly over men,
ruling in the fear of God,
he dawns on them like the morning light,
like the sun shining forth upon a cloudless morning,
like rain that makes grass to sprout from the earth.

2 Samuel 23: 2–4

Prayers of Solomon

'And now, O Lord my God, thou hast made thy servant king in place of 50
David my father, although I am but a little child; I do not know how to go out or come in. And thy servant is in the midst of thy people whom thou hast chosen, a great people, that cannot be numbered or counted for multitude. Give thy servant therefore an understanding mind to govern thy people, that I may discern between good and evil; for who is able to govern this thy great people?'

1 Kings 3: 7–9

'But will God indeed dwell on the earth? Behold heaven and the highest 51
heaven cannot contain thee; how much less this house which I have built! Yet have regard to the prayer of thy servant and to his supplication, O

Lord my God, hearkening to the cry and to the prayer which thy servant prays before thee this day; that thy eyes may be open night and day toward this house, the place of which, thou hast said, "My name shall be there", that thou mayest hearken to the prayer which thy servant offers toward this place. And hearken thou to the supplication of thy servant and of thy people Israel, when they pray toward this place; yea, hear thou in heaven thy dwelling place; and when thou hearest, forgive.'

1 Kings 8: 27–30

Prayers attributed to Solomon

52 'For thou lovest all the things that are,
and abhorrest nothing which thou hast made:
for never wouldest thou have made any thing if thou hadst hated it.
And how could any thing have endured,
if it had not been thy will?
or been preserved, if not called by thee?
But thou sparest all: for they are thine,
O Lord, thou lover of souls.'

Wisdom 11: 24–6 (AV)

53 'For thine incorruptible spirit is in all things. Wherefore thou convictest by little and little them that fall from the right way, and putting them in remembrance by the very things wherein they sin, dost thou admonish them, that escaping from their wickedness, they may believe on thee, O Lord.'

Wisdom 12: 1–2 (RV)

54 'O God of my fathers and Lord of mercy, who hast made all things by thy word, and by thy wisdom hast formed man, to have dominion over the creatures thou hast made, and rule the world in holiness and righteousness, and pronounce judgment in uprightness of soul, give me the wisdom that sits by thy throne, and do not reject me from among thy servants . . . With thee is wisdom, who knows thy works and was present when thou didst make the world, and who understands what is pleasing in thy sight and what is right according to thy commandments. Send her forth from the holy heavens, and from the throne of thy glory send her, that she may be with me and toil, and that I may learn what is pleasing to thee. For she knows and understands all things, and she will guide me wisely in my actions and guard me with her glory. Then my works will be acceptable, and I shall judge thy people justly, and shall be worthy of the

throne of my father. For what man can learn the counsel of God? Or who can discern what the Lord wills? . . . Who has learned thy counsel, unless thou hast given wisdom and sent thy holy Spirit from on high? And thus the paths of those on earth were set right, and men were taught what pleases thee, and were saved by wisdom.'

Wisdom 9: 1–4, 8–13, 17–18

Prayers of Isaiah

'Here am I! Send me.' 55

Isaiah 6: 8

'I will give thanks to thee, O Lord, 56
for though thou wast angry with me,
thy anger turned away,
and thou didst comfort me.
Behold, God is my salvation;
I will trust, and will not be afraid;
for the Lord God is my strength and my song,
and he has become my salvation.
With joy you will draw water from
the wells of salvation. And you will say in that day:
"Give thanks to the Lord,
call upon his name;
make known his deeds among the nations,
proclaim that his name is exalted.
Sing praises to the Lord, for he has done gloriously;
let this be known in all the earth.
Shout, and sing for joy, O inhabitant of Zion,
for great in your midst is the Holy One of Israel."'

Isaiah 12: 1b–5

'We have a strong city; he sets up salvation 57
as walls and bulwarks.
Open the gates, that the righteous nation
which keeps faith may enter in.
Thou dost keep him in perfect peace,
whose mind is stayed on thee,
because he trusts in thee.
Trust in the Lord for ever,
for the Lord God is an everlasting rock.'

Isaiah 26: 1b–4

58 'The way of the righteous is level;
thou dost make smooth the path of the righteous.
In the path of thy judgments,
O Lord, we wait for thee;
thy memorial name is the desire of our soul.
My soul yearns for thee in the night,
my spirit within me earnestly seeks thee.
For when thy judgments are in the earth,
the inhabitants of the world learn righteousness . . .

'O Lord, thou wilt ordain peace for us
thou hast wrought for us all our works.
O Lord our God,
other lords besides thee have ruled over us,
but thy name alone we acknowledge.' **Isaiah 26: 7–9, 12–13**

59 'Thy dead shall live, their bodies shall rise.
O dwellers in the dust, awake and sing for joy!
For thy dew is a dew of light,
and on the land of the shades thou wilt let it fall.' **Isaiah 26: 19**

Prayers of Jeremiah

60 Now the word of the Lord came to me saying,
'Before I formed you in the womb I knew you,
and before you were born I consecrated you;
I appointed you a prophet to the nations.'
Then I said, 'Ah, Lord God! Behold, I do not know how to speak, for I am only a youth.' But the Lord said to me,
'Do not say, "I am only a youth";
for to all to whom I send you you shall go,
and whatever I command you you shall speak.
Be not afraid of them,
for I am with you to deliver you, says the Lord.' **Jeremiah 1: 4–8**

61 'Thy words were found, and I ate them,
and thy words became to me a joy
and the delight of my heart;
for I am called by thy name,
O Lord, God of hosts.' **Jeremiah 15: 16**

'Heal me, O Lord, and I shall be healed; 62
save me, and I shall be saved;
for thou art my praise.'

Jeremiah 17: 14

'O Lord, thou hast deceived me, 63
and I was deceived;
thou art stronger than I,
and thou hast prevailed.
I have become a laughing-stock all the day;
everyone mocks me.
For whenever I speak, I cry out,
I shout, "violence and destruction!"
For the word of the Lord has become for me
a reproach and derision all day long.
If I say, "I will not mention him,
or speak any more in his name",
there is in my heart as it were a burning fire
shut up in my bones,
and I am weary with holding it in,
and I cannot.'

Jeremiah 20: 7–9

Jonah's prayer

'I called to the Lord, out of my distress, 64
and he answered me;
out of the belly of Sheol I cried,
and thou didst hear my voice.
For thou didst cast me into the deep,
into the heart of the seas,
and the flood was round about me;
all thy waves and thy billows
passed over me.
Then I said, "I am cast out
from thy presence;
how shall I again look
upon thy holy temple?"
The waters closed in over me,
the deep was round about me;
weeds were wrapped about my head
at the roots of the mountains.

I went down to the land
  whose bars closed upon me for ever;
yet thou didst bring up my life from the Pit,
  O Lord my God.
When my soul fainted within me,
  I remembered the Lord;
and my prayer came to thee,
  into thy holy temple.
Those who pay regard to vain idols
  forsake their true loyalty.
But I with the voice of thanksgiving
  will sacrifice to thee;
what I have vowed I will pay.
  Deliverance belongs to the Lord!'

Jonah 2: 2–9

65 But it displeased Jonah exceedingly, and he was angry. And he prayed to the Lord and said, 'I pray thee, Lord, is not this what I said when I was yet in my country? That is why I made haste to flee to Tarshish; for I knew that thou art a gracious God and merciful, slow to anger, and abounding in steadfast love, and repentest of evil. Therefore now, O Lord, take my life from me, I beseech thee, for it is better for me to die than to live.'

Jonah 4: 1–3

Habakkuk's prayer of trust

66 'Though the fig tree do not blossom,
  nor fruit be on the vines,
the produce of the olive fail
  and the fields yield no food,
the flock be cut off from the fold
  and there be no herd in the stalls,
yet I will rejoice in the Lord,
  I will joy in the God of my salvation.'

Habakkuk 3: 17–18

A prayer of Jesus Ben-Sirach

'Have mercy, O Lord, upon the people 67
called by thy name,
upon Israel, whom thou hast likened
to a first-born son.
Have pity on the city of thy sanctuary,
Jerusalem, the place of thy rest.
Fill Zion with the celebration of thy
wondrous deeds,
and thy temple with thy glory.
Bear witness to those whom thou
didst create in the beginning,
and fulfil the prophecies spoken in thy name.
Reward those who wait for thee,
and let thy prophets be found trustworthy.
Hearken, O Lord, to the prayer of thy servants,
according to the blessing of Aaron for thy people,
and all who are on the earth will know
that thou art the Lord, the God of the ages.'

Ecclesiasticus 36: 12–17

Ezra's prayer

'Nevertheless our fathers were disobedient and rebelled against thee and 68
cast thy law behind their back and killed thy prophets, who had warned them in order to turn them back to thee, and they committed great blasphemies. Therefore thou didst give them into the hand of their enemies, who made them suffer; and in the time of their suffering they cried to thee and thou didst hear them from heaven; and according to thy great mercies thou didst give them saviours who saved them from the hand of their enemies. But after they had rest they did evil again before thee, and thou didst abandon them to the hand of their enemies, so that they had dominion over them; yet when they turned and cried to thee thou didst hear from heaven, and many times thou didst deliver them according to thy mercies. And thou didst warn them in order to turn them back to thy law. Yet they acted presumptuously and did not obey thy commandments, but sinned against thy ordinances, by the observance of which a man shall live, and turned a stubborn shoulder and stiffened their neck and would not obey. Many years thou didst bear with them, and didst warn them by thy Spirit through thy prophets; yet they would not give ear . . . Nevertheless in thy great mercies thou didst not

make an end of them or forsake them; for thou art a gracious and merciful God. Now therefore, our God, the great and mighty and terrible God, who keepest covenant and steadfast love, let not all the hardship seem little to thee that has come upon us, upon our kings, our princes, our priests, our prophets, our fathers, and all thy people, since the time of the kings of Assyria until this day. Yet thou hast been just in all that has come upon us, for thou hast dealt faithfully and we have acted wickedly; our kings, our princes, our priests and our fathers have not kept thy law or heeded thy commandments and thy warnings which thou didst give them. They did not serve thee in their kingdom, and in thy great goodness which thou gavest them, and in the large and rich land which thou didst set before them; and they did not turn from their wicked works. Behold, we are slaves this day; in the land that thou gavest to our fathers to enjoy its fruit and its good gifts, behold, we are slaves. And its rich yield goes to the kings whom thou hast set over us because of our sins; they have power also over our bodies and over our cattle at their pleasure, and we are in great distress.

Because of all this we make a firm covenant and write it, and our princes, our Levites, and our priests set their seal to it.'

Nehemiah 9: 26–38

Prayers of Job

69 JOB'S OUTBURST

'Why did I not die at birth,
  come forth from the womb and expire?
Why did the knees receive me?
  Or why the breasts, that I should suck?
For then I should have lain down and been quiet;
  I should have slept; then I should have been at rest,
with kings and counsellors of the earth
  who rebuilt ruins for themselves,
or with princes who had gold,
  who filled their houses with silver.
Or why was I not as a hidden untimely birth,
  as infants that never see the light?
There the wicked cease from troubling,
  and there the weary are at rest.
There the prisoners are at ease together;
  they hear not the voice of the taskmaster.
The small and the great are there,
  and the slave is free from his master.

'Why is light given to him that is in misery,
and life to the bitter in soul,
who long for death, but it comes not,
and dig for it more than for hid treasures;
who rejoice exceedingly,
and are glad, when they find the grave?
Why is light given to a man whose way is hid,
whom God has hedged in?
For my sighing comes as my bread,
and my groanings are poured out like water.
For the thing that I fear comes upon me,
and what I dread befalls me.
I am not at ease, nor am I quiet;
I have no rest; but trouble comes.'

Job 3: 11–26

JOB'S PENITENCE

'I know that thou canst do all things, 70
and that no purpose of thine can be thwarted.
Who is this that hides counsel without knowledge?
Therefore I have uttered what I did not understand,
things too wonderful for me, which I did not know.
Hear, and I will speak;
I will question you, and you declare to me.
I had heard of thee by the hearing of the ear,
but now my eye sees thee;
therefore I despise myself,
and repent in dust and ashes.'

Job 42: 2–6

Daniel's prayer of penitence

'O Lord, the great and terrible God, who keepest covenant and steadfast 71
love with those who love him and keep his commandments, we have sinned and done wrong and acted wickedly and rebelled, turning aside from thy commandments and ordinances; we have not listened to thy servants the prophets, who spoke in thy name to our kings, our princes, and our fathers, and to all the people of the land. To thee, O Lord, belongs righteousness, but to us confusion of face, as at this day, to the men of Judah, to the inhabitants of Jerusalem, and to all Israel, those that are near and those that are far away, in all the lands to which thou hast driven them, because of the treachery which they have committed against thee. To us, O Lord, belongs confusion of face, to our kings, to our

princes and to our fathers, because we have sinned against thee. To the Lord our God belong mercy and forgiveness; because we have rebelled against him, and have not obeyed the voice of the Lord our God by following his laws, which he set before us by his servants the prophets. All Israel has transgressed thy law and turned aside, refusing to obey thy voice. And the curse and oath which are written in the law of Moses the servant of God have been poured out upon us, because we have sinned against him . . . O my God, incline thy ear and hear; open thy eyes and behold our desolations, and the city which is called by thy name; for we do not present our supplications before thee on the ground of our righteousness, but on the ground of thy great mercy. O Lord, hear; O Lord, forgive; O Lord, give heed and act; delay not, for thy own sake, O my God, because thy city and thy people are called by thy name.'

Daniel 9: 4b–11, 18–19

The Song of the Three Young Men

72 'Bless the Lord, all works of the Lord,
sing praise to him and highly exalt him for ever . . .
Bless the Lord, you angels of the Lord,
sing praise to him and highly exalt him for ever . . .
Let the earth bless the Lord; let it sing praise to him
and highly exalt him for ever . . .
Bless the Lord, you sons of men,
sing praise to him and highly exalt him for ever.
Bless the Lord, O Israel,
sing praise to him and highly exalt him for ever.
Bless the Lord, you priests of the Lord,
sing praise to him and highly exalt him for ever.
Bless the Lord, you servants of the Lord,
sing praise to him and highly exalt him for ever.
Bless the Lord, spirits and souls of the righteous,
sing praise to him and highly exalt him for ever.
Bless the Lord, you who are holy and humble in heart,
sing praise to him and highly exalt him for ever.
Bless the Lord, Hananiah, Azariah, and Misha-el,
sing praise to him and highly exalt him for ever;
for he has rescued us from Hades and
saved us from the hand of death,
and delivered us from the midst of
the burning fiery furnace;
from the midst of the fire he has delivered us.

Give thanks to the Lord, for he is good,
for his mercy endures for ever.
Bless him, all who worship the Lord,
the God of gods,
sing praise to him and give thanks to him,
for his mercy endures for ever.'

The Song of the Three Young Men: vv. 35, 37, 52, 60–8

Prayers of the Psalmists

73 Blessed is the man that hath not walked in the counsel of the ungodly, nor stood in the way of sinners: and hath not sat in the seat of the scornful.
But his delight is in the law of the Lord: and in his law will he exercise himself day and night.
And he shall be like a tree planted by the waterside: that will bring forth his fruit in due season.

Psalm 1: 1–3

74 For with thee is the well of life: and in thy light shall we see light.

Psalm 36: 9

75 What is man that you have been mindful of him,
Mortal man that you have taken note of him,
That you have made him little less than divine
And adorned him with glory and majesty;
You have made him master over your handiwork,
Laying the world at his feet?

Psalm 8: 5–7 (from a Jewish translation)

76 Be still then, and know that I am God.

Psalm 46: 10

77 Lord, who shall dwell in thy tabernacle: or who shall rest upon thy holy hill?
Even he, that leadeth an uncorrupt life: and doeth the thing which is right, and speaketh the truth from his heart.

He that hath used no deceit in his tongue, nor done evil to his neighbour: and hath not slandered his neighbour.
He that setteth not by himself, but is lowly in his own eyes: and maketh much of them that fear the Lord.
He that sweareth unto his neighbour, and disappointeth him not: though it were to his own hindrance.
He that hath not given his money upon usury: nor taken reward against the innocent.
Whoso doeth these things: shall never fall.

Psalm 15

78 I am thine, O save me: for I have sought thy commandments.

Psalm 119: 94

79 The law of the Lord is an undefiled law, converting the soul: the testimony of the Lord is sure, and giveth wisdom unto the simple.
The statutes of the Lord are right, and rejoice the heart: the commandment of the Lord is pure, and giveth light unto the eyes.
The fear of the Lord is clean, and endureth for ever: the judgments of the Lord are true, and righteous altogether.
More to be desired are they than gold, yea, than much fine gold: sweeter also than honey, and the honey-comb.
Moreover, by them is thy servant taught: and in keeping of them there is great reward.
Who can tell how oft he offendeth: O cleanse thou me from my secret faults.
Keep thy servant also from presumptuous sins, lest they get the dominion over me: so shall I be undefiled, and innocent from the great offence.
Let the words of my mouth, and the meditation of my heart: be alway acceptable in thy sight,
O Lord: my strength, and my redeemer.

Psalm 19: 7–15

80 Lord, what love have I unto thy law: all the day long is my study in it.

Psalm 119: 97

81 My God, my God, look upon me; why hast thou forsaken me: and art so far from my health, and from the words of my complaint? . . .
But thou art he that took me out of my mother's womb: thou wast my hope, when I hanged yet upon my mother's breasts.

I have been left unto thee ever since I was born: thou art my God even from my mother's womb.
O go not from me, for trouble is hard at hand: and there is none to help me . . .
But be not far from me, O Lord: thou art my succour, haste thee to help me . . .
I will declare thy Name unto my brethren: in the midst of the congregation will I praise thee.
O praise the Lord, ye that fear him: magnify him, all ye of the seed of Jacob, and fear him, all ye seed of Israel;
For he hath not despised, nor abhorred, the low estate of the poor: he hath not hid his face from him, but when he called unto him he heard him.
My praise is of thee in the great congregation: my vows will I perform in the sight of them that fear him.
The poor shall eat, and be satisfied: they that seek after the Lord shall praise him; your heart shall live for ever.
All the ends of the world shall remember themselves, and be turned unto the Lord: and all the kindreds of the nations shall worship before him.
For the kingdom is the Lord's: and he is the Governor among the people.
All such as be fat upon earth: have eaten, and worshipped.
All they that go down into the dust shall kneel before him: and no man hath quickened his own soul.
My seed shall serve him: they shall be counted unto the Lord for a generation.
They shall come, and the heavens shall declare his righteousness: unto a people that shall be born, whom the Lord hath made.

Psalm 22: 1, 9–11, 19, 22–32

Nevertheless, though I am sometime afraid: yet put I my trust in thee. 82

Psalm 56: 3

The Lord is my shepherd: therefore can I lack nothing. 83
He shall feed me in a green pasture: and lead me forth beside the waters of comfort.
He shall convert my soul: and bring me forth in the paths of righteousness, for his Name's sake.
Yea, though I walk through the valley of the shadow of death, I will fear no evil: for thou art with me; thy rod and thy staff comfort me.

Thou shalt prepare a table before me against them that trouble me: thou hast anointed my head with oil, and my cup shall be full.
But thy loving-kindness and mercy shall follow me all the days of my life: and I will dwell in the house of the Lord for ever.

Psalm 23

84 Into thy hands I commend my spirit: for thou hast redeemed me, O Lord, thou God of truth.

Psalm 31: 6

85 Have mercy upon me, O God, after thy great goodness: according to the multitude of thy mercies do away mine offences.
Wash me thoroughly from my wickedness: and cleanse me from my sin . . .
But lo, thou requirest truth in the inward parts: and shalt make me to understand wisdom secretly . . .
Make me a clean heart, O God: and renew a right spirit within me.
Cast me not away from thy presence: and take not thy holy Spirit from me.
O give me the comfort of thy help again: and stablish me with thy free Spirit . . .
Thou shalt open my lips, O Lord: and my mouth shall shew thy praise.
For thou desirest no sacrifice, else would I give it thee: but thou delightest not in burnt-offerings.
The sacrifice of God is a troubled spirit: a broken and contrite heart, O God, shalt thou not despise . . .

Psalm 51: 1–2, 6, 10–12, 15–17

86 I have gone astray like a sheep that is lost: O seek thy servant, for I do not forget thy commandments.

Psalm 119: 176

87 Thou, O God, art praised in Sion: and unto thee shall the vow be performed in Jerusalem.
Thou that hearest the prayer: unto thee shall all flesh come . . .
Thou shalt shew us wonderful things in thy righteousness,
O God of our salvation: thou that art the hope of all the ends of the earth, and of them that remain in the broad sea . . .

Thou visitest the earth, and blessest it: thou makest it very plenteous.
The river of God is full of water: thou preparest their corn, for so thou providest for the earth.
Thou waterest her furrows, thou sendest rain into the little valleys thereof: thou makest it soft with the drops of rain, and blessest the increase of it.
Thou crownest the year with thy goodness: and thy clouds drop fatness.
They shall drop upon the dwellings of the wilderness: and the little hills shall rejoice on every side.
The folds shall be full of sheep: the valleys also shall stand so thick with corn, that they shall laugh and sing.

Psalm 65: 1–2, 5, 9–14

God, thou art my God: early will I seek thee. 88

Psalm 63: 1

O how amiable are thy dwellings: thou Lord of hosts! 89
My soul hath a desire and longing to enter into the courts of the Lord: my heart and my flesh rejoice in the living God.
Yea, the sparrow hath found her an house, and the swallow a nest where she may lay her young: even thy altars, O Lord of hosts, my King and my God.
Blessed are they that dwell in thy house: they will be alway praising thee.
Blessed is the man whose strength is in thee: in whose heart are thy ways.
Who going through the vale of misery use it for a well: and the pools are filled with water.
They will go from strength to strength: and unto the God of gods appeareth every one of them in Sion.

Psalm 84: 1–7

Like as the hart desireth the water-brooks: so longeth my soul after thee, O God. 90

Psalm 42: 1a

Lord, thou hast been our refuge: from one generation to another. 91
Before the mountains were brought forth, or ever the earth and the world were made: thou art God from everlasting, and world without end . . .

The days of our age are threescore years and ten; and though men be so strong that they come to fourscore years: yet is their strength then but labour and sorrow; so soon passeth it away, and we are gone . . .
So teach us to number our days: that we may apply our hearts unto wisdom . . .
Shew thy servants thy work: and their children thy glory.
And the glorious Majesty of the Lord our God be upon us: prosper thou the work of our hands upon us, O prosper thou our handy-work.

Psalm 90: 1–2, 10, 12, 16–17

92 And now, Lord, what is my hope: truly my hope is even in thee.

Psalm 39: 8

93 O come, let us sing unto the Lord: let us heartily rejoice in the strength of our salvation.
Let us come before his presence with thanksgiving: and shew ourselves glad in him with psalms.
For the Lord is a great God: and a great King above all gods.
In his hand are all the corners of the earth: and the strength of the hills is his also.
The sea is his, and he made it: and his hands prepared the dry land.
O come, let us worship and fall down: and kneel before the Lord our Maker.

Psalm 95: 1–6

94 I will love thee, O Lord, my strength; the Lord is my rock, and my defence: my Saviour, my God, and my might, in whom I will trust.

Psalm 18: 1

95 O be joyful in the Lord, all ye lands: serve the Lord with gladness, and come before his presence with a song.
Be ye sure that the Lord he is God: it is he that hath made us, and not we ourselves: we are his people, and the sheep of his pasture.
O go your way into his gates with thanksgiving, and into his courts with praise: be thankful unto him, and speak good of his name.
For the Lord is gracious, his mercy is everlasting: and his truth endureth from generation to generation.

Psalm 100

Thou shalt shew me the path of life; in thy presence is the fulness of joy: and at thy right hand there is pleasure for evermore. 96

Psalm 16: 12

Praise the Lord, O my soul: and all that is within me praise his holy Name. 97
Praise the Lord, O my soul: and forget not all his benefits;
Who forgiveth all thy sin: and healeth all thine infirmities;
Who saveth thy life from destruction: and crowneth thee with mercy and loving-kindness;
Who satisfieth thy mouth with good things: making thee young and lusty as an eagle.
The Lord executeth righteousness and judgement: for all them that are oppressed with wrong.
He shewed his ways unto Moses: his works unto the children of Israel.
The Lord is full of compassion and mercy: long-suffering, and of great goodness.
He will not alway be chiding: neither keepeth he his anger for ever.
He hath not dealt with us after our sins: nor rewarded us according to our wickednesses.
For look how high the heaven is in comparison of the earth: so great is his mercy also toward them that fear him.
Look how wide also the east is from the west: so far hath he set our sins from us.
Yea, like as a father pitieth his own children: even so is the Lord merciful unto them that fear him.
For he knoweth whereof we are made: he remembereth that we are but dust.
The days of man are but as grass: for he flourisheth as a flower of the field.
For as soon as the wind goeth over it, it is gone: and the place thereof shall know it no more.
But the merciful goodness of the Lord endureth for ever and ever upon them that fear him: and his righteousness upon children's children.
Even upon such as keep his covenant: and think upon his commandments to do them.
The Lord hath prepared his seat in heaven: and his kingdom ruleth over all.
O praise the Lord, ye angels of his, ye that excel in strength: ye that fulfil his commandments, and hearken unto the voice of his words.
O praise the Lord, all ye his hosts: ye servants of his that do his pleasure.
O speak good of the Lord, all ye works of his, in all places of his dominion: praise thou the Lord, O my soul.

Psalm 103

98 I have said unto the Lord, thou art my God: I have no good beyond thee.

Psalm 16: 2 (RV)

99 O God, my heart is ready; my heart is ready: I will sing and give praise
with the best member that I have.
Awake, thou lute, and harp: I myself will awake right early.
I will give thanks unto thee, O Lord, among the people: I will sing praises
unto thee among the nations.
For thy mercy is greater than the heavens: and thy truth reacheth unto
the clouds.

Psalm 108: 1–4

The Prayers of Jesus

100 'Our Father who art in heaven,
Hallowed be thy name.
Thy kingdom come,
Thy will be done,
On earth as it is in heaven.
Give us this day our daily bread;
And forgive us our debts,
As we also have forgiven our debtors;
And lead us not into temptation,
But deliver us from evil.'

Matthew 6: 9b–13

101 'I thank thee, Father, Lord of heaven and earth, that thou hast hidden these things from the wise and understanding and revealed them to babes; yea, Father, for such was thy gracious will. All things have been delivered to me by my Father; and no one knows who the Son is except the Father, or who the Father is except the Son and anyone to whom the Son chooses to reveal him.'

Luke 10: 21b–22

102 'Father, I thank thee that thou hast heard me. I knew that thou hearest me always, but I have said this on account of the people standing by, that they may believe that thou didst send me.'

John 11: 41b–42

'Now is my soul troubled. And what shall I say? "Father, save me from 103
this hour?" No, for this purpose I have come to this hour. Father glorify thy Name.' Then a voice came from heaven, 'I have glorified it, and I will glorify it again.'

John 12: 27–8

Prayers of the Passion

IN THE UPPER ROOM 104

'Father, the hour has come; glorify thy Son that the Son may glorify thee . . .
I have manifested thy name to the men whom thou gavest me out of the world . . . I am praying for them . . . Holy Father, keep them in thy name, which thou hast given me, that they may be one, even as we are one . . . I do not pray that thou shouldst take them out of the world, but that thou shouldst keep them from the evil one . . . Sanctify them in the truth, thy word is truth . . . for their sake I consecrate myself, that they also may be consecrated in truth.
I do not pray for these only, but also for those who believe in me through their word, that they may all be one, even as thou, Father, art in me, and I in thee . . . that they also may be in us, so that the world may believe that thou hast sent me . . . and hast loved them even as thou hast loved me. Father, I desire that they . . . may be with me where I am, to behold my glory, which thou hast given me . . . I have made known thy name, and I will make it known, that the love with which thou hast loved me may be in them, and I in them.'

from John 17

IN GETHSEMANE 105

'Abba, Father, all things are possible to thee; remove this cup from me; yet not what I will, but what thou wilt.'

Mark 14: 36

AT THE NAILING 106

'Father, forgive them; for they know not what they do.'

Luke 23: 34

IN THE DARKNESS 107

'Eloi, Eloi, lama sabachthani?' which means, 'My God, my God, why hast thou forsaken me?'

Mark 15: 34

108 **IN THE MOMENT OF DEATH**

'Father, into thy hands I commit my spirit!'

Luke 23: 46

The first disciples under persecution

109 **'Lord, look upon their threats, and grant to thy servants to speak thy word with all boldness, while thou stretchest out thy hand to heal, and signs and wonders are performed through the name of thy holy servant Jesus.'**

Acts 4: 29–30

110 **STEPHEN'S PRAYER**

'Lord Jesus, receive my spirit . . . Lord, do not hold this sin against them.'

Acts 7: 59,60

The Prayers of Paul

111 **'Lord, what wilt thou have me to do?'** **Acts 22: 10 (A.V.)**

112 **'Now may our God and Father himself, and our Lord Jesus, direct our way to you; and may the Lord make you increase and abound in love to one another and to all men, as we do to you, so that he may establish your hearts unblameable in holiness before our God and Father, at the coming of our Lord Jesus with all his saints.'**

1 Thessalonians 3: 11–13

113 **'May the God of peace himself sanctify you wholly; and may your spirit and soul and body be kept sound and blameless at the coming of our Lord Jesus Christ.'**

1 Thessalonians 5: 23

114 **'Now may our Lord Jesus Christ himself, and God our Father, who loved us and gave us eternal comfort and good hope through grace, comfort your hearts and establish them in every good work and word.'**

2 Thessalonians 2: 16–17

'O the depths of the riches and wisdom and knowledge of God! How 115
unsearchable are his judgments and how inscrutable his ways! For who has known the mind of the Lord, or who has been his counsellor? Or who has given a gift to him that he might be repaid? For from him and through him and to him are all things. To him be glory for ever. Amen.'

Romans 11: 33–6

THANKSGIVING FOR GOD'S COMFORTING GRACE 116

'Blessed be the God and Father of our Lord Jesus Christ, the Father of mercies and God of all comfort, who comforts us in all our affliction, so that we may be able to comfort those who are in any affliction, with the comfort with which we ourselves are comforted by God. For as we share abundantly in Christ's sufferings, so through Christ we share abundantly in comfort too.'

2 Corinthians 1: 3–5

'The grace of the Lord Jesus Christ and the love of God and the 117
fellowship of the Holy Spirit be with you all.'

2 Corinthians 13: 14

FOR THE GALATIANS

'Grace to you and peace from God the Father and our Lord Jesus Christ, 118
who gave himself for our sins to deliver us from the present evil age, according to the will of our God and Father; to whom be the glory for ever and ever. Amen.'

Galatians 1: 3–4

FOR THE PHILIPPIANS 119

'I thank my God in all my remembrance of you, always in every prayer of mine for you all making my prayer with joy, thankful for your partnership in the gospel from the first day until now. And I am sure that he who began a good work in you will bring it to completion at the day of Jesus Christ. It is right for me to feel thus about you all, because I hold you in my heart, for you are all partakers with me of grace both in my imprisonment and in the defence and confirmation of the gospel. For God is my witness, how I yearn for you all with the affection of Christ Jesus. And it is my prayer that your love may abound more and more, with knowledge and all discernment, so that you may approve what is excellent, and may be pure and blameless for the day of Christ, filled with the fruits of righteousness which come through Jesus Christ, to the glory and praise of God.'

Philippians 1: 3–11

120 **FOR THE EPHESIANS**

'Blessed be the God and Father of our Lord Jesus Christ, who has blessed us in Christ with every spiritual blessing in the heavenly places, even as he chose us in him before the foundation of the world, that we should be holy and blameless before him. He destined us in love to be his sons through Jesus Christ, according to the purpose of his will, to the praise of his glorious grace which he freely bestowed on us in the Beloved. In him we have redemption through his blood, the forgiveness of our trespasses, according to the riches of his grace which he lavished upon us. For he has made known to us in all wisdom and insight the mystery of his will, according to his purpose which he set forth in Christ as a plan for the fullness of time, to unite all things in him, things in heaven and things on earth.'

Ephesians 1: 3–10

121 'For this reason I bow my knees before the Father, from whom every family in heaven and on earth is named, that according to the riches of his glory he may grant you to be strengthened with might through his Spirit in the inner man, and that Christ may dwell in your hearts through faith; that you, being rooted and grounded in love, may have power to comprehend with all the saints what is the breadth and length and height and depth, and to know the love of Christ which surpasses knowledge, that you may be filled with all the fulness of God. Now to him who by the power at work within us is able to do far more abundantly than all that we ask or think to him be glory in the church and in Christ Jesus to all generations, for ever and ever. Amen.'

Ephesians 3: 14–20

122 **FOR THE COLOSSIANS**

'. . . that you may be filled with the knowledge of his will in all spiritual wisdom and understanding, to lead a life worthy of the Lord, fully pleasing to him, bearing fruit in every good work and increasing in the knowledge of God. May you be strengthened with all power, according to his glorious might, for all endurance and patience with joy, giving thanks to the Father, who has qualified us to share in the inheritance of the saints in light.'

Colossians 1: 9–12

'The Blessed and only Sovereign, the King of kings and Lord of lords, 123
who alone has immortality and dwells in unapproachable light, whom no man has ever seen or can see. To him be honour and eternal dominion. Amen.'

1 Timothy 6: 15b–16

Other New Testament Prayers

PETER'S THANKSGIVING FOR THE RESURRECTION 124

'Blessed be the God and Father of our Lord Jesus Christ! By his great mercy we have been born anew to a living hope through the resurrection of Jesus Christ from the dead, and to an inheritance which is imperishable, undefiled, and unfading, kept in heaven for you, who by God's power are guarded through faith for a salvation ready to be revealed in the last time.'

1 Peter 1: 3–5

'Now may the God of peace who brought again from the dead our Lord 125
Jesus, the great shepherd of the sheep, by the blood of the eternal covenant, equip you with everything good that you may do his will, working in you that which is pleasing in his sight, through Jesus Christ; to whom be glory for ever and ever. Amen.'

Hebrews 13: 20–1

'Now to him who is able to keep you from falling and to present you 126
without blemish before the presence of his glory with rejoicing, to the only God, our Saviour through Jesus Christ our Lord, be glory, majesty, dominion, and authority, before all time and now and for ever. Amen.'

Jude: 24–5

The worship of Heaven

127 'Worthy is the Lamb who was slain, to receive power and wealth and wisdom and might and honour and glory and blessing! . . . To him who sits upon the throne and to the Lamb be blessing and honour and glory and might for ever and ever!'

Revelation 5: 12–13b

128 'Salvation belongs to our God who sits upon the throne, and to the Lamb! . . . Amen! Blessing and glory and wisdom and thanksgiving and honour and power and might be to our God for ever and ever! Amen.'

Revelation 7: 10, 12

129 'Worthy art thou, our Lord and God, to receive glory and honour and power, for thou didst create all things, and by thy will they existed and were created.'

Revelation 4: 11

130 'Great and wonderful are thy deeds, O Lord God the Almighty! Just and true are thy ways, O King of the ages! Who shall not fear and glorify thy name, O Lord? For thou alone art holy. All nations shall come and worship thee, for thy judgments have been revealed.'

Revelation 15: 3–4

131 Hallelujah! For the Lord our God the Almighty reigns. Let us rejoice and exult and give him the glory, for the marriage of the Lamb has come, and his Bride has made herself ready; it was granted her to be clothed with fine linen, bright and pure—for the fine linen is the righteous deeds of the saints.'

Revelation 19: 6b–8

A sheaf of arrow prayers

132 Behold, I am the handmaid of the Lord; be it unto me according to thy word (Luke 1: 38 AV).

Glory to God in the highest, and on earth peace among men (Luke 2: 14).

OTHER NEW TESTAMENT PRAYERS

Lord, now lettest thou thy servant depart in peace (Luke 2: 29).

Lord, I believe, help thou mine unbelief (Mark 9: 24 AV).

Abba, Father (Mark 14: 36).

Lord, save me (Matthew 14: 30).

God, be merciful to me a sinner (Luke 18: 13).

Jesus, remember me, when thou comest in thy Kingdom (Luke 23: 42 RV).

Stay with us, for it is toward evening and the day is now far spent (Luke 24: 29).

Sir, give me this water, that I thirst not (John 4: 15 AV).

Lord, give us this bread always (John 6: 34).

Lord, to whom shall we go? You have the words of eternal life (John 6: 68).

Lord, he whom you love is ill (John 11: 3).

Lord, show us the Father, and we shall be satisfied (John 14: 8).

Lord, you know that I love you (John 21: 16).

My Lord and my God! (John 20: 28).

Amen. Come, Lord Jesus (Revelation 22: 20).

III

PRAYERS OF CHRISTIANS: PERSONAL AND OCCASIONAL

Introduction

We have it on the authority of a poet that 'no man can say "I *will* write a poem"': the like may be asserted of a prayer. For what *is* a prayer but (like life for Henry Vaughan) 'a quickness that my God hath kiss'd'? The spiritual impetus is not to be had on demand, rather it is to be respected by those to whom, and for whom, it breathes.

In this section a framework of the phrases of the Lord's Prayer has been adopted, as set out below, to control the astonishing variety of the Christian personal and occasional prayers selected. Subheadings indicate the dominant concern of each group. Within the group the juxtaposition of authorship, period, length, and style is deliberate in an attempt to appreciate the contrasts held within the unity of intention. Inevitably it will be found that a few prayers could have been placed under more than one heading: the subject-index at the end of the book will give the reader further guidance. Where spelling and punctuation have been judged to represent the style, period, and tradition in any significant way they have been retained, but mainly such incidentals have been adapted to modern standards.

'OUR FATHER' *Dependence*

'WHO ART IN HEAVEN' *Affirmation*

'HALLOWED BE THY NAME' *Blessing and thanksgiving*

'THY KINGDOM COME' *Longing; Seeking; Doing; Serving; Peace*

'THY WILL BE DONE' *Dedication; Obedience*

'AS IT IS IN HEAVEN' *Guidance; Acceptance*

'GIVE US THIS DAY' *Daily; Graces*

'FORGIVE US OUR TRESPASSES' *Penitence*

'AS WE FORGIVE' *Relationships*

'LEAD US NOT INTO TEMPTATION' *Right living*

'DELIVER US FROM EVIL' *Protection; Suffering; Compassion*

'FOR THINE IS THE KINGDOM' *Devotion; Contemplation; Gifts of the Spirit; Sacraments*

'FOR EVER AND EVER' *Death and eternity; The Virgin, martyrs, and saints; Blessings*

Our Father, which art in heaven, Hallowed be thy Name. Thy kingdom 133
come. Thy will be done, in earth as it is in Heaven. Give us this day our

daily bread. And forgive us our trespasses, As we forgive them that trespass against us. And lead us not into temptation; But deliver us from evil: For thine is the kingdom, The power, and the glory, For ever and ever. Amen.

Book of Common Prayer

134 Our Father in heaven,
hallowed be your name,
your kingdom come,
your will be done,
on earth as in heaven.
Give us today our daily bread.
Forgive us our sins
as we forgive those who sin against us.
Lead us not into temptation
but deliver us from evil.
For the kingdom, the power, and the glory are yours
now and for ever Amen.

The Alternative Service Book 1980

'OUR FATHER'

Dependence

135 O Lord Jesu Christ, the maker and redeemer of mankind which hast said, that thou art the way, the truth and the life: the way by doctrine, precepts, and examples: the truth, in promises; and the life, in reward: I beseech thee for thine unspeakable love's sake, wherethrough thou hast vouchsafed to employ thyself wholly in thy saving of us, suffer me not at any time to stray from thee, which art the way; nor to distrust thy promises, which art the truth, and performest whatsoever thou promisest; nor to rest in any other thing than thee, which art the way, beyond which there is nothing to be desired, neither in heaven, nor in earth. By thee we have learned the sure and ready way to true salvation, to the intent we should not wander any longer up and down in the mazes of the world. Thou hast taught us thoroughly what to believe, what to do, what to hope, and wherein to rest.

Erasmus, 1466–1536

Save me Lord, king of eternal glory, you who have the power to save us all. Grant that I may long for, do and perfect those things which are pleasing to you and profitable for me. Lord, give me counsel in my anxiety, help in time of trial, solace when persecuted, and strength against every temptation. Grant me pardon, Lord, for my past wrongdoings and afflictions, correction of my present ones, and deign also to protect me against those in the future. 136

Latin, 11th century

Behold, Lord, an empty vessel that needs to be filled. My Lord, fill it. I am weak in the faith; strengthen thou me. I am cold in love; warm me and make me fervent that my love may go out to my neighbour. I do not have a strong and firm faith; at times I doubt and am unable to trust thee altogether. O Lord, help me. Strengthen my faith and trust in thee. In thee I have sealed the treasures of all I have. I am poor; thou art rich and didst come to be merciful to the poor. I am a sinner; thou art upright. With me there is an abundance of sin; in thee is the fulness of righteousness. Therefore, I will remain with thee of whom I can receive but to whom I may not give. Amen. 137

Martin Luther, 1483–1546

Lord, why should I doubt any more, when you have given me such assured pledges of your love? First, you are my creator, I your creature, you my master, I your servant. But hence arises not my comfort: you are my Father, I your child. 'You shall be my sons and daughters', says the Lord almighty. Christ is my brother: 'I ascend to my Father and your Father, to my God and your God; but, lest this should not be enough, your maker is your husband.' Nay, more, I am a member of his body, he my head. Such privileges—had not the Word of truth made them known, who or where is the man that dared in his heart have presumed to have thought it? So wonderful are these thoughts that my spirit fails in me at their consideration, and I am confounded to think that God, who has done so much for me, should have so little from me. But this is my comfort, that when I come to heaven, I shall understand perfectly what he has done for me, and then I shall be able to praise him as I ought. Lord, having this hope let me purify myself as you are pure, and let me be no more afraid of death, but even desire to be dissolved and be with you, which is best of all. 138

Anne Bradstreet, d. 1672

139 O son of man, to right my lot
Nought but thy presence can avail;
Yet on the road thy wheels are not,
Nor on the sea thy sail.

My fancied ways why should'st thou heed?
Thou com'st down thine own secret stair
Com'st down to answer all my need,
Yea, every bygone prayer!

George Macdonald, 1824–1905

140 Lord,
Keep my parents in your love.
Lord,
bless them and keep them.
Lord,
please let me have money and strength
and keep my parents for many more years
so that I can take care of them.

Prayer of a young Ghanaian Christian

141 Grant me, O most sweet and loving Jesus, to rest in Thee above every creature, above all health and beauty, above all glory and honour, above all power and dignity, above all knowledge and subtility, above all riches and arts, above all joy and exultation, above all fame and praise, above all sweetness and consolation, above all hope and promise, above all desert and desire, above all gifts and presents which Thou art able to bestow or infuse, above all joy and gladness which the mind is capable of receiving and feeling; finally, above Angels and Archangels, and above all the host of Heaven, above all things visible and invisible, and above all that falls short of Thyself, O Thou, my God!

Thomas à Kempis, 1380–1471

142 In the life which wells up in me and in the matter which sustains me, I find much more than Your gifts. It is You Yourself whom I find, You who makes me participate in Your being, You who moulds me. Truly in the ruling and in the first disciplining of my living strength, in the continually beneficent play of secondary causes, I touch, as near as possible, the two faces of Your creative action, and I encounter, and kiss, Your two marvellous hands—the one which holds us so firmly that it is

merged, in us, with the sources of life, and the other whose embrace is so wide that, at its slightest pressure, all the springs of the universe respond harmoniously together.

Teilhard de Chardin, SJ, 1881–1955

Lord, my heart is not large enough, 143
my memory is not good enough,
my will is not strong enough:
Take my heart and enlarge it,
Take my memory and give it quicker recall,
Take my will and make it strong
and make me conscious of thee
everpresent,
ever accompanying.

G.A.

O Lord Jesus Christ, Thou Word and Revelation of the Eternal Father, 144
come, we pray Thee, take possession of our hearts, and reign where Thou hast right to reign. So fill our minds with the thought and our imaginations with the picture of Thy love, that there may be in us no room for any desire that is discordant with Thy holy will. Cleanse us, we pray Thee, from all that may make us deaf to Thy call or slow to obey it, Who, with the Father and the Holy Spirit, art one God, blessed for ever.

William Temple, 1881–1944

Let me depend on God alone: 145
who never changes,
who knows what is best for me
so much better than I;
and gives in a thousand ways, at all times
all that the perfect Father can
for the son's good growth,
things needful, things salutary,
things wise, beneficent and happy.

Eric Milner-White, 1884–1964

'WHO ART IN HEAVEN'

Affirmation

146 I believe that God is real,
Even though I cannot realize Him;
That what I commit to Him, He will glorify, and use for his eternal purpose.
I believe that his will is love to all of us.
His ways are not our ways,
But we may come to Him
Through Jesus,
Through his Spirit,
Through all beauty, love and truth.

Margaret Cropper, 1886–1980

147 One goodness ruleth by its single will
All things that are, and have been, and shall be,
Itself abiding, knowing naught of change.
This is true health, this is the blessed life.
Here, O ye prisoners of empty hope,
Minds kept in bonds by pleasure, haste ye to return.
Here, here your rest, sure rest for all your hurt,
Eternal harbour for your quiet anchorage,
Shelter and refuge for unhappy men
That's always open.
This is the Father, and the Son, and the kind Holy Ghost,
One King omnipotent, one called the Trinity.
One love, O thou that readest, that shall be
Thine to eternity,
That sent this mighty gift of books
That reading, thou mightst recognize thy Maker,
King, Maker of all things, Father, Redeemer,
The Saviour Christ, to whom be glory.

Alcuin of York, 735–804

148 Lord,
I offer what I am
to what You are.
I stretch up to You in desire
my attention on You alone.

AFFIRMATION

I cannot grasp You
  explain You
  describe You
Only cast myself into the depths
  of your mystery
Only let your love pierce the
  cloud of my unknowing.
Let me forget all but You
You are what I long for
You are my chiefest good
You are my eager hope
You are my allness.

In the glimpses of your Eternity
  Your Unconditional Freedom
  Your Unfailing Wisdom
  Your Perfect Love
I am humble and worshipping
  warming to love and hope
  waiting and available
  for your Will
    dear Lord.

G.A.

Thou art my Lord: I have no good beyond thee. **Psalm 16: 2 (RV)** 149

HYMN TO MATTER 150

Blessed be you, harsh matter, barren soil, stubborn rock: you who yield only to violence, you who force us to work if we would eat. Blessed be you, perilous matter, violent sea, untameable passion: you who unless we fetter you will devour us. Blessed be you, mighty matter, irresistible march of evolution, reality ever new-born; you who, by constantly shattering our mental categories, force us to go ever further and further in our pursuit of the truth. Blessed be you, universal matter, unmeasurable time, boundless ether, triple abyss of stars and atoms and generations: you who by overflowing and dissolving our narrow standards of measurement reveal to us the dimensions of God . . .

Teilhard de Chardin, SJ, 1881–1955

I find thee throned in my heart, my Lord Jesus. It is enough. I know that 151
thou art throned in heaven. My heart and heaven are one.

Gaelic, tr. Alistair MacLean

152 As the rain hides the stars, as the autumn mist hides the hills, as the clouds veil the blue of the sky, so the dark happenings of my lot hide the shining of thy face from me. Yet, if I may hold thy hand in the darkness, it is enough. Since I know that, though I may stumble in my going, thou dost not fall.

Gaelic, tr. Alistair MacLean

153 Thou, O my God, art ever new, though thou art the most ancient—thou alone art the food for eternity. I am to live for ever, not for a time—and I have no power over my being; I cannot destroy myself, even though I were so wicked as to wish to do so. I must live on, with intellect and consciousness for ever, in spite of myself. Without thee eternity would be another name for eternal misery. In thee alone have I that which can stay me up for ever: thou alone art the food of my soul. Thou alone art inexhaustible, and ever offerest to me something new to know, something new to love . . . and so on for eternity I shall ever be a little child beginning to be taught the rudiments of thy infinite divine nature. For thou art thyself the seat and centre of all good, and the only substance in this universe of shadows, and the heaven in which blessed spirits live and rejoice—Amen.

John Henry Newman, 1801–90

154 And now, Lord, what is my hope: truly my hope is even in thee.

Psalm 39: 8

155 The sun has disappeared.
I have switched off the light,
and my wife and children are asleep.
The animals in the forest are full of fear,
and so are the people on their mats.
They prefer the day with your sun
to the night.
But I still know that your moon is there,
and your eyes and also your hands.
Thus I am not afraid.
This day again
you led us wonderfully.
Everybody went to his mat
satisfied and full.

Renew us during our sleep,
that in the morning
we may come afresh to our daily jobs.
Be with our brothers far away in Asia
who may be getting up now. Amen.

Prayer of a young Ghanaian Christian

God's thought in a man's brain, 156
God's love in a man's heart,
God's pain in a man's body,
I worship.

Margaret Cropper, 1886–1980

O God, the God of all goodness and of all grace, 157
who art worthy of a greater love
than we can either give or understand:
Fill our hearts, we beseech thee,
with such love toward thee
that nothing may seem too hard for us to do
or to suffer
in obedience to thy will;
and grant that thus loving thee,
we may become daily more like unto thee,
and finally obtain the crown of life
which thou hast promised to those that love thee;
through Jesus Christ our Lord.

Bishop Brooke Foss Westcott, 1825–1901

'HALLOWED BE THY NAME'

Blessing and Thanksgiving

O Thou who through the light of nature hast aroused in us a longing for 158
the light of grace, so that we may be raised in the light of Thy majesty, to Thee, I give thanks, Creator and Lord, that Thou allowest me to rejoice in Thy works. Praise the Lord ye heavenly harmonies, and ye who know the revealed harmonies. For from Him, through Him and in Him, all is, which is perceptible as well as spiritual; that which we know and that which we do not know, for there is still much to learn.

Johann Kepler, 1571–1630

159 Great is, O King, our happiness
in thy kingdom, thou, our King.

We dance before thee, Our King,
By the strength of thy kingdom.

May our feet be made strong;
Let us dance before thee, eternal.

Give you praise, all angels,
To him above who is worthy of praise.

Prayer in sacred dance of the Zulu Nazarite Church

160 I am as glad of thy word: as one that findeth great spoils.

Psalm 119: 162

161 Praise and glory be to the omnipotence of the eternal Father, who in his providence created the world out of nothing. Praise and glory be to the wisdom of his only-begotten Son, who redeemed the world with his blood. Praise and glory be to the living kindness of the Holy Spirit, who enlightened the world in faith. Praise and glory be to the holy and undivided Trinity, who formed us without our deserving it in their image. We give praise and glory to you, most blessed Trinity, for the blessing of our creation, by which you granted us bodies and souls, you adorned us with your image and likeness, and added us to your Christian flock, making us sound and whole in our senses and in our members, above all the creatures who are beneath the heavens, and gave us your holy angels as our guides and ministers. For all this be pleased that we may praise you, world without end.

Latin, 11th century

162 Shone to him the earth and sphere together,
God the Lord has opened a door;
Son of Mary Virgin, hasten thou to help me,
Thou Christ of hope, thou Door of joy,
Golden Sun of hill and mountain,
All hail! Let there be joy!

Gaelic, 6th century

163 The sun is shining . . . thank you Lord.
I mean it is shining: the sky and everything is warm and smiling.
But it is not only that . . . my heart is smiling.

I know that I am loved . . . and that I love too.
Thank you, Lord, the sun is shining. Michael Hollings and Etta Gullick

Teach me thy love to know; 164
That this new light, which now I see,
May both the work and workman show:
Then by a sunne-beam I will climbe to thee.

George Herbert, 1593–1633

God, who created me 165
Nimble and light of limb,
In three elements free,
To run, to ride, to swim;
Not when the sense is dim,
But now from the heart of joy,
I would remember him:
Take the thanks of a boy.

H. C. Beeching, 1859–1919

O Lord God, who hast given me the gift of sight, grant that I may see not only with the eyes of my head but with the eyes of the heart also, that I may perceive the beauty and meaning of all that I behold, and glorify Thee, the Creator of all, who art blessed for evermore. G.A. 166

For thy loving-kindness is better than the life itself: my lips shall praise thee. Psalm 63: 4 167

. . . Blessed be thy holy Name, 168
O Lord, my God!
For ever blessed be thy holy Name,
For that I am made
The work of thy hands,
Curiously wrought
By thy divine Wisdom,
Enriched
By thy Goodness,
Being more thine
Than I am mine own.
O Lord!

'HALLOWED BE THY NAME'

Thou hast given me a Body,
Wherein the glory of thy Power shineth,
Wonderfully composed above the Beasts,
Within distinguished into useful parts,
Beautified without with many Ornaments.
Limbs rarely poised,
And made for Heaven:
Arteries filled
With celestial spirits . . .

For all the art which thou hast hidden
In this little piece
Of red clay.
For the workmanship of thy hand,
Who didst thy self form man
Of the dust of the ground,
And breath into his nostrils
The breath of Life.
For the high Exaltation whereby thou hast glorified every body,
Especially mine,
As thou didst thy Servant
Adam's in Eden.
Thy Works themselves speaking to me the same thing that was said unto
him in the beginning,
WE ARE ALL THINE.

Thomas Traherne, 1636–74

169 Lead us, O God, from the sight of the lovely things of the world to the thought of thee their Creator; and grant that delighting in the beautiful things of thy creation we may delight in thee, the first author of beauty and the Sovereign Lord of all thy works, blessed for evermore.

G.A.

170 You are holy, Lord, the only God,
and your deeds are wonderful.
You are strong.
You are great.
You are the Most High,
You are almighty.
You, holy Father, are
King of heaven and earth.

You are Three and One,
Lord God, all good.
You are Good, all Good, supreme Good,
Lord God, living and true.
You are love,
You are wisdom.
You are humility,
You are endurance.
You are rest,
You are peace.
You are joy and gladness.
You are justice and moderation.
You are all our riches,
And you suffice for us.
You are beauty.
You are gentleness.
You are our protector,
You are our guardian and defender.
You are courage.
You are our haven and our hope.
You are our faith,
Our great consolation.
You are our eternal life,
Great and wonderful Lord,
God almighty,
Merciful Saviour.

St Francis of Assisi, 1181–1226

O God, I thank thee 171
for all the creatures thou hast made,
so perfect in their kind—
great animals like the elephant and the rhinoceros,
humorous animals like the camel and the monkey,
friendly ones like the dog and the cat,
working ones like the horse and the ox,
timid ones like the squirrel and the rabbit,
majestic ones like the lion and the tiger,
for birds with their songs.
O Lord give us such love for thy creation,
that love may cast out fear,
and all thy creatures see in man
their priest and friend,
through Jesus Christ our Lord.

G.A.

172 **BISHOP SERAPION'S PRAYER OF OBLATION**

It is right and proper that we should give you praise and hymns and glory O uncreated Father of Jesus Christ, who is your only Son.

We praise you, God uncreated, unsearchable, ineffable, beyond the grasp of any created being.

We praise you because you are known by the Only Son, proclaimed and explained by him to created beings and known in turn by them. We praise you because you know the Son and reveal to the saints the glories that are his. We praise you because you are known by the Word you begot and are seen by the saints and understood by them after a fashion.

We praise you, Father, invisible, Giver of immortality. You are the source of life and light, the source of all grace and truth; you love men and you love the poor, you seek reconciliation with all men and draw them all to you by sending your dear Son to visit them.

We beg you, make us really alive. Give us the spirit of light, that we may know you, the supremely true, and your envoy, Jesus Christ. Give us the Holy Spirit and enable us to discourse at large upon your ineffable mysteries.

May the Lord Jesus and the Holy Spirit speak in us and praise you through us, for you are high above all princedoms, powers, virtues and dominations, above everything that can be named, both in this world and in the world to come . . .

Holy, holy, holy is the Lord of hosts. Heaven and earth are full of your glory. Heaven is full, earth is full of your wonderful glory . . .

4th century

'THY KINGDOM COME'

Longing

173 Thou awakest us to delight in Thy praises; for Thou madest us for Thyself, and our heart is restless, until it repose in Thee.

St Augustine, 354–450

174 My spirit longs for thee
Within my troubled breast,
Though I unworthy be
Of so divine a Guest.

Of so divine a guest
Unworthy though I be,
Yet has my heart no rest
Unless it come from thee.

John Byrom, 1692–1763

Late have I loved Thee, O Beauty so ancient and so new; late have I loved 175
Thee: for behold Thou wert within me, and I outside; and I sought Thee outside and in my unloveliness fell upon those lovely things that Thou hast made. Thou wert with me, and I was not with Thee. I was kept from Thee by those things, yet had they not been in Thee, they would not have been at all. Thou didst call and cry to me to break open my deafness: and Thou didst send forth Thy beams and shine upon me and chase away my blindness: Thou didst breathe fragrance upon me, and I drew in my breath and do now pant for Thee: I tasted Thee, and now hunger and thirst for Thee: Thou didst touch me, and I have burned for Thy peace.

St Augustine, 354–450

Hunger and thirst, O Christ, for sight of thee 176
Came between me and all the feasts of earth.
Give thou Thyself the Bread, thyself the Wine,
Thou, sole provision for the unknown way.
Long hunger wasted the world wanderer,
With sight of thee may he be satisfied.

Radbod, Bishop of Utrecht, *c.* 900

As a hart longs for flowing streams, so longs my soul for thee, O God. My 177
soul thirsts for God, for the living God.

Psalm 42: 1–2 (RSV)

Lord, thou that wilt not be seen but by those that be clean of heart: I have 178
done that in me is, read and deeply thought and ensearched what it is, and on what manner I might best come to this cleanness that I might thee know somedeal. Lord, I have sought and thought with all my poor heart! And, Lord, in my meditation the fire of desire kindled for to know thee, not only the bitter bark without, but in feeling and tasting in my soul. And this unworthiness I ask not for me, for I am wretched and sinful and most unworthy of all other. But, Lord, as a whelp eateth of the crumbs

that fall from the board of his lord: of the heritage that is for to come, a crop of that heavenly joy to comfort my thirsty soul that burneth in love-longing to thee!

The Cloud of Unknowing, 14th century

179 God, of your goodness give me yourself for you are sufficient for me. I cannot properly ask anything less, to be worthy of you. If I were to ask less, I should always be in want. In you alone do I have all.

Julian of Norwich, 1342–1443

180 O Lord, prepare my heart, I beseech thee, to reverence thee, to adore thee, to love thee; to hate, for love of thee, all my sins and imperfections, short-comings, whatever in me displeaseth thee; and to love all which thou lovest, and whom thou lovest. Give me, Lord, fervour of love, shame for my unthankfulness, sorrow for my sins, longing for thy grace, and to be wholly united with thee. Let my very coldness call for the glow of thy love; let my emptiness and dryness, like a barren and thirsty land, thirst for thee, call on thee to come into my soul, who refreshest those who are weary. Let my heart ache to thee and for thee, who stillest the aching of the heart. Let my mute longings praise thee, crave to thee, who satisfiest the empty soul that waits on thee.

E. B. Pusey, 1800–82

181 O give me the comfort of thy help again and give me a willing spirit as my strength.

Psalm 51: 12

182 Lord, enfold me in the depths of your heart; and there hold me, refine, purge, and set me on fire, raise me aloft, until my own self knows utter annihilation.

Teilhard de Chardin, SJ, 1881–1955

183 My God,
I pray that I may so know you and love you
  that I may rejoice in you.
And if I may not do so fully in this life,
  let me go steadily on
  to the day when I come to that fulness . . .
  let me receive
That which you promised through your truth,
  that my joy may be full.

St Anselm, 1033–1109

LONGING

Lord, I want to be a Christian 184
in-na my heart
in-na my heart
Lord, I want to be a Christian
in-na my heart
in-na my heart
In-na my heart
in-na my heart
Lord, I want to be a Christian
in-na my heart.

Lord, I want to be more loving
in-na my heart
in-na my heart . . .

Lord, I want to be like Jesus
in-na my heart
in-na my heart
Lord, I want to be like Jesus
in-na my heart
In-na my heart
in-na my heart
Lord, I want to be like Jesus
in-na my heart.

Negro spiritual

O God of mountains, stars, and boundless spaces, 185
O God of freedom and of joyous hearts,
When thy face looketh forth from all men's faces,
There will be room enough in crowded marts!
Brood thou around me, and the noise is o'er,
Thy universe my closet with shut door.

George Macdonald, 1824–1905

The more I win thee, Lord, 186
the more for thee I pine;
Ah, such a heart of mine!

My eyes behold thee, and
are filled and straightway then
Their hunger wakes again!

My arms have clasped thee and
Should set thee free, but no,
I cannot let thee go!

'THY KINGDOM COME'

Thou dwell'st within my heart,
  Forthwith anew the fire
Burns of my soul's desire.

Lord Jesus Christ, beloved,
  tell, O tell me true,
What shall thy servant do?

Narayan Vaman Tilak, 1862–1919

Seeking

187 O great God, who art thou? Where art thou? Show thyself to me.

Venkayya, first outcaste convert in the Church of South India; prayer offered every day for three years

188 O Lord our God, grant us grace to desire thee with our whole heart, that so desiring, we may seek and find thee; and so finding thee we may love thee; and loving thee we may hate those sins from which thou hast redeemed us; for the sake of Jesus Christ.

St Anselm, 1033–1109

189 Lord Jesus Christ; Let me seek you by desiring you,
  and let me desire you by seeking you;
  let me find you by loving you,
  and love you in finding you.
  I confess, Lord, with thanksgiving,
  that you have made me in your image,
so that I can remember you, think of you, and love you.
But that image is so worn and blotted out by faults,
  and darkened by the smoke of sin,
  that it cannot do that for which it was made,
  unless you renew and refashion it.
Lord, I am not trying to make my way to your height,
for my understanding is in no way equal to that,
but I do desire to understand a little of your truth
  which my heart already believes and loves.
I do not seek to understand so that I can believe,
  but I believe so that I may understand;
    and what is more,
I believe that unless I do believe, I shall not understand.

St Anselm, 1033–1109

SEEKING

190 O my God how does it happen in this poor old world that thou art so great and yet nobody finds thee, that thou callest so loudly and yet nobody hears thee, that thou art so near and yet nobody feels thee, that thou givest thyself to everybody and yet nobody knows thy name? Men flee from thee and say they cannot find thee; they turn their backs and say they cannot see thee; they stop their ears and say they cannot hear thee.

Hans Denck, 16th century

191 I have gone astray like a sheep that is lost: O seek thy servant.

Psalm 119: 176

192 We have our treasure in earthen vessels, but thou, O Holy Spirit, when thou livest in a man, thou livest in what is infinitely lower. Thou Spirit of Holiness, thou livest in the midst of impurity and corruption; thou Spirit of Wisdom, thou livest in the midst of folly; thou Spirit of Truth, thou livest in one who is himself deluded. Oh, continue to dwell there, thou who dost not seek a desirable dwelling place, for thou wouldst seek there in vain, thou Creator and Redeemer, to make a dwelling for thyself; oh, continue to dwell there, that one day thou mayst finally be pleased by the dwelling which thou didst thyself prepare in my heart, foolish, deceiving, and impure as it is.

Søren Kierkegaard, 1813–55

193 Lord, I want to love you, yet I'm not sure.
I want to trust you, yet I'm afraid of being taken in.
I know I need you, yet I'm ashamed of the need.
I want to pray, yet I'm afraid of being a hypocrite.
I need my independence, yet I fear to be alone.
I want to belong, yet I must be myself.
Take me, Lord, yet leave me alone.
Lord, I believe; help thou my unbelief.
O Lord, if you are there, you do understand, don't you?
Give me what I need but leave me free to choose.
Help me work it out my own way, but don't let me go.
Let me understand myself, but don't let me despair.
Come unto me, O Lord—I want you there.
Lighten my darkness—but don't dazzle me.
Help me to see what I need to do and give me strength to do it.
O Lord, I believe; help thou my unbelief.

Bernard, SSF

194 Open thou mine eyes: that I may see the wondrous things of thy Law.

Psalm 119: 18

195 Eternal Light, shine into our hearts,
Eternal Goodness, deliver us from evil,
Eternal Power, be our support,
Eternal Wisdom, scatter the darkness of our ignorance,
Eternal Pity, have mercy upon us;
that with all our heart and mind and soul and strength
we may seek thy face and be brought by thine infinite mercy
to thy holy presence; through Jesus Christ our Lord.

Alcuin of York, 735–804

196 He whom I bow to only knows to whom I bow
When I attempt the ineffable Name, murmuring *Thou*,
And dream of Pheidian fancies and embrace in heart
Symbols (I know) which cannot be the thing thou art.
Thus always, taken at their word, all prayers blaspheme
Worshipping with frail images a folk-lore dream,
And all men in their praying, self-deceived, address
The coinage of their own unquiet thoughts, unless
Thou in magnetic mercy to Thyself divert
Our arrows, aimed unskilfully, beyond desert;
And all men are idolaters, crying unheard
To a deaf idol, if thou take them at their word.
Take not, oh Lord, our literal sense. Lord, in thy great,
Unbroken speech our limping metaphor translate.

C. S. Lewis, 1898–1963

197 Ah! Lord Jesus, King of bliss, how shall I be eased? Who shall teach me and tell me that [thing] me needeth to know, if I may not at this time see it in Thee?

Julian of Norwich, 1342–1443

Doing

198 Eternal God, in whose perfect kingdom no sword is drawn but the sword of righteousness, and no strength known but the strength of love . . . We

pray thee so mightily to shed and spread abroad thy Spirit, that all peoples and ranks may be gathered under one banner, of the Prince of Peace; as children of one God and Father of all; to whom be dominion and glory now and for ever. Amen.

Eric Milner-White, 1884–1964

Thou, O Father! who gavest the Visible Light as the first-born of thy Creatures, and didst pour into man the Intellectual Light as the top and consummation of thy workmanship, be pleased to protect and govern this work, which coming from thy Goodness returneth to thy Glory. Then, after thou hadst reviewed the works which thy hands had made, beheldest that 'everything was very good'; and thou didst rest with complacency in them. But man reflecting on the works which he had made, saw that 'all was vanity and vexation of Spirit', and could by no means acquiesce in them. Wherefore if we labour in thy works with the sweat of our brows, thou wilt make us partakers of thy Vision and thy Sabbath. We humbly beg that this mind may be steadfastly in us, and that thou, by our hands and also by the hands of others on whom thou shalt bestow the same Spirit, wilt please to convey a largeness of new alms to thy family of Mankind. These things we commend to thy everlasting love, by our Jesus, thy Christ, God with us. Amen. 199

Francis Bacon, 1561–1626

Almighty God, our heavenly Father, without whose help labour is useless, without whose light search is vain, invigorate my studies and direct my enquiries, that I may by due diligence and right discernment establish myself and others in thy holy Faith. Take not, O Lord, thy Holy Spirit from me, let not evil thoughts have dominion in my mind. Let me not linger in ignorance and doubt, but enlighten and support me for the sake of Jesus Christ our Lord. Amen. 200

Samuel Johnson, 1709–84

O God, who hast bound us together in this bundle of life, give us grace to understand how our lives depend upon the courage, the industry, the honesty, and the integrity of our fellow-men; that we may be mindful of their needs, grateful for their faithfulness, and faithful in our responsibilities to them; through Jesus Christ our Lord. 201

Reinhold Niebuhr, 1892–1971

202 O God, the God of all righteousness, mercy, and love: Give us all grace and strength to conceive and execute whatever may be for thine honour and the welfare of the nation; that we may become at last, through the merits and intercession of our common Redeemer, a great and a happy because a wise and understanding people; to thy honour and glory.

Lord Salisbury, 1830–1903

203 Lord, bless this kingdom, we beseech thee, that religion and virtue may season all sorts of men, that there may be peace within the gates, and plenty within the palaces of it. In peace, we beseech thee, so preserve it, that it corrupt not; in war, so defend it, that it suffer not; in plenty, so order it, that it riot not; in want, so pacify and moderate it, that it may patiently and peaceably see thee, the only full supply both of men and states; that so it may continue a place and a people to do thee service to the end of time; through Jesus Christ our only Saviour and Redeemer. Amen.

Archbishop William Laud, 1573–1645

204 Pour thy blessing, O God, we pray thee, upon Elizabeth our Queen that she may fulfil her calling as a Christian ruler. Support her in the ceaseless round of duty, inspire her in the service of many peoples. Give her wise and selfless ministers, bless her in home and family, and grant that through her the Commonwealth may be knit together in one great brotherhood, a strength and joy to all its members and an instrument of peace in our troubled world, through Jesus Christ, our Lord.

G.A.

205 PRAYER FOR THE PEOPLES OF THE MIDDLE EAST

O Lord Jesus, stretch forth thy wounded hands in blessing over thy people, to heal and to restore, and to draw them to thyself and to one another in love.

Church Missionary Society, exact source unknown

206 God bless Africa:
Guard her children,
Guide her rulers,
And give her peace.
For Jesus Christ's sake.

Bishop Huddleston's prayer for Africa

DOING

Lead us not into imitation. 207

Prayer of East Asia Christian Youth Consultation Council, in a report which bears on its cover a Coca-Cola bottle, superimposed on a map of Asia.

Grant, O Lord, that thy Spirit may permeate every sphere of human thought and activity. Let those who believe in thee take with them into their daily work the values of thy kingdom, the insights of the gospel and the love of their fellow-men. Hasten the time when justice and brotherhood shall be established and when all men shall be brought into the unity of thy Son, our Saviour Jesus Christ. 208

G.A.

Thou art never weary, O Lord, of doing us good. Let us never be weary of doing thee service. But, as thou hast pleasure in the prosperity of thy servants, so let us take pleasure in the service of our Lord, and abound in thy work, and in thy love and praise evermore. O fill up all that is wanting, reform whatever is amiss in us, perfect the thing that concerneth us. Let the witness of thy pardoning love ever abide in all our hearts. 209

John Wesley, 1703–91

Lord Jesus Christ 210
alive and at large in the world,
help me to follow and find you there today,
in the places where I work,
meet people,
spend money
and make plans.
Take me as a disciple of your kingdom,
to see through your eyes,
and hear the questions you are asking,
to welcome all men with your trust and truth
and to change the things that contradict God's love,
by the power of the Cross
and the freedom of your Spirit. Amen.

John Taylor, Bishop of Winchester

O God, make the door of this house wide enough to receive all who need human love and fellowship; narrow enough to shut out all envy, pride and strife. 211

Make its threshold smooth enough to be no stumbling-block to children, nor to straying feet, but rugged and strong enough to turn back the tempter's power. God make the door of this house the gateway to thine eternal kingdom.

on St Stephen's Walbrook, London. Bishop Thomas Ken, 1637–1711

212 We beg you, Lord, to help and defend us. Deliver the oppressed, pity the insignificant, raise the fallen, show yourself to the needy, heal the sick, bring back those of your people who have gone astray, feed the hungry, lift up the weak, take off the prisoners' chains. May every nation come to know that you alone are God, that Jesus Christ is your Child, that we are your people, the sheep that you pasture.

St Clement of Rome, *c.* 100

213 O Almighty God, the Father of all mankind, we pray thee to turn to thyself the hearts of all peoples and their rulers, that by the power of thy Holy Spirit peace may be established on the foundation of justice, righteousness and truth; through Him who was lifted up on the cross to draw all men unto Himself, even thy Son Jesus Christ our Lord.

William Temple, 1881–1944

214 God and Father of all, who from the beginning came to bring light and truth and love to man, by the Word, grant to us who deal with words and images, such a reverence for thee, that through careful and honest work, we may keep the coinage of our language sound. Give us humility to realize that we are called, not to be perfect but to be clear, not to be infallible but to be fair. Direct those who in this our generation speak where many listen, who write what many read, and who show what many see, that they may do their part in making the heart of our people wise, its mind sound, and its will righteous.

David B. Collins

215 O Lord and Saviour Christ, who comest not to strive nor cry, but to let thy words fall as the drops that water the earth; grant all who contend for the faith once delivered, never to injure it by clamour and impatience; but speaking thy precious truth in love so to present it that it may be loved, and that men may see in it thy goodness and thy beauty . . .

William Bright, 1824–1901

SERVING

O Lord, without whom our labour is but lost, and with whom thy little ones go forth as the mighty; be present to all works in thy Church which are undertaken according to thy will (*especially* . . .) and grant to thy labourers a pure intention, patient faith, sufficient success upon earth and the bliss of serving thee in heaven; through Jesus Christ our Lord. 216

William Bright, 1824–1901

Serving

Lord, make me an instrument of your peace. 217
Where there is hatred, let me sow love,
Where there is injury, pardon;
Where there is doubt, faith;
Where there is despair, hope;
Where there is darkness, light;
Where there is sadness, joy.
O divine Master, Grant that I may not so much seek
To be consoled, as to console,
To be understood, as to understand,
To be loved, as to love,
For it is in giving that we receive;
It is in pardoning that we are pardoned;
It is in dying that we are born to eternal life.

St Francis of Assisi, 1181–1226

Father, 218
who hast made all men in thy likeness
and lovest all whom thou hast made,
suffer not our family to separate itself from thee
by building barriers of race and colour.
As thy Son our Saviour was born of a Hebrew mother, but
rejoiced in the faith of a Syrian woman and of a Roman
soldier, welcomed the Greeks who sought him,
and suffered a man from Africa to carry his cross,
so teach us to regard the members of all races as
fellow-heirs of the kingdom of Jesus Christ our Lord. **Toc H**

Make us worthy, Lord, 219
To serve our fellow-men
Throughout the world who live and die
In poverty or hunger.

Give them, through our hands
this day their daily bread,
And by our understanding love,
Give peace and joy.

Mother Teresa, Calcutta

220 O Lord, I remember before thee tonight all the workers of the world:
Workers with hand or brain:
Workers in cities or in the fields:
Men who go forth to toil and women who keep house:
Employers and employees:
Those who command and those who obey:
Those whose work is dangerous:
Those whose work is monotonous or mean:
Those who can find no work to do:
Those whose work is the service of the poor
Or the healing of the sick
Or the proclamation of the gospel of Christ
At home or in foreign places.

John Baillie, 1886–1960

221 O God our Saviour, who willest that all men should be saved and come to the knowledge of the truth, prosper, we pray thee, our brethren who labour in distant lands. Protect them in all perils by land and sea, support them in loneliness and in the hour of trial; give them grace to bear faithful witness unto thee, and endue them with burning zeal and love, that they may turn many to righteousness and finally obtain a crown of glory; through Jesus Christ.

A prayer for missionaries. Scottish Book of Common Prayer, 1912

222 Lord, why did you tell me to love all men, my brothers?
I have tried, but I come back to you, frightened . . .
Lord, I was so peaceful at home, I was so comfortably settled.
It was well furnished, and I felt cosy.
I was alone, I was at peace,
Sheltered from the wind, the rain, the mud.
I would have stayed unsullied in my ivory tower.
But, Lord, you have discovered a breach in my defences,
You have forced me to open my door,
Like a squall of rain in the face, the cry of men has awakened me.

SERVING

Like a gale of wind a friendship has shaken me,
As a ray of light slips in unnoticed, your grace has stirred me
. . . and, rashly enough, I left my door ajar. Now, Lord, I am lost!
Outside men were lying in wait for me.
I did not know they were so near; in this house, in this street, in this office; my neighbour, my colleague, my friend.
As soon as I started to open the door I saw them, with outstretched hands, burning eyes, longing hearts, like beggars on church steps.

The first ones came in, Lord. There was after all some space in my heart.
I welcomed them. I would have cared for them and fondled them, my very own little lambs, my little flock.
You would have been pleased, Lord, I would have served and honoured you in a proper, respectable way.
Till then, it was sensible . . .
But the next ones, Lord, the other men, I had not seen them; they were hidden behind the first ones.
There were more of them, they were wretched; they overpowered me without warning.
We had to crowd in, I had to find room for them.
Now they have come from all over, in successive waves, pushing one another, jostling one another.
They have come from all over town, from all parts of the country, of the world; numberless, inexhaustible.
They don't come alone any longer but in groups, bound one to another.
They come bending under heavy loads; loads of injustice, of resentment and hate, of suffering and sin . . .
They drag the world behind them, with everything rusted, twisted, or badly adjusted.

Lord, they hurt me! They are in the way, they are everywhere.
They are too hungry, they are consuming me!
I can't do anything any more; as they come in, they push the door, and the door opens wider . . .
Lord! my door is wide open!
I can't stand it any more! It's too much! It's no kind of a life! What about my job? my family? my peace? my liberty? and me?
Lord, I have lost everything, I don't belong to myself any longer;
There's no more room for me at home.

Don't worry, God says, you have gained all.
While men came in to you,
I, your Father,
I, your God,
Slipped in among them.

Michel Quoist

223 **Lord, thou hast made us citizens of a fair city and inheritors of a valiant freedom. Grant that thy Spirit may invest our mightiest endeavours and our humblest toil. Nourish in us the fruits of the Spirit that the splendour of London may shine forth in the world, to thy honour and glory and the welfare of the brethren.**

A prayer for London. Cecil Hunt

Peace

224 **Lord, make this world to last as long as possible.**

Prayer of 11-year-old child on hearing of Sino-Indian border fighting

225 **O God of many names**
Lover of all nations
We pray for peace
in our hearts
in our homes
in our nations
in our world
The peace of your will
The peace of our need.

G.A.

226 **O sweet Child of Bethlehem, grant that we may share with all our hearts in this profound mystery of Christmas. Put into the hearts of men this peace for which they sometimes seek so desperately and which you alone can give them. Help them to know one another better, and to live as brothers, children of the same Father.**

Reveal to them also your beauty, holiness and purity. Awaken in their hearts love and gratitude for your infinite goodness. Join them all together in your love. And give us your heavenly peace.

Pope John XXIII, 1881–1963

227 **Lord, we pray for the power to be gentle; the strength to be forgiving; the patience to be understanding; and the endurance to accept the consequences of holding to what we believe to be right.**

May we put our trust in the power of good to overcome evil and the power of love to overcome hatred. We pray for the vision to see and the

faith to believe in a world emancipated from violence, a new world where fear shall no longer lead men to commit injustice, nor selfishness make them bring suffering to others.

Help us to devote our whole life and thought and energy to the task of making peace, praying always for the inspiration and the power to fulfil the destiny for which we and all men were created.

Week of Prayer for World Peace, 1978

God send that there may be an end at last; God send that there may be peace again. God in heaven send us peace. 228

Diary of Hartich Sierk, a peasant (1628)

Almighty God, in whose hands lies the destiny of men and nations, Let not the hopes of men perish, nor the sacrifices of men be in vain. 229

O holy and life-giving Spirit, enable us by thy grace to root out from our common life the bitterness of ancient wrongs and the thirst to avenge the betrayals of long ago. Save us from the tyranny of history and set us free in a new obedience to serve each other in the present hour.

Accepting the redemption wrought for us, we believe that all our sins of yesterday are covered by thy mercy; grant us therefore grace and courage to give and to receive the forgiveness which alone can heal today's wounds. Draw us, O Lord, towards loving kindness and guide us into the way of peace.

Anon.

O Lord, calm the waves of this heart; calm its tempests. Calm thyself, O my soul, so that the divine can act in thee. Calm thyself, O my soul, so that God is able to repose in thee, so that his peace may cover thee. Yes, Father in heaven, often have we found that the world cannot give us peace, O but make us feel that thou art able to give peace; let us know the truth of thy promise: that the whole world may not be able to take away thy peace. 230

Søren Kierkegaard, 1813–55

Let us not seek out of thee what we can 231
only find in thee, O Lord.
Peace and rest and joy and bliss,
which abide only in thine abiding joy.

Lift up our souls above the weary round of
harassing thoughts to thy eternal presence.
Lift up our minds to the pure, bright serene
atmosphere of thy presence,
that we may breathe freely,
there repose in thy love,
there be at rest from ourselves
and from all things that weary us:
and thence return, arrayed in thy peace,
to do and to bear
whatsoever shall best please thee,
O blessed Lord.

E. B. Pusey, 1800–82

232 Drop thy still dews of quietness,
Till all our strivings cease;
Take from our souls the strain and stress,
And let our ordered lives confess
The beauty of thy peace.

J. G. Whittier, 1807–92

233 Set free, O Lord, the souls of thy servants from all restlessness and anxiety. Give us that peace and power which flow from thee. Keep us in all perplexity and distress, that upheld by thy strength and stayed on the rock of thy faithfulness we may abide in thee now and evermore.

234 Almighty God, from whom all thoughts of truth and peace proceed, kindle, we pray thee, in the hearts of all men the true love of peace, and guide with thy pure and peaceable wisdom those who take counsel for the nations of the earth; that in tranquillity thy kingdom may go forward, till the earth be filled with the knowledge of thy love; through Jesus Christ our Lord.

Francis Paget, Bishop of Oxford, 1851–1911

235 Show us, good Lord,
the peace we should seek,
the peace we must give,
the peace we can keep,
the peace we must forgo,
and the peace you have given in Jesus our Lord.

From *Contemporary Prayers for Public Worship*, ed. Caryl Micklem

'THY WILL BE DONE'

Dedication

I delight to do thy will, O my God: thy law is within my heart. 236

Psalm 40: 8

Take, Lord, all my liberty. Receive my memory, my understanding and my whole will. Whatever I have and possess thou hast given to me; to thee I restore it wholly, and to thy will I utterly surrender it for thy direction. Give me the love of thee only, with thy grace, and I am rich enough; nor ask I anything beside. 237

St Ignatius Loyola, 1491–1556

O God, I know that if I do not love thee with all my heart, with all my mind, with all my soul and with all my strength, I shall love something else with all my heart and mind and soul and strength. Grant that putting thee first in all my lovings I may be liberated from all lesser loves and loyalties, and have thee as my first love, my chiefest good and my final joy. 238

G.A.

Thee, God, I come from, to thee go, 239
All day long I like fountain flow
From thy hand out, swayed about
Mote-like in thy mighty glow.

What I know of thee I bless,
As acknowledging thy stress
On my being and as seeing
Something of thy holiness.

Once I turned from thee and hid,
Bound on what thou hadst forbid;
Sow the wind I would; I sinned:
I repent of what I did.

Bad I am, but yet thy child.
Father, be thou reconciled.
Spare thou me, since I see
With thy might that thou art mild.

I have life left with me still
And thy purpose to fulfil;
Yea a debt to pay thee yet:
Help me, sir, and so I will . . .

Gerard Manley Hopkins, 1844–89

240 Forgive me Lord for thinking years ago that to serve you as a priest unmarried was service of a higher, better kind;
That love, the greatest of your gifts to man, was best sublimated, not expressed;
That marriage, with responsibility for family life, was a lower form of priestly service.
And now that years have passed, help me to bear the burden of the consequence, the burden of loving and longing to love more, yet bound by no gesture to indicate that love to those beloved.
Perhaps in some mysterious way, this means that the whole world can be my family, the object of my love.
But if this be what your loving providence demands, give me that love which is sensitive, compassionate, controlled, the kind of love, if such exists, that transcends the nature you have given me, reaching a plane which I do not, cannot, fully comprehend.
So that amidst the conventions, customs of this world you made and love and customs and conventions so often artificial—no harm may come from anything I do or don't do to those I love. But grant, good Lord, that from all contacts with the world, my family, all blessings possible may flow upon them and upon me.

Edward Maycock, 1907–72

241 Grant me, O Lord, an understanding heart, that I may see into the hearts of thy people, and know their strengths and weaknesses, their hopes and their despairs, their efforts and their failures, their need of love and their need to love. Through my touch with them grant comfort and hope and the assurance that now life begins at any age and on any day, redeeming the past, sanctifying the present and brightening the future with the assurance of thy unfailing love and grace brought to us in Jesus Christ, thy Son, our Lord.

G.A.

242 Prince-Archbishop, Father Adelhard,
Now at the pinnacle of priesthood,
I say to thee farewell.
Almighty God grant all go well with thee.

DEDICATION

Be an honour to the church, follow Christ's word,
 Clear in thy task and careful in thy speech.
Be thine an open hand, a merry heart,
 Christ in thy mouth, life that all men may know
A lover of righteousness and compassion.
 Let none come to thee and go sad away.
Hope of poor men, and solace to the sad,
 Go thou before God's people to God's realm,
That he who follows thee may come to the stars.
 Sow living seeds, words that are quick with life,
That faith may be the harvest in men's hearts.
 In word and in example let thy light
Shine in the black dark like the morning star.
 Let not the wealth of the world nor its dominion
Flatter thee into silence as to truth,
 Nor king, nor judge, yea, nor thy dearest friend
Muzzle thy lips from righteousness.

Alcuin of York, 735–804

When I found truth, there I found my God who is the truth. And there since the time I learned thee, thou abidest in my memory; and there I find thee, whensoever I call thee to remembrance, and delight in thee. 243

St Augustine, 354–430

Lord, take my lips and speak through them; take my mind and think through it; take my heart and set it on fire. 244

W. H. H. Aitken

My Father, I abandon myself to you. Do with me as you will. 245
Whatever you may do with me, I thank you.
I am prepared for anything, I accept everything.
Provided your will is fulfilled in me and in all
creatures I ask for nothing more my God.
I place my soul in your hands.
I give it to you, my God,
with all the love of my heart
because I love you.

And for me it is a necessity of love,
this gift of myself,
this placing of myself in your hands
without reserve
in boundless confidence
because you are my Father.

Charles de Foucauld, 1858–1916

246 Stay with me, and then I shall begin to shine as thou shinest: so to shine as to be a light to others. The light, O Jesus, will be all from thee. None of it will be mine. No merit to me. It will be thou who shinest through me upon others. O let me thus praise thee, in the way which thou dost love best, by shining on all those around me. Give light to them as well as to me; light them with me, through me. Teach me to show forth thy praise, thy truth, thy will. Make me preach thee without preaching—not by words, but by my example and by the catching force, the sympathetic influence, of what I do—by my visible resemblance to thy saints, and the evident fulness of the love which my heart bears to thee.

John Henry Newman, 1801–90

247 Let the healing grace of your love, O Lord, so transform me that I may play my part in the transfiguration of the world from a place of suffering, death and corruption to a realm of infinite light, joy and love. Make me so obedient to your Spirit that my life may become a living prayer, and a witness to your unfailing presence.

Martin Israel

248 Thou who art over us,
Thou who art one of us,
Thou who *art*—
Also within us,
May all see thee—in me also,
May I prepare the way for thee,
May I thank thee for all that shall fall to my lot,
May I also not forget the needs of others,
Keep me in thy love
As thou wouldest that all should be kept in mine
May everything in this my being be directed to thy glory
And may I never despair.
For I am under thy hand,
And in thee is all power and goodness.

DEDICATION

Give me a pure heart—that I may see thee,
A humble heart—that I may hear thee,
A heart of love—that I may serve thee,
A heart of faith—that I may abide in thee.

To love life and men as God loves them—for the sake of their infinite
possibilities,
to wait like him
to judge like him
without passing judgment,
to obey the order when it is given
and never look back—
then he can use you—then, perhaps, he will use you.
And if he doesn't use you—what matter. In his hand,
every moment has its meaning, its greatness, its glory,
its peace, its co-inherence.

Dag Hammarskjöld, 1905–61

Father, into thy hands I give the heart 249
Which left thee but to learn how good thou art.

George Macdonald, 1824–1905

Lord make thy will our will in all things. 250

Dean Vaughan, 1816–97

O thou who camest from above, 251
The pure celestial fire to impart,
Kindle a flame of sacred love
On the mean altar of my heart.

There let it for thy glory burn
With inextinguishable blaze,
And trembling to its source return
In humble prayer, and fervent praise.

Charles Wesley, 1707–88

My Father, do with me as thou wilt, only help me against myself and for 252
thee; I am thy child, the inheritor of thy spirit, thy being, a part of thyself, glorious in thee, but grown poor in me: let me be thy dog, thy horse, thy anything, anything thou willest; let me be thine in any shape the love that is my Father may please to have me; let me be thine in any way, and my own or another's in no way but thine.

George Macdonald, 1824–1905

253 Almighty God, who hast led men and women in this as in every age to surrender all that they possess, and to bind themselves in spiritual families for thy single service: accept their oblation and hallow their common life, we beseech thee most merciful Father: and move thy whole Church to press forward with them to the more perfect obedience of thy Son, our Saviour Jesus Christ, who with thee and the Holy Ghost liveth and reigneth one God, world without end.

Ascribed to Bishop Basil Roberts, 1887–1957

Obedience

254 Dearest Lord, teach me to be generous;
Teach me to serve thee as thou deservest;
To give and not to count the cost,
To fight and not to heed the wounds,
To toil and not to seek for rest,
To labour and not to seek reward,
Save that of knowing that I do thy will.

St Ignatius Loyola, 1491–1556

255 Lord, make me according to thy heart.

Brother Lawrence, 1611–91

256 O God, who by our great Master's example, hast taught us what labours and sufferings heaven deserves, and that we are to take it by force; confound in us, we beseech thee, the nice tenderness of our nature, which is averse to that discipline and hardship we ought to endure as disciples and soldiers of Jesus Christ; help us in our way thither, by self-denial and mortification, for the sake of our Lord Jesus Christ, who liveth and reigneth with thee and thy Holy Spirit, ever one God, world without end.

John Wesley, 1703–91

257 *Before* thee, Father,
  In righteousness and humility,
With thee, Brother,
  In faith and courage,
In thee, Spirit,
  In stillness.

Dag Hammarskjöld, 1905–61

OBEDIENCE

Grant unto us thy servants 258
To our God—a heart of flame
To our fellow men—a heart of love
To ourselves—a heart of steel.

Prayer adapted from St Augustine of Hippo, 354–430

That I am and how that I am, as in nature and in grace, all I have it of thee, Lord, and thou it art. And all I offer it unto thee, principally to the praising of thee, for the help of all mine even Christians and of me. 259

from *The Epistle of Privy Counsel*, by the author of *The Cloud of Unknowing*, 14th century

My Lord, I have nothing to do in this world, but to seek and serve thee; I have nothing to do with a heart and its affections, but to breathe after thee; I have nothing to do with my tongue and pen, but to speak to thee, and for thee, and to publish thy glory and thy will. 260

Richard Baxter, 1615–91

God of mercy, God of grace, 261
  teach me to hold my will attentive
  in the liberty thou gavest me,
  that I may will with thee to do thy will
  as thou dost show it me;
  draw me to respond to thee
  in each separate occasion of the passing time
that when the vanities of earth are passed
  I may remain for ever
in the loving rhythm of thy everlasting peace.

Fr Gilbert Shaw, 1886–1967

O God, thou knowest that I do not want anything else but to serve thee and men, always, all my life. 262

Temple Gairdner of Cairo, 1873–1928

O my Love, I cannot love thee but I must desire above all things to be like my Beloved. O give me grace to tread in thy steps and conform me to thy divine image, that the more I grow like thee, the more I may love thee, and the more I may be loved by thee. 263

Bishop Thomas Ken, 1637–1711

264 O God, hearken to my prayer,
Let my earnest petition come to thee,
For I know that thou art hearing me
As surely as though I saw thee with my eyes.

I am placing a lock upon my heart,
I am placing a lock upon my thoughts,
I am placing a lock upon my lips
And double-knitting them.

But mayest thou thyself, O God of life,
Be at my breast, be at my back,
Thou to me as a star, thou to me as a guide
From my life's beginning to my life's closing.

from *Carmina Gadelica*, tr. Alexander Carmichael

265 O Jesus
Be the canoe that holds me in the sea of life.
Be the steer that keeps me straight.
Be the outrigger that supports me in times of great temptation.
Let thy spirit be my sail that carries me through each day.
Keep my body strong,
so that I can paddle steadfastly on,
in the long voyage of life.

A New Hebridean prayer

266 O God, I am Mustafah the tailor and I work at the shop of Muhammad Ali. The whole day long I sit and pull the needle and the thread through the cloth. O God, you are the needle and I am the thread. I am attached to you and I follow you. When the thread tries to slip away from the needle it becomes tangled and must be cut so that it can be put back in the right place. O God, help me to follow you wherever you may lead me. For I am really only Mustafah the tailor, and I work at the shop of Muhammad Ali on the great square.

A Muslim's first prayer as a Christian

267 God stir the soil,
Run the ploughshare deep,
Cut the furrows round and round,
Overturn the hard, dry ground,
Spare no strength nor toil,
Even though I weep.

OBEDIENCE

In the loose, fresh mangled earth
Sow new seed.
Free of withered vine and weed
Bring fair flowers to birth.

Prayer from Singapore, Church Missionary Society

O Lord Jesus our God 268
Who called people from their daily work
Saying to them 'Come ye after me',
May your children today hear your voice
And gladly answer your call
To give their lives to you
To serve your Church
To offer their gifts
And give away their hearts
To you only.
Bless their hopes
The first tiny stirrings of desire
The little resolve to go forward
The small vision of what might be.
Deal gently with their fears
The hesitation of uncertainty
The darkness of the unknown
The lack of confidence in their own capacity
And turn it all to trust in you.

Gabrielle Hadingham, United Society for the Propagation of the Gospel

Whom have I in heaven but thee: there is none upon earth that I desire in 269
comparison of thee. Psalm 73: 24

When thou saidst, 'Seek ye my face', my heart said unto thee, 'Thy face, 270
Lord, will I seek.' Psalm 27: 8

Lord Jhesu Crist, that madest me, 271
That boughtest me on rode-tree
And fore-ordeinedst that I be,
Thou knowst what Thou wouldst do with me;
Do with me now as pleseth Thee.
Amen, Jhesu, for Thy pyte. King Henry VI, 1421–71

272 God be in my head, and in my understanding;
God be in my eyes, and in my looking;
God be in my mouth, and in my speaking;
God be in my heart, and in my thinking;
God be at my end, and at my departing.

Old Sarum Primer

273 Into thy hands, Almighty Father, who dost will peace and purpose loving kindness, we commend our spirits: our minds to know thee, our hearts to love thee, our wills to serve thee, for we are thine. Into thy hands, incarnate Saviour, who hast taught us that thou art the way, the truth and the life: receive us and draw us after thee, that we may follow thy steps: enlighten and guide us lest the night of sin and error overwhelm us: abide in us and quicken us by the power of thine indwelling: into thy hands, O Lord the spirit, who createst good and destroyest evil, take us and fashion us after thine image: let thy comfort strengthen, thy grace renew, and thy fire cleanse us. Soul and body, in life and in death, in this world of shadows and in thy changeless world of life eternal, now and for ever, Father, Son and Holy Ghost, into thy hands.

F. B. Macnutt 1873–1949

274 O King of glory and Lord of Valours, our warrior and our peace, who hast said 'Be of good cheer, I have overcome the world', be thou victorious in us thy servants, for without thee we can do nothing. Give us to will and to perform. Grant thy compassion to go before us, thy compassion to come behind us: before us in our undertaking, behind us in our ending. And what shall I now say, unless that thy will be done, who dost will that all men should be saved. Thy will is our salvation, our glory, and our joy.

Alcuin of York, 735–804

275 Lord, I believe thou art the way, the truth and the life. Make me so to walk with thee that by thee I may come to the Father; make my faith strong to believe all that thou hast revealed, for thou art the very truth. Give me thy life that I may say, 'I live, yet not I, but Christ liveth in me': by thy divine omnipotence direct and strengthen my faith: by thy divine wisdom instruct and enlighten it: by thy divine goodness sustain and perfect it, that I may abide in thee unchanging to the end.

S. C. Hughson

OBEDIENCE

Set our hearts on fire with love to thee, O Christ our God, that in its flame we may love thee with all our heart, with all our mind, with all our soul and with all our strength, and our neighbours as ourselves, so that, keeping thy commandments, we may glorify thee the giver of all good gifts. 276

Kontakion for love, Eastern Orthodox Church

O Lord Jesus Christ, only-begotten Son of thy eternal Father, thou hast said with thy most pure lips: Without me ye can do nothing. O Lord, my Lord, with faith I embrace in my heart and soul the words spoken by thee; help me, a sinner, to accomplish the task begun for thine own sake by me, in the name of the Father and of the Son and of the Holy Ghost. 277

Prayer before any acts, Eastern Orthodox Church

Lord Jesus Christ, Son of the living God, 278
teach us to walk in your way more trustfully,
to accept your truth more faithfully,
and to share your life more lovingly.
By the power of the Holy Spirit
guide us in our work for the Church,
so that we may come as one family
to the Kingdom of the Father,
where you live for ever.

National Pastoral Congress, Liverpool, 1980

O good Jesu, the word of the Father, the brightness of the Father's glory, whom angels desire to behold; teach me to do thy will; that guided by thy good spirit, I may come unto that blessed city where there is everlasting day and all are of one spirit; where there is certain security and secure eternity and eternal tranquillity and quiet felicity and happy sweetness and sweet pleasantness; where thou, with the Father and the Holy Ghost livest and reignest, world without end. 279

St Gregory, d. 638

Speak, Lord, for thy servant heareth. Grant us ears to hear, eyes to see, wills to obey, hearts to love; then declare what thou wilt, reveal what thou wilt, command what thou wilt, demand what thou wilt—Amen. 280

Christina G. Rossetti, 1830–94

'AS IT IS IN HEAVEN'

Guidance

281 O creator past all telling,
you have appointed from the treasures of your wisdom
the hierarchies of angels,
disposing them in wondrous order above the bright heavens,
and have so beautifully set out all parts of the universe.
You we call the true fount of wisdom
and the noble origin of all things.
Be pleased to shed on the darkness of mind in which I was born,
The twofold beam of your light
and warmth to dispel my ignorance and sin.
You make eloquent the tongues of children.
Then instruct my speech and touch my lips with graciousness.
Make me keen to understand, quick to learn,
able to remember;
make me delicate to interpret and ready to speak.
Guide my going in and going forward,
lead home my going forth.
You are true God and true man,
and live for ever and ever.

St Thomas Aquinas, 1225–74

282 O Holy Spirit, whose presence is liberty, grant us that freedom of the Spirit which will not fear to tread in unknown ways, nor be held back by misgivings of ourselves and fear of others. Ever beckon us forward to the place of thy will which is also the place of thy power, O ever-leading, ever-loving Lord.

G.A.

283 My Father, teach us not only thy will, but how to do it. Teach us the best way of doing the best thing, lest we spoil the end by unworthy means.

Revd J. H. Jowett, 1846–1923

284 Grant to me, O Lord, to know what I ought to know, to love what I ought to love, to praise what delights Thee most, to value what is precious in thy sight, to hate what is offensive to Thee. Do not suffer me to judge

according to the sight of my eyes, nor to pass sentence according to the hearing of the ears of ignorant men; but to discern with true judgement between things visible and spiritual, and above all things to enquire what is the good pleasure of thy will.

Thomas à Kempis, 1380–1471

Take away, O Lord, the veil of my heart while I read the scriptures. 285
Blessed art thou, O Lord: O teach me thy statutes! Give me a word, O Word of the Father: touch my heart: enlighten the understandings of my heart: open my lips and fill them with thy praise.

Bishop Lancelot Andrewes, 1555–1626

O God by whom the meek are guided in judgement, and light riseth up in 286
the darkness for the godly; grant us, in all our doubts and uncertainties, the grace to ask what thou wouldst have us do; that the Spirit of Wisdom may save us from all false choices and that in thy light we may see light, and in thy straight path may not stumble; through Jesus Christ our Lord.

William Bright (1824–1901), *Ancient Collects*

O Lord God, we thank thee that thy Spirit is ever urging the spirits of 287
men to higher achievements of wisdom and skill, love and goodness. We praise thee for the developing universe, by obeying whose laws men can circle the earth and reach towards the stars. Grant thy wisdom and protection to those who would go still further, and help them to know that they can never overtake thee nor pass out of thy care, through thy perfect Son, Jesus Christ, our Lord.

G.A.

Trusting in thy Word, O Lord, we wait for thy Spirit. Send him forth 288
from thy holy heaven to sanctify our deeps, which without him are empty and without form. Quicken us, O Lord, in thy loving kindness.

via G.A.

O eternal God, who hast made all things for man, and man for thy glory, 289
sanctify my body and soul, my thoughts and my intentions, my words and actions, that whatsoever I shall think, or speak, or do, may be by me designed to the glorification of thy name; and by thy blessing it may be effective and successful in the work of God, according as it can be

capable. Lord, turn my necessities into virtue; the works of nature into the works of grace, by making them orderly, regular, temperate, subordinate, and profitable to ends beyond their own proper efficacy; and let no pride or self-seeking, no covetousness or revenge, no impure mixture or unhandsome purposes, no little ends or low imaginations, pollute my spirit, and unhallow any of my words and actions: but let my body be a servant to my spirit, and both body and spirit servants of Jesus, that, doing all things for thy glory here, I may be partaker of thy glory hereafter, through Jesus Christ our Lord.

Jeremy Taylor, 1613–67

290 O Lord, who hast ordained labour to be the lot of man, and seest the necessities of all thy creatures, bless my studies and endeavours; feed me with food convenient for me; and if it shall be thy good pleasure to entrust me with plenty, give me a compassionate heart, that I may be ready to relieve the wants of others; let neither poverty nor riches estrange my heart from thee, but assist me with thy grace so to live that I may die in thy favour, for the sake of Jesus Christ.

Samuel Johnson, 1709–84

291 Almighty God, the giver of all good things, without whose help all labour is ineffectual, and without whose grace all wisdom is folly; grant, I beseech thee, that in this my undertaking, thy Holy Spirit may not be withheld from me, but that I may promote thy glory, and the salvation both of myself and others; grant this O Lord, for the sake of Jesus Christ. Lord bless me. So be it.

Samuel Johnson (1709–84) on *The Rambler*

292 In times of doubts and questionings, when our belief is perplexed by new learning, new teaching, new thought, when our faith is strained by creeds, by doctrines, by mysteries beyond our understanding, give us the faithfulness of learners and the courage of believers in thee; give us boldness to examine and faith to trust all truth; patience and insight to master difficulties; stability to hold fast our tradition with enlightened interpretation to admit all fresh truth made known to us, and in times of trouble, to grasp new knowledge readily and to combine it loyally and honestly with the old; alike from stubborn rejection of new revelations, and from hasty assurance that we are wiser than our fathers,

Save us and help us, we humbly beseech thee, O Lord.

Bishop George Ridding, 1828–1904

O most blessed Truth, to you I commit this decision, for you know all things, and your will is our peace. Deliver me from the false choices that come from self-interest, cowardice and lack of faith in you, and give me vision and strength to do your will. 293

Margaret Cropper, 1886–1980

Acceptance

I have calmed and quieted my soul, like a child quieted at its mother's breast: like a child that is quieted is my soul. 294

Psalm 131: 3

O Lord God, in whom we live, and move, and have our being, open our eyes that we may behold thy fatherly presence ever about us. Draw our hearts to thee with the power of thy love. Teach us to be careful for nothing, and when we have done what thou hast given us to do, help us, O God, our Saviour, to leave the issue to thy wisdom. Take from us all doubt and distrust. Lift our thoughts up to thee in heaven, and make us to know that all things are possible to us through thy Son, our Redeemer. 295

Bishop Brooke Foss Westcott, 1825–1901

Grant me, O most merciful Jesus, thy grace, that it may be with me, and labour with me, and abide with me even to the end. 296

Give me grace ever to desire and to will what is most acceptable to thee, and most pleasing in thy sight.

Let thy will be mine, and let my will ever follow thine, and fully accord with it.

Let there be between thee and me but one will, so that I may love what thou lovest, and abhor what thou hatest; and let me not be able to will any thing which thou dost not will, nor to dislike any thing which thou dost will.

Thomas à Kempis, 1380–1471

You love with an everlasting love because you are love. And so you are patiently effective always and everywhere, even when we cannot feel your presence. Teach us to love without wanting to control; to love without limit; to love you, our friends, and also our enemies. Teach us to be patient in love when love is not returned; teach us to be patient when even you are apparently far away. Teach us loving, waiting, patience when there is no answer to our questionings and our doubt. 297

Michael Hollings and Etta Gullick

298 I did not know you, my Lord, because I still desired to know and delight in things.

Well and good if all things change, Lord God, provided we are rooted in you.

If I go everywhere with you, my God, everywhere things will happen as I desire for your sake.

St John of the Cross, 1542–91

299 O Lord, I know not what to ask of thee. Thou alone knowest what are my true needs. Thou lovest me more than I myself know how to love. Help me to see my real needs which are concealed from me. I dare not ask either a cross or consolation. I can only wait on thee. My heart is open to thee. Visit and help me, for thy great mercy's sake. Strike me and heal me, cast me down and raise me up. I worship in silence thy holy will and thine inscrutable ways. I offer myself as a sacrifice to thee. I put all my trust in thee. I have no other desire than to fulfil thy will. Teach me how to pray. Pray thou thyself in me.

Metropolitan Philaret of Moscow, 1553–1633

300 Lord, give me patience in tribulation and grace in everything to conform my will to thine; that I may truly say: 'Fiat voluntas tua, sicut in coelo et in terra'.

The things, good Lord, that I pray for, give me thy grace to labour for.

St Thomas More, 1478–1535

301 God, give us grace to accept with serenity the things
that cannot be changed, courage to change the
things that should be changed, and the wisdom to
distinguish the one from the other

Reinhold Niebuhr, 1892–1971

302 Leave it all quietly to God, my soul, my rescue comes from him alone.

Psalm 62: 1, 2 (Moffatt)

303 O Lord God
when we pray unto thee
    desiring well and meaning truly,
if thou seest a better way
    to thy glory and our good,

then be thy will done,
  and not ours:
as with thy dear Son
  in the Garden of Agony,
even Jesus Christ our Lord.

Eric Milner-White, 1884–1964

Lord, I thank you for teaching me how to live in the present moment. In this way I enjoy each simple task as I do it without thinking that I must hurry on to the next thing. I do what I am doing with all my ability and all my concentration. My mind is no longer divided, and life is more peaceful. Thank you for teaching me how to do this, and please help me how to show others the way to learn to trust you more completely and to do everything which has to be done at your time and your speed. 304

Michael Hollings and Etta Gullick

O most blessed grace, which makest the poor in spirit, rich in virtues; and makest the rich in many goods, humble in heart! 305

Come thou, descend upon me, refresh me early with thy mercy and thy consolation, that my soul may not faint for weariness and dryness of spirit.

I beseech thee, O Lord, that I may find grace in thy sight, for thy grace is sufficient for me, though the things which nature desires be wanting.

Thomas à Kempis, 1380–1471

'GIVE US THIS DAY'

Daily

Good morning, Guvnor, and thank you. Hospital porter's prayer 306

A CHILD'S PRAYER 307

Ah, dearest Jesus, holy Child,
Make thee a bed, soft, undefiled,
Within my heart, that it may be
A quiet chamber kept for thee.

Martin Luther, 1483–1546

'GIVE US THIS DAY'

308 O God, grant that I may do and suffer all things this day for the glory of thy name.

Used by the Curé d'Ars, 1786–1859

309 My God, grant me the conversion of my parish; I am willing to suffer all my life whatsoever it may please thee to lay upon me; yes even for a hundred years am I prepared to endure the sharpest pains, only let my people be converted.

My God, convert my parish.

Curé d'Ars, 1786–1859

310 Father in heaven! When the thought of thee wakes in our hearts let it not awaken like a frightened bird that flies about in dismay, but like a child waking from its sleep with a heavenly smile.

Søren Kierkegaard, 1813–55

311 Blessed be the hour, O Christ, in which thou wast born, and the hour in which thou didst die:

Blessed be the dawn of thy rising again, and the high day of thine ascending. O most merciful and mighty redeemer Christ, let all times be the time of our presence with thee, and of thy dwelling in us.

Eric Milner-White, 1884–1964

312 Eternal Father of my soul, let my first thought today be of thee, let my first impulse be to worship thee, let my first speech be thy name, let my first action be to kneel before thee in prayer.

John Baillie, 1886–1960

313 O Lord Jesus Christ, which art the sun of the world, evermore arising, and never going down, which by thy most wholesome appearing and sight dost bring forth, preserve, nourish and refresh all things, as well that are in heaven, as also that are on earth; we beseech thee mercifully and favourably to shine into our hearts, that the night and darkness of sins, and the mists of errors on every side are driven away, thou brightly shining within our hearts, we may all our life space go without stumbling or offence, and may decently and seemly walk, (as in the day time) being pure and clean from the works of darkness, and abounding in all good

works which God hath prepared for us to walk in; which with the Father and with the Holy Ghost livest and reignest for ever and ever.

Thomas Cranmer, 1489–1556

O Lord, thou greatest and most true light, whence this light of the day 314
and of the sun doth spring! O Light, which dost lighten every man that cometh into the world! O Light, which knowest no night nor evening, but art always a mid-day most clear and fair, without whom all is most dark darkness, by whom all be most resplendent! O thou Wisdom of the eternal 'Father of mercies'! lighten my mind, that so soon as you behold the daylight pray: that I may only see those things that please thee, and may be blinded to all other things. Grant that I may walk in thy ways, and that nothing else may be light and pleasant unto me. Lighten mine eyes, O Lord, that I sleep not in death . . .

John Bradford, 1510–55

Most holy and eternal God, lord and sovereign of all the creatures, I 315
humbly present to thy divine majesty, myself, my soul and body, my thoughts and my words, my actions and intentions, my passions and my sufferings, to be disposed by thee to thy glory; to be blessed by thy providence; to be guided by thy counsel; to be sanctified by thy Spirit; and afterwards that my body and soul may be received into glory; for nothing can perish which is under thy custody, and the enemy of souls cannot devour, what is thy portion, nor take it out of thy hands. This day, O Lord, and all the days of my life, I dedicate to thy honour, and the actions of my calling to the uses of grace, and the religion of all my days to be united to the merits and intercession of my holy Saviour, Jesus; that, in him and for him, I may be pardoned and accepted.

Jeremy Taylor, 1613–67

The day returns and brings us the petty round of irritating concerns and 316
duties. Help us to play the man, help us to perform them with laughter and kind faces. Let cheerfulness abound with industry. Give us to go blithely on our business all this day, bring us to our resting beds weary and content and undishonoured, and grant us in the end the gift of sleep.

R. L. Stevenson, 1850–94

O Lord, thou knowest how busy I must be this day; if I forget thee, do 317
not thou forget me: for Christ's sake.

General Lord Astley (1579–1652), before the battle of Edgehill

318 O Jesus, Son of God, who wast silent before Pilate, do not let us wag our tongues without thinking of what we are to say and how to say it.

Irish Gaelic

319 O Christ, be with all who are facing death today in fear or loneliness.

United Society for the Propagation of the Gospel

320 Lord,
I sing your praise,
The whole day through until the night.
Dad's nets are filled,
I have helped him.
We have drawn them in,
Stamping the rhythm with our feet,
The muscles tense.
We have sung your praise.
On the beach, there were our mammies,
Who bought the blessing out of the nets,
Out of the nets into their baskets.
They rushed to the market,
Returned and bought again.
Lord, what a blessing is the sea
With fish in plenty.
Lord, that is the story of your grace.
Nets tear, and we succumb
Because we cannot hold them.
Lord, with your praise we drop off to sleep.
Carry us through the night,
Make us fresh for the morning.
Hallelujah for the day!
And blessing for the night!

A Ghanaian fisherman's prayer

321 The day is there and the sunshine,
With steamers in the harbour,
But is there work?
Others have friends,
Others have money.
They can drain their whisky bottle,
And I stand nearby unemployed.

Dear God, can't you give me work in the harbour?
To have money for wife and children.
To put my little bit in your basket next Sunday.
Please give me work, good Lord Jesus.
We praise you. Amen. Prayer of a Ghanaian harbour man out of work

Grant us, O Lord, to pass this day in gladness and in peace, without stumbling and without stain; that, reaching the eventide victorious over all temptation, we may praise thee, the eternal God, who art blessed, and dost govern all things, world without end. 322

Mozarabic

Abide with us, O Lord, for it is toward evening and the day is far spent; abide with us, and with thy whole Church. Abide with us in the evening of the day, in the evening of life, in the evening of the world. Abide with us and with all thy faithful ones, O Lord, in time and eternity. 323

Lutheran Manual of Prayer

May He support us all the day long, till the shades lengthen, and the evening comes, and the busy world is hushed, and the fever of life is over, and our work is done! Then in His mercy may He give us a safe lodging, and a holy rest, and peace at the last. 324

John Henry Newman, 1801–90

I am going now into the sleep, 325
Be it that I in health shall wake;
If death be to me in deathly sleep,
Be it that in thine own arm's keep,
O God of grace, to new life I wake;
O be it in thy dear arm's keep,
O God of grace, that I shall awake!

from *Poems of the Western Highlanders* (1900)

O God our Father, by whose mercy and might the world turns safely into darkness and returns again to light: We give into thy hands our unfinished task, our unsolved problems, and our unfulfilled hopes, knowing that only that which thou dost bless will prosper. To thy great love and protection we commit each other and all those we love knowing that thou alone art our sure defender, through Jesus Christ, our Lord. 326

The Church of South India

327 Be present, O merciful God, and protect us through the silent hours of this night, so that we who are wearied by the changes and chances of this fleeting world may rest upon thy eternal changelessness; through Jesus Christ our Lord.

An ancient Collect at Compline

328 Save us while waking, and defend us while sleeping, that when we awake we may watch with Christ, and when we sleep we may rest in peace.

Antiphon at Compline

329 —Night is drawing nigh—
For all that has been—Thanks!
For all that shall be—Yes!

Dag Hammarskjöld, 1905–61

330 Prayer when opening door:
I pray thee, Lord, to open the door of my heart to receive thee within my heart.

When washing clothes:
I pray thee, Lord, to wash my heart, making me white as snow.

When sweeping floors:
I pray thee, Lord, to sweep away my heart's uncleanness, that my heart may always be pure.

When pouring oil:
I pray thee, Lord, to give me wisdom like the wise virgins who always had oil in their vessels.

When posting a letter:
I pray thee, Lord, to add to me faith upon faith, that I may always have communication with thee.

When lighting lamps:
I pray thee, Lord, to make my deeds excellent like lamps before others, and more, to place thy true light within my heart.

When watering flowers:
I pray thee, Lord, to send down spiritual rain into my heart, to germinate the good seed there.

When boiling water for tea:
I pray thee, Lord, to send down spiritual fire to burn away the coldness of my heart and that I may always be hot-hearted in serving thee.

Prayer of Chinese Christian women

On building a wall: 331
I pray thee, Lord, to make my faith as firmly established as a house built upon a rock, so that neither rain, flood nor wind can ever destroy it.

On pruning a tree:
I pray thee, Lord, to purge me and take away my selfishness and sinful thoughts, that I may bring forth more fruits of the Spirit.

On tending sheep:
I pray thee, Lord, to protect me from evil and keep me from want, daily carrying me in thine arms like a lamb.

On winnowing grain:
I pray thee, Lord, to winnow away the chaff from my heart and make it like the true wheat, fit to be garnered in thy barn.

On sowing seed:
I pray thee, Lord, to sow the good seed of virtue in my heart, letting it grow by day and night and bring forth a hundredfold.

On writing a book:
I pray thee, Lord, by the precious blood of Jesus, to pay my debt of sin and write my name in heaven, making me free in body and soul.

On planing wood:
I pray thee, Lord, to make me smooth and straight, fit to be a useful vessel, pleasing to the Lord.

On drawing water:
I pray thee, Lord, to give living water to quench my thirst, and wash away the stains from my heart.

Prayer of Chinese Christian men

Mister God, this is Anna. 332

Fynn

Now, into the keeping of God I put 333
All doings of today.
All disappointments,
hindrances,
forgotten things,
negligences.
All gladness and beauty,
love,
delight,
achievement.

All that people have done for me,
All that I have done for them,
  my work and my prayers.

And I commit all the people whom I love
  to his shepherding,
  to his healing and restoring,
  to his calling and making;
    Through Jesus Christ our Lord.

Margaret Cropper, 1886–1980

334 O Lord God, the life of mortals, the light of the faithful, the strength of those who labour and the repose of the dead; grant us a tranquil night free from all disturbance; that after an interval of quiet sleep, we may, by thy bounty, at the return of light be endued with activity from the Holy Spirit, and enabled in security to render thanks to thee.

Mozarabic

Graces

335 Thou that givest food to all flesh,
which feedst the young ravens that cry unto thee
and hast nourished us from our youth up:
  fill our hearts with good and gladness
  and establish our hearts with thy grace.

Bishop Lancelot Andrewes, 1555–1626

336 And when thou art at thy meat, praise thy God:
in thought at ilke morsel and say thus in thy heart:
Loved be thou King
and thanked be thou King
and blessed be thou King.
Ihesu all my joying
of all thy giftes good
that for me spilt thy blood
and died on the rood.
Thou give me grace to sing
the song of thy loving
my praise to thee ay spring
withouten any feigning.

from *The Lay Folk's Mass Book*

GRACES

337
God! to my little meal and oil
Add but a bit of flesh, to boil:
And Thou my pipkinnet shalt see
Give a wave-offering unto Thee.

Robert Herrick, 1591–1674

338
Here, a little child, I stand,
Heaving up my either hand:
Cold as paddocks though they be,
Here I lift them up to thee,
For a benison to fall
On our meat and on our all.

Robert Herrick, 1591–1674

339
Lord God, we thank you for all the good things of your providing, and we pray for the time when people everywhere shall have the abundant life of your will, revealed to us in Jesus Christ, your Son, our Lord.

G.A.

340
Lord Christ, we pray thy mercy on our table spread,
And what thy gentle hands have given thy men
Let it by thee be blessed: whate'er we have
Came from thy lavish heart and gentle hand,
And all that's good is thine, for thou art good.
And ye that eat, give thanks for it to Christ,
And let the words ye utter be only peace,
For Christ loved peace: it was himself that said,
Peace I give unto you, my peace I leave with you.
Grant that our own may be a generous hand
Breaking the bread for all poor men, sharing the food.
Christ shall receive the bread thou gavest his poor,
And shall not tarry to give thee reward.

Alcuin of York, 735–804

'FORGIVE US OUR TRESPASSES'

Penitence

341 Make me a clean heart, O God, and renew a right spirit within me. Cast me not away from thy presence, and take not thy holy Spirit from me.

Psalm 51: 10, 11

342 O Jesus, my feet are dirty. Come even as a slave to me, pour water into your bowl, come and wash my feet. In asking such a thing I know I am overbold but I dread what was threatened when you said to me, 'If I do not wash your feet I have no fellowship with you.' Wash my feet then, because I long for your companionship. And yet, what am I asking? It was well for Peter to ask you to wash his feet, for him that was all that was needed for him to be clean in every part. With me it is different, though you wash me now I shall still stand in need of that other washing, the cleansing you promised when you said, 'there is a baptism I must needs be baptized with'.

Origen, *c.* 185–*c.* 254

343 Lord God, omnipotent Father, creator of all things, you gave me a body and a soul, and created me in your image before time was. O Lord, my God, I confess my offences to you; I have sinned before you and before your angels, and my sins are as numerous as the sands on the seashore. Yet for your love have mercy on me, God, let me not perish. Do not turn your face from me since I do not seek your forgiveness because I think I deserve it, but because of your mercy. Look down on me, Lord, from the holy seat of your majesty, and illumine the shadows of my heart with the radiance of your splendour. Protect me, Lord, with the shield of your truth and faith, so that the glowing darts of the devil may not pierce me. Have mercy, Saviour of the world, who live and reign for ever.

Latin, 10th century

344 Almighty and eternal God, who drew out a fountain of living water in the desert for your people, as they well knew, draw from the hardness of our hearts tears of compunction, that we may be able to lament our sins, and may merit to receive you in your mercy.

Latin, late 14th century

O spare me a little, that I may recover my strength: before I go hence, and be no more seen. 345

Psalm 39: 15

O God our Father, help us to nail to the cross of thy dear Son the whole body of our death, the wrong desires of the heart, the sinful devisings of the mind, the corrupt apprehensions of the eyes, the cruel words of the tongue, the ill employment of hands and feet; that the old man being crucified and done away, the new man may live and grow into the glorious likeness of the same thy Son Jesus Christ, who liveth and reigneth with thee and the Holy Ghost, one God, world without end. 346

Eric Milner-White, 1884–1964

God in Heaven, you have helped my life to grow like a tree. Now something has happened. Satan, like a bird, has carried in one twig of his own choosing after another. Before I knew it he had built a dwelling place and was living in it. Tonight, my Father, I am throwing out both the bird and the nest. 347

Prayer of a Nigerian Christian

When I look back upon my life nigh spent, 348
Nigh spent, although the stream as yet flows on,
I more of follies than of sins repent,
Less for offence than love's shortcomings moan.
With self, O Father, leave me not alone—
Leave not with the beguiler the beguiled;
Besmirched and ragged, Lord, take back thine own:
A fool I bring thee to be made a child.

George Macdonald, 1824–1905

Were you there when they crucified my Lord? 349
Were you there?
O sometimes it causes me to tremble, tremble, tremble,
Were you there when they crucified my Lord? . . .

Negro spiritual

350 Thou the Cross didst bear:
What bear I?
Thou the thorn didst wear:
What wear I?
Thou to death didst dare:
What dare I?
Thou for me dost care:
What care I?

ascribed to Laurence Housman, 1865–1959

351 O thou great Chief, light a candle in my heart, that I may see what is therein, and sweep the rubbish from thy dwelling place.

An African schoolgirl's prayer

352 Almighty God, Spirit of purity and grace, in asking thy forgiveness I cannot claim a right to be forgiven but only cast myself upon thine unbounded love.
I can plead no merit or desert:
I can plead no extenuating circumstances:
I cannot plead the frailty of my nature:
I cannot plead the force of the temptations I encounter:
I cannot plead the persuasions of others who led me astray:
I can only say, for the sake of Jesus Christ thy Son, my Lord. Amen.

John Baillie, 1886–1960

353 In these dark days when negation has so deeply entered into thought,
and the futility of life oppresses many souls,
when belief and unbelief appear indifferent
and what is left
is natural passion to express the pride of life,
or the empty void of nothingness
when the nerve to live and to create is weakened and suicides increase—
O Lord, forgive the failures of your Church to witness to the world
that justice should run down as water
and righteousness a mighty stream,
O Lord, forgive the failure of the Christian life
that lives so worldly
that few can see the life of Spirit
that must proclaim the kingdom of God's love
to glorify his Name.

Fr Gilbert Shaw, 1886–1967

Withhold not from me, O my God, the best, the Spirit of thy dear Son; that in that day when the judgement is set I may be presented unto thee not blameless, but forgiven, not effectual but faithful, not holy but persevering, without desert but accepted, because he hath pleaded the causes of my soul, and redeemed my life. 354

Eric Milner-White, 1884–1964

Lord, today you made us known to friends we did not know, 355
And you have given us seats in homes which are not our own.
You have brought the distant near,
And made a brother of a stranger,
Forgive us Lord . . .
We did not introduce you.

Prayer from Polynesia

God of our salvation, our rescue, our health: all things are yours and when we bring our hearts and hands and voices to worship, we bring you what is yours. 356

Yet we do not serve you as we should, and the world is racked by all the tensions and outright conflicts which come from the worship of that which is less than yourself. Our goodwill towards men has no firm foundation, and crumbles at the first tremor of real testing. In our personal affairs, and in our communal judgements, we try to heal deep wounds with superficial cures.

Father, forgive us. Confront us with your way of righting wrong, your strange work of redemption through the sacrificial love of Jesus. And help us to love one another as he has loved us.

from *Contemporary Prayers for Public Worship*, ed. Caryl Micklem

I have just hung up; why did he telephone? 357
I don't know . . . Oh! I get it . . .
I talked a lot and listened very little.

Forgive me, Lord, it was a monologue and not a dialogue.
I explained my idea and did not get his;
Since I didn't listen, I learned nothing,
Since I didn't listen, I didn't help,
Since I didn't listen, we didn't communicate.

Forgive me, Lord, for we were connected,
and now we are cut off.

Michel Quoist

'FORGIVE US OUR TRESPASSES'

358 **HYMN TO GOD THE FATHER**

Wilt thou forgive that sinn where I begunn,
Which is my sinn, though it were done before?
Wilt thou forgive those sinns, through which I runn,
And doe them still, though still I doe deplore?
When thou hast done, thou hast not done,
for I have more.

Wilt thou forgive that sinn, by which I have wonne
Others to sinn, and made my sinn their dore?
Wilt Thou forgive that sinn which I did shunne
A yeare, or twoe, but wallowed in a score?
When thou hast done, thou hast not done,
for I have more.

I have a sinn of fear, that when I have spunn
My last thred, I shall perish on the shore;
Sweare by thy selfe that at my Death thy Sunn
Shall shine as it shines nowe, and heretofore;
And having done that, thou hast done,
I have noe more.

John Donne, 1572–1631

359 From needing danger, to bee good,
From owing thee yesterdaies teares to day,
From trusting so much to thy blood,
That in that hope, wee wound our soule away,
From bribing thee with Almes, to excuse
Some sinne more burdenous,
From light affecting, in religion, newes,
From thinking us all soule, neglecting thus
Our mutuall duties, Lord deliver us.

from John Donne (1752–1631), 'The Litany'

360 I am heartily sorry, and beg pardon for my sins, especially for my little respect, and for wandering in my thoughts when in your presence, and for my continual infidelitys to your graces; for all which I beg pardon, by the merits of the Blood you shed for them.

Lady Lucy Herbert, 1669–1744

'AS WE FORGIVE'

Relationships

Lord, you return gladly and lovingly to lift up the one who offends you 361
and I do not turn to raise up and honour the one who angers me.

St John of the Cross, 1542–91

As the first martyr prayed to thee for his murderers, O Lord, so we fall 362
before thee and pray; forgive all who hate and maltreat us and let not one of them perish because of us, but may all be saved by thy grace, O God the all-bountiful.

Eastern Church

O God, if there are those who wish evil for me or do evil and are my 363
enemies and are my opponents and persecutors, grant to them, O Lord, indulgence and eternal rest, and bring them to your will. Lord, deign to convert their hearts to wholesome peace, to turn all the malice which they plot secretly or wish against me into good. Grant me your mercy and save me so that unharmed I might be able to thwart their every effort; and stand by me, that with a pure heart I may be able to scatter for your name's sake all those who sin against me, so that I may merit to accept remission of all my sins from you, and also, that I may be able to love a friend in you, and an enemy for your sake.

Latin, 15th century

Almighty God, have mercy on N. and N., and on all that bear me evil 364
will, and would me harm, and their faults and mine together, by such easy, tender, merciful means, as thine infinite wisdom best can devise, vouchsafe to amend and redress, and make us saved souls in heaven together where we may ever live and love together with thee and thy blessed saints, O glorious Trinity, for the bitter passion of our sweet Saviour Christ.

St Thomas More, 1478–1535

And I offer also for all those whom I have in any way grieved, vexed, 365
oppressed, and scandalized, by word or deed, knowingly or unknowingly; that thou mayest equally forgive us all our sins, and all our offences against each other.

Take away, O Lord, from our hearts all suspiciousness, indignation, anger, and contention, and whatever is calculated to wound charity, and to lessen brotherly love.

Have mercy, O Lord, have mercy on those who seek thy mercy; give grace to the needy; make us so to live, that we may be found worthy to enjoy the fruition of thy grace, and that we may attain to eternal life.

Thomas à Kempis, 1380–1471

366 O God, we are conscious that many centuries of blindness have blinded our eyes so that we no longer see the beauty of thy chosen people, nor recognize in their faces the features of our privileged brethren. We realize that the mark of Cain stands upon our foreheads. Across the centuries our brother Abel has lain in the blood which we drew or which we caused to be shed by forgetting thy love. Forgive us for the curse we falsely attached to their name as Jews. Forgive us for crucifying thee a second time in their flesh. For we knew not what we did.

Pope John XXIII, 1881–1963

367 O Lord, remember not only the men and women of good will, but also those of ill will. But do not remember all the suffering they have inflicted on us; remember the fruits we have bought, thanks to this suffering—our comradeship, our loyalty, our humility, our courage, our generosity, the greatness of heart which has grown out of all this, and when they come to judgement let all the fruits which we have borne be their forgiveness.

Prayer written by an unknown prisoner in Ravensbrück concentration camp and left by the body of a dead child

368 Most merciful and loving Father, which hatest not any of the things which thou hast made, but sufferest and bearest with men's misdoings, winking at them to provoke them to repentance: We beseech thee most humbly, even with our hearts, to pour out upon our enemies with bountiful hands whatsoever things thou knowest may do them good, and chiefly a sound and uncorrupt mind, wherethrough they may know thee and seek thee in true charity and with their whole heart, and love us, thy children, for thy sake.

Destroy them not, O Father, for their hatred towards us, but save them at our entreatance for them.

Elizabethan Prayer Book

I pray, O Master, that the flames of hell may not touch me nor any of those whom I love, and even that they may never touch anyone (and I know, my God, that you will forgive this bold prayer) . . . 369

Teilhard de Chardin, SJ, 1881–1955

O Lord give me strength to refrain from the unkind silence that is born of hardness of heart; the unkind silence that clouds the serenity of understanding and is the enemy of peace. 370

Give me strength to be the first to tender the healing word and the renewal of friendship, that the bonds of amity and the flow of charity may be strengthened for the good of the brethren and the furthering of thine eternal, loving purpose.

Cecil Hunt

Be gracious to all that are near and dear to me, and keep us all in thy fear and love. Guide us, good Lord, and govern us by the same Spirit, that we may be so united to thee here as not to be divided when thou art pleased to call us hence, but may together enter into thy glory, through Jesus Christ, our blessed Lord and Saviour, who hath taught us when we pray to say: Our Father . . . 371

John Wesley, 1703–91

O blessed Lord, who hast commanded us to love one another, grant us grace that having received thine undeserved bounty, we may love everyone in thee and for thee. We implore thy clemency for all; but especially for the friends whom thy love has given to us. Love thou them, O thou fountain of love, and make them to love thee with all their heart, that they may will, and speak, and do those things only which are pleasing to thee. 372

St Anselm, 1033–1109

Most glorious Lord of lyfe, that on this day, 373
Didst make thy triumph over death and sin:
and having harrowed hell, didst bring away
captivity thence captive us to win:
This joyous day, deare Lord, with joy begin,
and grant that we for whom thou diddest dye
being with thy deare blood clene washt from sin,
may live forever in felicity.

And that thy love we weighing worthily,
may likewise love thee for the same againe:
and for thy sake that all lyke deare didst buy,
with love may one another entertayne.
So let us love, deare Love, lyke as we ought,
love is the lesson which the Lord us taught.

Edmund Spenser, 1552–99

374 **PRAYER FOR A FIANCÉE OR WIFE**

That I may come near to her, draw me nearer to thee than to her; that I may know her, make me to know thee more than her; that I may love her with the perfect love of a perfectly whole heart, cause me to love thee more than her and most of all. Amen. Amen.

That nothing may be between me and her, be thou between us, every moment. That we may be constantly together, draw us into separate loneliness with thyself. And when we meet breast to breast, my God, let it be on thine own. Amen. Amen.

Temple Gairdner, 1873–1928, before his marriage

375 God, whose eternal mind
Rules the round world over,
Whose wisdom lies behind
All that men discover:
Grant that we, by thought and speech,
May grow nearer each to each;
Lord, let sweet converse bind
Lover unto lover.
Bless us, God of loving.

Godhead in human guise
Once to earth returning,
Daily through human eyes
Joys of earth discerning:
Grant that we may treasure less
Passion than true tenderness,
Yet never, Lord, despise
Heart to sweetheart turning.
Bless us, God of loving.

RIGHT LIVING

God, whose unbounded grace
Heaven and earth pervadeth,
Whose mercy doth embrace
All thy wisdom madeth:
Grant that we may, hand in hand,
All forgive, all understand;
Keeping, through time and space,
Trust that never fadeth.
Bless us, God of loving.

God, who art three in One,
All things comprehending,
Wise Father, valiant Son,
In the Spirit blending:
Grant us love's eternal three—
Friendship, rapture, constancy;
Lord, till our lives be done,
Grant us love unending.
Bless us, God of loving.

Jan Struther, 1901–53

O Lord God almighty who hast made us out of nothing, and redeemed us by the precious blood of thine only Son, preserve, I beseech thee, the work of thy hands, and defend both me and the tender fruit of my womb from all perils and evils. I beg of thee, for myself, thy grace, protection, and a happy delivery; and for my child, that thou wouldst preserve it for baptism, sanctify it for thyself, and make it thine for ever. Through Jesus Christ, thy Son, our Lord. 376

The Christian's Guide to Heaven, 1794

'LEAD US NOT INTO TEMPTATION'

Right Living

From the cowardice that dare not face new truth 377
From the laziness that is contented with half truth
From the arrogance that thinks it knows all truth,
Good Lord, deliver me.

Prayer from Kenya

378 O Lord, my maker and protector, who hast graciously sent me into this world, to work out my salvation, enable me to drive from me all such unquiet and perplexing thoughts as may mislead or hinder me in the practice of those duties which thou hast required. When I behold the works of thy hands and consider the course of thy providence, give me grace always to remember that thy thoughts are not my thoughts, nor thy ways my ways. And while it shall please thee to continue me in this world where much is to be done and little to be known, teach me by thy Holy Spirit to withdraw my mind from unprofitable and dangerous enquiries, from difficulties vainly curious and doubts impossible to be solved. Let me rejoice in the light which thou hast imparted, let me serve thee with active zeal and humble confidence, and wait with patient expectation for the time in which the soul which thou receivest shall be satisfied with knowledge. Grant this, O Lord, for Jesus Christ's sake, amen.

Samuel Johnson, 1709–84

379 Almighty God, who hast created man in thine own image, and made him a living soul that he might seek after thee and have dominion over thy creatures, teach us to study the works of thy hands that we may subdue the earth to our use, and strengthen our reason for thy service; and so to receive thy blessed word that we may believe on Him whom thou hast sent to give us the knowledge of salvation and the remission of our sins. All which we ask in the name of the same Jesus Christ our Lord.

James Clerk Maxwell, 1831–79

380 Look upon us and hear us, O Lord our God; and assist those endeavours to please thee which thou thyself hast granted to us; as thou hast given the first act of will, so give the completion of the work; grant that we may be able to finish what thou hast granted us to wish to begin; through Jesus Christ our Lord.

Mozarabic

381 O God Almighty, Father of our Lord Jesus Christ, grant us, we pray thee, to be grounded and settled in thy truth by the coming down of the Holy Spirit into our hearts. That which we know not, do thou reveal; that which is wanting in us, do thou fill up; that which we know, do thou confirm; and keep us blameless in thy service, through the same Jesus Christ our Lord.

St Clement of Rome, *c.* 100

Our Father in heaven, I thank thee that thou hast led me into the light. I thank thee for sending the Saviour to call me from death to life. I confess that I was dead in sin before I heard his call, but when I heard him, like Lazarus, I arose. But, O my Father, the grave clothes bind me still. Old habits that I cannot throw off, old customs that are so much a part of my life that I am helpless to live the new life that Christ calls me to live. Give me strength, O Father, to break the bonds; give me courage to live a new life in thee; give me faith, to believe that with thy help I cannot fail. And this I ask in the Saviour's name who has taught me to come to thee. 382

Prayer from Taiwan

Grant, O God, that we may wait patiently, as servants standing before their lord, to know thy will; that we may welcome all truth, under whatever outward form it may be uttered; that we may bless every good deed, by whomsoever it may be done; that we may rise above all strife to the contemplation of thy eternal truth and goodness; through Jesus Christ our Saviour. 383

ascribed to Charles Kingsley, 1819–75

O Lord, our Saviour, who hast warned us that thou wilt require much of those to whom much is given; grant that we whose lot is cast in so goodly a heritage may strive together the more abundantly by prayer, by almsgiving, by fasting, and by every other appointed means, to extend to others what we so richly enjoy; and as we have entered into the labours of other men, so to labour that in their turn other men may enter into ours, to the fulfilment of thy holy will, and our own everlasting salvation; through Jesus Christ our Lord. 384

St Augustine, 354–430

God give me work 385
Till my life shall end
And life
Till my work is done.

On the grave of Winifred Holtby, novelist, 1898–1935

Give me grace, O God, to hearken to thy calling, and to follow thy guiding. For thou leadest us to store of all good things: thou offerest thyself and all thy goods; give us grace to receive them. Thou shewest us the way to most singular benefits; suffer us not to turn aside, until we have taken possession of them. 386

Give us constancy and steadiness of purpose, that our thoughts may not be fleeting, fond and ineffectual, but that we may perform all things with an unmovable mind, to the glory of thy holy name. Through Jesus Christ our Lord.

Ludovicus Vives, 1492–1540

387 Almighty God, bestow upon us the meaning of words, the light of understanding, the nobility of diction and the faith of the true nature. And grant that what we believe we may also speak.

St Hilary, 315–67

388 O God, who hast ordained that whatever is to be desired should be sought by labour, and who by thy blessing bringest honest labour to good effect, look with mercy upon my studies and endeavours. Grant me, O Lord, to design only what is lawful and right; and afford me calmness of mind, and steadiness of purpose, that I may so do thy will in this short life, as to obtain happiness in the world to come, for the sake of Jesus Christ, our Lord.

Samuel Johnson, 1709–84

389 I have set God always before me: for he is on my right hand, therefore I shall not fall.

Psalm 16: 9

390 Lord God Almighty,
I pray thee for thy great mercy and by the token of the holy rood,
Guide me to thy will, to my soul's need, better than I can myself;
And shield me against my foes, seen and unseen;
And teach me to do thy will
that I may inwardly love thee before all things with a clean mind and a clean body.
For thou art my maker and my redeemer,
my help, my comfort, my trust, and my hope.
Praise and glory be to thee now, ever and ever, world without end.

King Alfred, 849–901

391 So teach us to number our days that we may get a heart of wisdom.

Psalm 90: 12

Help each one of us, gracious Father, to live in such magnanimity and restraint that the Head of the Church may never have cause to say to any one of us, This is my body, broken by you. 392

Prayer from China

O Lord, who has taught us that to gain the whole world and to lose our souls is great folly, grant us the grace so to lose ourselves that we may truly find ourselves anew in the life of grace, and so to forget ourselves that we may be remembered in your kingdom. 393

Reinhold Niebuhr, 1892–1971

Grant us grace, our Father, to do our work this day as workmen who need not be ashamed. Give us the spirit of diligence and honest enquiry in our quest for the truth, the spirit of charity in all our dealings with our fellows, and the spirit of gaiety, courage, and a quiet mind in facing all tasks and responsibilities. 394

Reinhold Niebuhr, 1892–1971

I asked for strength that I might achieve; 395
I was made weak that I might learn humbly to obey.

I asked for health that I might do greater things;
I was given infirmity that I might do better things.

I asked for riches that I might be happy;
I was given poverty that I might be wise.

I asked for power that I might have the praise of men;
I was given weakness that I might feel the need of God.

I asked for all things that I might enjoy life;
I was given life that I might enjoy all things.

I got nothing that I had asked for,
but everything that I had hoped for.

Almost despite myself my unspoken prayers were answered;
I am, among all men, most richly blessed.

Prayer of an unknown Confederate soldier

Teach me, O God, so to use all the circumstances of my life today that they may bring forth in me the fruits of holiness rather than the fruits of sin. 396

Let me use disappointments as material for patience:

Let me use success as material for thankfulness:
Let me use suspense as material for perseverance:
Let me use danger as material for courage:
Let me use reproach as material for longsuffering:
Let me use praise as material for humility:
Let me use pleasure as material for temperance:
Let me use pains as material for endurance. John Baillie, 1886–1960

397 Wonderful to come out living
From the fiery furnace-blast,
But yet more, that after testing
I shall be fine gold at last;
Time of cleansing! Time of winnowing!
Yet 'tis calm, without dismay;
He who soon shall be my refuge
Holds the winnowing-fan today.

Ann Griffiths, 1776–1805

398 O heavenly Father, open wide the sluice gate into my heart that I may receive thy living water and be fruitful. Prayer of a Punjabi Christian

399 Give me
The girdle, the helmet,
The breastplate, the shield,
The shoes, the sword,
over all, prayer.
Grant me the power and the opportunity of welldoing
that before the day of my decease
I may at all adventure effect some good thing
whereof the fruit may remain:
that I may be able to appear with righteousness
and be satisfied with glory.
Thou which didst add fifteen years to the life of Ezekias,
grant so much space of life,
at the least unto such a measure,
that I may be able therein to deplore my sins,
And grant me a good end—
What is above every gift—
a good and holy end of life,
a glorious and joyful resurrection. Bishop Lancelot Andrewes, 1555–1626

Take from us, O God, all pride and vanity, all boasting and forwardness, and give us the true courage that shows itself by gentleness; the true wisdom that shows itself by simplicity; and the true power that shows itself by modesty; through Jesus Christ our Lord. 400

Charles Kingsley, 1819–75

I will run the way of thy commandments: when thou hast set my heart at liberty. 401

Psalm 119: 32

Let no riches make me ever forget myself, no poverty make me to forget thee: let no hope or fear, no pleasure or pain, no accident without, no weakness within, hinder or discompose my duty, or turn me from the ways of thy commandments. O let thy Spirit dwell with me for ever, and make my soul just and charitable, full of honesty, full of religion, resolute and constant in holy purposes, but inflexible to evil. Make me humble and obedient, peaceable and pious: let me never envy any man's good, nor deserve to be despised myself: and if I be, teach me to bear it with meekness and charity. 402

Jeremy Taylor, 1613–67

Thou, therefore, O Lord Jesu Christ, which art the greatest of all lights, the only true light, the light from whence springeth the light of the day, and the sun: thou light, which enlighteneth every man that cometh into the world: thou light, whereon there cometh no night nor eventide, but continuest ever bright and clear, as at mid-day: thou light, wherewithout all things are deep darkness, and whereby all things were made lightsome: thou mind and wisdom of the heavenly Father, enlighten my mind, that (being blind to all other things) I may see nothing but that which belongeth to thee, and that I may thereby walk in thy ways, without fantasying or liking of any other light else. Lord, I beseech thee, enlighten mine eyes, that I may never slumber in darkness, lest my ghostly enemy say at any time, I have prevailed against him. 403

Ludovicus Vives, 1492–1540

Suffer me never to think that I have knowledge enough to need no teaching, wisdom enough to need no correction, talents enough to need no grace, goodness enough to need no progress, humility enough to need no repentance, devotion enough to need no quickening, strength sufficient without thy Spirit; lest, standing still, I fall back for evermore. 404

Eric Milner-White, 1884–1964

405 O Christ, you came so that we might have life, and have it more abundantly,
grant us power in our love,
strength in our humility,
purity in our zeal,
kindness in our laughter,
and your peace in our hearts at all times.

J. L. Cowie

406 Grant unto us, O Lord, the gift of modesty. When we speak, teach us to give our opinion quietly and sincerely. When we do well in work or play, give us a sense of proportion, that we be neither unduly elated nor foolishly self-deprecatory. Help us in success to realize what we owe to thee and to the efforts of others: in failure, to avoid dejection; and in all ways to be simple and natural, quiet in manner and lowly in thought: through Christ.

Joseph L. Bernardin

407 O Blessed Jesu Christ, who didst bid all who carry heavy burdens to come to thee, refresh us with thy presence and thy power. Quiet our understandings and give ease to our hearts, by bringing us close to things infinite and eternal. Open to us the mind of God, that in his light we may see light. And crown thy choice of us to be thy servants, by making us springs of strength and joy to all whom we serve.

Evelyn Underhill, 1875–1941

408 O Almighty God, from whom every good prayer cometh, and who pourest out on all who desire it, the Spirit of grace and supplications; deliver us, when we draw nigh to thee, from coldness of heart and wanderings of mind; that with steadfast thoughts and kindled affections, we may worship thee in spirit and in truth, through Jesus Christ, our Lord.

William Bright (1824–1901), *Ancient Collects*

409 Grant Lord, that I may not, for one moment, admit willingly into my soul any thought contrary to thy love.

E. B. Pusey, 1800–82

Eternal Father, source of life and light, whose love extends to all people, all creatures, all things: Grant us that reverence for life which becomes those who believe in you; lest we despise it, degrade it, or come callously to destroy it. Rather let us save it, secure it, and sanctify it, after the example of your Son, Jesus Christ our Lord. 410

Archbishop Robert Runcie

And give me, good Lord, an humble, lowly, quiet, peaceable, patient, charitable, kind and filial and tender mind, every shade, in fact, of charity, with all my words and all my works, and all my thoughts, to have a taste of thy holy blessed Spirit. 411

St Thomas More, 1478–1535

The things, good Lord, that we pray for, give us the grace to labour for. 412

St Thomas More, 1478–1535

'DELIVER US FROM EVIL'

Protection

Blessed are all thy Saints, O God and King, who have travelled over the tempestuous sea of this mortal life, and have made the harbour of peace and felicity. Watch over us who are still in our dangerous voyage; and remember such as lie exposed to the rough storms of trouble and temptations. Frail is our vessel, and the ocean is wide; but as in thy mercy thou hast set our course, so steer the vessel of our life toward the everlasting shore of peace, and bring us at length to the quiet haven of our heart's desire, where thou, O our God, are blessed, and livest and reignest for ever and ever. 413

St Augustine, 354–430

O God, who has been the refuge of my fathers through many generations, be my refuge today in every time and circumstance of need. Be my guide through all that is dark and doubtful. Be my guard against all that threatens my spirit's welfare. Be my strength in time of testing. Gladden my heart with thy peace; through Jesus Christ my Lord. 414

John Baillie, 1886–1960

415 **O Christ, guide and strengthen all who are tempted in this hour.**

United Society for the Propagation of the Gospel

416 **The Lord preserveth the simple: I was in misery, and he helped me.**

Psalm 116: 6

417 **Lord, give us grace to hold to you**
when all is weariness and fear
and sin abounds within, without
when love itself is tested by the doubt . . .
that love is false, or dead within the soul,
when every act brings new confusion, new distress,
new opportunities, new misunderstandings,
and every thought new accusation.

Lord, give us grace that we may know
that in the darkness pressing round
it is the mist of sin that hides your face,
that you are there
and you do know we love you still
and our dependence and endurance in your will
is still our gift of love.

Fr Gilbert Shaw, 1886–1967

418 **Blessed Lord, who wast tempted in all things like as we are, have mercy upon our frailty. Out of weakness give us strength. Grant to us thy fear, that we may fear thee only. Support us in time of temptation. Embolden us in the time of danger. Help us to do thy work with good courage, and to continue thy faithful soldiers and servants unto our life's end; through Jesus Christ our Lord.**

Bishop Brooke Foss Westcott, 1825–1901

419 **Dear Jesus, as a hen covers her chicks with her wings to keep them safe, do thou this dark night protect us under your golden wings.**

Prayer from India

420 **Like an ant on a stick both ends of which are burning, I go to and fro without knowing what to do and in great despair. Like the inescapable shadow which follows me, the dead weight of sin haunts me. Graciously look upon me. Thy love is my refuge.**

Prayer from India

O God that art the only hope of the world, 421
The only refuge for unhappy men,
Abiding in the faithfulness of heaven,
Give me strong succour in this testing place.
O King, protect thy man from utter ruin
Lest the weak faith surrender to the tyrant,
Facing innumerable blows alone.
Remember I am dust, and wind, and shadow,
And life as fleeting as the flower of grass.
But may the eternal mercy which hath shone
From time of old
Rescue thy servant from the jaws of the lion.
Thou who didst come from on high in the cloak of flesh,
Strike down the dragon with that two-edged sword,
Whereby our mortal flesh can war with the winds
And beat down strongholds, with our Captain God.

Bede, 672–735

Dear God, be good to me; 422
The sea is so wide,
And my boat is so small.

Breton fishermen's prayer

Guard for me my eyes, Jesus Son of Mary, lest seeing another's wealth make me covetous. 423

Guard for me my ears, lest they hearken to slander, lest they listen constantly to folly in the sinful world.

Guard for me my heart, O Christ, in thy love, lest I ponder wretchedly the desire of any iniquity.

Guard for me my hands, that they be not stretched out for quarrelling, that they may not, after that, practise shameful supplication.

Guard for me my feet upon the gentle earth of Ireland, lest, bent on profitless errands, they abandon rest.

Irish

He lay with quiet heart in the stern asleep: 424
Waking, commanded both the winds and sea.
Christ, though this weary body slumber deep,
Grant that my heart may keep its watch with thee.
O Lamb of God that carried all our sin,
Guard thou my sleep against the enemy.

Alcuin of York, 735–804

'DELIVER US FROM EVIL'

425 O Christ, who hast known fear, be with all who are afraid today.

United Society for the Propagation of the Gospel

426 O Lord, we beseech thee to deliver us from the fear of the unknown future; from fear of failure; from fear of poverty; from fear of bereavement; from fear of loneliness; from fear of sickness and pain; from fear of age; and from fear of death. Help us, O Father, by thy grace to love and fear thee only, fill our hearts with cheerful courage and loving trust in thee; through our Lord and Master Jesus Christ.

Akanu Ibaim, Nigeria

427 LAMENT FOR AQUILEIA DESTROYED, AND NEVER TO BE BUILT AGAIN

O Christ our King, the judge no man gainsays,
Look down in pity, turn away thy wrath.
Forbid a fate the like of this to fall
Again upon thy folk.

We bring thee hymns and prayers,
Rein in the peoples, curb the envious,
Protect us ever with thy strong right arm,
Thou that hast mercy on men everywhere.
Chasten us, Father, but be merciful.
Go thou before thy flock, and come behind:
Thy fold that walk upon the harmless road
Keep to eternity.

St Paulinus of Aquileia, 726–802

428 Three things are of the evil one:
An evil eye;
An evil tongue;
An evil mind.

Three things are of God, and these three are what Mary told to her Son, for she heard them in heaven:
The merciful word,
The singing word,
And the good word.

May the power of these three holy things be on all men and women of Erin for evermore.

Traditional Irish prayer

BLESSING FOR CAIRO'S NEW BRIDGE, 1972 429

May the eternal God bless this city,
guard it against all evil,
guide it in wisdom.

May he bless all who build the bridge,
and keep them faithful and safe in their work.

May the peoples of this city be united and godfearing,
happy and prosperous,
preserving the good heritage of the past,
and building the future on foundations of
righteousness and love.

And all glory be to the eternal God,
the Lord of the worlds,
the compassionate and merciful,
the ruler in history
and the lover of men,
the God and Father of Jesus Christ,
for ever and ever. Amen.

G.A.

Keep me as the apple of an eye: hide me under the shadow of thy wings. 430

Psalm 17: 8

Thou knowest my heart, Lord, and that whatsoever thou hast given to thy servant I desire to spend wholly on them and to consume it all in their service. Grant unto me then, O Lord my God, that thine eyes may be opened upon them day and night. Tenderly spread thy wings to protect them. Stretch forth thy holy right hand to bless them. Pour into their hearts thy Holy Spirit who may abide with them while they pray to refresh them with devout compunction, to stimulate them with hope, to make them humble with fear, and to inflame them with charity. May he, the kind consoler, succour them in temptation and help their weakness in all the trials and tribulations of this life. 431

Abbot Aelred, 1109–67, for his monks

Lord, 432
the motor under me is running hot.
Lord,
there are twenty-eight people
and lots of luggage in the truck.

'DELIVER US FROM EVIL'

Underneath are my bad tyres.
The brakes are unreliable.
Unfortunately I have no money,
and parts are difficult to get.
Lord,
I did not overload the truck.
Lord,
'Jesus is mine'
is written on the vehicle,
for without him I would not drive
a single mile.
The people in the back are relying on me.
They trust me because they see the words:
'Jesus is mine'.
Lord,
I trust you!

First comes the straight road
with little danger,
I can keep my eyes on the women,
children and chickens in the village.
But soon the road begins to turn,
it goes up and down,
it jumps and dances,
this death-road to Kumasi.
Tractors carrying mahogany trunks drive
as if there were no right or left.
Lord,
Kumasi is the temptation
to take more people than we should.
Let's overcome it!

The road to Accra is another problem.
Truck drivers try to beat the record,
although the road is poor
and has many holes
and there are many curves
before we come to the hills.

And finally to Akwasim.
Passing large churches in every village,
I am reminded of you, and in reverence
I take off my hat.
Now downhill in second gear.

One more temptation;
the straight road to Accra.
Lord, keep my feet steady on the pedals
Even on the straight road to Accra.

Lord,
I sing hallelujah
when the ride is ended
for you brought the truck and the people
in safety
through the hustle and bustle of Accra.
Lord, all is mercy,
because
'Jesus is mine'.
Hallelujah. Amen.

Truck driver's prayer by a young Ghanaian Christian

Christ, be with me, Christ before me, Christ behind me, 433
Christ in me, Christ beneath me, Christ above me,
Christ on my right, Christ on my left,
Christ where I lie, Christ where I sit, Christ where I arise,
Christ in the heart of every one who thinks of me,
Christ in the mouth of every one who speaks of me,
Christ in every eye that sees me,
Christ in every ear that hears me.
Salvation is of the Lord,
Salvation is of the Lord,
Salvation is of the Christ,
May your salvation, O Lord, be ever with us.

St Patrick, 389–461

O my God, thou art very near, in my heart and about my way; yet often 434
thou dost seem very far off and my soul fainteth for looking after thee: thou dost lead me through dark places and withdrawest thyself from me. In the desolate time, when I feel perplexed and forsaken, I would think upon the cross of my Saviour and his dreadful cry, that my faith may hold fast in his faith and that despair may not seize me. Help me to remember the days of vision and sure confidence, guide me to stay my soul in the revelations of thyself which thou hast given me in time past through all thy prophets and servants, and bring me out of the valley of the dark shade once more into the light of thy presence, through Jesus Christ our Lord.

W. R. Matthews, 1881–1973

435 O thou Chief of Chiefs, we kneel before thee in obeisance and adoration. Like the bird in the branches we praise thy heavenly glory. Like the village sharpening stone, thou art always available and never exhausted. Remove we pray thee, our sins that hide thy face. Thou knowest that we are poor and unlearned; that we often work when hungry. Send rain in due season for our gardens that our food may not fail. Protect us from the cold and danger by night. Help us to keep in health that we may rejoice in strength. May our villages be filled with children. Emancipate us from the fear of the fetish and the witch doctor and from all manner of superstitions. Save the people, especially the Christian boys and girls in the villages, from the evil that surrounds them. All this we ask in the name of Jesus Christ thy Son.

Prayer from Zaire

Suffering

436 O Christ, bless and uphold all who are in pain or sickness this day.

United Society for the Propagation of the Gospel

437 Lord, teach me the art of patience whilst I am well, and give me the use of it when I am sick. In that day either lighten my burden or strengthen my back. Make me, who so often in my health have discovered my weakness presuming on my own strength, to be strong in my sickness when I solely rely on thy assistance.

Thomas Fuller, 1608–61

438 Lord, comfort the sick, the hungry, the lonely and those who are hurt and shut in on themselves, by your presence in their hearts; use us to help them in a practical way. Show us how to set about this and give us strength, tact and compassion. Teach us how to be alongside them, and how to share in their distress deeply in our prayer. Make us open to them and give us courage to suffer with them, and that in so doing we share with you in the suffering of the world for we are your body on earth and you work through us.

Michael Hollings and Etta Gullick

439 O give us patience and steadfastness in adversity, strengthen our weakness, comfort us in trouble and distress, help us to fight; grant unto us that in true obedience and contentation of mind we may give over our

own wills unto thee our Father in all things, according to the example of thy beloved Son; that in adversity we grudge not, but offer up ourselves unto thee without contradiction . . . O give us a willing and cheerful mind, that we may gladly suffer and bear all things for thy sake.

Bishop Miles Coverdale, 1488–1568

PRAYER FOR POOR LABOURING FOLK

Humbly, simply, we come early, praise God's kindness, his great mercy. 440
Beg him pity our distress, grant forgiveness for each trespass. Bitter each day is our labour. As we worship in this temple, fill our souls with his great peace. Now we know God's grace will never cease. Sometimes we bear pain and suffering till our hearts are full of darkness. Father, never from us depart, keep us poor folk in your kind heart. God, give grace to us and gladness, bring us joy despite our sadness. May your mercy be our stay, may your love enlighten each day.

Chao Tzu-ch'en, China

O Christ, be with all who are facing death today in fear or loneliness. 441

United Society for the Propagation of the Gospel

O God, who hast in thy love kept me vigorously and joyfully at work in 442
days gone by, and dost now send me joyful and contented into silence and inactivity; grant me to find happiness in thee in all my solitary and quiet hours. In thy strength, O God, I bid farewell to all. The past thou knowest: I leave it at thy feet. Grant me grace to respond to thy divine call; to leave all that is dear on earth, and go alone to thee. Behold, I come quickly, saith the Lord. Come, Lord Jesus.

Prayer of an Indian priest in old age

I am not eager, bold 443
Or strong—all that is past.
I am ready *not* to do,
At last, at last!

St Peter Canisius, 1521–97

Having passed over this day, Lord, I give thanks unto thee. 444
The evening draweth nigh, make it comfortable.
An evening there is, as of the day, so of this life.

The evening of this life of old-age,
  Old-age hath seiz'd upon me;
  make that comfortable.
  Cast me not away in the time of age;
Forsake me not when my strength
  faileth me. (Psalm 71: 9)
Be thou with me until old-age and even
to hoar hairs do thou carrie me. (P. Isaiah 46: 4)

Do thou do it, do thou forgive,
Do thou receive and save me, O Lord.

Tarrie thou with me, O Lord,
for it is toward evening with me,
and the day is far spent, (Luke 24: 29)
of this my toilsom life.

Let thy strength be made
perfect in my weakness. (2 Corinthians 12: 9)

Bishop Lancelot Andrewes, 1555–1626

445 AT THE DOOR OF A CHRISTIAN HOSPITAL

O God,
make the door of this house wide enough
to receive all who need human love and
fellowship, and a heavenly Father's care;
  and narrow enough to shut out
all envy, pride and hate.
  Make its threshold smooth enough
to be no stumbling-block to children,
nor to straying feet,
  but rugged enough to turn back
the tempter's power:
  make it a gateway
  to thine eternal kingdom.

Bishop Thomas Ken, 1637–1711

446 Grant peace and eternal rest to all the departed, but especially to the millions known and unknown who died as prisoners in many lands, victims of the hatred and cruelty of man. May the example of their suffering and courage draw us closer to thee through thine own agony and passion, and thus strengthen us in our desire to serve thee in the sick, the unwanted and the dying wherever we may find them. Give us the grace so

to spend ourselves for those who are still alive, that we may prove most truly that we have not forgotten those who died.

Sue Ryder and Leonard Cheshire

I acknowledge, O Lord, that I am a sinner. Accept therefore what I now suffer in atonement of my sins. I offer myself and all that I have or am, to thee. Do with me, my God, whatever thou pleasest. Shall I not drink the cup which my Father hath given me? Not my will but thine be done! 447

The Christian's Guide to Heaven, 1794

Lord, since thou hast taken from me all that I had of thee, yet of thy grace leave me the gift which every dog has by nature, that of being true to thee in my distress, when I am deprived of all consolation. This I desire more fervently than thy heavenly kingdom. 448

Mechtild of Magdeburg, 1210–80

Dearest Lord, may I see you today and every day in the person of your sick, and whilst nursing them minister unto you. 449

Though you hide yourself behind the unattractive disguise of the irritable, the exacting, the unreasonable, may I still recognize you and say: 'Jesus, my patient, how sweet it is to serve you.'

Lord, give me this seeing faith, then my work will never be monotonous. I will ever find joy in humouring the fancies and gratifying the wishes of all poor sufferers.

O beloved sick, how doubly dear you are to me, when you personify Christ; and what a privilege is mine to be allowed to tend you.

Sweetest Lord, make me appreciative of the dignity of my high vocation, and its many responsibilities. Never permit me to disgrace it by giving way to coldness, unkindness, or impatience.

And, O God, while you are Jesus, my patient, deign also to be to me a patient Jesus, bearing with my faults, looking only to my intention, which is to love and serve you in the person of each of your sick.

Lord, increase my faith, bless my efforts and work, now and for evermore.

Daily prayer of Mother Teresa of Calcutta

When the signs of age begin to mark my body (and still more when they touch my mind); when the ill that is to diminish me or carry me off strikes from without or is born within me; when the painful moment comes in 450 which I suddenly awaken to the fact that I am ill or growing old; and above all at that last moment when I feel I am losing hold of myself and am absolutely passive within the hands of the great unknown forces that have formed me; in all those dark moments, O God, grant that I may understand that it is you (provided only my faith is strong enough) who are painfully parting the fibres of my being in order to penetrate to the very marrow of my substance and bear me away within yourself.

Teilhard de Chardin, SJ, 1881–1955

Compassion

451 O Lord, baptize our hearts into a sense of the needs and conditions of all.

George Fox, 1624–91

452 O God of goodness,
in the mystery of natural disasters we look to thee,
trusting that there is an explanation that will
satisfy our minds and hearts.
Accept our compassion for our fellow-men,
our desire for their relief,
and our hope for knowledge which shall control
the forces of nature.
Help us to help thee complete thy universse,
O creator Father,
to remove its flaws,
so that we may be sub-creators with thee of the
Kingdom of thy love in Jesus Christ. G.A.

453 Lord, give us grace
to see that pity wailing over suffering is not love,
that weeping without penitence is not life,
unless they lead to action,
the giving of ourselves to serve and suffer for the loved.
Lord, give us understanding of your way,
lead us to know the mystery of your pain,
that we may follow you
and plead with you
in this your sacrifice,
and enter in the gate of love
to walk love's way.

Fr Gilbert Shaw, 1884–1967

COMPASSION

Lord, the wounds of the world are too deep for us to heal. We have to bring men and women to you and ask you to look after them—the sick in body and mind, the withered in spirit, the victims of greed and injustice, the prisoners of grief. 454

And yet, our Father, do not let our prayers excuse us from paying the price of compassion.

Make us generous with the resources you have entrusted to us. Let your work of rescue be done in us and through us all.

from *Contemporary Prayers for Public Worship*, ed. Caryl Micklem

When you sit happy in your own fair house, 455
  Remember all poor men that are abroad,
That Christ, who gave this roof, prepare for thee
  Eternal dwelling in the house of God.

Alcuin of York, 735–804

O thou whose divine tenderness ever outsoars the narrow loves and charities of earth, grant me today a kind and gentle heart towards all things that live. Let me not ruthlessly hurt any creature of thine. Let me take thought also for the welfare of little children, and of those who are sick, and of the poor; remembering that what I do unto the least of these his brethren I do unto Jesus Christ my Lord. 456

John Baillie, 1886–1960

O merciful and loving Father of all, look down we pray thee on the many millions who are hungry in the world today and are at the mercy of disease. Grant that we who have lived so comfortably and gently all our lives may have true sympathy with them and do all in our power, as individuals and as a nation, to help them to that abundant life which is thy will for them; through Jesus Christ our Lord. 457

G.A.

A FATHER'S PRAYER UPON THE MURDER OF HIS SON 458

O God

We remember not only our son but also his murderers;

Not because they killed him in the prime of his youth and made our hearts bleed and our tears flow,

Not because with this savage act they have brought further disgrace on the name of our country among the civilized nations of the world;

But because through their crime we now follow thy footsteps more closely in the way of sacrifice.

The terrible fire of this calamity burns up all selfishness and possessiveness in us;

Its flame reveals the depth of depravity and meanness and suspicion, the dimension of hatred and the measure of sinfulness in human nature;

It makes obvious as never before our need to trust in God's love as shown in the cross of Jesus and his resurrection;

Love which makes us free from hate towards our persecutors;

Love which brings patience, forbearance, courage, loyalty, humility, generosity, greatness of heart;

Love which more than ever deepens our trust in God's final victory and his eternal designs for the Church and for the world;

Love which teaches us how to prepare ourselves to face our own day of death.

O God

Our son's blood has multiplied the fruit of the Spirit in the soil of our souls;

So when his murderers stand before thee on the day of judgement

Remember the fruit of the Spirit by which they have enriched our lives.

And forgive.

Bishop Dehqani-Tafti of Iran

'FOR THINE IS THE KINGDOM'

Devotion

459 Soul of Christ, be my sanctification;
Body of Christ, be my salvation;
Blood of Christ, fill all my veins;
Water of Christ's side, wash out my stains;
Passion of Christ, my comfort be;
O good Jesu, listen to me;
In thy wounds I fain would hide,
Ne'er to be parted from thy side;

Guard me, should the foe assail me;
Call me when my life shall fail me,
Bid me come to thee above,
With thy Saints to sing thy love,
World without end. Amen.

Anima Christi, 14th century,
tr. John Henry Newman, 1801–90

Grant me, O God, 460
the heart of a child,
pure and transparent as a spring;
a simple heart,
which never harbours sorrows;
a heart glorious in self-giving,
tender in compassion;
a heart faithful and generous,
which will never forget any good
or bear a grudge for any evil.

Make me a heart gentle and humble,
loving without asking any return,
large-hearted and undauntable,
which no ingratitude can sour
and no indifference can weary;
a heart penetrated by the love of Jesus
whose desire will only be satisfied in heaven.

Grant me, O Lord,
the mind and heart
of thy dear Son.

Translated from the French by G.A.

Father, behold thy child: 461
Creator, behold thy creature:
Master, behold thy disciple:
Saviour, behold thy redeemed one:
Spirit, behold thy cleansed one:
Comforter, behold one whom thou dost uphold:

So I come to thee,
O infinite and unimaginable,
To worship thee.

Margaret Cropper, 1886–1980

462 Grant me, even me, my dearest Lord, to know thee, and love thee, and rejoice in thee. And if I cannot do these perfectly in this life, let me at least advance to higher degrees every day, till I can come to do them in perfection. Let the knowledge of thee increase in me here, that it may be full hereafter. Let the love of thee grow every day more and more here, that it may be perfect hereafter; that my joy may be great in itself, and full in thee. I know, O God, that thou art a God of truth, O make good thy gracious promises to me, that my joy may be full. Amen.

St Augustine, 354–430

463 Eternal King, grant me true quietness
For thou art rest and quiet without end.
Eternal light, grant me the abiding light,
And may I live and quicken in thy good.

Angilbert, 8th century

464 O Jesu, king most wonderful,
Thou conqueror renowned,
Thou sweetness most ineffable,
In whom all joys are found!

When once thou visitest the heart,
Then truth begins to shine;
Then earthly vanities depart;
Then kindles love divine.

Latin, 11th century, tr. E. Caswall

465 Jesu to cast one thought upon
Makes gladness after He is gone;
But more than honey and honeycomb
Is to come near and take him home.

Latin, 12th century,
tr. Gerard Manley Hopkins, 1844–89

466 My God, I love thee; not because
I hope for heaven thereby,
Nor yet because who love thee not
Are lost eternally.

Not with the hope of gaining aught,
Not seeking a reward;
But as thyself hast loved me,
O ever-loving Lord!

E'en so I love thee, and will love,
And in thy praise will sing,
Solely because thou art my God,
and my eternal King.

Latin, 17th century, tr. E. Caswall

My joy, my life, my crown! 467
My heart was meaning all the day,
Somewhat it fain would say:
And still it runneth mutt'ring up and down
With onely this, *My joy, my life, my crown.*

George Herbert, 1593–1633

I am serene because I know thou lovest me. 468
Because thou lovest me, naught can move me from my peace.
Because thou lovest me, I am as one to whom all good has come.

Gaelic, tr. Alistair MacLean

As the hand is made for holding and the eye for seeing, thou hast fashioned me for joy. Share with me the vision that shall find it everywhere: in the wild violet's beauty; in the lark's melody; in the face of a steadfast man; in a child's smile; in a mother's love; in the purity of Jesus. 469

Gaelic, tr. Alistair MacLean

I will love thee, O Lord, my strength. 470

Psalm 18: 1

My spirit has become dry because it forgets to feed on you. 471

St John of the Cross, 1542–91

472 PRAYER OF A SOUL TAKEN WITH LOVE

Mine are the heavens and mine is the earth. Mine are the nations, the just are mine and mine the sinners. The angels are mine and the Mother of God and all things are mine; and God himself is mine and all for me, because Christ is mine and all for me.

What do you ask then and seek, my soul? Yours is all of this and all for you. Do not engage yourself in something less nor pay heed to the crumbs which fall from your Father's table. Go forth and exult in your glory! Hide yourself in it and rejoice, and you will obtain the supplications of your heart.

St John of the Cross, 1542–91

473 Him whom I love I greet
with my heart's blood,
but all my senses fail
in the wild storm of love.

Dutch, *c.* 1300, tr. Edmund Colledge

474 O Christ, who laid aside your glory and lived as a man, that all men might see the light of God shining through a human life; help us to be more like you and to lay aside all that hides you from the peoples of other races—our pride of race, of knowledge, of civilization; so that through our lives of prayer and communion and love, they may come to see you as you are, and hail you as their Lord.

Sister Ruth, SLG

475 Ah, Lord God, thou holy lover of my soul, when thou comest into my soul, all that is within me shall rejoice. Thou art my glory and the exultation of my heart; thou art my hope and refuge in the day of my trouble. Set me free from all evil passions, and heal my heart of all inordinate affections; that being inwardly cured and thoroughly cleansed, I may be made fit to love, courageous to suffer, steady to persevere. Nothing is sweeter than love, nothing more courageous, nothing fuller nor better in heaven and earth; because love is born of God, and cannot rest but in God, above all created things. Let me love thee more than myself, nor love myself but for thee; and in thee all that truly love thee, as the law of love commandeth, shining out from thyself. Amen.

Thomas à Kempis, 1380–1471

DEVOTION

O God, the God of all goodness and of all grace, who art worthy of a greater love than we can either give or understand, fill our hearts, we beseech thee, with such love toward thee, that nothing may seem too hard for us to do or to suffer in obedience to thy will; and grant that thus loving thee, we may become daily more like unto thee, and finally obtain the crown of life which thou hast promised to those that love thee; through Jesus Christ our Lord. 476

Farnham Hostel Manual, 19th century

Be thou my vision, O Lord of my heart; 477
Naught be all else to me, save that thou art,
Thou my best thought, by day or by night,
Waking or sleeping, thy presence my light.

Traditional Irish

Jesus, my Lord, 478
Come to me,
Comfort me, console me.
Visit the hearts
In strange lands
Yearning for you.
Visit the dying and those
Who have died without you.
Jesus, my Lord,
Visit also those
Who persecute you.
Lord Jesus, you are my light
In the darkness.
You are my warmth
In the cold.
You are my happiness
In sorrow . . .

Anon.

Here, dying for the world, the world's life hung, 479
Laving a world's sin in that deathly tide;
That downbent head raised earth above the stars:
O timeless wonder! Life, because One died.

Alcuin of York, 735–804

480 Lord, before the mystery of your dying I am silent, dumb, I do not know what to say or do. All I can do is adore silently, without words, without even emotion. Yet, Lord, I want to understand more deeply and love more fully, but somehow I am empty and drained of feeling. Accept then my dumb adoration, and silent offering of myself for this is all I have to give.

Michael Hollings and Etta Gullick

481 Lord, let us be with you, wherever you are crucified today,
Wherever the will of man crosses the will of God:
For being God and man, you are stretched out on the cross of God's purpose, and our rebellion.
Where the will to use armed force crosses God's will for peace,
Where lying and corruption cross God's will for truth,
Where greed and possessiveness cross the use of God's plenty,
Where we live not for others but for ourselves,
Where ugliness and disease cross the will of God for beauty and well-being,
There let us find you, racked on the cross,
And there let us be with you, and share your pain,
And bring about with you, in union with your sacrifice,
That redemption, which you are accomplishing in your passion.

Margaret Cropper, 1886–1980

482 TO JESUS CRUCIFIED

Lovely tears of lovely eyes—
Why dost thou me so woe?
Sorrowful tears of sorrowful eyes—
Thou breakest my heart in two.

Thou sighest sore;
Thy sorrow is more
Than man's tongue can tell;
Thou singest of sorrow,
Mankind to borrow
Out of the pit of hell.

I proud and keen,
Thou meek and clean
Without woe or wile;
Thou art dead for me,
And I live for thee,
So blessed be thy will.

Thy mother seeth
How woe thou beest,
Therefore she yearns apart;
To her thou speakest,
Her sorrow thou slakest—
Sweet prayer won thy heart.

Thy heart is rent,
Thy body is bent
Upon the rood tree;
The tempest is spent,
The devil is schent,
Christ, by the might of thee.

Lovely tears of lovely eyes—
Why dost thou me so woe?
Sorrowful tears of sorrowful eyes—
Thou breakest my heart in two.

Anon., 14th century

Good Lord, give me the grace, in all my fear and agony, to have recourse to that great fear and wonderful agony that thou, my sweet Saviour, hadst at the Mount of Olivet before thy most bitter passion, and in the meditation thereof, to conceive ghostly comfort and consolation profitable for my soul. 483

St Thomas More, 1475–1535

Blessed be thy name, O Jesu, Son of the most high God; blessed be the sorrow thou sufferedst when thy holy hands and feet were nailed to the tree; and blessed thy love when, the fullness of pain accomplished, thou didst give thy soul into the hands of the Father; so by thy cross and precious blood redeeming all the world, all longing souls departed and the numberless unborn; who now livest and reignest in the glory of the eternal Trinity, God for ever and ever. 484

Eric Milner-White, 1884–1964

O Lord, let me rest the ladder of gratitude against thy cross and, mounting, kiss thy feet. 485

Prayer of an Indian Christian

'FOR THINE IS THE KINGDOM'

486 O most gracious and loving Jesu, my Lord and my God, fountain of all grace, come into my soul with the fullness of thy grace. Jesu most patient, too long have I made thee wait for me, yet come to me: endure me a sinner, and make me, through thy patience, to endure all things, and to be patient with all. Jesu most humble, make me through thy humility so humble that I may never lift up myself, for anything against anything, as to any one. Jesu most loving, come with all thy love into my soul, that I may love thee with a burning love, and love all and each with thine own love.

E. B. Pusey, 1800–82

487 Father, we pray thee to fill this house with thy Spirit. Here may the strong renew their strength and seek for their working lives a noble consecration. Here may the poor find succour and the friendless friendship. Here may the tempted find power, the sorrowing comfort and the bereaved find the truth that death hath no dominion over their beloved. Here let the fearing find a new courage and the doubting have their faith and hope confirmed. Here may the careless be awakened and all that are oppressed be freed. Hither may many be drawn by thy love and go hence, their doubts resolved and faith renewed, their sins forgiven and their hearts aflame with thy love. Through Jesus Christ our Lord.

From the chapel porch, Pleshey Retreat House

488 You love with an everlasting love because you are love. And so you are patiently effective always and everywhere, even when we cannot feel your presence. Teach us to love without wanting to control; to love without limit; to love you, our friends, and also our enemies. Teach us to be patient in love when love is not returned; teach us to be patient when even you are apparently far away. Teach us loving, waiting, patience when there is no answer to our questionings and our doubt.

Michael Hollings and Etta Gullick

489 All my fresh springs shall be in thee.

Psalm 87: 7b

490 O thou beloved:
Love eternal, my whole good, happiness which hath
no bounds, I desire to appropriate thee with the
most vehement desire, and the most worthy reverence.

I desire to reserve nothing unto myself.
O everlasting light, surpassing all created
luminaries, flash forth thy lightning from above,
piercing all the most inward parts of my heart.
Make clean, make glad, make bright and make alive
my spirit, with all the powers thereof, that I
may cleave unto thee in ecstasies of joy. Thomas à Kempis, 1380–1471

491 My soul hath desired thee all night, O eternal wisdom! and in the early morning I turn to thee from the depths of my heart. May thy holy presence remove all dangers from my soul and body. May thy many graces fill the inmost recesses of my heart, and inflame it with thy divine love. O most sweet Jesus! turn thy face towards me, for this morning with all the powers of my soul I fly to thee and salute thee, beseeching thee, that the thousand times a thousand angels who minister to thee may praise thee for me, and that the thousand times ten thousand blessed spirits who surround thy throne may glorify thee for me today. May all that is beautiful and amiable in creatures praise thee for me, and may all creation bless thy holy name, our consoling protection in time and in eternity. Blessed Henry Suso, *c.* 1295–1366

492 Almighty Father, Son and Holy Ghost, eternal ever blessed gracious God; to me the least of saints, to me allow that I may keep a door in paradise. That I may keep even the smallest door, the furthest, the darkest, coldest door, the door that is least used, the stiffest door. If so it be but in thine house, O God, if so be that I can see thy glory even afar, and hear thy voice O God, and know that I am with thee, thee O God. St Columba, 521–97

493 Jesus, the Saviour of mankind, who was fastened to the cross with three nails, fasten my heart to the same cross with the three nails of faith, hope, and charity. Fr Adrian Parviliers, SJ

494 Thanks be to thee, O Lord Jesus Christ, for all the benefits which thou hast given us; for all the pains and insults which thou hast borne for us. O most merciful redeemer, friend and brother, may we know thee more clearly, love thee more dearly, and follow thee more nearly; for thine own sake. St Richard of Chichester, 1197–1253

Contemplation

495 Lord Jesus Christ, who returned from this world to the Father and loved those who were here in this world, make my mind turn from worldly preoccupations to the contemplation of heaven, to despise everything transitory and to yearn only for celestial things, and to burn with the glowing fire of your love. And you, Lord, who deemed yourself worthy to wash the feet of your holy apostles with your sacred hands, cleanse also my heart by pouring in the radiance of the Holy Spirit, so that I may be able to love you, our Lord Jesus Christ, in all things and above all else.

Latin, 11th century, tr. Bernard Muir

496 Father in heaven! Thou dost speak to man in many ways; thou to whom alone belongeth wisdom and understanding yet desirest thyself to be understood by man. Even when thou art silent, still thou speakest to him, for the one who saith nothing, yet speaketh in order to examine the disciple; the one who saith nothing, yet speaketh in order to try the beloved one; the one who saith nothing, yet speaketh so that the hour of understanding may be more profound. Is it not thus, Father in heaven! Oh, in the time of silence when man remains alone, abandoned when he does not hear thy voice, it seems to him doubtless that the separation must last forever. Oh, in the time of silence when a man consumes himself in the desert in which he does not hear thy voice, it seems to him doubtless that it is completely extinguished. Father in heaven! It is only a moment of silence in an intimacy of conversation. Bless then this silence as thy word to man; grant that he never forgets that thou speakest also when thou art silent; give him this consolation if he waits on thee, that thou art silent through love and that thou speakest through love, so that in thy silence as in thy word thou art still the same Father and that it is still the same paternal love that thou guidest by thy voice and that thou dost instruct by thy silence.

Søren Kierkegaard, 1813–55

497 ST DENIS'S PRAYER

You are wisdom, uncreated and eternal,
the supreme first cause, above all being,
sovereign Godhead, sovereign goodness,
watching unseen the God-inspired wisdom of Christian people.
Raise us, we pray, that we may totally respond
to the supreme, unknown, ultimate, and splendid height
of your words, mysterious and inspired.
There all God's secret matters lie covered and hidden
under darkness both profound and brilliant, silent and wise.

You make what is ultimate and beyond brightness
  secretly to shine in all that is most dark.
In your way, ever unseen and intangible,
  you fill to the full with most beautiful splendour
  those souls who close their eyes that they may see.
And I, please, with love that goes on beyond mind
  to all that is beyond mind,
  seek to gain such for myself through this prayer.

from *The Cloud of Unknowing*, 14th century

O Christ, my Lord, again and again 498
I have said with Mary Magdalene,
'They have taken away my Lord
and I know not where they have laid him.'
I have been desolate and alone.
And thou hast found me again, and I know
that what has died is not thou, my Lord,
but only my idea of thee,
the image which I have made to preserve
what I have found, and to be my security.
I shall make another image, O Lord,
better than the last.
That too must go, and all successive images,
until I come to the blessed vision of thyself,
O Christ, my Lord.

G.A.

O our Saviour! of ourselves we cannot love thee, cannot follow thee, 499
cannot cleave to thee;
  but thou didst come down
  that we might love thee
  didst ascend
  that we might follow thee,
  didst bind us round thee as thy girdle
  that we might be held fast unto thee;
Thou who hast loved us, make us to love thee,
Thou who hast sought us, make us to seek thee,
Thou who, when lost, didst find us,
  be thou thyself the way,
  that we may find thee
  and be found in thee,
  our only hope, and our everlasting joy.

E. B. Pusey, 1800–82

500 I pause upon the brink of the unknown;
I am neither there nor here.
On this side, as in a dream, men move,
Doing the phantom things we do on earth;
On that side, through the silence, something stirs,
A wave of living surges and is gone.
The one I see as figures on a screen,
Things without substance;
The other hear, and yet hear not,
As one that has no ears.
To the known I cannot return, for I have passed
Where knowledge is not;
Yet the unknown I cannot touch,
Save as a pebble the sea which covers it.
O God, unknown to me, life to my death,
See how, forgetting, thou rememberest me;
Can I forget, and so remember thee?

Sister Ruth, SLG

Gifts of the Spirit

501 O Holy Spirit, whose presence is liberty, grant us that freedom of the spirit, which will not fear to tread in unknown ways, nor be held back by misgivings of ourselves and fear of others. Ever beckon us forward to the place of thy will which is also the place of thy power, O ever-leading, ever-loving Lord.

G.A.

502 O God who dost teach the hearts of thy faithful people by sending to us the light of thy Holy Spirit: Grant us by that same Spirit to be enlightened in our minds, sanctified in our hearts, kindled in love and strengthened by grace, through Jesus Christ, thy blessed Son, our Lord.

The Book of Common Prayer adapted by G.A.

503 Spirit of promise, Spirit of unity, we thank thee that thou art also the Spirit of renewal. Renew in the whole Church, we pray thee, that passionate desire for the coming of thy kingdom which will unite all Christians in one mission to the world. May we all grow up together into him, who is our head, the Saviour of the world, and our only Lord and master.

Olive Wyon, 1881–1966

GIFTS OF THE SPIRIT

Enter my heart, O Holy Spirit, 504
come in blessed mercy and set me free.
Throw open, O Lord, the locked doors of my mind;
cleanse the chambers of my thought for thy dwelling:
light there the fires of thine own holy brightness in new understandings of truth,
O Holy Spirit, very God, whose presence is liberty,
grant me the perfect freedom
to be thy servant
today, tomorrow, evermore.

Eric Milner-White, 1884–1964

505

Come thou Holy Spirit	Veni, Sancte Spiritus,
Send from highest heaven	Et emitte coelitus
Radiance of thy light.	Lucis tuae radium.
Come, Father of the poor	Veni, pater pauperum,
Come, giver of all gifts	Veni, dator munerum,
Come, light of every heart.	Veni, lumen cordium.
Of comforters the best	Consolator optime,
Dear guest of every soul	Dulcis hospes animae,
Refreshment ever sweet.	Dulce refrigerium.
In our labour rest	In labore requies,
Coolness in our heat	In aestu temperies,
Comfort in our grief.	In fletu solatium.
O most blessed light	O lux beatissima,
Fill the inmost hearts	Remple cordis intima
Of thy faithful ones.	Tuorum fidelium.
Without thy holy presence	Sine tuo numine,
All is dark	Nihil est in lumine
Nothing free from sin.	Nihil est innoxium.
What is soiled cleanse	Lava quod est sordidum,
What is dry refresh	Riga quod est aridum,
What is wounded heal.	Sana quod est saucium.
What is rigid bend	Flecte quod est rigidum,
What is frozen warm	Fove quod est frigidum,
Guide what goes astray.	Rege quod est devium.
Give thy faithful ones	Da tuis fidelibus,
Who in thee confide	In te confidentibus,
Sevenfold hallowing.	Sacrum septenarium.

Give goodness its reward	Da virtutis meritum,
Give journey safe through death	Da salutis exitum,
Give joy that has no end.	Da perenne gaudium.

A 13th-century hymn by an anonymous writer, tr. G.A.

506 O holy Spirit . . . which with thy holy breath cleansest men's minds, comforting them when they be in sorrow, cheering them up with pure gladness, when they be in heaviness, leading them into all truth, when they be out of the way, kindling in them the fire of charity, when they be a cold, knitting them together with the glue of peace, when they be at variance, and garnishing and enriching them with sundry gifts, which by thy means profess the name of the Lord Jesus: by whose working all things live, which live in deed: whose delight is to dwell in the hearts of the simple, which thou hast vouchsafed to consecrate for temples, to thyself. I beseech thee, maintain thy gifts in me, and increase the things daily, which thou hast vouchsafed to bestow upon me, that by thy governance the lusts of the flesh may die more and more in me and the desire of the heavenly life more quicken and increase. Let me so pass through the misty desert of this world by thy light going before me; as I may neither be defiled with Sathan's wiles, nor be entangled with any errors disagreeing from thy truth which the true catholic Church hath delivered us by the instinct of thee, which livest and reignest everlastingly with the Father and the Son.

Erasmus, 1466–1536

507 VENI CREATOR SPIRITUS

Creator Spirit, by whose aid
The world's foundations first were laid,
Come visit ev'ry pious mind;
Come pour thy joys on human kind:
From sin, and sorrow set us free;
And make thy temples worthy thee.

O, source of uncreated light,
The Father's promis'd *Paraclete*!
Thrice holy fount, thrice holy fire,
Our hearts with heav'nly love inspire;
Come, and thy sacred unction bring
To sanctifie us, while we sing!

GIFTS OF THE SPIRIT

Plenteous of grace, descend from high,
Rich in thy sev'n-fold energy!
Thou strength of his almighty hand,
Whose pow'r does heav'n and earth command:
Proceeding Spirit, our defence,
Who do'st the gift of tongues dispence,
And crown'st thy gift, with eloquence!

Refine and purge our earthy parts;
But, oh, inflame and fire our hearts!
Our frailties help, our vice controul;
Submit the senses to the soul;
And when rebellious they are grown,
Then, lay thy hand, and hold 'em down.

Chace from our minds th' infernal foe;
And Peace, the fruit of love, bestow:
And, lest our feet shou'd step astray,
Protect, and guide us in the way.

Make us eternal truths receive,
And practise, all that we believe:
Give us thy self, that we may see
The Father and the Son, by thee.

Immortal honour, endless fame
Attend th'almighty Father's name:
The saviour Son, be glorify'd,
Who for lost man's redemption dy'd:
and equal adoration be
Eternal *Paraclete*, to thee.

Translated in paraphrase by John Dryden, 1631–1701

Fire of the Spirit, life of the lives of creatures, 508
spiral of sanctity, bond of all natures,
glow of charity, lights of clarity, taste
of sweetness to sinners, be with us and hear us . . .

Composer of all things, light of all the risen,
key of salvation, release from the dark prison,
hope of all unions, scope of chastities, joy
in the glory, strong honour, be with us and hear us.

St Hildegarde, 12th century,
freely translated by Charles Williams, 1886–1945

509 O Holy Ghost, O faithful Paraclete,
Love of the Father and the Son.
In whom begetter and begotten meet . . .
Bond that holdeth God to man.
Power that welds in one
Humanity and Deity.
God making all that is
Before our day.
God guiding all that's made
Throughout our day.
Gift that abides through an eternity
Of giving, and is made no less.
Thy going forth preceded time,
Thy pouring forth took place in time.
The one, the well-spring of power and the river of grace,
The other, the flowing, the giving, the light on our face.
Thou camest forth from thy transcendent day,
To make for us this shining feasting day.
Thou who alone
Art worthily adored
With Father and with Son.
To thee in heart and word
Be honour, worship, grace,
Here and in every place,
World without end.

Hildebert, 1056–1133

510 O come, Holy Spirit, inflame my heart, set it on fire with love. Burn away my self-centredness so that I can love unselfishly. Breathe your life-giving breath into my soul so that I can live freely and joyously, unrestricted by self-consciousness, and may be ready to go wherever you may send me. Come like a gentle breeze and give me your still peace so that I may be quiet and know the wonder of your presence, and help diffuse it in the world. Never let me shut you out; never let me try to limit you to my capacity; act freely in me and through me, never leave me, O Lord and giver of life!

Michael Hollings and Etta Gullick

511 O Spirit of God, mighty river,
flow over me, in me, through me.
O Spirit of God, cleanse me,
purify the channels of my life.

O Spirit of God, bear me along
with thy flood of live-giving service.
O Spirit of God, mighty river,
bear me down to the ocean,
the ocean of thy love.
O Spirit of God, mighty fire,
glow in me, burn in me,
until thy radiance fills my soul.
O Spirit of God, mighty fire,
may thy light illumine my mind.
O Spirit of God, mighty fire,
may thy heat consume my will
until I burn for thee.
May the flames of thy love
ever blaze upon the altar
of my heart.

Charles Devanesan

On your last days on earth 512
you promised
to leave us the Holy Spirit
as our present comforter.
We also know that your Holy Spirit blows over this earth.
But we do not understand him.
Many think
he is only wind or a feeling.
Let your Holy Spirit
break into our lives.
Let him come like blood into our veins,
so that we will be driven
entirely by your will.
Let your Spirit
blow over wealthy Europe and America,
so that men there will be humble.
Let him blow over the poor parts of the world,
so that men there need suffer no more.
Let him blow over Africa,
so that men here may understand
what true freedom is.
There are a thousand voices and spirits
in this world,
but we want to hear only your voice,
and be open only to your Spirit.

Prayer of a young Ghanaian Christian

513 Grant, O merciful Father, that thy divine Spirit may enlighten, inflame, and cleanse our hearts; that he may penetrate us with his heavenly dew, and make us fruitful in good works. Through Jesus Christ our Lord.

from *The Golden Manual*

514 O Spirit of God, brooding over the formless world: brood over my spirit.
Blest Holy Spirit.

O Spirit of God, giving form to the formless: fashion my spirit.
Blest Holy Spirit.

O Spirit of God, bringing order out of chaos: order my spirit.
Blest Holy Spirit.

O Spirit of God, giving life to the lifeless: give life to my spirit.
Blest Holy Spirit.

O Spirit of the Lord, inspiration of the prophets: speak to my spirit.
Blest Holy Spirit.

O Holy Spirit, author of holiness: sanctify my spirit.
Blest Holy Spirit.

O Holy Spirit, knowing the deep things of God: move in the depths of my being.
Blest Holy Spirit.

Fire of the Spirit! Burn all that is not holy.
Blest Holy Spirit.

Fire of the Spirit! Shine with thy light.
Blest Holy Spirit.

Fire of the Spirit! Kindle with thy warmth.
Blest Holy Spirit.

Fire of the Spirit! Generate in us power.
Blest Holy Spirit.

Fire of the Spirit! Inflame us with love.
Blest Holy Spirit.

Wind of the Spirit! Breathe in us thy gentleness.
Blest Holy Spirit.

Wind of the Spirit! Blow in thy strength.
Blest Holy Spirit.

Let us pray for the gift of the Spirit.

The gift of the Spirit is wisdom and understanding, resourcefulness and spiritual strength, knowledge and true godliness, and holy fear. Grant us thy sevenfold gift, O Holy Spirit.
Blest Holy Spirit.

GIFTS OF THE SPIRIT

Let us pray for the fruit of the Spirit.

The harvest of the Spirit is love, joy, peace, good temper, gentleness, goodness, humility and self-control. Produce in us thy harvest, O Holy Spirit.

Blest Holy Spirit.

G.A.

O Holy Spirit, 515
Giver of light and life,
impart to us thoughts higher than our own thoughts,
and prayers better than our own prayers,
and powers beyond our own powers,
that we may spend and be spent
in the ways of love and goodness,
after the perfect image
of our Lord and Saviour Jesus Christ.

Eric Milner-White, 1884–1964, and G. W. Briggs, 1875–1959

O God, the Holy Spirit, 516
come to us, and among us:
come as the wind, and cleanse us;
come as the fire, and burn;
come as the dew, and refresh:
convict, convert, and consecrate
many hearts and lives
to our great good
and thy greater glory,
and this we ask for Jesus Christ's sake.

Eric Milner-White, 1884–1964

O Holy Ghost, my King, I worship thee; 517
Creator of the world I kneel to thee;
O light of uncreated majesty,
O love of God in threefold unity,
O spouse of virgin souls, I lean on thee;
O gracious Paraclete, I worship thee.

O Holy Ghost, thou most sweet charity—
Thou sevenfold ray of God's great majesty,
Thou sevenfold beauty of the unity;
Thou sevenfold glory of the Trinity;
Thou sevenfold gift from God's eternity,
O Holy Ghost, I praise and worship thee.

O Holy Ghost, who givest life to me;
O Holy Ghost, who givest strength to me,
O Holy Ghost, who givest gifts to me;
Who willest all thy gifts to give to me;
Who willest I should correspond with thee;
O Holy Ghost, vouchsafe to live in me,
That this my heart may be a home for thee.

Spirit of wisdom, let me learn from thee
The falsehoods of the world to leave for thee;
Spirit of understanding, I would be
Enlightened with the fire that burns in thee,
Spirit of counsel, do thou set me free
From tangled judgements that are not of thee,
And guide me in the way of liberty.

Spirit of fortitude, O come to me,
In all my trials do thou strengthen me;
Spirit of heavenly knowledge, give to me
The grace divine to use this world for thee.
And thou, O spirit meek of piety,
Make this my heart a home of peace to be,
A spring of overflowing charity.

Spirit of holy fear, O I would be
Plunged in thy very depths, all steeped in thee,
That sin may never more find place in me;
That imperfection may grow less in me;
That thought of self may pass away from me;
That God's eternal light may rest on me;
That I may live in thee and thou in me.

Great ruler of the Church, I worship thee,
The giver of her gifts art thou to me;
Her sacramental graces flow from thee;
All power in heaven and earth she draws from thee;
Thou art her breath, her soul, she lives by thee.
O Holy Ghost, O gift of God to me!
O Holy Ghost, with joy I worship thee.

Origin unknown

Sacraments

518 Lord, I am not worthy that thou shouldest enter under my roof: but speak the word only, and my soul shall be healed.

based on Luke 7: 6–7

Almighty, everlasting God, I draw near to the sacrament of your only-begotten Son, our Lord Jesus Christ. I who am sick approach to the physician of life. I who am unclean come to the fountain of mercy; blind, to the light of eternal brightness; poor and needy, to the Lord of heaven and earth. Therefore, I implore you, in your boundless mercy, to heal my sickness, cleanse my defilement, enlighten my blindness, enrich my poverty, and clothe my nakedness. Then shall I dare to receive the bread of angels, the King of kings and Lord of lords, with reverence and humility, contrition and love, purity and faith, with the purpose and intention necessary for the good of my soul. Grant, I beseech you, that I may receive not only the Body and Blood of the Lord, but also the grace and power of the sacrament. Most merciful God, enable me so to receive the Body of your only-begotten Son, our Lord Jesus Christ, which he took from the Virgin Mary, that I may be found worthy to be incorporated into his mystical Body, and counted among his members. Most loving Father, grant that I may one day see face to face your beloved Son, whom I now intend to receive under the veil of the sacrament, and who with you and the Holy Spirit, lives and reigns for ever, one God, world without end. 519

from the New Roman Missal

Godhead here in hiding, whom I do adore 520
Masked by these bare shadows, shape and nothing more,
See, Lord, at thy service low lies here a heart
Lost, all lost in wonder at the God thou art . . .
Jesu whom I look at shrouded here below,
I beseech thee send me what I thirst for so,
Some day to gaze on thee face to face in light
And be blest for ever with thy glory's sight.

Latin, 13th century, tr. Gerard Manley Hopkins, 1844–89

Lord Jesus Christ, king of glory, Son of the living God, who for sinners gave your body over into the hands of enemies, and deigned to surrender yourself to death, I implore you in your pity mercifully to rescue me from the hands of all my enemies, by your glorious body which we here adore in the form of bread, by your blood through which today the world is sanctified. And I beg too, O Lord, that I and all my friends and my enemies and all Christians, at the separation of body and soul, may be led through true faith into eternal life. 521

Latin, 14th century, tr. Edmund Colledge

522 FOR THE KINDLING OF THE LIGHT ON EASTER EVE

Good captain, maker of the light
Who dost divide the day and night,
The sun is drowned beneath the sea,
Chaos is on us, horribly.
O Christ, give back to faithful souls the light!

Prudentius, 348–c. 410

523 The word went forth
Yet from his Father never went away:
Came to his work on earth
And laboured till the twilight of his day.

Men envied him: he went to death
By his own man betrayed:
Yet first to his own men himself had given,
In wine and broken bread.

O victim slain for us and our salvation,
Opening the door of light,
The warring hosts are set on our damnation:
Give us the strength to fight.

St Thomas Aquinas, 1225–74

524 I am not worthy, Master and Lord, that thou shouldest come beneath the roof of my soul: yet, since thou in thy love toward all men, dost wish to dwell in me, in boldness I come. Thou commandest, Open the gates—which thou alone hast forged; and thou wilt come in with love toward all men, as is thy nature; thou wilt come in and enlighten my darkened reasoning. I believe that thou wilt do this: for thou didst not send away the harlot who came to thee with tears; nor cast out the repenting publican; nor reject the thief who acknowledged thy kingdom; nor forsake the repentant persecutor, a yet greater act; but all of those who came to thee in repentance, didst thou count in the band of thy friends, who alone abidest blessed forever, now, and unto the endless ages.

St John Chrysostom, c. 347–407

525 Since once again, Lord, as in another time in the forests along the Aisne, I have neither bread nor wine nor altar here on the Asian steppes, I lift myself far above symbols, to the pure majesty of the Real; and I, your

priest, offer to you on the altar of the entire earth, the travail and suffering of the world. Yonder breaks the sun, to light the uttermost east, and then to send its sheets of fire over the living surface of the earth, which wakens, shudders, and resumes its appalling struggle . . .

Teilhard de Chardin, SJ, 1881–1955

For the bread that we have eaten 526
For the wine that we have tasted
For the life that you have given:
  Father, Son and Holy Spirit,
  We will praise you.

For the life of Christ within us
Turning all our fears to freedom
Helping us to live for others:
  Father, Son and Holy Spirit,
  We will praise you.

For the strength of Christ to lead us
In our living and our dying,
In the end with all your people
  Father, Son and Holy Spirit,
  We will praise you.

from *Contemporary Prayers for Public Worship*, ed. Caryl Micklem

Strengthen, O Lord, the hands that holy things have taken, that they may daily bring forth fruit to thy glory. Grant, O Lord, that the lips which have sung thy praise within the sanctuary, may glorify thee for ever; that the ears which have heard the voice of thy songs, may be closed to the voice of clamour and dispute; that the eyes which have seen thy great love, may also behold thy blessed hope; that the tongues which have sung the sanctus, may ever speak the truth. Grant that the feet that have trod in thy holy courts may ever walk in the light, and that the souls and bodies, which have tasted of thy living body and blood, may ever be restored in newness of life. 527

Liturgy of Malabar

What reward shall I give unto the Lord for all the benefits that he hath done unto me? I will receive the cup of salvation and call upon the name of the Lord. 528

Psalm 116: 12–13

529 O God, who in this wondrous sacrament hast left unto us a memorial of thy passion; grant us so to venerate the sacred mysteries of thy body and blood, that we may ever continue to feel within ourselves the blessed fruit of thy redemption. Who livest and reignest God, for ever and ever.

St Thomas Aquinas, 1225–74, from *The Golden Manual*

530 Nothing has been capable, dear Lord, to hinder you from being all mine, neither heaven, nor your divinity, nor the gibbet of the cross: grant me the grace, that nothing may hinder me from being all yours, to whom I owe myself both for creation and redemption.

'Twas never heard that in your mortal life, you lodg'd with any, which you did not liberally reward with your gifts: I beg you will do the same to your present habitation, which is my heart: let the touch of yours, which consecrates all things, sanctify my heart that it may be grateful to you.

Lady Lucy Herbert, 1669–1744

531 Finished and perfected,
so far forth as is in our power,
O Christ our God,
is the mystery of thy dispensation.
For we have held the remembrance of thy death,
we have seen the figure of thy resurrection,
we have been filled with thine unending life,
we have had fruition of thine inexhaustible delight,
whereof in the world to come withal
be Thou pleased that we all
be accounted worthy.

Bishop Lancelot Andrewes, 1555–1626

532 Let all mortal flesh keep silence, and with fear and trembling stand;
Ponder nothing earthly-minded, for with blessings in his hand,
Christ our God to earth descendeth, our full homage to command.

Liturgy of St James

533 O my Lord and God
the journey is too great for me
unless
thou feed me with bread from heaven
and wine of life

unless
thou share with me thine own life
victorious over sin,
hatred, pain, and death.
Let thy blood
flow through my veins
thy strength
be my strength
thy love
be my love
And the father's will
be my will as well as thine
Let me be one with thee
in heart, mind, and will.

G.A.

534

Lord God,
in return for thy great love
I would bring an offering,
But there is only one worthy offering
The perfect obedience of thy Son
even unto death.

Lord God,
I remember that offering,
I plead it before thee,
And though it be all-sufficient
I add to it
the offering of myself,
body, mind, and spirit,
mind, heart and will,
all that I have,
all that I am,
all that by thy grace I can become.
Accept, O Lord God,
this unworthy sacrifice
and cleanse
and sanctify
and use it
in the service of thy kingdom
for his dear sake.

G.A.

535 Lord, this is thy feast,
prepared by thy longing,
spread at thy command,
attended at thine invitation,
blessed by thine own Word,
distributed by thine own hand,
the undying memorial of thy sacrifice
upon the Cross,
the full gift of thine everlasting love,
and its perpetuation till time shall end.

Lord, this is Bread of heaven,
Bread of life,
that, whoso eateth, never shall hunger more
And this the cup of pardon, healing, gladness,
strength,
that whoso drinketh, thirsteth not again.

So may we come, O Lord, to thy table;
Lord Jesus, come to us.

Eric Milner-White, 1884–1964

'FOR EVER AND EVER'

Death and eternity

536 Give me thy grace, good Lord, to make death no stranger to me. Give me, good Lord, a longing to be with thee, not for the avoiding of the calamities of this wretched world; nor so much for the avoiding of the pains of purgatory, nor of the pains of hell neither, nor so much for the attaining of the joys of heaven in respect of mine own commodity, as even for a very love to thee.

St Thomas More, 1475–1535

537 Know that the Lord cometh and that today you shall see his glory, and there shall be in that day a great light . . . O Lord, I trust in thee, O Lord in eternity, I shall not be confounded. I believe . . . in the life eternal.

Joseph Müller, priest, last prayer in the face of death, 11 Sept. 1944

538 O God, early in the morning I cry to you.
Help me to pray
And to concentrate my thoughts on you:
I cannot do this alone.

In me there is darkness,
But with you there is light;
I am lonely, but you do not leave me;
I am feeble in heart, but with you there is help;
I am restless, but with you there is peace.
In me there is bitterness, but with you there is patience;
I do not understand your ways,
But you know the way for me . . .

Restore me to liberty,
And enable me so to live now
That I may answer before you and before me.
Lord, whatever this day may bring,
Your name be praised.

Dietrich Bonhoeffer, written while awaiting execution in a Nazi prison

O Lord our God, from whom neither life nor death can separate those 539
who trust in thy love, and whose love holds in its embrace thy children in this world and the next; so unite us to thyself that in fellowship with thee we may always be united to our loved ones whether here or there; give us courage, constancy and hope; through him who died and was buried and rose again for us, Jesus Christ our Lord.

William Temple, 1881–1944

O Lord, governor of heaven and earth, in whose hands are embodied and 540
departed spirits, if thou hast ordained the souls of the dead to minister to the living, and appointed my departed wife to have care of me, grant that I may enjoy the good effects of her attention and ministration, whether exercised by appearance, impulses, dreams, or in any other manner agreeable to thy government; forgive my presumption, enlighten my ignorance, and however meaner agents are employed, grant me the blessed influences of thy Holy Spirit, through Jesus Christ our Lord.

Samuel Johnson, 1709–84

We give back, to you, O God, those whom you gave to us. You did not lose 541
them when you gave them to us, and we do not lose them by their return to you. Your dear Son has taught us that life is eternal and love cannot die. So death is only an horizon, and an horizon is only the limit of our sight. Open our eyes to see more clearly, and draw us closer to you that

we may know that we are nearer to our loved ones, who are with you. You have told us that you are preparing a place for us: prepare us also for that happy place, that where you are we may also be always, O dear Lord of life and death.

William Penn, 1644–1718

542 Incline us O God! to think humbly of ourselves, to be saved only in the examination of our own conduct, to consider our fellow-creatures with kindness, and to judge of all they say and do with the charity which we would desire from them ourselves.

Jane Austen, 1775–1817

543 O Lord, you have made us very small, and we bring our years to an end like a tale that is told; help us to remember that beyond our brief day is the eternity of your love.

Reinhold Niebuhr, 1892–1971

544 Grant us, O Lord, not to mind earthly things, but to love things heavenly; and even now, while we are placed among things that are passing away, to cleave to those that shall abide; through Jesus Christ our Lord.

Leonine Sacramentary, 5th century

545

Here lie I, Martin Elginbrodde:
Have mercy on my soul, Lord God,
As I would do, were I Lord God
and You were Martin Elginbrodde.

Epitaph in Elgin Cathedral

546 Father of all, I commend to thy mercy all my friends who have died, especially . . . Grant them more light and further opportunities for progress in the knowledge of thee. If it be possible, may they pray for me as I do now for them. Unite us in the communion of Saints and the fellowship of the Holy Spirit, for Jesus' sake.

W. R. Matthews, 1881–1973

Bring us, O Lord God, at our last awakening into the house and gate of heaven, to enter into that gate and dwell in that house, where there shall be no darkness nor dazzling, but one equal light; no noise nor silence, but one equal music; no fears nor hopes, but one equal possession; no ends nor beginnings, but one equal eternity; in the habitations of thy glory and dominion world without end. 547

John Donne, 1572–1631

O God, who broughtest me from the rest of last night 548
Unto the joyous light of this day,
Be thou bringing me from the new light of this day
Unto the guiding light of eternity.
Oh! from the new light of this day
Unto the guiding light of eternity.

from *Carmina Gadelica*, tr. Alexander Carmichael (1961)

The Virgin, martyrs, and saints

Hail Mary, full of grace, the Lord is with thee. Blessed art thou among women, and blessed is the fruit of thy womb Jesus: Holy Mary, Mother of God, pray for us sinners now and at the hour of our death. 549

Ave Maria, based on Luke 1: 28, 42

Hail, holy Lady, 550
Most holy Queen,
Mary, Mother of God,
Ever Virgin;
Chosen by the most holy Father in heaven,
Consecrated by him,
With his most holy beloved Son
And the Holy Spirit, the comforter.
On you descended and in you still remains
All the fullness of grace
And every good.
Hail, his Palace.
Hail, his Tabernacle.
Hail, his Robe.
Hail, his Handmaid.
Hail, his Mother.

And hail, all holy virtues,
  Who, by the grace
  And inspiration of the Holy Spirit,
  Are poured into the hearts of the faithful
So that, faithless no longer,
They may be made faithful servants of God
through you.

St Francis of Assisi, 1182–1226

551 O most loving Mary, star of the sea, most glorious mother of mercy, dwelling place of chasteness, pray for us to our Lord Jesus Christ your Son, that he may rescue us from evil, that he may make us rejoice in good, that he may cleanse us of vices and may strengthen us with virtues, that he may bring us tranquillity and may preserve us in a peaceful life with those who are his own. We entreat you that we may escape Satan's terrors, and that we may have you for our guide as we make our way to our home, lest the subtle enemy ensnare us on our road.

Latin, 14th century, tr. Edmund Colledge

552 THE FIVE SORROWS OF THE VIRGIN

Gracious lady, God's mother, for the sorrow that you had when Simeon said that the sword of sorrow would pass through your heart, implore your dear Son that I may have forgiveness for my sinful life, and that I may be received with his blessed children into endless bliss. And good Jesus, for your mother's love and for this first sorrow, comfort us in all our needs, bodily and spiritual, and especially those who pray for me and trust in my prayers. *Our Father*, *etc.*

Blessed mother of God, for that grievous sorrow which you had when you had lost your Son, seeking hastily, weeping and mourning, pray for me to him our Lord, that I may have grace to seek for him with tears of love and penitence, and that I may grow in love and come to perfect charity. And good Jesus, God's Son, for your mother's love and for this her second sorrow, comfort us all in our need, bodily and spiritual, and especially those who pray for me and trust in my prayers for them. *Our Father*, *etc.*

Blessed lady, mother of God, for that dreadful sorrow when in your soul you saw how your Son was arrested by wicked Jews, deliver me from every kind of fear of bodily and spiritual enemies, that by grace I may live and die pleasingly to him. And good Jesus, for that dreadful arrest and for this third sorrow of your mother, comfort us all in our need, bodily and spiritual, and especially those who pray for me and trust in my prayers for them. *Our Father*, *etc.*

Blessed lady, at the Passion of your Son, for that great sorrow which you suffered in all his pains and his lamentable death, ask grace for me to love that Lord so fervently that through the heat of burning love I may always keep in mind his Passion, for the health of my soul and the overthrow of the devil. And good Jesus, God's Son, for your mother's love and for this her fourth sorrow, comfort us in all our needs, bodily and spiritual, and especially those who pray for me and trust in my prayers for them. *Our Father, etc.*

Sorrowful lady, standing mourning in the sight of your dear Son, for the great pain that you had to look on that good Lord and all his bloody wounds, by your power obtain for me both grace and mercy, and accept me into your keeping, and govern me in body and in soul, to the honour of your dear Son and for my salvation. And good Jesus, God's Son, for your mother's love and for this her fifth sorrow, comfort us in all our need, bodily and spiritual, and especially those who pray for me and trust in my prayers. *Our Father, etc.*

English, 14th century, tr. Edmund Colledge

TO THE BLESSED VIRGIN 553

. . .

Be thou then, O thou dear
Mother, my atmosphere;
My happier world, wherein
To wend and meet no sin;
Above me, round me lie
Fronting my froward eye
With sweet and scarless sky;
Stir in my ears, speak there
Of God's love, O live air,
Of patience, penance, prayer:
Worldmothering air, air wild,
Wound with thee, in thee isled,
Fold home, fast fold thy child.

Gerard Manley Hopkins, 1844–89

I am God's wheat. May I be ground by the teeth of the wild beasts until I become the fine wheat bread that is Christ's. My passions are crucified, there is no heat in my flesh. A stream flows murmuring inside me; deep down in me it says: Come to the Father. 554

St Ignatius of Antioch, before his martyrdom in 107

555 May God the Father, and the eternal High Priest Jesus Christ, build us up in faith and truth and love, and grant to us our portion among the saints with all those who believe on our Lord Jesus Christ. We pray for all saints, for kings and rulers, for the enemies of the Cross of Christ, and for ourselves we pray that our fruit may abound and we be made perfect in Christ Jesus our Lord.

Bishop Polycarp, 69–155

556 O God, who hast brought us near to an innumerable company of angels and to the spirits of just men made perfect; grant us in our pilgrimage to abide in their fellowship, and in our heavenly country to become partakers of their joy; through Jesus Christ our Lord.

William Bright, 1824–1901

557 O King, eternal, immortal, invisible, who in the righteousness of thy saints hast given us an example of godly life, and in their blessedness a glorious pledge of the hope of our calling, we beseech thee that, being compassed about with so great a cloud of witnesses, we may run with patience the race that is set before us, and with them receive the crown of glory that fadeth not away; through Jesus Christ our Lord.

Anon.

558 We thank thee, O God, for the saints of all ages; for those who in times of darkness kept the lamp of faith burning; for the great souls who saw visions of larger truth and dared to declare it; for the multitude of quiet and gracious souls whose presence has purified and sanctified the world; and for those known and loved by us, who have passed from this earthly fellowship into the fuller light of life with thee.

Anon.

559 O eternal Lord God, we thy children lift grateful thanks to thee for our elder brethren in the household of faith:

For Abraham the father of the faithful:
Blessed be thou, Lord God of Israel.

For the patriarchs who succeeded him in faith:
Blessed be thou, Lord God of Israel.

For Moses, who under thee led thy people to freedom and gave them thy law:
Blessed be thou, Lord God of Israel.

For the prophets to whom thy Word came:
Blessed be thou, Lord God of Israel.

For David, the first singer of thy praises:
Blessed be thou, Lord God of Israel.

For those who gave their lives to preserve thy law:
Blessed be thou, Lord God of Israel.

For Jesus, thy Christ, thy Word in person, Mediator of the new covenant, Saviour of men, King of Saints:
Praise be to thee, O God, and to thy Christ.

For the first disciples who left all to follow him:
Praise be to thee, O God, and to thy Christ.

For the apostles, who in obedience to him carried the Gospel to many lands:
Praise be to thee, O God, and to thy Christ.

For thy servant Paul, who so richly experienced the grace of the Risen Lord, and interpreted him to the nations:
Praise be to thee, O God, and to thy Christ.

For the evangelists who recorded the apostles' memories of their Lord and their own faith in him:
Praise be to thee, O God, and to thy Christ.

For the messengers, known and unknown, who brought the good news to our own country:
Praise be to thee, O God, and to thy Christ.

For all who have gone to the ends of the earth to share thy love in Christ Jesus:
Praise be to thee, O God, and to thy Christ.

For the noble army of martyrs who faced death for love of thee and in thy power:
Praise be to thee, O King of Saints.

For the saints in every age who reflected thee in their lives and ever since:
Praise be to thee, O King of Saints.

Who stood fast in the faith and worked the works of love:
Praise be to thee, O King of Saints.

For the succession of quiet and gracious souls, whose presence has sweetened and sanctified the world:
Praise be to thee, O King of Saints.

For the mighty company of every race and nation who worship in thy presence:
Praise be to thee, O King of Saints.

Amen. Blessing, and glory, and wisdom, and thanksgiving, and honour, and power, and might be unto our God for ever and ever. Amen.

G.A.

Blessings

560 Unto God's gracious mercy and protection we commit you. The Lord bless you and keep you. The Lord make his face to shine upon you, and be gracious to you. The Lord lift his countenance upon you, and give you peace.

The Aaronic blessing, Numbers 6: 24–6

561 May the God of peace himself sanctify you wholly; and may your spirit and soul and body, be kept sound and blameless at the coming of our Lord Jesus Christ.

1 Thessalonians 5: 23

562 The God of peace, that brought again from the dead our Lord Jesus, that great shepherd of the sheep, through the blood of the everlasting covenant, make us perfect in every good work to do his will, working in us that which is well-pleasing in his sight; through Jesus Christ, to whom be glory for ever and ever.

Hebrews 13: 20, 21

563 May the Lord bless you with all good and keep you from all evil; may He give light to your heart with loving wisdom, and be gracious to you with eternal knowledge; may He lift up his loving countenance upon you for eternal peace.

Dead Sea Scrolls

564 May God, the Lord, bless us with all heavenly benediction, and make us pure and holy in his sight.

May the riches of his glory abound in us.

May He instruct us with the word of truth, inform us with the Gospel of salvation, and enrich us with his love, Through Jesus Christ, our Lord.

Gelasian Sacramentary

BLESSINGS

May the eternal God bless and keep us, guard our bodies, save our souls, direct our thoughts, and bring us safe to the heavenly country, our eternal home, where Father, Son and Holy Spirit ever reign, one God for ever and ever. 565

Sarum Breviary

The Lord Jesus Christ be near to defend thee, within thee to refresh thee, around thee to preserve thee, before thee to guide thee, behind thee to justify thee, above thee to bless thee; who liveth and reigneth with the Father and the Holy Spirit, God for evermore. 566

Anon., 10th century

The peace of God which passeth all understanding, keep your hearts and minds in the knowledge and love of God, and of his Son Jesus Christ our Lord, and the blessing of God Almighty, the Father, the Son and the Holy Ghost, be amongst you and remain with you always. 567

Book of Common Prayer, 1549

May the right hand of the Lord keep us ever in old age, the grace of Christ continually defend us from the enemy. O Lord, direct our heart in the way of peace; through Jesus Christ our Lord. 568

from the *Book of Cerne*, the prayerbook of Bishop Aedelwald, 8th century

I saw a stranger today 569
I put food for him in the eating-place
And drink in the drinking-place
And music in the listening-place.
In the Holy Name of the Trinity
He blessed myself and my house
My goods and my family.
And the lark said in her warble
Often, often, often
Goes Christ in the stranger's guise
O, oft and oft and oft,
Goes Christ in the Stranger's guise.

A rune of hospitality

570 May the road rise to meet you.
May the wind be always at your back.
May the sun shine warm upon your face.
May the rains fall softly upon your fields
until we meet again
May God hold you in the hollow of his hand.

Old Gaelic blessing

571 May God in the plenitude of his love pour upon you the torrents of his grace, bless you and keep you in his holy fear, prepare you for a happy eternity, and receive you at last into immortal glory.

Blessing at the Consecration of Coventry Cathedral

572 May the love of the Lord Jesus
draw us to himself;
May the power of the Lord Jesus
strengthen us in his service;
May the joy of the Lord Jesus
fill our souls.
May the blessing of God almighty,
the Father, the Son, and the Holy Ghost,
be amongst you
and remain with you
always.

William Temple, 1881–1944

573 May our Lady and all the Saints pray for you, and the holy guardian angels watch over you and keep you in their safe protection, and the blessing of God almighty, the Father, the Son and the Holy Spirit descend upon you and remain with you always.

via Fr Anthony de Vere

574 Seed we bring
Lord, to thee, wilt thou bless them, O Lord!
Gardens we bring
Lord, to thee, wilt thou bless them O Lord!
Hoes we bring
Lord, to thee, wilt thou bless them, O Lord!

Knives we bring
Lord, to thee, wilt thou bless them, O Lord!
Hands we bring
Lord, to thee, wilt thou bless them, O Lord!
Ourselves we bring
Lord, to thee, wilt thou bless us, O Lord!

East African hymn used at seed consecration service

May the Cross of the Son of God who is mightier than all the hosts of Satan, and more glorious than all the angels of heaven, abide with you in your going out and your coming in! By day and night, at morning and at evening, at all times and in all places, may it protect and defend you! From the wrath of evil men, from the assaults of evil spirits, from foes invisible, from the snares of the devil, from all low passions that beguile the soul and body, may it guard, protect, and deliver you. 575

The Christarakana: Book of Common Prayer,
Church of India, Pakistan, Burma and Ceylon

The blessing of the Lord rest and remain upon all his people, in every land, of every tongue; the Lord meet in mercy all that seek him; the Lord comfort all who suffer and mourn; the Lord hasten his coming, and give us, his people, the blessing of peace. 576

Bishop Handley Moule, 1841–1920

IV

PRAYERS OF THE CHURCH

Introduction

This section, like the book as a whole, is an anthology and not a compendium of public worship, and, as space is limited, the Church's prayer is represented here by content and not by structure. But it should be understood that each of the prayers selected forms part of a definite liturgical structure or 'shape' of worship, and it sustains its full weight and depth of meaning by virtue of its place in that structure where it is part of an organic whole, related to every other part. This is most obviously the case where the prayer is, for example, a snatch of psalmody or Old Testament prophecy which, once placed in a Christian liturgical setting, is drawn into the full light of revelation. An outstanding example of this is Psalm 22 as it is used in a variety of ways in the Passiontide liturgy, but it is equally true of every component of a given pattern of worship, including those specially written for it. In its liturgical function not even the most perfect unit of prayer is independent; it belongs somewhere, and for the purposes of this anthology such units have been detached from one setting and inserted, on a temporary basis, in another.

So what is illustrated here is not the whole pattern of the Church's prayer, but some of its details. It is hoped that the one who prays will be drawn by dwelling on these details to rediscover many of them in their proper setting, and to recognize them repeatedly in his own experience as a member of the worshipping community. Such an anthology calls for a background and arrangement of its own, and this one has lent itself to provisional arrangement, as set out below, under the headings of the clauses of the Apostles' Creed.

The Creed is a statement of belief expressed both in precise, historical terms ('suffered under Pontius Pilate') and, as far as the resources of language allow, in supra-temporal terms ('the Communion of Saints . . . life everlasting'). So there are included under the headings prayers directed to the eternal being and love of God as well as prayers formulated from exact knowledge of how and where and when that eternal love and being were manifested in Jesus Christ. This dual reference to time and eternity characterizes all liturgical prayer.

The Prayers of the Church are the voice of the Messianic people. This is a corporate voice in which everything that is human finds utterance, in such a way that one speaks with the voice of all, and all speak with the voice of each one. No prayer (not even the most public or ceremonious) is ever anything but personal, for prayer implies by definition a movement of the heart towards God. It has been said that 'Liturgical forms which are authentic are born from the personal prayer of an individual with his Creator and then fixed in forms suited to communal expression. The Psalter is the most typical example of this.' This means that the Church's prayer, by catching up each and every human experience and offering it for cleansing, healing, and reconciling, or for thanksgiving and praising, or for dedication and sacrifice and service, is affirming the eternal value and significance of all that happens within the human life that has been experienced also by the Son of God.

The inexhaustible wealth of Christian liturgical prayer has led the compilers to make their selection on the basis of what is known, familiar, and readily available in the various traditions. There has been no attempt to search out remote or curious samples of liturgy; and while much has been supplied by specialists, the actual compilation is not the work of liturgical scholars. Although the selection inevitably reflects the English-speaking (and indeed Anglican) background of the compilers, no preference has been consciously given to any one tradition.

One difficulty in compiling the section has arisen from the present state of liturgical studies and practice. More than forty years of liturgical renewal, reform, and experiment in the Western Churches has reached a point of stability. In the Roman Catholic Church Latin has been largely abandoned, a new missal and new breviaries have been authorized, and many new prayers composed as well as translated. Several parts of the Anglican Communion have authorized new prayerbooks allowing great diversity, attempts have been made to modernize the language of Anglican liturgy, numerous alternative versions of the Psalms and of the Bible are available and widely used. Throughout their task the compilers have attempted to choose the best. In the liturgical section this has generally come to mean choosing what has stood the test of time. This has not been done out of wilful conservatism, but because there are as yet no means of knowing to what extent the new material and the new forms and versions of the old material are lodging themselves in the memory of praying people, so that the impulses of the heart come to be expressed spontaneously in these forms. The solid benefits of renewal and revision are probably most apparent in the sacramental and especially Eucharistic rites, and where the new is very good we have been glad to include it.

The Church is a worshipping community, and through its communal forms and liturgies not only expresses its faith and devotion but also submits the whole body to the cleansing, humbling, sanctification, and inspiration of the Spirit of God. In the worship forms of its branches it has a wonderful treasury of devotion, to which members of each tradition can contribute, learn from other traditions, and so join in a Sanctus embracing all believers in earth and heaven, who are dedicated to the spreading of his eternal saving love, in an ever-deepening Gloria.

INTRODUCTION

'I BELIEVE IN GOD THE FATHER ALMIGHTY, MAKER OF HEAVEN AND EARTH'

Praises of God the Creator; God in his self-revelation as Father, Son and Spirit:

The Hallowing of Time: Morning, noon and night offered back to God in thanksgiving; prayers for protection and the fulfilment of God's promise.

'I BELIEVE IN JESUS CHRIST HIS ONLY SON OUR LORD'

The mysteries of the incarnate life in the Church's year: the Christmas cycle; the Paschal cycle.

'I BELIEVE IN THE HOLY GHOST'

The gift and promise of the Father, the Spirit of Jesus Christ his Son: Pentecost; prayers for the continual presence of the Holy Spirit, his gifts and fruits.

'I BELIEVE IN THE HOLY CATHOLIC CHURCH'

A spiritual house. A chosen race, a royal priesthood: baptism and confirmation; priesthood and ministry; forms of life consecrated by the Church.

A holy nation, God's own people: prayers for all men and women and the hallowing of human affairs.

That you may declare the wonderful deeds of Him who called you out of darkness into his marvellous light: the sacrament of the Eucharist; preparation; the great thanksgiving prayer; before and after communion.

Who had not obtained mercy, but have now obtained mercy: penitence and forgiveness; prayers for healing and restoration.

'I BELIEVE IN THE COMMUNION OF SAINTS, THE FORGIVENESS OF SINS, THE RESURRECTION OF THE BODY, AND THE LIFE EVERLASTING'

Prayers for the dying and the dead; the angels and the saints; life in the Kingdom.

Note on Sources

There is probably no error-proof or ideal method of accurately ascribing origin and authorship to prayers that are drawn from the whole range of Christian public prayer. The references in the text are given to indicate to the user the tradition and sometimes the liturgical place in which the prayer is most commonly used, but such references do not imply that its use is confined to this tradition.

Within the several mainstream traditions of Christian worship the following broad distinctions have been observed: prayers taken from

Russian and Greek service books are designated simply 'Orthodox'; prayers that are used widely throughout the Eastern Churches are designated 'Eastern Orthodox'; where a prayer is known to belong to one Eastern tradition specifically, it is designated e.g. 'Syrian (or Armenian) Orthodox'.

In the West, the 2nd Vatican Council of the Roman Catholic Church has been a watershed, sharply dividing old from new. Prayers that have enjoyed widespread use in the Western Churches are designated 'Western Rite'. Where more precision is called for they are ascribed to, e.g., 'Roman Rite', 'Western Breviary', 'Book of Common Prayer', 'Scottish Prayer Book', etc.

'Roman Rite' refers to liturgical uses of the Roman Church as authorized by the Council of Trent, and especially the Roman Missal issued in 1570 by Pope Pius V. We have used the 1961 edition of this. 'Western Breviary' covers prayers taken from the Monastic Breviary as revised under Pope Paul V (1612) and used also in Breviaries and forms of Divine Office compiled for numerous religious and lay groups and congregations of the Roman Catholic, Anglican, and Reformed Churches. We have used the 1916 edition of this.

Where the word 'new' occurs in the title, e.g. 'New Roman Missal', 'New American Prayer Book', etc., the reference is to the authorized book issued by the respective Churches in the years since the 2nd Vatican Council. Where the author of a prayer is known, or where there is a strong claim to authorship, the name is given. Certain prayers of universal provenance, e.g. Te Deum Laudamus, Gloria in Excelsis, are simply designated by their titles.

577 I believe in God the Father Almighty, Maker of heaven and earth:

And in Jesus Christ his only Son our Lord, Who was conceived by the Holy Ghost, Born of the Virgin Mary, Suffered under Pontius Pilate, Was crucified, dead, and buried, He descended into hell; The third day he rose again from the dead, He ascended into heaven, And sitteth on the right hand of God the Father Almighty; From thence he shall come to judge the quick and the dead.

I believe in the Holy Ghost; The holy Catholick Church; The Communion of Saints; The Forgiveness of sins; The Resurrection of the body; And the life everlasting. Amen.

'I BELIEVE IN GOD THE FATHER ALMIGHTY'

Christian belief in God is belief in three Persons, one in essence, Father, Son and Holy Spirit: a divine society of mutual love which overflows in the creation of all that is. All Christian prayer is Trinitarian. No one Person can be addressed without involving the other two. Morning, noon, and night, creation responds to its maker through the heart and lips of man, who bears the image and likeness of God and is its appointed spokesman.

We praise thee, O God: we acknowledge thee to be the Lord. All the 578
earth doth worship thee: the Father everlasting. To thee all Angels cry aloud: the Heavens, and all the Powers therein.
To thee Cherubim and Seraphim: continually do cry,
Holy, Holy, Holy: Lord God of Sabaoth;
Heaven and earth are full of the Majesty: of thy Glory.
The glorious company of the Apostles: praise thee.
The goodly fellowship of the Prophets: praise thee.
The noble army of Martyrs: praise thee.
The holy Church throughout all the world: doth acknowledge thee;
The Father: of an infinite Majesty;
Thine honourable, true: and only Son;
Also the Holy Ghost: the Comforter . . .

Te Deum Laudamus

Come, true light. 579
Come, life eternal.
Come, hidden mystery.
Come, treasure without name.
Come, reality beyond all words.
Come, person beyond all understanding.
Come, rejoicing without end.
Come, light that knows no evening.
Come, unfailing expectation of the saved.
Come, raising of the fallen.
Come, resurrection of the dead.
Come, all-powerful, for unceasingly you create, refashion and change all things by your will alone.
Come, invisible whom none may touch and handle.
Come, for you continue always unmoved, yet at every instant you are wholly in movement; you draw near to us who lie in hell, yet you remain higher than the heavens.

Come, for your name fills our hearts with longing and is ever on our lips; yet who you are and what your nature is, we cannot say or know.
Come, Alone to the alone.
Come, for you are yourself the desire that is within me.
Come, my breath and my life.
Come, the consolation of my humble soul.
Come, my joy, my glory, my endless delight.

St Symeon the New Theologian

580 Thee, O God, the Father unbegotten; thee, O only-begotten Son; thee, O Holy Spirit, the Paraclete; holy and undivided Trinity: with our whole heart and mouth we confess thee, we praise thee and bless thee: to thee be glory for ever and ever.

Trinity Sunday, Western Breviary

581 Great art thou, O Lord, and marvellous are thy works: no words suffice to sing the praise of thy wonders.
For thou by thine own will hast brought all things out of nothingness into being: by thy power thou dost hold together the creation and by thy providence thou dost govern the world.
Of four elements hast thou compounded the creation: with four seasons hast thou crowned the circuit of the year.
All the spiritual powers tremble before thee.
The sun sings thy praises;
The moon glorifies thee;
The stars supplicate before thee;
The light obeys thee;
The deeps are afraid at thy presence;
The fountains are thy servants.
Thou hast stretched out the heavens like a curtain;
Thou hast established the earth upon the waters;
Thou hast walled about the sea with sand.
Thou hast poured forth the air that living things may breathe.
The angelic powers minister to thee; the choirs of archangels worship thee; the many-eyed cherubim and the six-winged seraphim, standing round thee and flying about thee, hide their faces in fear of thine unapproachable glory . . .
By the elements, by the angels and by men, by things visible and invisible, may thy most holy name be glorified, together with the Father and the Holy Spirit, now and ever, and to the ages of ages. Amen.

At the Blessing of the Waters, Epiphany, Orthodox

'I BELIEVE IN GOD THE FATHER'

Father, in whom we live, 582
In whom we are, and move,
The glory, power and praise receive
Of thy creating love.
Let all the angel throng
Give thanks to God on high;
While earth repeats the joyful song,
And echoes to the sky.

Incarnate Deity,
Let all the ransomed race
Render in thanks their lives to thee
For thy redeeming grace.
The grace to sinners showed
Ye heavenly choirs proclaim,
And cry: Salvation to our God,
Salvation to the Lamb!

Spirit of Holiness,
Let all thy saints adore
Thy sacred energy, and bless
Thine heart-renewing power.
Not angel tongues can tell
Thy love's ecstatic height,
The glorious joy unspeakable,
The beatific sight.

Eternal, triune Lord!
Let all the hosts above,
Let all the sons of men, record
And dwell upon thy love.
When heaven and earth are fled
Before thy glorious face,
Sing all the saints thy love hath made
Thine everlasting praise.

Charles Wesley

O Father, my hope 583
O Son, my refuge
O Holy Spirit, my protection.
Holy Trinity, glory to Thee.

Compline, Eastern Orthodox, St Joannikios

584 O thou who coverest thy high places with the waters,
Who settest the sand as a bound to the sea
And dost uphold all things:
The sun sings thy praises,
The moon gives thee glory,
Every creature offers a hymn to thee,
His author and creator, for ever. Eastern Orthodox

585 Almighty and everlasting God, who hast given unto us thy servants grace by the confession of a true faith to acknowledge the glory of the eternal Trinity, and in the power of the Divine Majesty to worship the Unity; We beseech thee, that thou wouldest keep us steadfast in this faith, and evermore defend us from all adversities, who livest and reignest, one God, world without end. Book of Common Prayer

586 Almighty God, Father of all mercies, we thine unworthy servants do give thee most humble and hearty thanks for all thy goodness and loving-kindness to us, and to all men; We bless thee for our creation, preservation, and all the blessings of this life; but above all, for thine inestimable love in the redemption of the world by our Lord Jesus Christ; for the means of grace, and for the hope of glory. And, we beseech thee, give us that due sense of all thy mercies, that our hearts may be unfeignedly thankful, and that we shew forth thy praise, not only with our lips, but in our lives: by giving up ourselves to thy service, and by walking before thee in holiness and righteousness all our days; through Jesus Christ our Lord, to whom with thee and the Holy Ghost be all honour and glory, world without end. General Thanksgiving, BCP

The Hallowing of Time

587 By night arising let us all keep vigil
Praying to God with ready hearts and voices
In psalms and praises singing to his glory.

May He our King, the Holy One we worship,
With all the blessed make us also worthy
To share the life of his eternal kingdom.

Grant this we pray thee, Trinity all-holy,
Father and Son and Spirit we adore thee,
With all creation echoing thy glory.

Hymn at Mattins, Western Breviary

Open to us, Lord, your great door, O Fountain of all mercy, hear our prayer and have mercy on our souls. Lord of the morning and ruler of all seasons, hear our prayer and have mercy on our souls. Shine upon me, Lord, and I shall be light like the day; I will sing your praise in light while I marvel; may the morning awaken me to the praise of your Godhead and I will pursue the study of your word all the day long. With the day may your light shine on our thoughts and may it drive away the shadows of error from our souls. The creation is full of light, give light also to our hearts that they may praise you with the day and the night. 588

Syrian Orthodox

Rise up, O children of light, and let us give glory to the Lord who alone can save our souls. O Lord, as you withdraw sleep from the eyes of our body, grant us wakefulness of mind so that we may stand before you in awe and sing your praises worthily. 589

Syrian Orthodox

To thee, O Master who lovest all men, I hasten on rising from sleep; by thy mercy I go forth to do thy work, and I make my prayer to thee, help me at all times and in all things; deliver me from every evil thing of this world and from pursuit by the devil; save me and bring me to thy eternal kingdom. For thou art my Creator, thou dost inspire all good thoughts in me; in thee is all my hope, and to thee I ascribe glory, now and for ever, and unto the ages of ages. 590

Eastern Orthodox, St Macarius the Great

Blessed be the Lord God of Israel: for he hath visited and redeemed his people; 591
And hath raised up a mighty salvation for us: in the house of his servant David;
As he spake by the mouth of his holy Prophets: which have been since the world began;
That we should be saved from our enemies: and from the hands of all that hate us;
To perform the mercy promised to our forefathers: and to remember his holy Covenant;
To perform the oath which he sware to our forefather Abraham: that he would give us;
That we being delivered out of the hand of our enemies: might serve him without fear;

In holiness and righteousness before him: all the days of our life.
And thou, child, shalt be called the Prophet of the Highest: for thou shalt go before the face of the Lord to prepare his ways;
To give knowledge of salvation unto his people: for the remission of their sins,
Through the tender mercy of our God: whereby the day-spring from on high hath visited us;
To give light to them that sit in darkness, and in the shadow of death: and to guide our feet into the way of peace.

Benedictus. (See Luke 1: 68–79.)

592 Now unto the King eternal, immortal, invisible, the only wise God, be honour and glory for ever and ever.

Office of Prime, Western Breviary

593 O Lord, our heavenly Father, almighty and everlasting God, who hast safely brought us to the beginning of this day; defend us in the same with thy mighty power; and grant that this day we fall into no sin, neither run into any kind of danger; but that all our doings may be ordered by thy governance, to do always that is righteous in thy sight; through Jesus Christ our Lord.

Mattins, BCP

594 O Christ, you are continually worshipped in heaven and on earth, in all times and at all hours; you are patience, compassion and mercy; you love the righteous, you have mercy on sinners, and you call all men to salvation, promising them all things to come: receive our prayer, this day at noon, and make our life conform to your will; sanctify our souls and our bodies, order our thoughts, and give us victory in all trials and sadness; protect us and bless us, so that we may come to unity of faith and knowledge of your glory, for you live and reign, with the Father and the Holy Spirit, God now and forever.

Mid-day Office, Taizé Community

595 For ye are bought with a price: therefore glorify God in your body, and in your spirit, which are God's.
O cleanse thou me from my secret faults:
Keep thy servants also from presumptuous sins.

Office of None, Roman Breviary

In the evening Abraham called upon you on the mountain top and you answered him, O lover of men; and in the evening we call upon you, come to our aid, O God, full of mercy, halleluia, and have mercy upon us. 596

Office of Vespers, Syrian Orthodox

My soul doth magnify the Lord: and my spirit hath rejoiced in God my Saviour. 597
For he hath regarded: the lowliness of his hand-maiden.
For behold, from henceforth: all generations shall call me blessed.
For he that is mighty hath magnified me: and holy is his Name.
And his mercy is on them that fear him: throughout all generations.
He hath shewed strength with his arm: he hath scattered the proud in the imagination of their hearts.
He hath put down the mighty from their seat: and hath exalted the humble and meek.
He hath filled the hungry with good things: and the rich he hath sent empty away.
He remembering his mercy hath holpen his servant Israel: as he promised to our forefathers, Abraham and his seed, for ever.

The Magnificat. (See Luke 1: 46–55.)

Hail, gladdening Light, of his pure glory poured 598
Who is the immortal Father, heavenly, blest,
Holiest of Holies, Jesus Christ our Lord!
Now we are come to the sun's hour of rest,
The lights of evening round us shine,
We hymn the Father, Son, and Holy Spirit divine.
Worthiest art thou at all times to be sung
With undefiled tongue,
Son of our God, giver of life, alone:
Therefore in all the world thy glories, Lord, we own.

Vespers, Eastern Orthodox

O God, from whom all holy desires, all good counsels, and all just works do proceed; give unto thy servants that peace which the world cannot give; that both our hearts may be set to obey thy commandments, and also that by thee we being defended from the fear of our enemies may pass our time in rest and quietness; through the merits of Jesus Christ our Saviour. 599

Evensong, BCP

600 Holy Father, keep us in your truth; holy Son, protect us under the wings of your cross; holy Spirit, make us temples and dwelling places for your glory; grant us your peace all the days of our lives, O Lord.

Office of Compline, Maronite Church

601 O eternal God, King of all creation who hast brought me to this hour, forgive me the sins which I have committed this day in thought, word, and deed, and cleanse, O Lord, my humble soul from every stain of flesh and spirit. Grant me, O Lord, to pass through the sleep of this night in peace, to rise from my lowly bed, to please thy holy Name all the days of my life, and to vanquish the enemies both bodily and spiritual that contend against me. Deliver me, O Lord, from the vain thoughts that stain me, and from evil desires. For thine is the kingdom and the power, and the glory, of the Father, and the Son, and the Holy Ghost, now and for ever and unto the ages of ages.

Eastern Orthodox, St Macarius the Great

602 Lighten our darkness, we beseech thee, O Lord; and by thy great mercy defend us from all perils and dangers of this night; for the love of thy only Son, our Saviour, Jesus Christ.

Evensong, BCP

603 O Lord Jesus Christ, son of the living God, who at this evening hour didst rest in the sepulchre, and didst thereby sanctify the grave to be a bed of hope to thy people: make us to abound in sorrow for our sins, which were the cause of thy passion, that when our bodies lie in the dust, our souls may live with thee; who livest and reignest with the Father and the Holy Ghost, one God, world without end.

Compline, BCP (1928)

604
Servant of God, remember
The stream thy soul bedewing,
The grace that came upon thee
Anointing and renewing.

When kindly slumber calls thee,
Upon thy bed reclining,
Trace thou the Cross of Jesus,
Thy heart and forehead signing.

THE HALLOWING OF TIME

The Cross dissolves the darkness,
And drives away temptation;
It calms the wavering spirit
By quiet consecration.

Begone, begone, the terrors
Of vague and formless dreaming;
Begone, thou fell deceiver,
With all thy boasted scheming.

Begone, thou crooked serpent,
Who, twisting and pursuing,
By fraud and lie preparest
The simple soul's undoing;

Tremble, for Christ is near us,
Depart, for here he dwelleth,
And this, the Sign thou knowest,
Thy strong battalions quelleth.

Then while the weary body
Its rest in sleep is nearing,
The heart will muse in silence
On Christ and his appearing.

To God, eternal Father,
To Christ, our King, be glory,
And to the Holy Spirit,
In never-ending story.

Compline, Western Rite, Prudentius

Save us, O Lord, while waking, and guard us while sleeping: that awake we may watch with Christ, and asleep we may rest in peace. 605

Compline, Sarum Breviary

Lord, now lettest thou thy servant depart in peace: according to thy word. 606
For mine eyes have seen: thy salvation,
Which thou hast prepared: before the face of all people;
To be a light to lighten the Gentiles: and to be the glory of thy people Israel.

The Nunc Dimittis. (See Luke 2: 29–32.)

'I BELIEVE IN JESUS CHRIST'

607 Grant us thy light, O Lord: that the darkness of our hearts being done away, we may come to the true light, even Christ our Saviour.

Compline, Sarum Breviary

'I BELIEVE IN JESUS CHRIST HIS ONLY SON'

Jesus Christ is the supreme gift and word of God to man. He is the beginning and the end. In him the timeless love of God is disclosed in terms of the created order in which a human life unfolds. The events of his life are more than historical facts, they are mysteries of revelation, permanent possessions of mankind. Within the conditions of time and space the Church renews year by year her remembrance of these mysteries, entering thereby into the life of God Himself through Jesus Christ who is the door.

The Christmas Cycle

608 Today is the crown of our salvation and the manifestation of the mystery that is from all eternity. The Son of God becomes Son of the Virgin, and Gabriel announces the good tidings of grace. Therefore let us also join him and cry aloud to the Mother of God: Hail, thou who art full of grace: the Lord is with thee.

Hymn for the Annunciation, Orthodox

609 Almighty God, give us grace that we may cast away the works of darkness, and put upon us the armour of light, now in the time of this mortal life, in which thy Son Jesus Christ came to visit us in great humility; that in the last day, when he shall come again in his glorious Majesty to judge both the living and the dead, we may rise to the life immortal, through him who liveth and reigneth with thee and the Holy Ghost, now and ever.

Advent Sunday, BCP

610 O Wisdom, who camest out of the mouth of the Most High, and reachest from one end to another, mightily and sweetly ordering all things: Come and teach us the way of prudence.

O Adonai, and leader of the house of Israel, who didst appear in the bush to Moses in a flame of fire, and gavest him the law on Sinai: Come and redeem us with an outstretched arm.

O Root of Jesse, who standest for an ensign of the people, at whom kings shall shut their mouths, unto whom shall the gentiles seek: Come and deliver us, and tarry not.

O Key of David, and sceptre of the house of Israel, who openest and no man shutteth, and shuttest and no man openeth: Come, and bring the prisoners out of the prison-house, them that sit in darkness and the shadow of death.

O Day-spring, brightness of the light everlasting, and sun of righteousness: Come and enlighten them that sit in darkness and the shadow of death.

O King of nations, and their desire; the cornerstone, who makest both one: Come and save mankind, whom thou hast formed of clay.

O Emmanuel, our King and lawgiver, the desire of all nations and their salvation: Come and save us, O Lord our God.

O Virgin of virgins, how shall this be? for neither before thee was any seen like thee, nor shall there be after. Daughters of Jerusalem, why do you marvel at me? The thing which you behold is a divine mystery.

The Greater Antiphons Vespers, Western Rite

While all things were in quiet silence, and night was in the midst of her swift course, thine Almighty Word, O Lord, leaped down out of thy royal throne, alleluia. 611

Christmas Vespers, Western Rite

What shall we offer thee, O Christ, 612
Who for our sakes hast appeared on earth as man?
Every creature made by thee offers thee thanks.
The angels offer thee a hymn;
The heavens a star;
The magi, gifts;
The shepherds, their wonder;
The earth, its cave;
The wilderness, the manger:
And we offer thee a Virgin Mother.
O God from everlasting, have mercy upon us.

Eastern Orthodox

Of the Father's heart begotten, 613
Ere the world from chaos rose,
He is Alpha: from that fountain
All that is and hath been flows:
He is Omega, of all things
Yet to come the mystic close.
Evermore and evermore.

'I BELIEVE IN JESUS CHRIST'

By his word was all created;
He commanded and 'twas done;
Earth and sky and boundless ocean,
Universe of three in one,
All that sees the moon's soft radiance,
All that breathes beneath the sun.
Evermore and evermore.

O how blest that wondrous birthday
When the Maid the curse retrieved,
Brought to birth mankind's salvation,
By the Holy Ghost conceived;
And the Babe, the world's Redeemer,
In her loving arms received.
Evermore and evermore.

This is he, whom seer and sybil
Sang in ages long gone by;
This is he of old revealed
In the page of prophecy;
Lo! he comes, the promised Saviour;
Let the world his praises cry!
Evermore and evermore.

Sing, ye heights of heaven, his praises;
Angels and Archangels, sing!
Wheresoe'er ye be, ye faithful,
Let your joyous anthems ring,
Every tongue his name confessing,
Countless voices answering.
Evermore and evermore.

Christmas Processional, Western Rite, Prudentius

614 Christ is born, give glory. Christ comes from heaven, meet him. Christ is on earth, be exalted. O all the earth, sing unto the Lord, and sing praises in gladness, O all you people, for he has been glorified.

Wisdom and Word and Power, Christ our God is the Son and the Brightness of the Father; and unknown to the powers both above and upon the earth, he was made man, and so has won us back again: for he has been glorified.

Eastern Orthodox

O God who hast made this most hallowed night resplendent with the glory of the true Light; grant that we who have known the mysteries of that Light on earth, may enter into the fullness of his joys in heaven. 615

Christmas midnight, Western Rite

It is very meet and right, just and for salvation, that we should at all times and in all places give thanks unto thee: O Lord, holy Father, almighty everlasting God: because through the mystery of the incarnate Word the light of thy glory hath shone anew upon the eyes of our mind: that while we acknowledge God made visible, we may be caught up through him to the love of things invisible. And therefore with angels and archangels, with thrones and dominations and with all the host of the heavenly army we sing the hymn of thy glory, evermore saying: Holy, Holy, Holy Lord God of Hosts, Heaven and earth are full of thy glory. Hosanna in the highest. Blessed is he who cometh in the name of the Lord. Hosanna in the highest. 616

Preface of the Nativity, Roman Rite

Almighty God, who hast poured upon us the new light of thine Incarnate Word; grant that the same light enkindled in our hearts may shine forth in our lives; through Jesus Christ our Lord. 617

Mass of Christmas at Dawn, Sarum Rite

Almighty God, who hast given us thy only-begotten Son to take our nature upon him, and as at this time to be born of a pure Virgin; Grant that we being regenerate, and made thy children by adoption and grace, may daily be renewed by thy Holy Spirit; through the same our Lord Jesus Christ, who liveth and reigneth with thee and the same Spirit, ever one God, world without end. 618

Christmas Day, BCP

Before the morning star begotten, and Lord from everlasting, our Saviour is made manifest unto the world today. 619

Epiphany, Office of Lauds, Western Rite

Almighty God, who at the baptism of thy blessed Son Jesus Christ in the river Jordan didst manifest his glorious Godhead; Grant, we beseech thee, that the brightness of his presence may shine in our hearts, and his glory be set forth in our lives; through the same Jesus Christ our Lord. 620

Epiphany, Scottish Prayer Book

621 The mighty Rain comes forth in flesh to the streams of the river, desiring baptism. Filled with amazement, the Forerunner said to him: 'How shall I baptize thee who hast no stain at all? How shall I stretch out my right hand upon thy head, before which all things tremble?'

O Christ my saviour, the enlightenment of those who lie in darkness, the salvation of all in despair, I seek thee early in the morning: enlighten me with thy brightness, O King of peace, for I know no other God save thee.

Feast of the Forerunner, Orthodox

622 Now do we celebrate a holy day adorned by three miracles: today a star led the wise men to the manger; today water was made wine at the wedding feast; today Christ vouchsafed to be baptized of John in Jordan that he might save us, alleluia. Epiphany, Vespers, Western Rite

623 Prepare your bridal chamber, O Sion, to receive Christ the King: welcome with love Mary, the gate of heaven, for it is she who brings you the King of light and glory. There stands the Virgin, holding in her arms the Son begotten before the morning star: and Simeon, taking him into his arms, proclaims to all the nations that he is the Lord of life and death, and the saviour of the world.

Feast of the Presentation, Western Rite

624 Come, and with divine songs let us also go to meet Christ and let us receive him whose salvation Simeon saw. This is he whom David announced: this is he whose words the prophets uttered, who for our sakes has taken flesh and speaks to us in the law. Let us worship him.

Orthodox

625 O God, whose only-begotten Son was this day presented in the temple in our flesh, grant that as we joyfully receive him for our Redeemer, so we may with sure confidence behold Him when he shall come to be our Judge. Feast of the Presentation, Gelasian Sacramentary

626 We beseech thee, O Lord, pour thy grace into our hearts; that, as we have known the incarnation of thy Son Jesus Christ by the message of an angel, so by his cross and passion we may be brought into the glory of his resurrection; through the same Jesus Christ our Lord.

Feast of the Annunciation, Western Rite

The Paschal Cycle—Lent to Ascension

Almighty and everlasting God, who, of thy tender love towards mankind, hast sent thy Son, our Saviour Jesus Christ, to take upon him our flesh, and to suffer death upon the cross, that all mankind should follow the example of his great humility: Mercifully grant, that we may both follow the example of his patience, and also be made partakers of his resurrection; through the same Jesus Christ our Lord. 627

Palm Sunday, BCP

Come, let us enter the inner chamber of our soul, offering prayers to the Lord and crying aloud: Our Father, who art in heaven, remit and forgive our debts, for thou alone art compassionate. 628

Showing joyfulness of soul in the fast, let us not be of a sad countenance; for the change in our way of life during these blessed days will help us to gain holiness.

Giving wings to our soul through abstinence, let us all offer acceptable prayers to the Lord in heaven.

In a spirit of compunction, let us weep for the deliverance of our souls and sing the praises of Christ for ever.

We bless the Lord, Father, Son and Holy Spirit.

Consubstantial Trinity, uncreated Unity, the God of all, we exalt thee above all for ever.

Mattins in Lent, Orthodox

O Lord, who for our sake didst fast forty days and forty nights; Give us grace to use such abstinence, that our flesh being subdued to the Spirit, we may ever obey thy godly inspirations in righteousness, and true holiness, to thy honour and glory, who livest and reignest with the Father and the Holy Ghost, one God, world without end. 629

First Sunday in Lent, BCP

Grant to us O Lord, to enter upon this holy fast with the armour of Christian warfare: that we who are to fight against spiritual wickedness, may be fortified by the power of self-denial. Through Christ, our Lord. 630

Ash Wednesday, Roman Missal

631 O God, who before the Passion of thine only-begotten Son didst reveal his glory upon the holy mountain: grant unto us thy servants, that in faith beholding the light of his countenance, we may be strengthened to bear the cross, and be changed into his likeness from glory to glory; through the same Jesus Christ our Lord.

Feast of the Transfiguration, BCP (1928)

632 Thou wast transfigured upon the mountain, and thy disciples beheld thy glory, O Christ our God, as far as they were able to do so: that when they saw thee crucified, they might know that thy suffering was voluntary, and might proclaim unto the world that thou art truly the brightness of the Father.

Orthodox

633 Behold, the Bridegroom comes in the middle of the night; and blessed is the servant whom he shall find watching, but unworthy is he whom he shall find in slothfulness. Beware, then, O my soul, and be not overcome by sleep, lest thou be given over to death and shut out from the kingdom. But return to soberness and cry aloud: Holy, holy, holy art thou, O God: through the Mother of God have mercy upon us.

Hymn for Holy Week, Orthodox

634 My God, my God, look upon me; why hast thou forsaken me: and art so far from my health, and from the words of my complaint?

O my God, I cry in the daytime, but thou hearest not: and in the night-season also I take no rest.

And thou continuest holy: O thou worship of Israel.

Our fathers hoped in thee: they trusted in thee, and thou didst deliver them.

They called upon thee, and were holpen: they put their trust in thee, and were not confounded.

But as for me, I am a worm, and no man: a very scorn of men, and the outcast of the people.

All they that see me laugh me to scorn: they shoot out their lips, and shake their heads, saying,

He trusted in God, that he would deliver him: let him deliver him, if he will have him.

But thou art he that took me out of my mother's womb: thou wast my hope, when I hanged yet upon my mother's breasts.

I have been left unto thee ever since I was born: thou art my God even from my mother's womb.

O go not from me, for trouble is hard at hand: and there is none to help me.

Many oxen are come about me: fat bulls of Basan close me in on every side.

They gape upon me with their mouths: as it were a ramping and a roaring lion.

I am poured out like water, and all my bones are out of joint: my heart also in the midst of my body is even like melting wax.

My strength is dried up like a potsherd, and my tongue cleaveth to my gums: and thou shalt bring me into the dust of death.

For many dogs are come about me: and the council of the wicked layeth siege against me.

They pierced my hands and my feet; I may tell all my bones: they stand staring and looking upon me.

They part my garments among them: and cast lots upon my vesture. But be not thou far from me, O Lord: thou art my succour, haste thee to help me.

Deliver my soul from the sword: my darling from the power of the dog.

Save me from the lion's mouth: thou hast heard me also from among the horns of the unicorns.

I will declare thy Name unto my brethren: in the midst of the congregation will I praise thee.

O praise the Lord, ye that fear him: magnify him, all ye of the seed of Jacob, and fear him, all ye seed of Israel.

For he hath not despised, nor abhorred, the low estate of the poor: he hath not hid his face from him, but when he called unto him he heard him.

My praise is of thee in the great congregation: my vows will I perform in the sight of them that fear him.

The poor shall eat, and be satisfied: they that seek after the Lord shall praise him; your heart shall live for ever.

All the ends of the world shall remember themselves, and be turned unto the Lord: and all the kindreds of the nations shall worship before him.

For the kingdom is the Lord's: and he is the Governor among the people.

My seed shall serve him: they shall be counted unto the Lord for a generation.

They shall come, and the heavens shall declare his righteousness: unto a people that shall be born, whom the Lord hath made.

Psalm 22, Passiontide, Western Rite

635 All glory, laud, and honour
To thee, Redeemer, King,
To whom the lips of children
Made sweet hosannas ring.

Thou art the King of Israel,
Thou David's royal Son,
Who in the Lord's name comest,
The King and blessed One.

The company of angels
Are praising thee on high,
And mortal men and all things
Created make reply.

The people of the Hebrews
With palms before thee went;
Our praise and prayer and anthems
Before thee we present.

To thee before thy passion
They sang their hymns of praise;
To thee now high exalted
Our melody we raise.

Thou didst accept their praises,
Accept the prayers we bring,
Who in all good delightest,
Thou good and gracious King.

Processional hymn, Palm Sunday, Western Rite

636 Thirty years among us dwelling,
His appointed time fulfilled,
Born for this, he meets his Passion,
For that this he freely willed:
On the Cross the Lamb is lifted,
Where his life-blood shall be spilled.

Hymn for Passiontide, Western Rite

637 Almighty God, whose most dear Son went not up to joy but first he suffered pain, and entered not into glory before he was crucified; Mercifully grant that we, walking in the way of the cross, may find it none other than the way of life and peace; through the same thy Son Jesus Christ our Lord.

American Prayer Book

Christ for us became obedient unto death, even the death of the cross. Wherefore God also hath highly exalted him: and given him a name which is above every name. 638

Holy Week, Western Rite

At thy mystical supper, son of God, today receive me as a partaker: for I will not speak of the mystery to thine enemies; I will not give thee a kiss like Judas; but like the thief I will acknowledge thee: Remember me, Lord, when thou comest in thy Kingdom. 639

Hymn for Holy Thursday, Orthodox

Now my tongue the mystery telling, 640
Of the glorious Body sing,
And the Blood, all price excelling,
Which the world's eternal King,
In a noble womb once dwelling
Shed for this world's ransoming.

Word made flesh, by word he maketh
Very bread his flesh to be;
Man in wine Christ's blood partaketh:
And if senses fail to see,
Faith alone, the true heart waketh
To behold the mystery.

Therefore we, before him bending,
This great sacrament revere;
Types and shadows have their ending,
For the newer rite is here;
Faith, our outward sense befriending,
Makes the inward vision clear.

Maundy Thursday, Western Rite

Almighty Father, whose dear Son, on the night before he suffered, did institute the Sacrament of his Body and Blood; mercifully grant that we may thankfully receive the same in remembrance of him, who in these holy mysteries giveth us a pledge of life eternal; the same thy Son Jesus Christ our Lord, who now liveth and reigneth with thee and the Holy Spirit ever one God, world without end. 641

American Prayer Book

642 The wisdom of God that restrains the untamed fury of the waters that are above the firmament, that sets a bridle on the deep and keeps back the seas, now pours water into a basin; and the Master washes the feet of his servants.

The Master shows to his disciples an example of humility; he who wraps the heaven in clouds girds himself with a towel; and he in whose hand is the life of all things kneels down to wash the feet of his servants.

Holy Thursday, Mattins, Orthodox

643 Let us all draw near in fear to the mystical table, and with pure souls let us receive the Bread; let us remain at the Master's side, that we may see how he washes the feet of the disciples and wipes them with a towel; and let us do as we have seen, subjecting ourselves to each other and washing one another's feet. For such is the commandment that Christ himself gave to his disciples; but Judas, slave and deceiver, paid no heed.

Orthodox

644 *Where charity and love are, there is God.*
The Love of Christ has gathered us as one.
Let us rejoice and be glad in him.
Let us fear and love the living God
And in purity of heart let us love one another.

Where charity and love are, there is God.
When therefore we are gathered together
Let us not be divided in spirit.
Let bitter strife and discord cease between us;
Let Christ our God be present in our midst.

Where charity and love are, there is God.
With all the blessed may we see for ever
Thy face in glory, Jesus Christ our God.
Joy that is infinite and undefiled
For all the ages of eternity.

At the Feet Washing, Maundy Thursday, Western Rite

645 Almighty God, we beseech thee graciously to behold this thy family, for which our Lord Jesus Christ was contented to be betrayed, and given up into the hands of wicked men, and to suffer death upon the cross, who now liveth and reigneth with thee and the Holy Ghost, ever one God, world without end.

Good Friday, Western Rite

O Lord God, our heavenly Father, regard, we beseech thee, with thy divine pity the pains of all thy children, and grant that the passion of our Lord and his infinite merits may make fruitful for good the miseries of the innocent, the sufferings of the sick and the sorrows of the bereaved; through him who suffered in our flesh and died for our sake, thy Son our Saviour Jesus Christ. 646

Scottish Prayer Book

We venerate the wood of thy Cross, O thou who lovest mankind, for upon it thou, the life of all, wast nailed. O Saviour, thou hast opened paradise to the thief who turned to thee in faith, and thou hast counted him worthy of blessedness when he confessed to thee crying, 'O Lord remember me'. Accept us like him, as we cry: We all have sinned, in thy merciful kindness despise us not. 647

Feast of the Exaltation of the Cross, Orthodox

Today he who hung the earth upon the waters is hung upon the Cross. 648
He who is King of the angels is arrayed in a crown of thorns.
He who wraps the heaven in clouds is wrapped in the purple of mockery.
He who in Jordan set Adam free receives blows upon his face.
The Bridegroom of the Church is transfixed with nails.
The Son of the Virgin is pierced with a spear.
We venerate thy Passion, O Christ.
Show us also thy glorious Resurrection.

Hymns for Good Friday, Orthodox

O my people, what have I done unto thee? or wherein have I wearied thee? Answer me! 649
Because I brought thee forth from the land of Egypt: thou hast prepared a Cross for thy Saviour.

Holy God.
Holy, mighty.
Holy and immortal, have mercy upon us.

The Reproaches, Good Friday, Western Rite

650 Sing, my tongue, the glorious battle,
Sing the ending of the fray;
Now above the Cross, the trophy,
Sound the loud triumphant lay:
Tell how Christ, the world's Redeemer,
As a Victim won the day.

Faithful Cross, above all other,
One and only noble tree,
None in foliage, none in blossom,
None in fruit thy peer may be.
Sweetest wood and sweetest iron
Sweetest weight was hung on thee.

Hymn for Passiontide, Western Rite

651 We adore thee O Christ, and we bless thee, because by thy Cross thou hast redeemed the world.

O Saviour of the world: who by thy Cross and precious Blood hast redeemed us, save us and help us, we humbly beseech thee, O our God.

Antiphons on Good Friday, Western Rite

652 Remember me, O Lord, when thou comest into thy kingdom.

Refrain in Passiontide (Luke 23: 42)

653 Today a tomb holds him who holds the creation in the hollow of his hand; a stone covers him who covered the heavens with glory. Life sleeps and hell trembles, and Adam is set free from his bonds. Glory to thy dispensation, whereby thou has accomplished all things, granting us an eternal Sabbath, thy most holy Resurrection from the dead.

What is this sight that we behold? What is this present rest? The King of the ages, having through his passion fulfilled the plan of salvation, keeps Sabbath in the tomb, granting us a new Sabbath. Unto him let us cry aloud: Arise, O Lord, judge thou the earth, for measureless is thy great mercy and thou dost reign for ever.

Come, let us see our Life lying in the tomb, that he may give life to those that in their tombs lie dead. Come, let us look today on the Son of Judah as he sleeps, and with the prophet let us cry aloud to him: Thou hast slept as a lion; who shall awaken thee, O King? But of thine own free will do thou rise up, who willingly dost give thyself for us. O Lord, glory to thee.

Mattins, Holy Saturday, Orthodox

Going down to death, O Life immortal, thou hast slain hell with the dazzling light of thy divinity. And when thou hast raised up the dead from their dwelling place beneath the earth, all the powers of heaven cried aloud: 'Giver of Life, O Christ our God, glory to thee.' 654

Hymn for Holy Saturday, Orthodox

Grant, O Lord, that as we are baptized into the death of thy blessed Son our Saviour Jesus Christ, so by continual mortifying our corrupt affections we may be buried with him; and that through the grave, and gate of death, we may pass to our joyful resurrection; for his merits, who died, and was buried, and rose again for us, thy Son Jesus Christ our Lord. 655

Easter Eve, BCP

Christ yesterday and today, the beginning and the end, Alpha and Omega. His are all times and all ages; to him be glory and dominion through all the ages of eternity. Amen. 656

By his holy and glorious wounds, may Christ our Lord guard us and keep us.

May the light of Christ, rising in glory, scatter the darkness of our heart and mind.

Blessing of the New Fire, Roman Missal

Most blessed of all nights, chosen by God 657
to see Christ rising from the dead!

Of this night scripture says:
'The night will be as clear as day:
it will become my light, my joy.'

The power of his holy night
dispels all evil, washes guilt away,
restores lost innocence, brings mourners joy;
it casts out hatred, brings us peace, and humbles earthly pride.

Night truly blessed when heaven is wedded to earth
and man is reconciled with God!

Therefore, heavenly Father, in the joy of this night,
receive our evening sacrifice of praise,
your Church's solemn offering.

Accept this Easter candle,
a flame divided but undimmed,
a pillar of fire that glows to the honour of God.

Let it mingle with the lights of heaven
and continue bravely burning
to dispel the darkness of this night!

May the Morning Star which never sets find this flame still burning:
Christ, that Morning Star, who came back from the dead,
and shed his peaceful light on all mankind,
your Son who lives and reigns for ever and ever. Amen.

Exsultet, Easter Vigil, The Roman Missal

658 Christ is risen from the dead: trampling down death by death; and upon those in the tombs bestowing life.

Though thou didst go down into the grave, O Immortal One, yet thou didst put down the power of hades and didst rise a conqueror, O Christ our God: thou spakest clearly to the myrrh-bearing women, Rejoice; thou didst bestow peace upon thine apostles, and to the fallen hast thou brought resurrection.

Orthodox

659 Hail to thee, Festival Day! blest day that art hallowed for ever;
Day wherein God destroyed hell, rising again from the dead.

He who was nailed to the Cross is God and the Ruler of all things;
All things created on earth worship the Maker of all.

God of all pity and power, let thy word be assured to the doubting;
Light on the third day returns: rise, Son of God, from the tomb.

Ill doth it seem that thy limbs should linger in lowly dishonour,
Ransom and price of the world, veiled from the vision of men.

Ill doth it seem that thou, by whose hand all things are encompassed,
Captive and bound should remain, deep in the gloom of the rock.

Rise now, O Lord, from the grave and cast off the shroud that enwrapped thee;
Thou are sufficient for us: nothing exists without thee.

Mourning they laid thee to rest, who art Author of life and creation;
Treading the pathway of death, life thou bestowest on man.

Show us thy face once more, that all times may exult in thy brightness;
Give us the light of day, darkened on earth at thy death.

Out of the prison of death thou art rescuing numberless captives;
Freely they tread in the way whither their Maker has gone.

Jesus has harrowed hell; he has led captivity captive:
Darkness and chaos and death flee from the face of the light.

Easter Processional, Western Rite, Venantuis Fortunatus

Love's redeeming work is done; 660
Fought the fight, the battle won:
Lo, our Sun's eclipse is o'er!
Lo, he sets in blood no more.

Vain the stone, the watch, the seal,
Christ has burst the gates of hell;
Death in vain forbids his rise;
Christ has opened Paradise.

Lives again our glorious King;
Where, O death, is now thy sting?
Dying once, he all doth save;
Where thy victory, O grave?

Charles Wesley

Peace be unto you, it is I, alleluia: be not afraid, alleluia. 661

Antiphon in Eastertide, Western Rite

We have seen the resurrection of Christ; let us worship the holy Lord 662
Jesus, who alone is without sin. We venerate thy Cross, O Christ, and we praise and glorify thy holy resurrection. For thou art our God: we know no other save thee; upon thy name we call. Come, all ye faithful, let us venerate the holy resurrection of Christ: for lo, through the Cross joy has come to all the world. Ever blessing the Lord, we sing the praises of his resurrection: for he endured the Cross on our behalf, and has destroyed death by death. Sunday Vigil, Orthodox

Almighty God, who through thine only-begotten Son Jesus Christ hast 663
overcome death, and opened unto us the gate of everlasting life: We humbly beseech thee, that as by thy grace preventing us thou dost put into our minds good desires, so by thy continual help we may bring the same to good effect; through Jesus Christ our Lord, who liveth and reigneth with thee and the Holy Ghost, ever one God, world without end.

Easter Day, BCP

664 Abide with us, Lord, for it is toward evening and the day is far spent, alleluia.

Vespers in Eastertide, Western Rite

665 The Lord ascended into heaven so that he could send the Comforter into this world. The heavens prepared his throne, and the angels marvelled at the sight of a human being more exalted and more glorious than themselves. Today the Father receives again in his bosom the One who was in him from all eternity, and the Holy Spirit gives a command to all the angels: 'Lift up your gates, O you princes.'—O you nations of the earth, clap your hands, for Christ has gone up to the place where he had been from all eternity.

Ascension Day, Orthodox

666 Grant, we beseech thee, almighty God, that like as we do believe thy only-begotten Son our Lord Jesus Christ to have ascended into the heavens; so we may also in heart and mind thither ascend, and with him continually dwell, who liveth and reigneth with thee and the Holy Ghost, one God, world without end.

Ascension Day, BCP

667 Sing ye to the Lord, who ascended above the heaven of heavens, to the Sunrising, alleluia.

Communion antiphon, Ascension Day, Roman Rite

668 The head that once was crowned with thorns
Is crowned with glory now:
A royal diadem adorns
The mighty Victor's brow.

The highest place that heaven affords
Is his, is his by right,
The King of kings and Lord of lords,
And heaven's eternal Light;

The joy of all who dwell above,
The joy of all below,
To whom he manifests his love,
And grants his name to know . . .

T. Kelly

O Christ you ascended in glory on the Mount of Olives in the presence of your disciples. O you who penetrate all things with your divinity, you were enthroned at the right hand of your Father and sent down upon your disciples the Holy Spirit who enlightens, strengthens and saves our souls. 669

Vespers of Ascension, Orthodox

'I BELIEVE IN THE HOLY GHOST'

The Spirit who brooded on the face of the waters at creation, the Spirit of the Lord who enlightened the prophets, is the Spirit who rested on the Son of God throughout his life on earth and who descended in tongues of fire upon the disciples at Pentecost, the birthday of the Church. Only through Jesus Christ do we know the Spirit as Person. The Church welcomes him with inexpressible joy as the living bond of her union with the Father and the Son, and the unfailing source of her renewal.

The Spirit of the Lord fills the whole world, alleluia, alleluia. In him all things have their being. Every sound that is uttered, he knows. Alleluia, alleluia. 670

Feast of Pentecost, Western Rite

The Holy Spirit is light and life, 671
A living fountain of knowledge,
Spirit of wisdom,
Spirit of understanding,
Loving, righteous, filled with knowledge and power,
Cleansing our offences,
Divine, and making us divine;
Fire that comes forth from Fire,
Speaking, working, distributing gifts of grace.
By him were all the prophets, the apostles of God and the martyrs crowned.
Strange were the tidings, strange was the vision of Pentecost:
Fire came down, bestowing gifts of grace on each.

Vespers of Pentecost, Orthodox

672 Holy Spirit, Creator, who in the beginning didst move on the face of the waters, through thy breath all things come to life, and without thee every living creature dies and returns to nothingness.

R. Come Holy Spirit, and enter into us!

Holy Spirit, counsellor, by thine inspiration men of God and prophets of old, spoke and acted; thou didst clothe them with thy power, that they might bear witness to thy Word (*R*)

Holy Spirit, thou art the power who didst overshadow the Virgin Mary; that she might become the mother of the Son of God, thou didst prepare a perfect dwelling-place for him (*R*)

Holy Spirit, consecrator, by thine action Jesus grew in wisdom and in grace; thou didst descend upon him in the form of a dove, on the day of his baptism, that he might be made holy and armed with power, as a faithful witness of the Father (*R*)

Holy Spirit, eternal God, through thee, Christ, our High Priest, offered himself up as a blameless victim, that we might be delivered from the powers of death to serve the living God (*R*)

Holy Spirit, defender, thou didst descend upon the apostles, in the form of tongues of fire, and thou didst speak through them when they bore witness to Christ and his resurrection, before kings and all nations (*R*)

Holy Spirit, comforter, through thee we are born as children of God, thou makest us living temples of thy presence, and thou intercedest within us, with words that cannot be uttered (*R*)

Holy Spirit, giver of life, by whom the whole body of the Church is animated, guided and sanctified, thou dwellest in all its members, in order to give life one day to our mortal bodies (*R*)

Litany of the Holy Spirit, Taizé Community

673 God, who as at this time didst teach the hearts of thy faithful people, by the sending to them the light of thy Holy Spirit; Grant us by the same Spirit to have a right judgement in all things, and evermore to rejoice in his holy comfort; through the merits of Christ Jesus our Saviour, who liveth and reigneth with thee, in the unity of the same Spirit, one God, world without end.

Pentecost, BCP

674 Send out wisdom from the throne of thy glory, O Lord, that being present she may labour with me: that I may know at all times what is pleasing to thee.

Respond at Mattins, Western Breviary

'I BELIEVE IN THE HOLY GHOST'

Alleluia, alleluia. Send forth thy Spirit and they shall be created, and thou shalt renew the face of the earth. Alleluia. Come, Holy Ghost, fill the hearts of thy faithful: and kindle in them the fire of thy love. 675

Feast of Pentecost, Western Rite

Come thou Holy Spirit	Veni, Sancte Spiritus	676
Send from highest heaven	Et emitte coelitus	
Radiance of thy light.	Lucis tuae radium.	
Come, father of the poor	Veni, pater pauperum,	
Come, giver of all gifts	Veni, dator munerum,	
Come, light of every heart.	Veni, lumen cordium.	
Of comforters the best	Consolator optime,	
Dear guest of every soul	Dulcis hospes animae,	
Refreshment ever sweet.	Dulce refrigerium.	
In our labour rest	In labore requies,	
Coolness in our heat	In aestu temperies,	
Comfort in our grief.	In fletu solatium.	
O most blessed light	O lux beatissima,	
Fill the inmost hearts	Remple cordis intima	
Of thy faithful ones.	Tuorum fidelium.	
Without thy holy presence	Sine tuo numine,	
All is dark	Nihil est in lumine,	
Nothing free from sin.	Nihil est innoxium.	
What is soiled cleanse	Lava quod est sordidum,	
What is dry refresh	Riga quod est aridum,	
What is wounded heal.	Sana quod est saucium.	
What is rigid bend	Flecte quod est rigidum,	
What is frozen warm	Fove quod est frigidum,	
Guide what goes astray.	Rege quod est devium.	
Give thy faithful ones	Da tuis fidelibus,	
Who in thee confide	In te confidentibus,	
Sevenfold hallowing.	Sacrum septenarium.	
Give goodness its reward	Da virtutis meritum,	
Give journey safe through death	Da salutis exitum,	
Give joy that has no end.	Da perenne gaudium.	

Sequence, Feast of Pentecost, Stephen Langton

O living God, come and make our souls temples of thy Spirit. 677
R. Sanctify us, O Lord!

Baptize thy whole Church with fire, that the divisions soon may cease, and that it may stand before the world as a pillar and buttress of thy truth. (*R*)

Grant us all the fruits of thy Holy Spirit: brotherly love, joy, peace, patience, good will and faithfulness. (*R*)

May thy Holy Spirit speak by the voice of thy servants, here and everywhere, as they preach thy word. (*R*)

Send thy Holy Spirit, the comforter, to all who face adversity, or who are the victims of men's wickedness. (*R*)

Preserve all nations and their leaders from hatred and war, and build up a true community among nations, through the power of thy Spirit. (*R*)

Holy Spirit, Lord and source of life, giver of the seven gifts,
R. Sanctify us, O Comforter.

Spirit of wisdom and understanding, Spirit of counsel and strength, (*R*)

Spirit of knowledge and devotion, Spirit of obedience to the Lord. (*R*)

Litany of the Holy Spirit, Taizé Community

678 O Almighty God, who on the day of Pentecost didst send the Holy Ghost the Comforter to abide in thy Church unto the end: Bestow upon us and upon all thy faithful people his manifold gifts of grace, that with minds enlightened by his truth and hearts purified by his presence, we may day by day be strengthened with power in the inward man; through Jesus Christ our Lord, who with thee and the same Spirit liveth and reigneth, one God world without end.

Scottish Prayer Book

679 Behold, we celebrate today the Feast of Pentecost, the descent of the Holy Spirit, the fulfilment of the promise and the realization of hope. How noble and how full of awe is this great mystery! Wherefore, O Lord and Creator of all, we cry out: 'Glory to thee!'

Orthodox

680 Glory to thee, O Lord, Glory to thee!
Heavenly King, Comforter, Spirit of truth,
Who art everywhere present and fillest all things,
Treasury of all good and giver of life,
Come and dwell within us;
Cleanse us from all unrighteousness,
And of thy goodness, save our souls.

Daily Office, Orthodox

'I BELIEVE IN THE HOLY GHOST'

O King enthroned on high, 681
Thou comforter divine,
Blest Spirit of all truth, be nigh
And make us thine.

Thou art the source of life,
Thou art our treasure-store;
Give us thy peace and end our strife
For evermore.

Descend, O heavenly Dove,
Abide with us alway;
And in the fullness of thy love
Cleanse us, we pray.

8th century, tr. J. Brownlie

O Lord, who hast taught us that all our doings without love are nothing worth; Send thy Holy Spirit, and pour into our hearts that most excellent gift of love, the very bond of peace and of all virtues, without which whosoever liveth is counted dead before thee: Grant this for thine only Son Jesus Christ's sake. 682

Book of Common Prayer

O thou who camest from above, 683
The pure celestial fire to impart,
Kindle a flame of sacred love
On the mean altar of my heart.

There let it for thy glory burn
With inextinguishable blaze,
And trembling to its source return
In humble prayer, and fervent praise.

Jesus, confirm my heart's desire
To work, and speak, and think for thee;
Still let me guard the holy fire,
And still stir up thy gift in me.

Ready for all thy perfect will,
My acts of faith and love repeat,
Till death thy endless mercies seal,
And make my sacrifice complete.

Charles Wesley

'I BELIEVE IN THE HOLY CATHOLIC CHURCH'

Under the Old Covenant Solomon was allowed to build a temple, 'a spiritual house' set apart for worship and sacrifice. In the fullness of time Jesus Christ made the one perfect sacrifice to God in the temple of his human nature, drawing all men as 'living stones' of that temple with him to the Father. St Peter addresses the young Church in these words:

> 'But you are a chosen race, a royal priesthood, a holy nation, God's own people, that you may declare the wonderful deeds of him who called you out of darkness into his marvellous light. Once you were no people but now you are God's people; once you had not received mercy but now you have received mercy.' (1 Peter 2: 9–10)

A Spiritual House

684 But will God in very deed dwell with men on the earth? Behold, heaven and the heaven of heavens cannot contain thee; how much less this house which I have builded! Yet have thou respect unto the prayer of thy servant, and to his supplication, O Lord my God, to hearken unto the cry and to the prayer which thy servant prayeth before thee: That thine eyes may be open toward this house day and night, even toward the place whereof thou hast said that thou wouldest put thy name there; to hearken unto the prayer which thy servant shall pray toward this place. And hearken thou to the supplications of thy servant and of thy people Israel, when they shall pray toward this place: yea, hear thou from thy dwelling place, even from heaven; and when thou hearest, forgive.

Dedication of a Church, Roman Breviary, (See 2 Chronicles 6: 18–21.)

685 Christ is made the sure foundation,
And the precious Corner-stone,
Who, the two walls underlying,
Bound in each, binds both in one,
Holy Sion's help for ever,
And her confidence alone.

All that dedicated City,
Dearly loved by God on high,
In exultant jubilation
Pours perpetual melody:
God the One and God the Trinal,
Singing everlastingly.

A CHOSEN RACE

To this temple, where we call thee,
Come, O Lord of Hosts, today;
With thy wonted loving-kindness
Hear thy people as they pray;
And thy fullest benediction
Shed within its walls for ay.

Dedication of a Church, Western Rite, tr. J. M. Neale

Give heed O Lord to our prayers; be with us in this mystic service, be thou present to the devout labours of thy servants, and to us who implore thy mercy. May thy Holy Spirit, in the overflowing fulness of his sevenfold grace, come down on this thy church which we, though unworthy, do now consecrate . . . that whenever thy holy name shall be called upon in this house of thine thou, loving Lord, mayest hear the prayers of them that call upon thee . . . Purify, bless, and consecrate this church of thine by the unceasing outpouring of thy hallowing virtue. May thy priests offer to thee in this place the sacrifice of praise, and thy faithful people here pay their vows. May the burden of sin be here cast off, and fallen believers be restored. We beseech thee, O Lord, that in this house of thine, by the grace of the Holy Ghost, the sick may be healed, the ailing recover strength, the lame be cured, the lepers cleansed, the blind regain their sight, the devils be cast out. By thy favour, O Lord, may all who are afflicted here find relief, and the bonds of all sinners be loosed, that all who shall come into this temple duly to entreat thy loving kindness may rejoice at having obtained their desire. Through our Lord Jesus Christ. 686

Consecration of an altar, Roman Rite

O almighty God, who hast built thy Church upon the foundation of the apostles and prophets, Jesus Christ himself being the head corner-stone: Grant us so to be joined together in unity of spirit by their doctrine, that we may be made an holy temple acceptable unto thee; through Jesus Christ our Lord. 687

Book of Common Prayer

A Chosen Race, A Royal Priesthood

O mystery deep, unsearchable, eternal, who hast decked with splendour the heavenly dominions, the legions of flaming spirits in the chamber of light unapproachable. 688

With wonderful power thou didst create Adam in a glorious image and didst clothe him with grace and excellence in the garden of Eden, wherein are all delights.

Through the sufferings of thine Only-Begotten all creatures are renewed and man hath once more been made immortal, clad in a garment that none can take away from him.

O chalice of fiery rain poured out on the apostles in the upper room, O Holy Ghost pour thy wisdom also upon us as we put on these vestments.

Holiness becometh thine house, thou who art clothed with majesty. As thou art girt about with the glory of holiness, so gird us also with thy truth.

O thou who didst spread thy creating arms to the stars, strengthen our arms with power to intercede when we lift up our hands to thee.

Bind our thoughts as the crown wreathes our head, and our senses with the stole adorned with the cross and woven, like Aaron's, with gold and flowers for the honour of the sanctuary.

Supreme, divine Sovereign of all beings, thou hast covered us with a robe as with love to be ministers of thy holy mystery.

Heavenly King, keep thy Church immoveable, and preserve in peace all them that worship thy Holy Name.

Hymn at the Vesting, Armenian Orthodox

689 Father, you give us grace through sacramental signs,
which tell us of the wonders of your unseen power.

In baptism we use your gift of water,
which you have made a rich symbol
of the grace you give us in this sacrament.

At the very dawn of creation
your Spirit breathed on the waters,
making them the wellspring of all holiness.

The waters of the great flood
you made a sign of the waters of baptism,
that make an end of sin and a new beginning of
goodness.

Through the waters of the Red Sea
you led Israel out of slavery,
to be an image of God's holy people
set free from sin by baptism.

A CHOSEN RACE

In the waters of the Jordan
your Son was baptized by John
and anointed with the Spirit.

Your Son willed that water and blood
should flow from his side
as he hung upon the cross.

After his resurrection he told his disciples:
'Go out and teach all nations,
baptizing them in the name of the Father
and of the Son and of the Holy Spirit.'

Father, look now with love upon your Church,
and unseal for her the fountain of baptism.

By the power of the Spirit
give to the water of this font
The grace of your Son.

You created man in your own likeness:
cleanse him from sin in a new birth of innocence
by water and the Spirit.

Blessing of water, The Roman Missal

Make thyself manifest, O Lord, in this water and grant to him who is baptized in it so to be transformed, that he may put off the old man, which is corrupted by deceitful lusts, and may put on the new man, which is formed fresh according to the image of the Creator. Grafted through baptism into the likeness of thy death, may he become a partaker also in thy resurrection. May he guard the gift of thy Holy Spirit, may he increase the measure of grace which has been entrusted to him, and so may he receive the prize which is God's calling to life above, being numbered among the first born whose names are written in heaven. 690

Blessing of baptismal font, Eastern Orthodox

We receive this child into the congregation of Christ's flock; and do sign him with the sign of the Cross, in token that hereafter he shall not be ashamed to confess the faith of Christ crucified, manfully to fight under his banner, against sin, the world and the devil; and to continue Christ's faithful soldier and servant unto his life's end. 691

Book of Common Prayer

692 Blessed is God, who desires that all men should be saved and come to the knowledge of the truth.

Blessed is God, who gives light and sanctification to every man that comes into the world.

Blessed are they whose transgressions are forgiven and whose sins are covered: blessed is the man to whom the Lord imputes no sin, and in whose mouth there is no deceit.

O Christ our God, rich in mercy, who clothest thyself with light as with a garment, grant unto me a robe that is radiant with light.

Baptism, Eastern Orthodox

693

God of eternal truth and love,
Vouchsafe the promised aid we claim;
Thine own great ordinance approve,
The child baptized into thy name
Partaker of thy nature make,
And give him all thine image back.

Father, if such thy sovereign will,
If Jesus did the rite enjoin,
Annex thy hallowing Spirit's seal,
And let the grace attend the sign;
The seed of endless life impart,
Take for thine own this infant's heart.

In presence of thy heavenly host
Thyself we faithfully require:
Come, Father, Son, and Holy Ghost,
By blood, by water and by fire,
And fill up all thy human shrine,
And seal our souls for ever thine.

Charles Wesley

694 Almighty and everliving God, who hast vouchsafed to regenerate these thy servants by water and the Holy Ghost, and hast given unto them forgiveness of all their sins: Strengthen them, we beseech thee, O Lord, with the Holy Ghost the comforter, and daily increase in them thy manifold gifts of grace; the spirit of wisdom and understanding; the spirit of counsel and ghostly strength; the spirit of knowledge and true godliness; and fill them, O Lord, with the spirit of thy holy fear, now and for ever.

Confirmation, BCP

These are the new-born lambs who have proclaimed, alleluia, they came but just now to the well. They are all filled with light, alleluia, alleluia. They stand before the Lamb, clothed in white robes with palms in their hands. They are all filled with light, alleluia, alleluia. 695

Mattins in Eastertide, Roman Breviary

Defend, O Lord, this thy child with thy heavenly grace, that he may continue thine for ever; and daily increase in thy Holy Spirit, more and more, until he come unto thy everlasting kingdom. 696

Confirmation, BCP

I am no longer my own, but thine. 697
Put me to what thou wilt, rank me with whom thou wilt:
Put me to doing: put me to suffering:
Let me be employed for thee, or laid aside for thee:
Exalted for thee, or brought low for thee:
Let me be full, let me be empty:
Let me have all things: let me have nothing:
I freely and heartily yield all things to thy pleasure and disposal.
And now, O glorious and blessed God, Father, Son and Holy Spirit,
Thou art mine and I am thine. So be it.
And the covenant which I have made on earth let it be ratified in heaven.

Methodist Covenant Service

Most gracious Father, who callest us to the Holy Table of our Saviour, to show His death and to receive His gift of life; enable us to come with earnest faith and kindled devotion. Help us to make the memorial of our Saviour's sacrifice with adoration and praise. Open our eyes to behold the vision of his love and pour into our souls the fullness of his grace. And grant that, yielding ourselves to Thee, we may henceforth live as those who are not their own, but are bought with a price; through Jesus Christ our Lord, to whom with Thee and the Holy Spirit be all honour and glory, world without end. Amen. 698

Church of Scotland *Book of Common Order*

Come Holy Ghost, our souls inspire, 699
And lighten with celestial fire.
Thou the anointing Spirit art,
Who dost they sevenfold gifts impart.

Thy blessèd unction from above,
Is comfort, life, and fire of love.
Enable with perpetual light
The dulness of our blinded sight.

Anoint and cheer our soilèd face
With the abundance of thy grace.
Keep far our foes, give peace at home;
Where thou art guide, no ill can come.

Teach us to know the Father, Son,
And thee, of both, to be but One.
That, through the ages all along,
This may be our endless song:

Praise to thy eternal merit,
Father, Son, and Holy Spirit.

Veni Creator Spiritus

700 Almighty and everlasting God, who alone workest great marvels: Send down upon our bishops, and clergy, and all congregations committed to their charge, the healthful spirit of thy grace: and that they may truly please thee, pour upon them the continual dew of thy blessing. Grant this, O Lord, for the honour of our advocate and mediator, Jesus Christ.

Book of Common Prayer (1928)

701 Almighty Father, give to these your servants grace and power to fulfil their ministry. Make them faithful to serve, ready to teach, constant in advancing your gospel; and grant that, always having full assurance of faith, abounding in hope, and being rooted and grounded in love, they may continue strong and steadfast in your Son Jesus Christ our Lord; to whom, with you and your Holy Spirit, belong glory and honour, worship and praise, now and for ever.

Ordination of deacons, Alternative Service Book 1980

702 Vouchsafe, O Lord, to consecrate and sanctify these hands by this anointing and by our blessing, that whatsoever they shall bless may be blessed, and whatsoever they shall consecrate may be consecrated and sanctified, in the name of our Lord Jesus Christ.

Anointing of the hands, Roman Ordinal

O God you are great from eternity, you have knowledge of what is hidden, you created everything by the power of your word; you guide and control all things by the gentle movement of your will, always bringing to effect much more than we ask or imagine, in accordance with your power which works within us; you acquired your holy church through the precious blood of your beloved Son, our Lord Jesus Christ, establishing in it apostles, prophets, teachers and priests through whom you might increase that knowledge of the truth which your only-begotten Son gave to humanity; do you, O Lord, make your face to shine now as well upon this servant of yours, making his election holy through the anointing of the Holy Spirit, so that he may be a perfect priest, one who imitates the true High Priest who gave his life for our sakes: strengthen him with the Spirit of Holiness in this ministry which he is entering; grant to him, O God the Father of truth, all holy and glorious, that he may shepherd your flock with an upright heart, preaching the unerring word of truth; may he be a source of light to those who sit in darkness, a guide for the uncertain, a teacher for the young and the children; clothe him, Lord, with power from on high, so that all those who are sick may be healed by the laying on of his hand, so that mighty deeds may be performed in him in your holy name to the honour of your glorious Godhead; through the power of your gift may he make priests, deacons, sub-deacons, readers, and deaconesses for the ministry of your holy church; may he gather together and increase your people, the sheep of your flock; may he bring to perfection all the souls entrusted to him in reverence of God and in purity; may he stand with confidence before your dread judgement seat, and be held worthy to receive from you that reward which was promised to the stewards who were diligent, through the grace and mercies of your only-begotten Son. To you and to him and to the Holy Spirit let us offer up praise, honour, thanksgiving and worship, now and for eternal ages, Amen. 703

Consecration of a bishop, Chaldean Rite

Receive this ring as a sign of your consecration and of the covenant of faithful and eternal love between you and your Lord. 704
Receive this cross, the token of your life-long stability. May he to whom your life is offered give you through the cross, joy and fortitude in perseverance.

At the profession of a nun, Western Rite

Lo, that which I desired, now I see; that for which I hoped I now possess; I am united in heaven unto him, whom on earth I loved with a perfect devotion. 705

Consecration of virgins, Roman Rite

706 Make haste to open thy fatherly arms to me:
For as the prodigal I have wasted my life.
O Saviour, remember the inexhaustible riches of thy mercy
And despise not a heart now in poverty.
For to thee, O Lord, with contrite heart I cry:
Father, I have sinned against heaven and before thee.

Hymn at monastic profession, Orthodox

707 Now I have renounced the world, with its life and its ways. I flee to thee, O Christ, I make my vow to be one with thee. I guard this treasure now bestowed on me to the day of my death. Thou art all the hope of my sojourn here below as long as I live, for thou art my God: I will confess thee, for thou hast heard my calling. Thou hast prepared my hands for the battle and my fingers for the fire of the conflict with the enemy. By thy divine power thou wilt save me from hell, at the very same moment when thou wilt receive me at the end of my life, when I shall come to thee.

Consecration of a hermit (based on Orthodox sources)

708 We thank thee, O Lord God almighty, who art before the ages, master of the universe, who didst adorn the heavens by thy word, and didst lay the foundations of the earth and all that is therein; who didst gather together those things which were separate into union, and didst make the twain one. Now again, our Master, we beseech thee, may thy servants be worthy of the mark of the sign of thy Word through the bond of betrothal, their love for one another inviolable through the firm sureness of their union. Build them, O Lord, upon the foundation of thy holy Church, that they may walk in accordance with the bond of the word which they have vowed one to another; for thou art the bond of their love, and the ordainer of the law of their union. Thou who hast brought about the oneness, by the union of the twain by thy words, complete, O Lord, the ordinance of thine only-begotten Son Jesus Christ our Lord, through whom and together with the all-Holy Spirit be praise to thee now and always.

Marriage service, Coptic Orthodox

709 O eternal God, creator and preserver of all mankind, giver of all spiritual grace, the author of everlasting life: Send thy blessing upon these thy servants, this man and this woman, whom we bless in thy name; that, as

Isaac and Rebecca lived faithfully together, so these persons may surely perform and keep the vow and covenant betwixt them made, (whereof this ring given and received is a token and pledge,) and may ever remain in perfect love and peace together, and live according to thy laws; through Jesus Christ our Lord.

Book of Common Prayer

May God by whose will the world and all creation have their being, and 710
who wills the life of all men—may Christ, the true bridegroom, seal your marriage in the truth of his love. As he finds joy in his Church, so may you find your happiness in one another; that your union may abound in love and your coming together in purity. May his angel guide you, may his peace reign between you, that in all things you may be guarded and guided, so that you may give thanks to the Father who will bless you, the Son who will rejoice in you, and the Spirit who will protect you, now and for ever and world without end.

Blessing from marriage service, Syrian Orthodox

Heavenly Father, maker of all things, you enable us to share in your work 711
of creation. Bless this couple in the gift and care of children, that their home may be a place of love, security and truth, and their children grow up to know and love you in your Son, Jesus Christ our Lord.

Alternative Service Book 1980

Almighty and everlasting God, by whose Spirit the whole body of the 712
Church is governed and sanctified: Receive our supplications and prayers, which we offer before thee for all in thy holy Church, that every member of the same, in his vocation and ministry, may truly and godly serve thee; through our Lord and Saviour Jesus Christ.

Book of Common Prayer

A Holy Nation, God's Own People

Merciful Lord, we beseech thee to cast thy bright beams of light upon thy 713
Church, that it being enlightened by the doctrine of thy blessed apostle and evangelist Saint John may so walk in the light of thy truth, that it may at length attain to the light of everlasting life; through Jesus Christ our Lord.

Book of Common Prayer

714 God, the Father in heaven,
God, the Son, redeemer of the world,
God, the Holy Spirit,
Holy Trinity, One God, have mercy on us.
Be gracious to us. Spare us, good Lord.
Be gracious to us. Spare us, good Lord.

From all sin, from all error, from all evil; from the cunning assaults of the devil; from an unprepared and evil death;
From war, bloodshed, and violence; from corrupt and unjust government; from sedition and treason;
From epidemic, drought, and famine; from fire and flood, earthquake, lightning and storm; and from everlasting death:
Good Lord, deliver us.
By the mystery of your incarnation; by your holy birth:
By your baptism, fasting and temptation; by your agony and bloody sweat; by your cross and suffering; by your death and burial:
By your resurrection and ascension; by the gift of the Holy Spirit:
Help us, good Lord.

In all time of our tribulation; in all time of our prosperity; in the hour of death; and in the day of judgement:
Save us, good Lord.
Though unworthy, we implore you to hear us, Lord our God.

To rule and govern your holy catholic Church; to guide all servants of your Church in the love of your word and in holiness of life; to put an end to all schisms and causes of offence to those who would believe; and to bring into the way of truth all who have gone astray:
R. We implore you to hear us, good Lord.

To beat down Satan under our feet; to send faithful workers into your harvest; to accompany your Word with your Spirit and power; to raise up those who fall and to strengthen those who stand; and to comfort and help the fainthearted and the distressed: (*R*)

To give to all nations justice and peace; to preserve our country from discord and strife; to direct and guard those who have civil authority; and to bless and guide all our people: (*R*)

To behold and help all who are in danger, need or tribulation; to protect and guide all who travel; to preserve and provide for all women in childbirth; to watch over children and to guide the young; to heal the sick and to strengthen their families and friends; to bring reconciliation to families in discord; to provide for the unemployed and for all in need; to be merciful to all who are imprisoned; to support, comfort and guide all orphans, widowers, and widows; and to have mercy on all your people: (*R*)

To forgive our enemies, persecutors, and slanderers, and to reconcile us to them; to help us use wisely the fruits and treasures of the earth, the sea, and the air; and graciously to hear our prayers: (*R*)

Book of Lutheran worship, USA

Almighty God, from whom all thoughts of truth and peace proceed: 715
Kindle, we pray thee, in the hearts of all men the true love of peace; and guide with thy pure and peaceable wisdom those who take counsel for the nations of the earth; that in tranquility thy kingdom may go forward, till the earth is filled with the knowledge of thy love; through Jesus Christ our Lord.

Book of Common Prayer (1928)

O God, the Father of our Lord Jesus Christ, our only Saviour, the Prince 716
of Peace; Give us grace seriously to lay to heart the great dangers we are in by our unhappy divisions. Take away all hatred and prejudice, and whatsoever else may hinder us from godly union and concord: that as there is but one Body and one Spirit, and one hope of our calling, one Lord, one faith, one baptism, one God and Father of us all, so we may henceforth be all of one heart and of one soul, united in one holy bond of truth and peace, of faith and charity, and may with one mind and one mouth glorify thee; through Jesus Christ our Lord.

Accession Service, BCP

Lord of all power and might, who art the author and giver of all good 717
things: Graft in our hearts the love of thy name, increase in us true religion, nourish us with all goodness, and of thy great mercy keep us in the same; through Jesus Christ our Lord.

Book of Common Prayer

Almighty God, who hast given us grace at this time with one accord to 718
make our common supplications unto thee; and dost promise that when two or three are gathered together in thy name thou wilt grant their requests: Fulfil now, O Lord, the desires and petitions of thy servants, as may be most expedient for them; granting us in this world knowledge of thy truth, and in the world to come life everlasting.

Book of Common Prayer (ascribed to St John Chrysostom)

That you may declare the wonderful Deeds of Him who has called you out of the Darkness into His marvellous light: The Sacrament of the Eucharist

719 Almighty God, unto whom all hearts be open, all desires known, and from whom no secrets are hid: Cleanse the thoughts of our hearts by the inspiration of thy Holy Spirit, that we may perfectly love thee, and worthily magnify thy holy name; through Christ our Lord.

Book of Common Prayer (Gregorian Sacramentary)

720 Kyrie Eleison, Christe Eleison, Kyrie Eleison.
Lord have mercy, Christ have mercy, Lord have mercy;

Kyrie Eleison, Christe Eleison, Kyrie Eleison.
Lord have mercy, Christ have mercy, Lord have mercy.

Kyrie Eleison, Christe Eleison, Kyrie Eleison
Lord have mercy, Christ have mercy, Lord have mercy.

721 In peace let us pray to the Lord.
R. Lord, have mercy upon us.

For peace from on high, and for the salvation of our souls, let us pray to the Lord. (*R*)

For the peace of the whole world, for the good estate of the holy Churches of God, and for the union of all, let us pray to the Lord. (*R*)

For this holy house, and for them that with faith, reverence, and godly fear enter herein, let us pray to the Lord. (*R*)

For our Patriarch (or Metropolitan), for our Archbishop (or Bishop), for the honourable order of priesthood, for the diaconate which is in Christ, for all the clergy and people, let us pray to the Lord. (*R*)

For this city and for all cities and countries, for them that in faith dwell therein, let us pray to the Lord. (*R*)

For temperate weather, abundance of fruits of the earth, and for peaceful seasons, let us pray to the Lord. (*R*)

For them that travel by land, air, or water, for the sick and the suffering, for prisoners and captives, and for their preservation, let us pray to the Lord. (*R*)

For our deliverance from all affliction, violence, danger, and necessity, let us pray to the Lord. (*R*)

Protect us, save us, have mercy upon us, and preserve us, O God, by thy grace.

Let us commend our most holy, most pure, most blessed and glorious Lady, Mary ever Virgin and Mother of God, with all the saints, we commend ourselves, and one another, and our whole life unto Christ our God.

To thee, O Lord.

Liturgy of St John Chrysostom

Glory be to God on high, and in earth peace, good will towards men. We 722
praise thee, we bless thee, we worship thee, we glorify thee, we give thanks to thee for thy great glory, O Lord God, heavenly King, God the Father almighty.

O Lord, the only-begotten Son Jesu Christ; O Lord God, Lamb of God, Son of the Father, that takest away the sins of the world, have mercy upon us. Thou that takest away the sins of the world, have mercy upon us. Thou that takest away the sins of the world, receive our prayer. Thou that sittest at the right hand of God the Father, have mercy upon us.

For thou only art holy; thou only art the Lord; thou only, O Christ, with the Holy Ghost, art most high in the glory of God the Father.

Book of Common Prayer

O God, our Master and our Lord, who hast appointed the heavenly 723
orders and the hosts of angels and archangels for the service of thy glory: Grant that thy holy angels may enter with us as we enter, that they with us may serve thee and glorify thy goodness.

The entrance, Liturgy of St John Chrysostom

O God who didst wonderfully create and yet more wonderfully renew the 724
dignity of man's nature: Grant that by the mystery of this water and wine we may be sharers of his divinity, who humbled himself to be partaker of our humanity, Jesus Christ thy Son our Lord.

Offertory prayer, Roman Missal

Blessed are you, Lord, God of all creation. Through your goodness we 725
have this bread to offer, which earth has given and human hands have made. It will become for us the bread of life.

Blessed are you, Lord, God of all creation. Through your goodness we have this wine to offer, fruit of the vine and work of human hands. It will become our spiritual drink.

Offertory prayers, The Roman Missal

726 We who in a mystery represent the Cherubim and sing the thrice-holy hymn to the life-giving Trinity: Let us lay aside the cares of this world; for now we are to receive the King of all who comes accompanied by unseen hosts of angels, Alleluia, alleluia, alleluia.

Liturgy of St John Chrysostom

727 We do not presume to come to this thy table, O merciful Lord, trusting in our own righteousness, but in thy manifold and great mercies. We are not worthy so much as to gather up the crumbs under thy table. But thou art the same Lord, whose nature is always to have mercy: Grant us therefore, gracious Lord, so to eat the flesh of thy dear Son Jesus Christ, and to drink his blood, . . . that we may evermore dwell in him, and he in us.

Alternative Service Book 1980, Rite B

728 Let all mortal flesh keep silence, and with fear and trembling stand;
Ponder nothing earthly-minded, for with blessing in his hand,
Christ our God to earth descendeth, our full homage to demand.

King of kings, yet born of Mary, as of old on earth he stood,
Lord of lords, in human vesture—in the Body and the Blood—
He will give to all the faithful his own Self for heavenly food.

Rank on rank the host of heaven spreads its vanguard on the way,
As the Light of light descendeth from the realms of endless day,
That the powers of hell may vanish as the darkness clears away.

At his feet the six-winged Seraph; Cherubim with sleepless eye,
Veil their faces to the Presence, as with ceaseless voice they cry,
Alleluia, alleluia, alleluia, Lord most high.

Liturgy of St James

The Eucharistic Prayer

The Lord's Prayer is rightly taken to be the model for the Christian's prayer. Yet it is also true to say that the typical prayer of the Church is the prayer recited over the bread and wine in the eucharist. Celebrated in obedience to the Lord's command given at the Last Supper, the eucharist is both the memorial of what God has done 'for us men and for our salvation', and the Church's responsive offering in faith and love. Its central prayer utters the Church's praise and thanksgiving for all God's mighty works; it recalls what the Lord did at supper the night before he died; it commemorates the saving events of his death and resurrection; and it asks that the Church may share in the fruits of his redeeming love.

The precise content of the eucharistic prayer has varied from time to time and from place to place, reflecting the different ways in which the Church has understood the eucharist. By the end of the fourth century eastern and western traditions had diverged in several ways. The eastern prayer came to be known as the 'anaphora', a title which reflected an understanding of the eucharist as a sacrifice offered to God. The western prayer, no less concerned with offering the gifts, retained the title 'canon', the first word of the Latin phrase meaning 'fixed way of giving thanks', reflecting an earlier emphasis on praise and thanksgiving as the sacrifice offered in the eucharist.

In the sixteenth century the Anglican reformers drastically reshaped the canon of the Latin mass, while others retained from it only the narrative of the institution of the eucharist at the Last Supper. In the present century liturgical renewal in the Roman Catholic Church and in the churches influenced by the Reformation has led to a remarkable convergence of traditions. In part this has stemmed from the desire to return to the early sources of eucharistic worship, and from the greater knowledge of the early traditions which liturgical study has placed at our disposal; in part it has been the fruit of growing ecumenical contact between the churches of east and west, and the openness of the west to eastern influence.

For reasons of space it has been possible to include here only six eucharistic prayers, representing some of the traditions, older and newer, of both east and west. For further notes on the development of eucharistic prayers, see the appendix on pp. 375–80.

(i) St Basil the Great

PRIEST: The grace of our Lord Jesus Christ, and the love of God, and the fellowship of the Holy Spirit, be with you all. 729

And with thy spirit.

Lift up your hearts.

We lift them up unto the Lord.

Let us give thanks unto the Lord.

Meet and right is it that we should adore the Father, the Son, and the Holy Spirit, the Trinity, one in essence and undivided.

O thou who in verity existest, Master, Lord God, Father Almighty adorable: Meet is it, in truth, and just and befitting the majesty of thy holiness, that we should magnify thee, praise thee, bless thee, adore thee, give thanks unto thee and glorify thee, the only God which verily existeth, and offer unto thee, with contrite heart and humbleness of spirit, this our reasonable service: for it is thou who hast graciously bestowed upon us the knowledge of thy truth. And who hath power enough to express thy mighty acts, to make all thy praises to be heard, or to utter forth all thy wonders at all times, O Master, O Sovereign Master of all things, Lord of heaven and earth, and of all created beings both visible and invisible; who sittest on the throne of glory and beholdest the depths; who art from everlasting, invisible, inscrutable, ineffable, immutable, the Father of our Lord Jesus Christ, our great God and the Saviour, our hope, who is the image of thy goodness, the seal of equal type, in himself showing forth thee, the Father, the living Word, the true God, the wisdom before all the ages, the life, the sanctification, the might, and the true light, through whom, also, the Holy Spirit was manifested; the spirit of truth, the gift of adoption, the earnest of an inheritance to come, the first-fruits of eternal good things, the life-giving power, the fountain of holiness; by whom enabled every creature endowed with reason and intelligence doth serve thee, and evermore doth send up unto thee an everlasting tribute of praise; for all things are thy servants. For Angels and Archangels, Thrones, Dominions, Principalities, Authorities, Powers, and the many-eyed Cherubim do laud thee. Before thee, round about, stand the Seraphim, having each six wings; for with twain do they cover their faces, and with twain their feet, and with twain do they fly, crying one to another continually, with never-ceasing praises.

Singing the triumphant song, crying, calling aloud, and saying:
Holy, holy, holy, Lord of Sabaoth: heaven and earth are full of thy glory: hosanna in the highest: blessed is he that cometh in the name of the Lord. Hosanna in the highest.

With these blessed Powers, O Master who lovest mankind, we sinners also do cry aloud and say: Holy art thou, of a truth, and all-holy, and there are no bounds to the majesty of thy holiness, and just art thou in all thy works; for in righteousness and true judgement hast thou ordered all things for us. When thou hadst created man, and hadst fashioned him from the dust of the earth, and hadst honoured him with thine own image, O God, thou didst set him in the midst of a Paradise of plenty, promising him life eternal and the enjoyment of everlasting good things in keeping thy commandments. But when he disobeyed thee, the true God, who had created him, and was led astray by the guile of the serpent, and rendered subject to death through his own transgressions, thou didst banish him, in thy righteous judgement, O God, from Paradise into this present world, and didst turn him again to the earth from which he was taken, providing for him the salvation of regeneration, which is in thy Christ himself. For thou didst not turn thyself away forever from thy creature, whom thou hadst made, O Good One, neither didst thou forget the work of thy hands; but thou didst visit him in divers manners, through the tender compassion of thy mercy. Thou didst send forth Prophets; thou didst perform mighty works by the Saints who, in every generation, were well-pleasing unto thee: thou didst speak to us by the mouths of thy servants the Prophets, who foretold unto us the salvation which was to come; thou didst give us the Law to aid us; thou didst appoint guardian Angels. And when the fulness of time was come, thou didst speak unto us by thy Son himself, by whom also thou madest the ages; who, being the Brightness of thy glory, and the Express Image of thy Person, and upholding all things by the word of his power, thought it no robbery to be equal to thee, the God and Father. But albeit he was God before all the ages, yet he appeared upon earth and dwelt among men; and was incarnate of a Holy Virgin, and did empty himself, taking on the form of a servant, and becoming conformed to the fashion of our lowliness, that he might make us conformable to the image of his glory. For as by man sin entered into the world, and by sin death, so it seemed good unto thine Only-begotten Son, who is in thy bosom, our God and Father, to be born of a woman, the holy Birth-giver of God and ever-virgin Mary; to be born under the Law, that he might condemn sin in his flesh; that they who were dead in Adam might be made alive in thy Christ. And becoming a dweller in this world, and giving commandments of salvation, he released us from the delusions of idols, and brought us unto a knowledge of thee, the true God and Father, having won us unto himself for a peculiar people, a royal priesthood, a holy nation; and being purified with water, and sanctified with the Holy Spirit, he gave himself a ransom to Death, whereby we were held, sold into bondage under sin. And having descended into Hell through the Cross, that he might fill all things with himself, he loosed the pains of death, and rose again from the dead on the third day, making a way for all flesh through the Resurrection from the dead—for it was not possible that the Author of Life should be holden of corruption—that he might be the first-fruits of those who have fallen asleep, the first-born from the dead; and he shall be all things, the first in all things. And ascending into heaven, he sat down at the right hand of thy Majesty on high; and he shall come again to render unto every man according to his works. And he hath left with us, as memorials of his saving Passion, these Things which we have spread forth according to his commandment. For when he was about to go forth to his voluntary, and ever-memorable, and life-creating death, in the night in which he gave himself for the life of the world, he took bread in his holy and stainless hands, and when he had shown it unto thee, his God and Father, he gave thanks, blessing it, sanctifying it, and breaking it, he gave it to his holy disciples and apostles, saying:

Take, eat, this is my Body which is broken for you, for the remission of sins. *Amen.*

In like manner, having taken the cup of the fruit of the vine, and mingled it, given thanks, blessed it, and sanctified it, He gave it to his holy disciples and apostles, saying:

Drink ye all of this; for this is my Blood of the New Testament, which is shed for you, and for many for the remission of sins. This do, in remembrance of me: for as often as ye shall eat this Bread and drink of this Cup ye do proclaim my death and confess my Resurrection.

Wherefore, we also, O Master, having in remembrance his redeeming Passion and life-giving Cross, his three days' Burial, and his Resurrection from the dead, his Ascension into Heaven, and his Sitting on the right hand of thee, the God and Father, and his glorious and terrible Coming-again:

Thine own, of thine own, we offer unto thee, in behalf of all, and for all.

We praise thee, we bless thee, we give thee thanks unto thee, O Lord, and we pray unto thee, O our God.

Wherefore, O all-holy Master, we also, thy sinful and unworthy servants, whom thou hast graciously permitted to minister at thy holy Altar, not through our own righteousness (for we have done no good deed on earth), but because of thy mercies and bounties, which thou hast richly poured out upon us, now have boldness to draw near unto this, thy holy Altar; and presenting unto thee the holy emblems of the sacred Body and Blood of thy Christ, we pray thee and implore thee, O Holy of Holies, by the favour of thy goodness, that thy Holy Spirit may descend upon us, and upon these Gifts here spread forth before thee, and bless them, and sanctify and manifest them.

For this bread is in very truth the precious Body of our Lord, and God, and Saviour, Jesus Christ.

For this chalice is, in very truth the precious Blood of our Lord and God, and Saviour, Jesus Christ, which was poured out for the life of the world.

Transmuting them by thy Holy Spirit.

And unite all us who partake of the one Bread and the one Cup, one to another in the communion of the Holy Spirit: and grant that no one of us may partake of that holy Body and Blood of thy Christ unto judgement or unto condemnation; but that we may find mercy and grace, together with all the Saints who, in all the ages, have been acceptable unto thee, our ancestors, fathers, the Patriarchs, Prophets, Apostles, Preachers, Evangelists, Martyrs, Confessors, Teachers; and with all righteous souls who have died in the faith.

(Here follows the Intercession.)

And grant that with one mouth and one heart we may glorify and praise thine all-honourable and majestic Name, of the Father, and of the Son, and of the Holy Spirit, now, and ever, and unto ages of ages. *Amen.*

(*ii*) *St John Chrysostom*

PRIEST: The grace of our Lord Jesus Christ, and the love of God, and 730
the fellowship of the Holy Spirit, be with you all.

And with thy Spirit.

Lift up your hearts.

We lift them up unto the Lord.

Let us give thanks unto the Lord.

Meet and right is it that we should adore the Father, the Son, and the Holy Spirit, the Trinity, one in essence and undivided.

It is meet and right that we should laud thee, bless thee, praise thee, give thanks unto thee, and adore thee in all places of thy dominion: for thou art God ineffable, incomprehensible, inconceivable; thou art from everlasting and art changeless, thou, and thine Only-begotten Son, and thy Holy Spirit. Thou from nothingness hast called us into being; and when we had fallen away from thee, thou didst raise us up again; and thou hast not ceased to do all things until thou hadst brought us back to heaven, and hadst endowed us with thy kingdom which is to come. For all which things we give thanks unto thee, and thine Only-begotten Son, and thy Holy Spirit; for all the things whereof we know, and whereof we know not; for all thy benefits bestowed upon us, both manifest and unseen. And we render thanks unto thee for this ministry which thou dost deign to accept at our hands, although before thee stand thousands of Archangels and myriads of Angels, with the Cherubim, and Seraphim, six-winged, many-eyed, who soar aloft, borne on their pinions,

Singing the triumphant song, crying, calling aloud, and saying:

Holy, holy, holy, Lord of Sabaoth; heaven and earth are full of thy glory: hosanna in the highest: blessed is he that cometh in the name of the Lord. Hosanna in the highest.

And we also, O Lord who lovest mankind, in company with these blessed Powers do cry aloud and say: Holy art thou, and all-holy thou, and thine

Only-begotten Son, and thy Holy Spirit; holy and all-holy; and majestic is thy glory. Who hast so loved thy world that thou gavest thine Only-begotten Son, that whosoever believeth on him should not perish, but should have everlasting life; who, when he had come and had performed all the dispensation for us, in the night in which he was given up,—in the which, rather, he did give himself for the life of the world,—took bread in his holy and pure and sinless hands; and when he had given thanks, and blessed it, and so sanctified it, he gave it to his holy disciples and apostles, saying: Take, eat, this is my Body which is broken for you, for the remission of sins. *Amen.*

And in like manner, after supper he took the cup, saying: Drink ye all of this: for this is my Blood of the New Testament, which is shed for you, and for many, for the remission of sins. *Amen.*

Bearing in remembrance, therefore, this commandment of salvation, and all those things which came to pass for us; the Cross, the Grave, the Resurrection on the third day, the Ascension into Heaven, the Sitting on the right hand, the Second and glorious Coming-again:

Thine own, of thine own, we offer unto thee, in behalf of all, and for all.

We praise thee, we bless thee, we give thanks unto thee, O Lord, and we pray unto thee, O our God.

Again we offer unto thee this reasonable and unbloody service. And we beseech and implore thee, and offer our supplications unto thee, that thou wilt send thy Holy Spirit upon us, and upon these Gifts here spread forth.

And make this bread the precious Body of thy Christ.

And make that which is in this chalice the precious Blood of thy Christ.

Transmuting them by thy Holy Spirit.

That to those who shall partake thereof they may be unto soberness of soul, unto the remission of sins, unto the fellowship of thy Holy Spirit, unto the fulfilling of the kingdom of Heaven, and unto boldness toward thee; and not unto judgement or unto condemnation.

(Here follows the Intercession).

And grant that with one mouth and one heart we may glorify and praise thine all-honourable and majestic Name, of the Father, and of the Son, and of the Holy Spirit, now, and ever, and unto ages of ages. *Amen.*

(iii) Old Roman Canon

731 PRIEST: Brethren, pray that my sacrifice and yours may be acceptable to God the Father Almighty.

May the Lord receive the sacrifice from thy hands, to the praise and glory of his name, to our benefit, and to that of all his holy church.

The Lord be with you.

And with thy Spirit.

Lift up your hearts.

We lift them up unto the Lord.

Let us give thanks unto our Lord God.

It is meet and right so to do.

It is very meet, right, and our bounden duty, that we should at all times and in all places, give thanks unto thee, O Lord, Holy Father, Almighty, Everlasting God. Through Christ our Lord: by whom the Angels laud, the Dominations adore, the Powers do hold in awe thy Majesty, the Heavens and the heavenly Virtues, together with the blessed Seraphim, in exultation celebrate thy praise. With whom, we pray thee, let us join our voices, humbly saying:

Holy, holy, holy, Lord God of hosts, heaven and earth are full of thy glory; Glory be to thee, O Lord most high.

Blessed is he that cometh in the Name of the Lord. Hosanna in the highest.

Therefore, O most merciful Father, we humbly pray and beseech thee, through Jesus Christ thy Son, our Lord, to accept and to bless these gifts, these offerings, these holy, unspotted sacrifices, which we offer unto thee, firstly, for thy holy Catholick Church, which may it please thee to keep in peace, to preserve, unite and govern throughout all the world, and also for thy servant N. our Pope, N. our Bishop, and for all orthodox believers and professors of the Catholic and Apostolic Faith.

Be mindful, O Lord, of thy servants and handmaidens, N. and N.

And of all here present, whose faith thou knowest, and whose devotion thou beholdest; for whom we do offer, or who do themselves offer unto thee this sacrifice of praise for themselves, for all their kinsfolk, for the redemption of their souls, for the hope of their safety and salvation, and do pay their vows unto thee, the eternal God, the living and the true.

Joining in communion with, and reverencing the memory, firstly of the glorious and ever-Virgin Mary, Mother of our God and Lord Jesus Christ; and also of the blessed Apostles and Martyrs, Peter and Paul, Andrew, James John, Thomas, James, Philip, Bartholomew, Matthew, Simon and Thaddeus; Linus, Cletus, Clement, Sixtus, Cornelius, Cyprian, Laurence, Chrysogonus, John and Paul, Cosmas and Damian, and of all thy Saints; by whose merits and prayers do thou grant that in all things we may be defended by the help of thy protection. Through the same Christ our Lord. Amen.

This oblation, therefore, of our service, and also of thy whole family, we beseech thee, O Lord, graciously to accept; and do thou order our days in thy peace, deliver us from eternal damnation, and suffer us to be numbered in the flock of thine elect. Through Christ our Lord. Amen.

Which oblation do thou, O God, vouchsafe in all things to make blessed, approved, ratified, reasonable, and acceptable, that it may become to us the Body and Blood of thy most dearly beloved Son, Jesus Christ our Lord.

Who the day before he suffered took bread into his holy and venerable hands, and lifting his eyes to heaven, to thee, O God, his Father Almighty, when he had given thanks he blessed it and brake it and gave it to his disciples, saying, Take, eat ye all of this; *for this is my Body.*

Likewise after supper he took this glorious Cup into his holy and venerable hands, and when he had given thanks to thee he blessed it and gave it to his disciples, saying, Take and drink ye all of this; *for this is the Cup of the New and Eternal Testament in my Blood; the mystery of faith; which is shed for you and for many for the remission of sins.* As often as ye shall do this ye shall do it in remembrance of me.

Wherefore, O Lord, we thy servants, and thy holy people, mindful of the ever-blessed passion of the same Christ thy Son our Lord, his resurrection from the dead, and glorious ascension into heaven, do offer unto thy most glorious majesty, of thine own bounteous gifts, a pure offering, a holy offering, a spotless offering, even the holy Bread of eternal life, and the Cup of everlasting salvation.

Upon which vouchsafe to look with a favourable and gracious countenance, and to accept them, even as it pleased thee to accept the gifts of thy righteous servant Abel, and the sacrifice of our patriarch Abraham, and the holy sacrifice, the spotless offering which thy high priest Melchisedech offered unto thee.

We humbly beseech thee, Almighty God, to command that these be carried by the hands of thy holy angel to thy altar on high, in the sight of thy divine majesty, that as many of us as by participation at this altar shall receive the most sacred Body and Blood of thy Son may be filled with all heavenly benediction and grace. Through the same Christ our Lord. Amen.

Be mindful also, O Lord, of thy servants, and handmaidens N. and N. who are gone hence before us with the sign of faith, and do now rest in the sleep of peace. To them, O Lord, and to all that rest in Christ, grant, we beseech thee, a place of refreshment, of light and of peace. Through Christ our Lord.

And to us, also, thy sinful servants, trusting in the multitude of thy mercies, vouchsafe to grant some part and fellowship with thy holy Apostles and Martyrs; with John, Stephen, Matthias, Barnabas, Ignatius, Alexander, Marcellinus, Peter, Felicity, Perpetua, Agatha, Lucy, Agnes, Cicely, Anastasia, and with all thy Saints: into whose company we beseech thee to admit us, not weighing our merits, but pardoning our offences. Through Christ our Lord.

By whom, O Lord, thou dost ever create, sanctify, quicken, bless, and bestow upon us all these good things.

Through whom and with whom and in whom, be unto thee, O God, the Father Almighty, in the unity of the Holy Ghost, all honour and glory, world without end. *Amen.*

(*iv*) *The Roman Missal, Fourth Eucharistic Prayer* 732

PRIEST: The Lord be with you.

And also with you.

Lift up your hearts.

We lift them up to the Lord.

Let us give thanks to the Lord our God.

It is right to give him thanks and praise.

Father in heaven,
it is right that we should give you thanks and glory:
you alone are God, living and true.
Through all eternity you live in unapproachable light.
Source of life and goodness, you have created all things,
to fill your creatures with every blessing
and lead all men to the joyful vision of your light.
Countless hosts of angels stand before you to do your will;
they look upon your splendour
and praise you, night and day.
United with them,
and in the name of every creature under heaven,
we too praise your glory as we say:
Holy, holy, holy Lord, God of power and might,
heaven and earth are full of your glory.
Hosanna in the highest.
Blessed is he who comes in the name of the Lord.
Hosanna in the highest.

'I BELIEVE IN THE HOLY CATHOLIC CHURCH'

PRAISE TO THE FATHER

**Father, we acknowledge your greatness:
all your actions show your wisdom and love.
You formed man in your own likeness
and set him over the whole world
to serve you, his creator,
and to rule over all creatures.
Even when he disobeyed you and lost your friendship
you did not abandon him to the power of death,
but helped all men to seek and find you.
Again and again you offered a covenant to man,
and through the prophets taught him to hope for salvation.
Father, you so loved the world
that in the fullness of time you sent your only Son to be our Saviour.
He was conceived through the power of the Holy Spirit,
and born of the Virgin Mary,
a man like us in all things but sin.
To the poor he proclaimed the good news of salvation,
to prisoners, freedom,
and to those in sorrow, joy.
In fulfilment of your will
he gave himself up to death;
but by rising from the dead,
he destroyed death and restored life.
And that we might live no longer for ourselves but for him,
he sent the Holy Spirit from you, Father,
as his first gift to those who believe,
to complete his work on earth
and bring us the fullness of grace.**

INVOCATION OF THE HOLY SPIRIT

**Father, may this Holy Spirit sanctify these offerings.
Let them become the body and blood of Jesus Christ our Lord
as we celebrate the great mystery
which he left us as an everlasting covenant.**

THE LORD'S SUPPER

**He always loved those who were his own in the world.
When the time came for him to be glorified by you, his heavenly Father,
he showed the depth of his love.
While they were at supper,
he took bread, said the blessing, broke the bread
and gave it to his disciples, saying:**

Take this, all of you, and eat it:
this is my body which will be given up for you.

In the same way, he took the cup, filled with wine.
He gave you thanks, and giving the cup to his disciples, said:
Take this, all of you, and drink from it:
This is the cup of my blood,
The blood of the new and everlasting covenant.
It will be shed for you and for all men
so that sins may be forgiven.
Do this in memory of me.

Let us proclaim the mystery of faith:

Christ has died,
Christ is risen,
Christ will come again.

Dying you destroyed our death,
Rising you restored our life.
Lord Jesus, come in glory.

When we eat this Bread and drink this Cup,
we proclaim your death, Lord Jesus,
until you come in glory.

Lord, by your cross and resurrection
you have set us free.
You are the saviour of the world.

THE MEMORIAL PRAYER

Father, we now celebrate this memorial of our redemption.
We recall Christ's death, his descent among the dead,
his resurrection, and his ascension to your right hand;
and, looking forward to his coming in glory,
we offer you his body and blood,
the acceptable sacrifice
which brings salvation to the whole world.

INTERCESSIONS: FOR THE CHURCH

Lord, look upon this sacrifice which you have given to your Church;
and by your Holy Spirit, gather all who share this bread and wine
into the one body of Christ, a living sacrifice of praise.

Lord, remember those for whom we offer this sacrifice,
especially N. our Pope,
N. our bishop, and bishops and clergy everywhere.
Remember those who take part in this offering,
those here present and all your people,
and all who seek you with a sincere heart.

FOR THE DEAD
Remember those who have died in the peace of Christ
and all the dead whose faith is known to you alone.

IN COMMUNION WITH THE SAINTS
Father, in your mercy grant also to us, your children,
to enter into our heavenly inheritance
in the company of the Virgin Mary, the Mother of God,
and your apostles and saints.
Then, in your kingdom, freed from the corruption of sin and death,
we shall sing your glory with every creature through Christ our Lord,
through whom you give us everything that is good.

FINAL DOXOLOGY: IN PRAISE OF GOD
Through him,
with him,
in him,
in the unity of the Holy Spirit,
all glory and honour is yours,
almighty Father, for ever and ever. *Amen.*

(*v*) *The Episcopal Church of the USA. Rite I, First Eucharistic Prayer*

733 CELEBRANT: The Lord be with you.
And with thy spirit.
Lift up your hearts.
We lift them up unto the Lord.
Let us give thanks unto our Lord God.
It is meet and right so to do.

It is very meet, right, and our bounden duty, that we should at all times, and in all places, give thanks unto thee, O Lord, holy Father, almighty, everlasting God.

Therefore with Angels and Archangels, and with all the company of heaven, we laud and magnify thy glorious Name; evermore praising thee, and saying,

Holy, holy, holy, Lord God of Hosts:
heaven and earth are full of thy glory.
Glory be to thee, O Lord most high.

Blessed is he that cometh in the name of the Lord.
Hosanna in the highest.

All glory be to thee, Almighty God, our heavenly Father, for that thou, of thy tender mercy, didst give thine only Son Jesus Christ to suffer death upon the cross for our redemption, who made there, by his one oblation of himself once offered, a full, perfect, and sufficient sacrifice, oblation, and satisfaction, for the sins of the whole world; and did institute, and in his holy Gospel command us to continue, a perpetual memory of that his precious death and sacrifice, until his coming again.

For in the night in which he was betrayed, he took bread; and when he had given thanks, he brake it, and gave it to his disciples, saying, 'Take, eat, this is my Body, which is given for you. Do this in remembrance of me.'

Likewise, after supper, he took the cup; and when he had given thanks, he gave it to them, saying, 'Drink ye all of this; for this is my Blood of the New Testament, which is shed for you, and for many, for the remission of sins. Do this, as oft as ye shall drink it, in remembrance of me.'

Wherefore, O Lord and heavenly Father, according to the institution of thy dearly beloved Son our Saviour Jesus Christ, we, thy humble servants, do celebrate and make here before thy divine Majesty, with these thy holy gifts, which we now offer unto thee, the memorial thy Son hath commanded us to make; having in remembrance his blessed passion and precious death, his mighty resurrection and glorious ascension; rendering unto thee most hearty thanks for the innumerable benefits procured unto us by the same.

And we most humbly beseech thee, O merciful Father, to hear us; and, of thy almighty goodness, vouchsafe to bless and sanctify, with thy Word and Holy Spirit, these thy gifts and creatures of bread and wine; that we, receiving them according to thy Son our Saviour Jesus Christ's holy institution, in remembrance of his death and passion, may be partakers of his most blessed Body and Blood.

And we earnestly desire thy fatherly goodness mercifully to accept this our sacrifice of praise and thanksgiving; most humbly beseeching thee to grant that, by the merits and death of thy Son Jesus Christ, and through faith in his blood, we, and all thy whole Church, may obtain remission of our sins, and all other benefits of his passion.

And here we offer and present unto thee, O Lord, ourselves, our souls and bodies, to be a reasonable, holy, and living sacrifice unto thee; humbly beseeching thee that we, and all others who shall be partakers of this Holy Communion, may worthily receive the most precious Body and Blood of thy Son Jesus Christ, be filled with thy grace and heavenly benediction, and made one body with him, that he may dwell in us, and we in him.

And although we are unworthy, through our manifold sins, to offer unto thee any sacrifice, yet we beseech thee to accept this our bounden duty

and service, not weighing our merits, but pardoning our offenses, through Jesus Christ our Lord;
By whom, and with whom, in the unity of the Holy Ghost, all honor and glory be unto thee, O Father Almighty, world without end. *Amen.*

(vi) Church of England Alternative Service Book 1980. Rite A, Third Eucharistic Prayer

734 PRESIDENT: The Lord be with you.
And also with you.
Lift up your hearts.
We lift them to the Lord.
Let us give thanks to the Lord our God.
It is right to give him thanks and praise.
Father, we give you thanks and praise
through your beloved Son Jesus Christ,
your living Word through whom you have created all things;
Who was sent by you, in your great goodness, to be our Saviour;
by the power of the Holy Spirit he took flesh
and, as your Son, born of the blessed Virgin,
was seen on earth
and went about among us;
He opened wide his arms for us on the cross;
he put an end to death by dying for us
and revealed the resurrection by rising to new life;
so he fulfilled your will and won for you a holy people.
Therefore with angels and archangels,
and with all the company of heaven,
we proclaim your great and glorious name,
for ever praising you and saying:
Holy, holy, holy Lord,
God of power and might,
heaven and earth are full of your glory.
Hosanna in the highest.
Blessed is he who comes in the name of the Lord.
Hosanna in the highest.
Lord, you are holy indeed, the source of all holiness;
grant that, by the power of your Holy Spirit,

and according to your holy will,
these gifts of bread and wine
may be to us the body and blood of our Lord Jesus Christ.
Who in the same night that he was betrayed,
took bread and gave you thanks;
he broke it and gave it to his disciples, saying,
Take, eat; this is my body which is given for you;
do this in remembrance of me.
In the same way, after supper
he took the cup and gave you thanks;
he gave it to them, saying,
Drink this, all of you;
this is my blood of the new covenant,
which is shed for you and for many for the forgiveness of sins.
Do this, as often as you drink it,
in remembrance of me.

Christ has died:
Christ is risen:
Christ will come again.

And so, Father, calling to mind his death on the cross,
his perfect sacrifice made once for the sins of all men,
rejoicing at his mighty resurrection and glorious ascension,
and looking for his coming in glory,
we celebrate this memorial of our redemption;
we thank you for counting us worthy
to stand in your presence and serve you;
we bring before you this bread and this cup;

We pray you to accept this our duty and service,
a spiritual sacrifice of praise and thanksgiving.

Send the Holy Spirit on your people
and gather into one in your kingdom
all who share this one bread and one cup,
so that we, in the company of all the saints,
may praise and glorify you for ever,
through him from whom all good things come,
Jesus Christ our Lord;

By whom, and with whom, and in whom,
in the unity of the Holy Spirit,
all honour and glory be yours, almighty Father,
for ever and ever. *Amen.*

735 Agnus Dei, qui tollis peccata mundi:
Misere nobis.
Agnus Dei, qui tollis peccata mundi:
Misere nobis.
Agnus Dei, qui tollis peccata mundi:
Dona nobis pacem.

Western Rite

Lamb of God, you take away the sins of the world:
have mercy on us.
Lamb of God, you take away the sins of the world:
have mercy on us.
Lamb of God, you take away the sins of the world:
grant us peace.

The Roman Missal

736 O Lord Jesus Christ, who didst say to thine apostles: Peace I leave with you, my peace I give unto you: regard not our sins, but the faith of thy Church; and grant her that peace and unity which is according to thy will: Who livest and reignest God, throughout all ages, world without end.

The Roman Missal

737 Lord, I am not worthy that thou shouldst come under my roof, but speak the word only and my soul shall be healed.

Prayer before communion, Western Rite

738 Holy things unto them that are holy.
R. One is holy, one is Lord, Jesus Christ, to the glory of God the Father.

Orthodox

739 O Lord our God, the bread from heaven, the food of the whole universe, I have sinned against heaven and before thee, and I am not worthy to receive thy most holy mysteries. But, in thy compassion, grant me by thy grace uncondemned to partake of thy holy body and thy precious blood, unto remission of sins and life eternal.

Liturgy of St James

The Body of our Lord Jesus Christ, which was given for thee, preserve thy body and soul unto everlasting life. Take and eat this in remembrance that Christ died for thee, and feed on him in thy heart by faith with thanksgiving. 740

Book of Common Prayer

We have seen the true light, we have received the heavenly Spirit, we have found the true faith, we worship the undivided Trinity: for the Trinity has saved us. 741

Liturgy of St John Chrysostom

Let our mouth be filled with thy praise, O Lord, that we may sing of thy glory, because thou hast counted us worthy to partake of thy holy, divine, immortal and life-giving mysteries: preserve us in thy holiness, that we may learn of thy righteousness all the day long. Alleluia, alleluia, alleluia. 742

Liturgy of St John Chrysostom

O Lord and heavenly Father, we thy humble servants entirely desire thy fatherly goodness mercifully to accept this our sacrifice of praise and thanksgiving; most humbly beseeching thee to grant, that by the merits and death of thy Son Jesus Christ, and through faith in his blood, we and all thy whole Church may obtain remission of our sins, and all other benefits of his passion. And here we offer and present unto thee, O Lord, ourselves, our souls and bodies, to be a reasonable, holy, and lively sacrifice unto thee; humbly beseeching thee, that all we, who are partakers of this holy Communion, may be fulfilled with thy grace and heavenly benediction. And although we be unworthy, through our manifold sins, to offer unto thee any sacrifice, yet we beseech thee to accept this our bounden duty and service; not weighing our merits, but pardoning our offences, through Jesus Christ our Lord; by whom, and with whom, in the unity of the Holy Ghost, all honour and glory be unto thee, O Father almighty, world without end. 743

Thanksgiving after Communion, BCP

Finished and perfected, so far as we are able, is the mystery of thy incarnate work, O Christ our God. 744
For we have kept the memorial of thy death,
We have seen the figure of thy resurrection,
We have been filled with thine unending life,
We have rejoiced in thine unfailing joy.
Grant that we may be counted worthy of that same joy also in the age to come.

Liturgy of St Basil the Great

'I BELIEVE IN THE HOLY CATHOLIC CHURCH'

745 Father of all, we give you thanks and praise, that when we were still far off you met us in your Son and brought us home. Dying and living, he declared your love, gave us grace, and opened the gate of glory. May we who share Christ's body live his risen life; we who drink his cup bring life to others; we whom the Spirit lights give light to the world. Keep us firm in the hope you have set before us, so we and all your children shall be free, and the whole earth live to praise your name; through Christ our Lord.

Alternative Service Book 1980

746 With thankful hearts we remember before Thee all thy saints who have entered into rest, especially those with whom we have had communion here, and whom Thou hast called to the closer communion that awaits the faithful within the veil . . . Keep us united with them in one fellowship of spirit, and at the last gather us together with them into the joy of thy heavenly kingdom; through Jesus Christ our Lord.

Book of Common Order Church of Scotland

747 The peace of God, which passeth all understanding, keep your hearts and minds in the knowledge and love of God, and of his Son Jesus Christ our Lord: and the blessing of God almighty, the Father, the Son, and the Holy Ghost, be amongst you and remain with you always.

Book of Common Prayer

748 Keep us in peace O Christ our God, under the protection of thy holy and venerable Cross; save us from enemies visible and invisible and account us worthy to glorify thee with thanksgiving, with the Father and the Holy Ghost now and ever and world without end.

Dismissal, Armenian Orthodox

Who had not obtained Mercy, but have now obtained Mercy

749 Almighty and everlasting God who hatest nothing that thou hast made, and dost forgive the sins of all them that are penitent: Create and make

in us new and contrite hearts, that we worthily lamenting our sins, and acknowledging our wretchedness, may obtain of thee, the God of all mercy, perfect remission and forgiveness through Jesus Christ our Lord.

Book of Common Prayer

I will arise, and go to my Father, and will say unto him, Father, I have sinned against heaven, and before thee, and am no more worthy to be called thy son. 750

Sentences at Morning and Evening Prayer, BCP

O Lord and Master of my life, take from me the spirit of sloth, faint-heartedness, lust of power and idle talk. But give rather the spirit of chastity, humility, patience and love to thy servant. Yea, O Lord and King, grant me to see my own errors and not to judge my brother, for thou art blessed from all ages to all ages. 751

Orthodox prayer in Lent

Almighty God, our heavenly Father, 752
we have sinned against you and against our fellow men,
in thought and word and deed,
through negligence, through weakness,
through our own deliberate fault.
We are truly sorry
and repent of all our sins.
For the sake of your Son Jesus Christ, who died for us,
forgive us all that is past;
and grant that we may serve you in newness of life;
to the glory of your name.

Confession, Alternative Service Book 1980

May God who pardoned David through Nathan the prophet when he confessed his sins, and Peter weeping bitterly for his denial, and the sinful woman weeping at his feet, and the publican and the prodigal son, may the same God forgive thee all things, through me a sinner, both in this world and in the world to come, and set thee uncondemned before his terrible judgement seat. Have no further care for the sins which thou hast confessed, depart in peace. 753

Absolution, Orthodox

754 Our Lord Jesus Christ, who hath left power to his Church to absolve all sinners who truly repent and believe in him, of his great mercy forgive thee thine offences: And by his authority committed to me, I absolve thee from all thy sins. In the Name of the Father, and of the Son, and of the Holy Ghost. Amen.

Absolution, Western Rite

755 O Saviour of the world, who by thy Cross and precious Blood hast redeemed us, Save us, and help us, we humbly beseech thee, O Lord.

Good Friday liturgy, Western Rite

756 As with visible oil your body outwardly is anointed, so our heavenly Father, Almighty God, grant of his infinite goodness that your soul inwardly may be anointed with the Holy Ghost, who is the Spirit of all strength, relief and gladness. May he, according to his blessed will, restore to you full strength and health of body, mind and spirit that you may withstand all temptations and in Christ's victory triumph over evil, sin and death: Through Jesus Christ our Lord, who by his death hath overcome the prince of death; and with the Father and the Holy Spirit evermore liveth and reigneth God, world without end.

The sacrament of anointing, Western Rite

757 I adjure you by the Tree of Life in the midst of Paradise; and again I bind you by him who sits in the heavenly Jerusalem, both I and the whole holy church, that if there should be here any of the house of Behemoth within these doors of the sanctuary, let him leave and depart from what is the dwelling place of men and not of beasts. Flee, unclean spirit, at this time when the church is signing her children with the name of the Only-Begotten, our Lord, Jesus Christ, along with that of his hidden Begetter and of his Spirit the Paraclete, three persons, one God, unsearchable, unknowable, incomprehensible, to whom be praise now and always and for eternal ages, Amen.

Baptismal exorcism, Syrian Orthodox

758 In the Name of Jesus of Nazareth, Son of the most high God, I find you, evil spirit, and command you to leave this person N., to harm no one, and to go to your own place, never to return.

Our Lord Jesus Christ, present with us now in his risen power, enter into your body, mind and spirit, protecting you from all that harms, and filling you with his healing and his peace, for his Name's sake. Amen. 759

Prayers of exorcism (Anglican)

O God grant me a prayer that is steadfast and recollection of mind, that I may pray with faith in thy gracious promises. 760

Grant me clearness in my thoughts and understanding; enlighten my heart that I may understand only what is pure.

That I may hear thy everlasting mysteries which thou hast prepared for mankind in the grace of thy Christ.

O Lord graciously grant me a pure heart that I may pray unto thee without hindrance.

And that I may ask with watchful understanding for the good things thou hast promised me, which eye hath not seen, nor ear heard, neither have they entered into the heart of man.

Which thou hast prepared for them that love thy holy Name.

O God grant me the love of thy Holy Spirit, to draw my understanding to love thee with all my heart and all my soul and all my strength; and to love my neighbour as myself, according to thy saying: This is the whole of the law and the prophets.

It is written: the Lord is my light and my salvation. Yes, Lord, draw me to thyself. Thou art a faithful God, a merciful Father, the giver of all that is good, and the instructor of the heart. Coptic Orthodox

O God, who hast prepared for them that love thee such good things as pass man's understanding: Pour into our hearts such love toward thee, that we, loving thee above all things, may obtain thy promises, which exceed all that we can desire; through Jesus Christ our Lord. 761

Book of Common Prayer

O God of unchangeable power and eternal light, look favourably on thy whole Church, that wonderful and sacred mystery; and by the tranquil operation of thy perpetual providence carry out the work of man's salvation; and let the whole world feel and see that things which were cast down are being raised up, and things which had grown old are being made new, and all things are returning to perfection through him from whom they took their origin, even Jesus Christ our Lord. Amen. 762

Gelasian Sacramentary

'I BELIEVE IN THE COMMUNION OF SAINTS, THE FORGIVENESS OF SINS, THE RESURRECTION OF THE BODY, AND THE LIFE EVERLASTING'

Death is the narrow passage out of time, place and experience into what is utterly unknown. It is the supreme crisis of human life, to the eyes of the onlooker a total severance, the final stilling of all responses. But for the child of God there is no ultimate loneliness. The Church gathers around one who is dying to take leave of him, commending him to the saints who wait to welcome him and the angels who fortify and uphold him as he prepares to enter into the mercy of God and the fulfilment of the faith, hope and love of his baptismal endowment.

763 Go forth, Christian soul, from this world in the name of God the Father almighty, who created thee; in the name of Jesus Christ, the Son of the living God, who suffered for thee; in the name of the Holy Ghost, who was poured out upon thee; in the name of the holy and glorious Mother of God, the Virgin Mary; in the name of blessed Joseph; in the name of angels and archangels; in the name of thrones and dominations; in the name of principalities and powers; in the name of cherubim and seraphim; in the name of the patriarchs and prophets; in the name of the holy apostles and evangelists; in the name of the holy martyrs and confessors; in the name of the holy monks and hermits; in the name of the holy virgins and of all the saints of God: today let thy place be in peace, and thine abode in holy Sion. Through the same Christ our Lord.

Commendation of a soul, Western Rite

764 Make speed to aid him, ye saints of God; come forth to meet him, ye angels of the Lord; Receiving his soul, Presenting him before the face of the most highest. May Christ receive thee, who hath called thee; and may angels bear thee into the bosom of Abraham. Receiving his soul; Presenting him before the face of the most highest. Rest eternal grant unto him, O Lord, and let light perpetual shine upon him. Presenting him before the face of the most highest.

Commendation of a soul, Western Rite

765 With the souls of the righteous dead, give rest, O Saviour, to the soul of thy servant N., preserving him unto the life of blessedness which is with thee, O thou who lovest mankind.

In the place of thy rest, where all thy saints repose, give rest also to the soul of thy servant N., for thou alone lovest mankind.
Glory be to the Father . . .
Thou art the God who didst descend into hell and loose the bonds of the captives. Do thou give rest also to the soul of thy servant N.

Both now and ever . . .
O Virgin, alone pure and undefiled, who without seed didst bring forth God, pray thou that his soul may be saved.

With the saints give rest, O Christ, to the soul of thy servant N., where there is neither sickness, nor sorrow, nor sighing, but life everlasting.

Prayers for the dead, Orthodox

Unto him who is gone hence, O my Saviour, open thou, we beseech thee, 766
the door of thy mercy, O Christ; that he may rejoice in glory, as he partaketh of the joys of thy kingdom.
What pleasure in this life remains unmarked by sorrow? What glory can endure upon this earth unchanged? All is feebler than a shadow, more deceptive than a dream; for death in a single moment takes all things away. But in the light of thy countenance, O Christ, and in the joy of thy beauty, give rest to those whom thou hast chosen, for thou lovest mankind.

Prayers for the dead, Orthodox

Blessed is the path thou goest on this day, for a place of rest is prepared 767
for thee.

Burial of the dead, Orthodox

O Father of all, we pray to thee for those whom we love, but see no 768
longer. Grant them thy peace; let light perpetual shine upon them; and in thy loving wisdom and almighty power work in them the good purpose of thy perfect will; through Jesus Christ our Lord.

Book of Common Prayer (1928)

Almighty God, Father of all mercies and giver of all comfort: Deal 769
graciously, we pray thee, with those who mourn, that casting every care on thee, they may know the consolation of thy love; through Jesus Christ our Lord.

Book of Common Prayer (1928)

'I BELIEVE IN THE COMMUNION OF SAINTS'

770 The souls of the righteous are in the hand of God and there shall no torment touch them. In the sight of the unwise they seemed to die, but they are in peace. Alleluia.

Offertory, Feast of All Saints, Western Rite

771 For an angel of peace, faithful guardian and guide of our souls and our bodies, we beseech thee, O Lord.

Orthodox

772 Seven archangels stand glorifying the Almighty and serving the hidden mystery.

Michael the first, Gabriel the second, and Raphael the third, symbol of the Trinity.

Surael, Sakakael, Saratael and Ananael. These are the shining ones, the great and pure ones, who pray to God for mankind.

The cherubim, the seraphim, the thrones, dominions, powers, and the four living creatures bearing the chariot of God.

The twenty-four elders in the Church of the Firstborn, praise him without ceasing, crying out and saying:

Holy is God; heal the sick. Holy is the Almighty; give rest to the departed. Holy is the Immortal; bless thine inheritance. May thy mercy and thy peace be a stronghold unto thy people.

Holy, holy, holy, Lord of hosts. Heaven and earth are full of thy glory.

Intercede for us O angels our guardians, and all heavenly hosts, that our sins may be forgiven.

Coptic Orthodox

773 O everlasting God, who hast ordained and constituted the services of angels and men in a wonderful order; Mercifully grant, that as thy holy angels alway do thee service in heaven, so by thy appointment they may succour and defend us on earth; through Jesus Christ our Lord.

Book of Common Prayer

774 In the presence of the angels I will sing praise unto thee, O my God. I will worship toward thy holy temple, and praise thy name.

Western Breviary

Gabriel, the greatest and most godlike of the spiritual powers, shining with heavenly brightness, who with the hosts on high gazes upon the light of the Three-fold Sun, came to the Virgin and announced to her the glad tidings of the divine mystery full of awe; and he intercedes for our souls. 775

To thee alone, O Gabriel, was entrusted the great mystery, till then unknown to the angels and hid from all eternity: coming to Nazareth, thou hast not dared to impart it to any save the pure Virgin alone. Pray with her that our souls may be granted peace and great mercy.

Thou who art ever filled with light, who doest the will and fulfillest the decrees of the almighty, O leader of the angels, Gabriel the all-perfect, preserve those who honour thee with love, and ask at all times that our souls may be granted peace and great mercy.

Orthodox

O my Lady, the holy Virgin Mary, thou hast been likened to many things, yet there is nothing which compares with thee. Neither heaven can match thee, nor the earth equal as much as the measure of thy womb. For thou didst confine the Unconfinable, and carry him whom none has power to sustain. 776

The cherubim are but thy Son's chariot bearers, and even the seraphim bow down in homage at the throne of thy Firstborn. How sublime is the honour of thy royal estate.

O holy Virgin, instrument of our strength and power, our grace, deification, joy, and fortune; glory of our human race! Thou wast the means whereby the salvation of the world was accomplished, and through whom God was reconciled to the sons of mankind. And it was through thee that created human nature was united in indivisible union with the Divine Being of the Creator.

What an unheard of thing for the potter to clothe himself in a clay vessel, or the craftsman in a handicraft. What humility beyond words for the Creator to clothe himself in the body of a human creature.

And now I cry unto thy Son, O Virgin, saying:

O thou who hast preferred the humble estate of men to the high rank of angels, do not reject thy servant because of the sins I have committed.

Thou whose desire was to partake of earthly rather than heavenly beings, let me share in the secret of thy flawless Divine Being.

Thou to whom Jacob was more comely than Esau, do not scorn me because of my transgressions. For against thee only have I sinned, and much sin have I heaped up upon me.

Thou didst create me pure and righteous, yet of my own will I became unclean, and through the persuasion of the wicked one went astray. Thou didst adorn me with gifts of priceless worth which I cast away in favour of unrighteousness.

Make speed, O Lord, to build me into a fortress for the Holy Spirit, Raise me up lest I crumble into a desolate ruin of sin. Make speed to forgive for forgiveness is with thee.

O Lord, thou knowest the balm to heal my wounds, the help to strengthen my weakness, the path to prosper my progress. Thou knowest all that is expedient to fulfil my life, as the potter knows how to contrive his own vessel's perfection. For the work is wrought according to the design and wisdom of its maker.

O Lord, renew thy vessel with the power of the Holy Spirit. Make the work of thy hands to be lovely and indestructible.

O Lord, remember thy descent from the heights of Heaven and thine indwelling within the womb of the Holy Virgin.

Remember thy birth from her while she was a virgin, and the suckling of her who wast chaste.

Remember how thou wast laid in a manger, wrapped in swaddling clothes, in a stable.

O Lord remembering all this, do not disregard thy sinful servant. Help me with thy deliverance and cover me with the shield of thy salvation for the sake of Mary thy Mother; for the sake of her breasts which suckled thee and her lips which kissed thee; for the sake of her hands which touched thee and her arms which embraced thee; for the sake of her spirit and flesh which thou didst take from her to be part of thyself . . .

I believe, O Lord, that thou art the Son of the Father in thy Godhead, and the Son of Man in thy humanity . . .

I believe, O Lord, that thou art the Firstborn Only Son to him who begat thee and the only Son of her who gave birth to thee. Thy birth in Heaven was unique, and thy birth on earth was unique.

I have sought but could not comprehend the mystery of thy first birth. I contemplate thy second birth and marvel in wonder. I give glory to the former though it is beyond my understanding. I give homage to the second in prostrate adoration.

And now without doubt, and in the fullness of faith, I glorify thy birth from the Father and give praise to thy birth from the Virgin. The Virgin's womb is greater than the mystical chariot of light, loftier than the heights of the firmament, more sublime than the distances of space, more glorious than the seraphim and cherubim.

The Virgin's womb was the gateway to Heaven, which, without being opened, became the way in and way out of the Son of Righteousness . . .

The Virgin's womb was the ark and dwelling-place of the Lord God Adonay.

And now let us praise God, saying: Glory to thee; glory to him who sent thee; and glory to the Holy Spirit who is co-equal with thee.

Honour to her who bore thee; homage to her who gave birth to thee; devotion to thy mother; and holiness to her who tended thee.

Hymn to the Blessed Virgin, Ethiopian Orthodox

O God most high who didst endue with wonderful virtue and grace the Blessed Virgin Mary, the Mother of our Lord: Grant that we who now call her blessed, may be made very members of the heavenly family of him who was pleased to be called the first-born among many brethren: who liveth and reigneth with Thee and the Holy Spirit, one God world without end. 777

Canadian Prayer Book

Hail, for through thee joy shall shine forth: 778
Hail, for through thee the curse shall cease:
Hail, recalling of fallen Adam:
Hail, deliverance from the tears of Eve.
Hail, height hard to climb for the thoughts of men:
Hail, depth hard to scan, even for the eyes of angels.
Hail, for thou art the throne of the King:
Hail, for thou holdest Him who upholds all.
Hail, star causing the Sun to shine:
Hail, womb of the divine Incarnation.
Hail, for through thee the creation is made new:
Hail, for through thee the Creator becomes a newborn child.
Hail, Bride without bridegroom!

Akathist hymn, Orthodox

As the lover of the Spirit, the swallow that brings divine tidings of grace, O Forerunner, thou hast clearly made known to mankind the dispensation of the King, who shone forth in brightness from a pure Virgin into the restoration of men. Thou dost banish the dominion of dark and evil ways, and guidest towards eternal life the hearts of those baptized in repentance, O blessed Prophet inspired by God. 779

Vespers of St John the Forerunner, Orthodox

'I BELIEVE IN THE COMMUNION OF SAINTS'

780 O almighty God, whom truly to know is everlasting life; Grant us perfectly to know thy Son Jesus Christ to be the way, the truth, and the life; that, following the steps of thy holy apostles, Saint Philip and Saint James, we may steadfastly walk in the way that leadeth to eternal life; through the same thy son Jesus Christ our Lord. Amen.

Book of Common Prayer

781 Almighty God, who didst call Luke the Physician, whose praise is in the Gospel, to be an Evangelist, the Physician of the soul; May it please thee that, by the wholesome medicines of the doctrine delivered by him, all the diseases of our souls may be healed; through the merits of thy Son Jesus Christ our Lord.

Book of Common Prayer

782 Great is the power of thy Cross, O Lord! It was set up in the place of the skull, and it prevails in all the world; it made the fishermen into apostles and the Gentiles into martyrs, that they might intercede for our souls.

Great is the power of thy martyrs, O Christ! Though they lie in their tombs, they drive out evil spirits and fight in defence of true devotion, subduing the dominion of the enemy through faith in the Trinity.

The prophets, the apostles of Christ and the martyrs have taught mankind to sing the praises of the consubstantial Trinity; they have given light to the nations that were gone astray, and they have made the sons of men the companions of the angels.

Vespers in Holy Week, Orthodox

783 O almighty God, who dost will to be glorified in thy Saints, and didst raise up thy servant N. to shine as a light in the world: Shine we pray thee in our hearts, that we also in our generation may show forth thy praises, who hast called us out of darkness into thy marvellous light; through Jesus Christ our Lord.

Canadian Prayer Book

784 O almighty God, who hast knit together thine elect in one communion and fellowship, in the mystical body of thy Son Christ our Lord; Grant us grace so to follow thy blessed Saints in all virtuous and godly living, that we may come to those unspeakable joys, which thou hast prepared for them that unfeignedly love thee; through Jesus Christ our Lord.

Book of Common Prayer

'I BELIEVE IN THE COMMUNION OF SAINTS'

Hail, Mary full of grace, the Lord is with thee. Blessed art thou among women, and blessed is the fruit of thy womb, Jesus. Holy Mary, Mother of God, pray for us sinners, now and in the hour of our death. 785

Angelic salutation (See Luke 1.)

Glory to the Father, who has woven garments of glory for the resurrection; worship to the Son, who was clothed in them at his rising; thanksgiving to the Spirit, who keeps them for all the Saints; one nature in three, to him be praise. 786

Syrian Orthodox

O King, all glorious amid thy saintly company, who ever shalt be praised yet overpassest utterance: thou O Lord, art in the midst of us, and we are called by thy holy Name; leave us not, O Lord our God; that in the day of judgement it may please thee to place us in the number of thy Saints and chosen ones, King most blessed. 787

Antiphon at Compline, Sarum Rite

O what their joy and their glory must be, 788
Those endless Sabbaths the blessed ones see!
Crown for the valiant; to weary ones rest;
God shall be all, and in all ever blest.

Truly Jerusalem name we that shore,
'Vision of peace', that brings joy evermore!
Wish and fulfilment can severed be ne'er,
Nor the thing prayed for come short of the prayer.

We, where no trouble distraction can bring,
Safely the anthems of Sion shall sing;
While for thy grace, Lord, their voices of praise
Thy blessed people shall evermore raise.

Low before him with our praises we fall,
Of whom, and in whom, and through whom are all;
Of whom, the Father; and through whom, the Son;
In whom, the Spirit, with these ever One.

Peter Abelard, tr. J. M. Neale

It is very meet and right, just and for salvation, that we should at all times and in all places give thanks unto thee: O Lord, holy Father, almighty everlasting God: Who didst anoint thine only-begotten Son, our Lord Jesus Christ, with the oil of gladness, to be a Priest for ever and the King 789

of all the world: that, offering himself an unspotted sacrifice of peace upon the altar of the cross, he might accomplish the mystery of the redemption of mankind: and making all creatures subject to his governance, might deliver up to thine infinite Majesty an eternal and universal kingdom. A kingdom of truth and life: a kingdom of sanctity and grace: a kingdom of justice, love and peace. And therefore with Angels and Archangels, with Thrones and Dominations and with all the host of the heavenly army we sing the hymn of thy glory, evermore saying: Holy, Holy, Holy Lord God of Hosts. Heaven and earth are full of thy glory. Hosanna in the highest. Blessed is he that cometh in the name of the Lord. Hosanna in the highest.

Preface of Christ the King, Roman Missal

V

PRAYER AS LISTENING

Introduction

Prayer is relationship with God. Such relationship presupposes communication from both sides. Not only does a person pray to God in words or unspoken thoughts, but also God communicates with the person in intuitions, often so clear that they can be interpreted into direct speech. At such times God's initiative is clearly apparent, and the heart is moved to respond in prayer or silent worship, or in inspired and obedient word or action.

Kierkegaard wrote: 'The "immediate" person thinks and imagines that 790
when he prays, the important thing, the thing he must concentrate upon, is that God should hear what *he* is praying for. Yet in the true, eternal sense it is just the reverse: the true relation in prayer is not when God hears what is prayed for, but when the person praying continues to pray until he is the one who hears, who hears what God wills. The "immediate" person, therefore, . . . makes demands in his prayers; the true man of prayer only attends.'

Julian of Norwich wrote that her Shewings of Divine Love came to her in 791
three ways: 'By bodily sight, by word forming in the understanding, and by ghostly sight.'

Simone Weil wrote: 'I saw that the carrying out of a vocation differed 792
from the actions dictated by reason or inclination in that it was due to an impulse of an essentially and manifestly different order; and not to follow such an impulse when it made itself felt, even if it demanded impossibilities, seemed to me the greatest of all ills. Hence my conception of obedience.'

Old Testament

Abraham, the founding patriarch of biblical religion: 'The Lord said to 793
Abram, "Go from your country and your kindred and your father's house

to the land that I will show you. And I will make of you a great nation . . . and by you all the families of the earth shall bless themselves."'

Genesis 12: 1–3

794 Moses at the burning bush: 'God called to him out of the bush . . . "I am the God of your father, the God of Abraham, the God of Isaac and the God of Jacob . . . I have seen the affliction of my people who are in Egypt . . . I will send you to Pharaoh . . . I AM WHO I AM." Say "I AM has sent me to you."'

Exodus 3: 4–14

795 Elijah at the cave on Horeb: 'after the wind . . . the earthquake . . . and the fire, a still small voice, "What are you doing here, Elijah? . . . Go, return on your way to the wilderness of Damascus . . .".'

1 Kings 19: 11–15

796 Job, seeking to understand the mystery of suffering, argued with God and with his 'comforters': 'Then the Lord answered Job out of the whirlwind: "Where were you when I laid the foundations of the earth? Tell me, if you have understanding . . . Shall a faultfinder contend with the Almighty? . . . Will you even put me in the wrong . . . that you may be justified? . . ." Then Job answered the Lord, "I have uttered what I did not understand . . . I had heard of thee by the hearing of the ear, but now my eye sees thee; therefore I despise myself and repent . . .".'

Job 38: 1, 4; 40: 2, 8; 42: 3–6

797 Isaiah, after his vision in the Temple: 'I heard the voice of the Lord saying, "Whom shall I send, and who will go for us?" Then I said, "Here am I! send me."'

'Thus says the high and lofty One . . . "I dwell in the high and holy place, and also with him who is of a contrite and humble spirit".'

Isaiah 6: 8; 57: 15

798 Hosea: 'What shall I do with you, O Ephraim? What shall I do with you, O Judah? Your love is like a morning cloud, like the dew that goes early away . . . I desire steadfast love and not sacrifice, the knowledge of God rather than burnt offerings.'

Hosea 6: 4, 6

Micah speaks for the Lord: 'He has showed you, O man, what is good: and what does the Lord require of you but to do justice and to love kindness, and to walk humbly with your God?' 799

Micah 6: 8

Amos: the Lord's message to his privileged people: '"You only have I known of all the families of the earth; therefore I will punish you for all your iniquities."' 800

Amos 3: 2

Jeremiah: 'The word of the Lord came to me saying, "Before I formed you in the womb I knew you, and before you were born I consecrated you; I appointed you a prophet to the nations." . . . "Ah, Lord God, behold I do not know how to speak, for I am only a youth." . . . "Do not say, 'I am only a youth'; for to all to whom I send you, you shall go, and whatever I command you you shall speak."' 801

Jeremiah 1: 4–7

Ezekiel, after his vision by the river: 'I heard him speaking to me . . . "Son of man, I send you to the people of Israel, to a nation of rebels . . . And whether they hear or refuse to hear . . . they will know that there has been a prophet among them."' 802

'"Son of man, can these bones live?" . . . "O Lord God, thou knowest." . . . "Prophesy to these bones . . ."'

Ezekiel 2: 2–3, 5; 37: 3, 4

Jonah resented Nineveh's repentance and the withering of the gourd: 'And the Lord said, "Do you do well to be angry?" . . . "I do well to be angry, angry enough to die." And the Lord said, "You pity the plant, for which you did not labour . . . [and] which came into being in a night, and perished in a night. And should not I pity Nineveh, that great city, in which there are more than a hundred and twenty thousand persons who do not know their right hand from their left, and also much cattle?"' 803

Jonah 4: 4, 9b–11

New Testament

804 Mary of Nazareth heard the Angel's annunciation: 'You will conceive . . . and bear a son, and you shall call his name Jesus.' . . . And Mary said ". . . I am the handmaid of the Lord; let it be to me according to your word."'

Luke 1: 31, 38

805 Jesus, after his baptism: 'a voice came from heaven, "Thou art my beloved Son; with thee I am well pleased."'

at his transfiguration: 'a voice came out of the cloud, "This is my beloved Son; listen to him."'

after his entry into Jerusalem: '"Now is my soul troubled. And what shall I say? 'Father, save me from this hour'? No, for this purpose I have come to this hour. Father, glorify thy name." Then a voice came from heaven, "I have glorified it, and I will glorify it again."'

Mark 1: 11; Mark 9: 7; John 12: 27, 28

806 Saul of Tarsus, struck blind on the road to Damascus, 'heard a voice saying to him, "Saul, Saul, why do you persecute me?" And he said, "Who are you, Lord?" And he said, "I am Jesus, whom you are persecuting".'

Acts 9: 4–5

807 Peter: 'There came a voice to him, "Rise, Peter; kill and eat." But Peter said, "No, Lord; for I have never eaten anything that is common or unclean." And the voice came to him again . . . "What God has cleansed, you must not call common."'

Acts 10: 13–15

808 John on Patmos, heard the words: '"I am the first and the last, and the living one; I died, and behold I am alive for evermore, and I have the keys of Death and Hades."'

Later a great voice from the throne said: '"Behold, the dwelling of God is with men . . . and they shall be his people . . . he will wipe away every tear from their eyes, and death shall be no more, neither shall there be mourning nor crying nor pain any more, for the former things have passed away . . . Behold, I make all things new."'

Revelation 1: 17–18; 21: 3, 4, 5

In the Christian Era

Antony of Egypt (3rd century): God spoke to him through the Gospel read in Church: 'If thou wilt be perfect, go, sell all that thou hast and give to the poor, and take up thy cross and follow me.' 809

Later, experiencing the direct conflict with evil, he cried out, 'Where were you, Lord, while I went through such tribulations?' A voice answered, 'I was here by your side, Antony, I have never left you . . . I will be your guide and comforter . . .'

Francis of Assisi (early 13th century), while praying before the crucifix in the ruined church of San Damiano, heard the words: 'Francis, go, repair my house, which, as you see, is falling completely to ruin.' 810

Thomas Aquinas (13th century), when pressed by his secretary, Reginald of Piperno, to explain why he had broken off his unfinished work, the *Summa Theologica*, said: 'All that I have written seems like straw compared to what has now been revealed to me.' 811

According to tradition, in his vision he heard the Lord say, 'Thomas, you have written well of me: what shall be your reward?' and his reply was, 'No reward but yourself, Lord.'

Dante (late 13th century) at the climax of his great vision: 812

For now my sight, clear and yet clearer grown,
  Pierced through the ray of that exalted light,
  Wherein, as in itself, the truth is known.

O light supreme, by mortal thought unscanned . . .

Make strong my tongue that in its words may burn
  One single spark of all Thy glory's light
  For future generations to discern.

Catherine of Siena (14th century), tormented by temptations and evil visions, cried: 'O good and sweet Jesus, where wert thou while my soul was being so sorely tempted?' The answer came, 'I was in thy heart, Catherine, for I will not leave anyone who does not first leave me.' 813

814 Julian of Norwich (14th century). When she was thirty years old this anchoress had a serious illness which she had prayed God to send her, during which she received sixteen 'revelations of divine love', on which she meditated for the rest of her life.

'He shewed me a little thing, the quantity of a hazel-nut, in the palm of my hand. I thought "What may this be?" and it was generally answered, "It is all that is made." I marvelled how it might last . . . and I was answered in my understanding: "It lasteth and ever shall last for that God loveth it." And so all things hath Being by the love of God.'

'Then said our good Lord Jesus Christ: "Art thou well paid that I suffered for thee?" I said: "Yea, Lord, blessed mayest thou be." Then said Jesus, our kind Lord: "If thou art paid, then I am paid: it is a joy, a bliss, and endless liking to me that ever suffered I passion for thee . . .".'

'Methought: "If sin had not been, we should all have been clean and like to our Lord, as he made us." But Jesus . . . answered: "It behoved that there should be sin; but all shall be well, and all manner of thing shall be well."'

'After sin and contrition, then sheweth our courteous Lord himself to the soul: "My darling, I am glad thou art come to me: in all thy woe I have ever been with thee." And this word that he said is an endless comfort: "I keep thee securely."'

'I am ground of thy beseeching . . . Pray inwardly, though thee thinketh it savour thee not: for it is profitable, though thou feel not . . .'

'"Thou shalt not be overcome", was said full clearly . . . He said not, "Thou shalt not be tempested, thou shalt not be travailed, thou shalt not be dis-eased", but he said, "Thou shalt not be overcome."'

815 Blaise Pascal (17th century):
The year of grace 1654,
Monday, 23 November, Feast of Saint Clement,
  Pope and Martyr . . .
From about half-past-ten in the evening until
  half-past-midnight,
    FIRE
'God of Abraham, God of Isaac, God of Jacob',
  not of philosophers and scholars,
Certainty, certainty, heartfelt, joy, peace.
God of Jesus Christ.
God of Jesus Christ.
'My God and your God,'
'Thy God shall be my God.'

The world forgotten, and everything except God.
He can only be found by the ways taught in the Gospels.
Greatness of the human soul.
'O righteous Father, the world had not known thee,
but I have known thee.'
Joy, joy, joy, tears of joy.
I have cut myself off from him.
'They have forsaken me, the fountain of living waters.'
My God wilt thou forsake me?
Let me not be cut off from him for ever!
'And this is life eternal, that they might know thee, the
only true God, and Jesus Christ whom thou hast sent.'
Jesus Christ.
Jesus Christ . . .

Ann Griffiths (18th-century Welsh hymn writer): 'O to continue to drink 816
deep of the streams of the great salvation, until I wholly lose the thirst for the passing things of earth; to live watching for my Lord, to be wide awake when he comes, to open to him quickly and enjoy his likeness to the full.'

Dag Hammarskjöld (20th century): 'I don't know who—or what—put 817
the question, I don't know when it was put. I don't even remember answering. But at some moment I did answer Yes to Someone—or Something—and from that hour I was certain that existence is meaningful and that, therefore, my life in self-surrender, had a goal. From that moment I have known what it means "not to look back", and "to take no thought for the morrow".'

Simone Weil (20th century): 'I heard by chance of the existence of those 818
English poets of the seventeenth century who are named metaphysical. I discovered the poem . . . called "Love". I learnt it by heart. Often . . . I make myself say it over, concentrating all my attention upon it, and clinging with all my soul to the tenderness it enshrines. I used to think I was merely reciting it as a beautiful poem, but without my knowing it the recitation had the virtue of a prayer. It was during one of these recitations that, as I told you, Christ himself came down and took possession of me.

Until last September I had never once prayed to God in all my life.'

819 LOVE

Love bade me welcome; yet my soul drew back,
  Guilty of dust and sin.
But quick-eyed Love, observing me grow slack
  From my first entrance in,
Drew nearer to me, sweetly questioning
  If I lack'd anything.

'A guest,' I answer'd, 'worthy to be here:'
  Love said, 'You shall be he.'
'I, the unkind, ungrateful? Ah, my dear,
  I cannot look on Thee.'
Love took my hand and smiling did reply,
  'Who made the eyes but I?'

'Truth, Lord, but I have marr'd them: let my shame
  Go where it doth deserve.'
'And know you not,' says Love, 'Who bore the blame?'
  'My dear, then I will serve.'
'You must sit down,' says Love, 'and taste my meat.'
  So I did sit and eat.

George Herbert, 1593–1633

VI

PRAYERS FROM OTHER TRADITIONS OF FAITH

Introduction

This anthology might well have been entitled 'The Prayers of Mankind', for it includes prayers not only of Christians but also of people of other traditions of faith. Any who pray will be interested to learn how other people pray. Primal people do not have written records and the prayers are largely handed down in oral form from one generation to another. Eastern religions emphasize meditation, whether of the mind or in silent stillness. So it will be understood that there is not available the same body of prayers from which to select. Yet there is enough available to give Christians the taste or feeling of the prayers of other religious people, and perhaps provide evidence that if others can pray such prayers of beauty and devotion they must have some experience of the Transcendent Reality with which those praying are hoping to enter into loving communion, by whatever name they may call that Supreme Absolute. There is the further expectation that as people in different traditions get to know each other better they will be able to share their spiritual treasures, and further still the hope that they may be able to pray some of the prayers of others.

Jewish

Individual prayers and meditations from the period of the Talmud

A MORNING PRAYER 820

When he wakes he says: 'My God, the soul which Thou hast placed in me is pure. Thou hast fashioned it in me, Thou didst breathe it into me, and Thou preservest it within me, and Thou wilt one day take it from me, and restore it to me in the time to come. So long as the soul is within me I give thanks unto Thee, O Lord, my God, and the God of my fathers, Sovereign of all worlds, Lord of all souls. Blessed art Thou, O Lord, who restorest souls to dead corpses.' When he hears the cock crowing he should say: 'Blessed is He who has given to the cock understanding to distinguish between day and night.' When he opens his eyes he should say: 'Blessed is He who opens the eyes of the blind.' When he stretches himself and sits up, he should say: 'Blessed is He who looseneth the bound.' When he dresses he should say: 'Blessed is He who clothes the naked.' When he draws himself up he should say: 'Blessed is He who raises the bowed.' When he steps on to the ground he should say: 'Blessed is He who spread the earth on the waters.' When he commences to walk he should say: 'Blessed is He who makes firm the steps of man.' When he ties his shoes he should say: 'Blessed is he who has supplied all my wants.' When he fastens his girdle, he should say: 'Blessed is He who girds Israel with might.' When he spreads a kerchief over his head he should say: 'Blessed is He who crowns Israël with glory.' When he wraps himself with the fringed garment he should say: 'Blessed is He who hast sanctified us with His commandments and commanded us to enwrap ourselves in the fringed garment.' When he puts the tefillin on his arm he should say: 'Blessed is He who has sanctified us with His commandments and commanded us to put on tefillin.' When he puts it on his head he should say: 'Blessed is He who has sanctified with His commandments and commanded us concerning the commandment of tefillin.' When he washes his hands he should say: 'Blessed is He who has sanctified us with His commandments and commanded us concerning the washing of hands.' When he washes his face he should say: 'Blessed is He who has removed the bands of sleep from mine eyes and slumber from mine eyes. And may it be Thy will O Lord, my God, to habituate me to Thy law and make me cleave to Thy commandments, and do not bring me into sin, or into iniquity, or into temptation, or into contempt, and bend my inclination to be subservient unto Thee, and remove me far from a bad man and a bad companion, and make me cleave to the good inclination and to a good companion in Thy world, and let me obtain this day and every day grace, favour, and mercy in Thine eyes, and in the eyes of all that see me, and show loving-kindness unto me. Blessed art Thou, O Lord, who bestowest loving-kindness upon Thy people Israel.'

Berakoth

821 A favourite saying of the Rabbis of Jabneh was: I am God's creature and my fellow is God's creature. My work is in the town and his work is in the country. I rise early for my work and he rises early for his work. Just as he does not presume to do my work, so I do not presume to do his work. Will you say, I do much and he does little? We have learnt: One may do much or one may do little; it is all one, provided he directs his heart to heaven.

Berakoth

PRAYER IN ACTION 822

These are the things whose interest a man enjoys in this world, while the capital remains for him in the world to come—this is what they are:

Respecting one's father and mother,
Acts of generosity and love,
Coming early to the Synagogue for morning and evening study,
Giving hospitality to strangers,
Visiting the sick,
Assisting the bride,
Attending the dead,
Devotion in prayer,
Working peace between a man and his companion.
And the study of the Torah leads to them all.

Mishnah

Close mine eyes from evil, 823
And my ears from hearing idle words,
And my heart from reflecting on unchaste thoughts,
And my veins from thinking of transgression.

Guide my feet to walk in thy commandments
And thy righteous ways,
And may thy mercies be turned upon me.

Berakoth

Rabbi Eleazer on concluding his prayer used to say the following: May it 824
be Thy will, O Lord our God, to cause to dwell in our lot love and brotherhood and peace and friendship, and mayest Thou make our borders rich in disciples and prosper our latter end with good prospect and hope, and set our portion in Paradise, and confirm us with a good companion and a good impulse in Thy world, and may we rise early and obtain the yearning of our heart to fear Thy name, and mayest Thou be pleased to grant the satisfaction of our desires!

Berakoth

Rabbi Johanan on concluding his prayer added the following: May it be 825
Thy will, O Lord our God, to look upon our shame, and behold our evil plight, and clothe Thyself in Thy mercies, and cover Thyself in Thy strength, and wrap Thyself in Thy loving-kindness, and gird Thyself with Thy graciousness, and may the attribute of Thy kindness and gentleness come before Thee!

Berakoth

826 Rabbi Safra on concluding his prayer added the following: May it be Thy will, O Lord our God, to establish peace among the celestial family, and among the earthly family, and among the disciples who occupy themselves with Thy Torah whether for its own sake or for other motives; and may it please Thee that all who do so for other motives may come to study it for its own sake!

Berakoth

827 Rab on concluding his prayer added the following: May it be Thy will, O Lord our God, to grant us long life, a life of peace, a life of good, a life of blessing, a life of sustenance, a life of bodily vigour, a life in which there is fear of sin, a life free from shame and confusion, a life of riches and honour, a life in which we may be filled with the love of Torah and the fear of heaven, a life in which Thou shalt fulfil all the desires of our heart for good!

Berakoth

828 Mar the son of Rabina on concluding his prayer added the following: My God, keep my tongue from evil and my lips from speaking guile. May my soul be silent to them that curse me and may my soul be as the dust to all. Open Thou my heart in Thy law, and may my soul pursue Thy commandments, and deliver me from evil hap, from the evil impulse and from all evils that threaten to come upon the world. As for all that design evil against me, speedily annul their counsel and frustrate their designs! May the words of my mouth and the meditation of my heart be acceptable before Thee, O Lord, my rock and my redeemer!

Berakoth

829 May you behold your world during your lifetime—your end be in life eternal—and your hope endure throughout the generations. May your heart meditate understanding, your mouth speak wisdom and your tongue sing joyously. May your eyelids look straight before you, your eyes themselves be enlightened by the Torah and your face shine like the brightness of the firmament. May your lips utter knowledge, your reins rejoice in uprightness and your steps run to hear and to understand the message of the Ancient of Days.

Berakoth

JEWISH

Blessed art Thou, O Lord our God, King of the universe, 830
Who makest the bands of sleep to fall upon mine eyes,
And slumber upon mine eyelids.

May it be Thy will, O Lord my God and God of my fathers,
To suffer me to lie down in peace
And to let me rise up again in peace.

Let not my thoughts trouble me,
Nor evil dreams, nor evil fancies,
But let my rest be perfect before Thee.

O lighten mine eyes, lest I sleep the sleep of death,
For it is Thou who givest light to the apple of the eye.
Blessed art Thou, O Lord,
Who givest light to the whole world in Thy glory.

Berakoth

Individual Prayers and Meditations—Mediaeval and Modern

Wherever I go—only Thou! Wherever I stand—only Thou! Just Thou; again Thou! always Thou! Thou, Thou, Thou! When things are good, Thou! when things are bad—Thou! Thou, Thou, Thou! 831

An early Hasidic song

Sometimes I feel lonely, and from the depths I cry unto Thee, and within me, Thy voice answers me, and I know that Thou, Eternal Friend, art near me. 832

Sometimes the sense of failure seizes me, and I am disheartened. Unto Thee do I raise mine eyes, and the light of my heavenly Father shines upon me, and bids me to persevere.

Sometimes my daily life oppresses me. Unto Thee do I lift up my soul, and I realize that by doing my duty manfully and cheerfully I am serving Thee, Divine Master, and my task is revealed to me as something good and sacred.

Sometimes I am sad and sick at heart, but when I think of Thee, Spirit of perfect righteousness and love, a wonderful joy comes to me, for I know that Thou art guiding me. O Lord God of Hosts, surely Thou wilt ever comfort me. Blessed be Thy Name for ever and ever. Amen.

from the Fratres Book of Prayer

833 **THE MEDICAL OATH**

Your eternal providence has appointed me to watch over the life and health of Your creatures. May the love for my art actuate me at all times; may neither avarice nor miserliness, nor the thirst for glory or for a great reputation engage my mind, for the enemies of truth and philanthropy could easily deceive me and make me forgetful of my lofty aim of doing good to Your children. May I never see in a patient anything but a fellow creature in pain. Grant me strength, time and opportunity always to correct what I have acquired, always to extend its domain, for knowledge is immense and the spirit of man can extend indefinitely to enrich itself daily with new requirements.

Today he can discover his errors of yesterday and tomorrow he may obtain new light on what he thinks himself sure of today.

O God, You have appointed me to watch over the life and death of Your creatures. Here I am, ready for my vocation.

Maimonides, 1135–1204

834
When all within is dark,
and former friends misprise;
from them I turn to you,
and find love in Your eyes.
When all within is dark,
and I my soul despise;
from me I turn to You,
and find love in Your eyes.

When all Your face is dark,
and Your just angers rise;
From You I turn to You,
and find love in Your eyes.

Israel Abrahams, based on Ibi Gabirol

835 Lord, let Your light be only for the day,
And the darkness for the night.
And let my dress, my poor humble dress
Lie quietly over my chair at night.
Let the church-bells be silent,
My neighbour Ivan not ring them at night.
Let the wind not waken the children
Out of their sleep at night.

Let the hen sleep on its roost, the horse in the stable
All through the night.
Remove the stone from the middle of the road
That the thief may not stumble at night.

Let heaven be quiet during the night,
Restrain the lightning, silence the thunder,
They should not frighten mothers giving birth
To their babies at night.

And me too protect against fire and water,
Protect my poor roof at night.
Let my dress, my poor humble dress
Lie quietly over my chair at night.

Nechum Bronze

A Selection of Prayers which are part of the Daily Service

Master of existence, and Lord of lords, we do not rely on our own good deeds but on Your great mercy as we lay our needs before You. Lord, hear! Lord, pardon! Lord, listen and act! What are we? What is our life? What is our love? What is our justice? What is our success? What is our endurance? What is our power? Lord our God, and God of our fathers, what can we say before You, for in Your presence are not the powerful as nothing, the famous as if they had never existed, the learned as if without knowledge, and the intelligent as if without insight. To You most of our actions are pointless and our daily life is shallow. Even the superiority of man over the beasts is nothing. For everything is trivial except the pure soul which must one day give its account and reckoning before the judgement seat of Your glory. 836

Cause us, our Father, to lie down in peace, and rise again to enjoy life. Spread over us the covering of Your peace, guide us with Your good counsel and save us for the sake of Your name. Be a shield about us, turning away every enemy, disease, violence, hunger and sorrow. Shelter us in the shadow of Your wings, for You are a God who guards and protects us, a ruler of mercy and compassion. Guard us when we go out and when we come in, to enjoy life and peace both now and forever, and spread over us the shelter of Your peace. Blessed are You Lord, who spreads the shelter of peace over us, over His people Israel, and over all the world. 837

838 Lord, open my lips and my mouth shall declare Your praise.

Blessed are You, Lord our God, and God of our fathers, God of Abraham, God of Isaac, and God of Jacob, the great, the mighty, and the awesome God, God beyond, generous in love and kindness, and possessing all. He remembers the good deeds of our fathers, and therefore in love brings rescue to the generations, for such is His being. The King who helps and saves and shields. Blessed are You Lord, the shield of Abraham. You, O Lord, are the endless power that renews life beyond death; You are the greatness that saves. You care for the living with love. You renew life beyond death with unending mercy. You support the falling, and heal the sick. You free prisoners, and keep faith with those who sleep in the dust. Who can perform such mighty deeds, and who can compare with You, a King who brings death and life, and renews salvation. You are faithful to renew life beyond death. Blessed are You Lord, who renews life beyond death.

839 Heal us, Lord, and we shall be healed; save us, and we shall be saved; for it is You we praise. Send relief and healing for all our diseases, our sufferings and our wounds; for You are a merciful and faithful healer. Blessed are You Lord, who heals the sick.

840 Grant us peace, goodness and blessing; life, grace and kindness; justice and mercy. Our Father, bless us all together with the light of Your presence, for in the light of Your presence You give us, Lord our God, law and life, love and kindness, justice and mercy, blessing and peace. And in Your eyes it is good to bless Your people Israel with great strength and peace. Blessed are You Lord, who blesses His people Israel with peace.

841 It is our duty to praise the Lord of all, to recognize the greatness of the creator of first things, who has chosen us from all peoples by giving us His Torah. Therefore we bend low and submit, and give thanks before the King above the kings of kings, the Holy One, blessed be He. He extends the limits of space and makes the world firm. His glory extends through the universe beyond, and the presence of His strength into farthest space. He is our God; no other exists. Our King is truth; the rest is nothing. It is written in His Torah: 'Realize this today and take it to heart—it is the Lord who is God in the heavens above and on the earth beneath; no other exists.'

Therefore, Lord our God, we put our hope in You. Soon let us witness the glory of Your power; when the worship of material things shall pass away from the earth, and prejudice and superstition shall at last be cut off; when the world will be set right by the rule of God, and all mankind shall speak out in Your name, and all the wicked of the earth shall turn to You. Then all who inhabit this world shall meet in understanding, and shall know that to You alone each one shall submit, and pledge himself in every tongue. In Your presence, Lord our God, they shall bow down and be humble, honouring the glory of Your being. All shall accept the duty of building Your kingdom, so that Your reign of goodness shall come soon and last forever. For Yours alone is the true kingdom, and only the glory of Your rule endures forever. So it is written in Your Torah:

'The Lord shall rule forever and ever.'

So it is prophesied:

'The Lord shall be as a king over all the earth. On that day the Lord shall be One, and known as One.'

THE KADDISH 842

Let us magnify and let us sanctify the great name of God in the world which He created according to His will. May His kingdom come in your lifetime, and in your days, and in the lifetime of the family of Israel— quickly and speedily may it come. Amen.

May the greatness of His being be blessed from eternity to eternity.

Let us bless and let us extol, let us tell aloud and let us raise aloft, let us set on high and let us honour, let us exalt and let us praise the Holy One—blessed be He!—though He is far beyond any blessing or song, any honour or any consolation that can be spoken of in this world. Amen.

May great peace from heaven and the gift of life be granted to us and to all the family of Israel. Amen.

May He who makes peace in the highest bring this peace upon us and upon all Israel. Amen.

A Selection of Sabbath prayers

BLESSING FOR THE SABBATH (*'Kiddush'*)

Blessed are You, Lord our God, King of the universe, who makes us holy 843
through doing His commands, and delights in us. Willingly and with love He gives us His holy Sabbath to inherit, for it recalls the act of creation. This is the first day of holy gatherings, a reminder of the exodus from

Egypt. Because You chose us to be holy among all peoples, willingly and with love You gave us Your holy Sabbath to inherit. Blessed are You Lord, who makes the Sabbath holy.

844 Lord of all creation, You have made us the masters of Your world, to tend it, to serve it, and to enjoy it. For six days we measure and we build, we count and carry the real and the imagined burdens of our task, the success we earn and the price we pay.

On this, the Sabbath day, give us rest.

For six days, if we are weary or bruised by the world, if we think ourselves giants or cause others pain, there is never a moment to pause, and know what we should really be.

On this, the Sabbath day, give us time.

For six days we are torn between our private greed and the urgent needs of others, between the foolish noises in our ears and the silent prayer of our soul.

On this, the Sabbath day, give us understanding and peace.

Help us, Lord, to carry these lessons, of rest and time, of understanding and peace, into the six days that lie ahead, to bless us in the working days of our lives. Amen.

845 Our God and God of our fathers, may our rest be pleasing to You. Make us holy by doing Your commands and let us share in the work of Your Torah. Make us content with Your goodness and let our souls know the joy of Your salvation. Purify our hearts to serve You in truth. In Your love and goodwill let us inherit Your holy Sabbath and may all Israel who seek holiness find in it their rest. Blessed are You Lord, who makes the Sabbath holy.

846 PRAYER AT SUNSET ON SATURDAY

Sovereign of the universe,
Father of mercy and forgiveness,
Grant that we begin the working days
Which are drawing nigh unto us, in peace;
Freed from all sin and transgression;
Cleansed from all iniquity, trespass and wickedness;
And clinging to the study of Thy Teaching,
And to the performance of good deeds.

JEWISH

Cause us to hear in the coming week
Tidings of joy and gladness.
May there not arise in the heart of any man envy of us.
Nor in us envy of any man.
O, our King, our God, Father of mercy,
Bless and prosper the work of our hands.

And all who cherish towards us and thy people Israel
Thoughts of good, strengthen and prosper them,
And fulfil their purpose;
But all who devise against us and thy people Israel
Plans which are not for good, O frustrate them
And make their designs of none effect;
As it is said,
Take counsel together, and it shall be brought to nought;
Speak the word, and it shall not stand;
For God is with us.

Open unto us, Father of mercies and Lord of forgiveness,
In this week and in the weeks to come,
The gates of light and blessing,
Of redemption and salvation,
Of heavenly help and rejoicing,
Of holiness and peace,
Of the study of thy Torah and of prayer.

In us also let the Scripture be fulfilled:
How beautiful upon the mountains
Are the feet of him that bringeth good tidings,
That announceth peace,
The harbinger of good tidings,
That announceth salvation;
That saith unto Zion,
Thy God reigneth! Amen.

A Selection from High Holy Day Prayers

PRAYER IN DARKNESS OF SPIRIT 847

O Merciful God, who answerest the poor,
  Answer us,
O Merciful God, who answerest the lowly in spirit,
  Answer us,
O Merciful God, who answerest the broken of heart,
  Answer us.

O Merciful God,
Answer us.
O Merciful God,
Have compassion.
O Merciful God,
Redeem.
O Merciful God,
Save.
O Merciful God, have pity upon us,
Now,
Speedily,
And at a near time.

Day of Atonement

848 God of Holiness

To You, our God, these prayers of holiness ascend.
You are the true and only King.

We declare how profound is the holiness of this day, for it arouses in us the deepest awe. Today the power of Your kingdom stirs within us. Love is the foundation of Your throne, and the spirit of truth rests upon it.

Truly You are the one who judges and tests, who probes and bears witness. You record and seal, You count and measure. You remember all that is forgotten. You open the book of memory, and it speaks for itself, for every man has signed it by his life.

The great *shofar* sounds, and a still small voice is heard. God's messengers feel the alarm. Also possessed by fear and trembling, they announce: 'Behold the Day of Judgement!' For judgement comes upon the heavens as well as the world, for neither can stand before Your judgement. This day all who enter the world pass before You like a flock of sheep. And as a shepherd gathers his flock and makes them pass beneath his staff, everything that lives passes in front of You, and You record, and count, and consider them. You set a limit to the life of every creature, and determine its destiny.

ON ROSH HASHANA [New Year] WE CONSIDER HOW JUDGEMENT IS FORMED ON YOM KIPPUR [Day of Atonement] WE CONSIDER HOW JUDGEMENT IS SEALED, for all who pass away and all who are born, for all who live and all who die, for those who complete their normal span and those who do not—who perish by fire or water, by the violence of man or beast, by hunger or thirst, by disaster, plague or execution; for those who rest and those who wander, for the secure and the tormented, for those who become poor and those who become rich, for the failures and the famous.

YET REPENTANCE AND PRAYER AND GOOD DEEDS
CAN TRANSFORM THE HARSHNESS IN OUR DESTINY.

JEWISH

PRAYER FOR ALL MANKIND 849

Our God and God of our fathers,
Reign over the whole universe in thy glory,
And in Thy splendour be exalted over all the earth.

Shine forth in the majesty of thy triumphant strength,
Over all the inhabitants of thy world,
That every form may know that Thou hast formed it,
And every creature understand that Thou hast created it,
And that all that hath breath in its nostrils may say:

The Lord God of Israel is King
And his dominion ruleth over all.

New Year Liturgy

Our God and God of our fathers, let our prayer reach You—do not turn away from our pleading. For we are not so arrogant and obstinate to claim that we are indeed righteous people and have never sinned. But we know that both we and our fathers have sinned. 850

We have abused and betrayed. We are cruel.
We have destroyed and embittered other people's lives.
We were false to ourselves.
We have gossiped about others and hated them.
We have insulted and jeered. We have killed. We have lied.
We have misled others and neglected them.
We were obstinate. We have perverted and quarrelled.
We have robbed and stolen.
We have transgressed through unkindness.
We have been both violent and weak.
We have practised extortion.
We have yielded to wrong desires, our zeal was misplaced.

We turn away from Your commandments and good judgement but it does not help us. Your justice exists whatever happens to us, for You work for truth, but we bring about evil. What can we say before You—so distant is the place where You are found? And what can we tell You—Your being is remote as the heavens? Yet You know everything, hidden and revealed. You know the mysteries of the universe and the intimate secrets of everyone alive. You probe our body's state. You see into the heart and mind. Nothing escapes You, nothing is hidden from Your gaze. Our God and God of our fathers, have mercy on us and pardon all our sins; grant atonement for all our iniquities, forgiveness for all our transgressions.

Day of Atonement

851 **MORNING LITANY**

This day wilt Thou strengthen us. Amen
This day wilt Thou bless us. Amen
This day wilt Thou uplift us. Amen
This day wilt Thou visit us for good. Amen
This day wilt Thou inscribe us for happy life. Amen
This day wilt Thou hear our cry. Amen
This day wilt Thou accept our prayer in mercy and favour. Amen
This day wilt Thou support us with Thy righteous hand. Amen

New Year

Indian

852 From the unreal lead me to the real!
From darkness lead me to light!
From death lead me to immortality!

Brihad-Aranyaka Upanishad

853 I magnify God, the Divine Fire,
the Priest, Minister of the sacrifice,
the Offerer of oblation, supreme Giver of treasure.

This and the following eleven prayers come from Raimundo Panikkar's collection *The Vedic Experience*

854 We meditate upon the glorious splendour
of the Vivifier divine.
May he himself illumine our minds!

855 May the Wind breathe healing upon us,
prolong our life-span,
and fill our hearts with comfort!

You are our father, O Wind,
our friend and our brother.
Give us life that we may live.

From that immortal treasure, O Lord,
which is hidden in your abode,
impart to us that we may live.

I am the Way, the supporter; your Lord and your witness, 856
home, refuge, and friend,
origin and dissolution, foundation and treasure-house,
imperishable seed.

On those who meditate on Me and worship
with undivided heart,
I confer attainment of what they have not,
and preserve what they have.

No devotee of mine is ever lost.
Taking refuge in Me,
lowly born, women, artisans, even servants,
reach the highest goal.

Let your mind and your heart, your offerings and worship,
to Me be devoted.
With your self thus controlled you shall strive toward Me
and to Me you shall come.

May the Lord of the clouds protect our stores, 857
piled high in our homes!

May the Lord of the clouds give us vitality in our homes,
granting goods and riches.

O generous God, Lord of thousandfold Abundance
impart to us now a share of Abundance;
may we have a share in prosperity!

From that which we fear, O Lord, make us fearless. 858
O bounteous One, assist us with your aid.
Drive far the malevolent, the foeman.

May the atmosphere we breathe
breathe fearlessness into us:
fearlessness on earth
and fearlessness in heaven!
May fearlessness guard us
behind and before!
May fearlessness surround us
above and below!

May we be without fear
of friend and foe!
May we be without fear
of the known and the unknown!
May we be without fear
by night and by day!
Let all the world be my friend!

859 O God, you are our Providence, our Father.
We are your brothers, you our Source of life.

You are called Father, caring for the humble;
supremely wise, you teach the simple wisdom.

860 O God, grant us of boons the best,
a mind to think and a smiling love,
increase of wealth, a healthy body,
speech that is winsome and days that are fair.

861 Love is the firstborn, loftier than the Gods,
the Fathers and men,
You, O Love, are the eldest of all,
altogether mighty.
To you we pay homage!

Greater than the quarters and directions, the expanses
and vistas of the sky,
you, O Love, are the eldest of all,
altogether mighty.
To you we pay homage!

Greater than all things moving and inert,
than the Ocean, O Passion,
you, O Love, are the eldest of all,
altogether mighty.
To you we pay homage!

In many a form of goodness, O Love,
you show your face.
Grant that these forms may penetrate
within our hearts.
Send elsewhere all malice!

God the Rescuer 862
God the Saviour,
almighty, whom always we joyfully adore,
powerful God,
invoked by all men,
may he, the bounteous, grant us his blessings!

You, O Lord, are the body's protector. 863
My body protect.
You, O Lord, are the giver of life.
Grant life to me.
From you, O Lord, comes brilliance of mind.
Illumine my mind.
Whatever is lacking to my being, O Lord,
supply that to me.

O Lord of the home, best finder of riches
for our children are you.
Grant to us splendour and strength,
O Master of our home.
A bounteous bestower of plenty is the God
who is Master of our herds.
Grant to us splendour and strength,
O Lord and Master.

You are the expiation for the sin of the Gods, *Svaha!* [*Amen*] 864
You are the expiation for the sin of men, *Svaha!*
You are the expiation for the sin of the Ancestors, *Svaha!*
You are the expiation for the sin of myself, *Svaha!*
You are the expiation for the sin of all. *Svaha!*

May there be peace in the higher regions; may there be peace in the firmament; may there be peace on earth. May the waters flow peacefully; may the herbs and plants grow peacefully; may all the divine powers bring unto us peace. The supreme Lord is peace. May we all be in peace, peace, and only peace; and may that peace come unto each of us. 865

Shanti [Peace]—*Shanti*—*Shanti!*

The Vedas

866 Thou my mother, and my father thou.
Thou my friend, and my teacher thou.
Thou my wisdom, and my riches thou.
Thou art all to me, O God of all gods.

Ramanuja, *c.* 14th century

867 Reveal thyself to me, reveal thyself to me.
I seek not wealth nor power, I yearn to see thee alone.
O God, I care not for renunciation or enjoyment, I yearn to see thee alone.
O God, I am neither anxious for home, nor for the forest of life;
I only yearn to see thee.
Yea I seek for nought save thee, O God, I yearn for thy vision alone; grant my prayer.

Dadu, 16th-century Hindu poet and mystic

868 O Lord give me strength that the whole world look to me with the eyes of a friend. Let us ever examine each other with the eyes of a friend.

Yayurveda

Four Sikh prayers

869 My soul hearken unto me!
Love thy Lord as the lotus loves water
Buffeted by waves its affection does not falter.
Creatures that have their being in water,
Taken out of water, die.

My soul if thou hast not such love
How wilt thou obtain release?
If the Word of the Guru is within us
We shall accumulate a store of devotion.

My soul hearken unto me!
Love thy Lord as a fish loves water.
The more the water, the greater its joy,
Greater the tranquillity of its body and mind.
Without water it cannot live one watch of the day
Only God knows the anguish of its heart.

My soul hearken unto me!
Love thy Lord as water loves milk.

It takes on the heat, boils and evaporates before the milk can suffer.
He alone unites, He alone separates
He alone bestows true greatness.

Without the Guru, love cannot be born
The dross of ego cannot be rinsed away.
He who recognizes the God within
Understands the secret of the Word and is happy.
O Nanak! there is but one gate to the Lord's mansion
And there is no other sanctuary. via Harmindar Singh

870 Having heard of Thy greatness
All say Thou art great;
How great Thou art
Shall be known only when we see Thee;
Thy worth cannot be valued
Thy praise not put into words;
Those who tried to speak of Thee were merged in Thee.
O Great Master of mine! of wisdom profound,
Of virtues a treasure!
Of Thy great apron none hath the measure.

All learned men with their loads of Vedic learning,
All evaluations put together;
Scholars, thinkers, teachers and those whom teachers teach
Could not even a sesame seed of Thy greatness gauge.
All charities and giving of alms;
All penances, all that good deeds gain;
Praises by Sidhas who perform miracles:
all, all are in vain.
Without Thy aid Siddhas could not miracles make.
None can come between us if Thou art compassionate.
Sorry is the plight of one who tries to contain in words;
Thy treasure is replete with words of praise.
Whom Thou givest the power need try no other ways.
'This truth have I beheld', Nanak says. via Harmindar Singh

871 By the grace of God's Name
May humanity find itself lifted higher and higher.
In thy dispensation O Lord,
Let there be good in all humanity.

Guru Nanak, 1489–1559, founder of Sikhism

872 O kind Father, loving Father, through Thy mercy we have spent our day in peace and happiness; grant that we may, according to Thy will, do what is right.

Give us light, give us understanding, so that we may know what pleases Thee.

We offer this prayer in Thy presence, O wonderful Lord:

Forgive us our sins. Help us in keeping ourselves pure. Bring us into the fellowship of those in whose company we may remember Thy name.

[Through Nanak] may Thy name forever be on the increase, and may all men prosper by Thy grace.

Guru Gobind Singh, 1666–1708

873 Master! for there is no one like Thee!

For thy devotees Thou dost choose the best: and though we ask for brass Thou givest gold.

The hungry Thou dost feed with good things; the thirsty go to Thee for nectar; and to the naked Thou dost give shining robes of love.

There is no one, Master, like Thee for us!

As the cow keeps by her calf, so art Thou ever with Thine own:

Thou, O gracious Lord, dost honour even humble offerings. Thy loving hand is outstretched to receive a straw, if only true love doth offer it!

All-generous! All-wise! according to Thy riches Thou dost satisfy our needs:

In the day of affliction Thou dost hasten to help us, to make suffering pleasant.

Thou art ever faithful to Thy promises.

There is no one like Thee for us, my Master!

Surdas, 15th century

874 Like the bounding stag I have sought sensual pleasures and fallen into the lake.

I am the greatest sinner among sinners, unwilling to part with even a grain of rice to the noisy crow.

Like the fly buzzing about without any rest, I seek. O, Father, tell me what to do that I may not die, and grant me Thy grace to support me.

Like the bull bearing heavy burdens, I have toiled carrying the load of my own grief.

Not knowing anything, I have roamed like the unclean animal feeding upon the refuse of the streets.
I am lower than the dog, which tires itself out with barking in uttter thoughtlessness.
Holy One, what can I do to obtain Thy grace to support me in my distress?
I have taken pride in regarding my darkness as light and my desire as the great goal.
I have wandered with the monkey of my mind in the darkness of the jungle, mistaking it for my kindred.
Oh, Thou who dwellest in the hearts of Thy saints, I have not the mind to seek the great object of life.
Father, what can I do to get Thy grace? Rule me with Thy grace.
I do not know the medicine, the jewel, the *mantra*, the knowledge, the rule and conduct of life.
I do not know the way of repentance, the power of Thy grace and the path of righteousness.
I do not know the place where I can live the controlled life, nor how to enter into the society of the wise, nor how to approach the holy place where the Lord resides.
I do not know the direction in which to go. How can I enter? Whom can I speak to? What can I do? I know not anything.
I have not abandoned the toils of caste, creed and sect.
I have not abandoned plunging into the mire of theological wrangling.
I do not know the beginning nor the end, nor how to abide in the waveless sea of Thy bliss.
I have not walked in the way of holiness, nor do I know the inward will of Him who abides in the assembly of the holy ones.
How can I enter the world of my foes? To whom can I speak?
What can I do? I know not.

Ramalinga Swami, 19th century

Dost Thou behold me perishing? 875
O haste and come, my God and King!

I die unless Thou succour bring,
O haste and come, my God and King!

To help me is a trifling thing;
Yet Thou must haste, my God and King!

O come (how Nama's clamours ring)
O haste and come, my God and King!

Namdev, *c.* 17th century

876 Thou didst ask of me love, purity and truth; but I was envious, sinful and untrue.
Show me mercy, Merciful! for if Thou refuse, no hope of deliverance have I!
Nay, my defeat I own: do with me according to Thy own good pleasure.
Pardon if Thou wilt; or if Thou wilt, seize and scourge Thy erring bride.
Alas! for Thy worship I offered not my head: what have I done!
I have not even quaffed the nectar of Thy love; nor with Thy colour dyed my heart; nor sung Thy praises with my lips:
I have achieved nothing for Thy service; regrets alone remain to mock my woe.
I followed in the wake of my desires, because I had not found my Love, my Lord: and O! there is no health in me.
My hope is stayed on Thee alone. No other can my troubled soul relieve.

Dadudayal, 17th century

877 I am unreal! My heart is unreal! My devotion is unreal! Sinner as I am, I can attain Thee if I but cry for Thee! O Sweet Lord! O Honey! O Clear Juice of the Sugar Cane! Be gracious, that I may reach Thee!

Manikka Vachakar, 10th century

878 The wrong of ignorance, the wrong of thoughtlessness,
The wrong of not having followed Thee with a melting heart,
The wrong of not having meditated upon Thee,
The wrong of not having prayed and worshipped Thee,
O Supreme Almighty, forgive me of all, all my wrongs!

Pattinatar, 10th century

879 Let me not wander in vain.
Let me not labour in vain.
Let me not mingle with the prejudiced.
Let me not leave the company of the virtuous.
Let me not fly into anger.
Let me not stray off the path of goodness.
Let me not seek for this day or for the morrow.
Give me such a wealth, O Almighty!

Pattinatar, 10th century

880 Glory unto Thee, O Source of all! O Omniscient!
Glory unto Thee, O Origin of Scriptures, O Pure Land!
Glory unto Thee, O King! O Nectar, Glory unto Thee!

Glory unto Thee, O Ocean of Eternal Bliss! Glory unto Thee!
O Lord, Thou art beyond birth and death, Glory unto Thee!
O Lord of all countries, Glory unto Thee!
Thou ever givest us redemption, Glory unto Thee!

Manikka Vachakar, 10th century

Thou art the life of the Universe; to me 881
The light of day thou art, and the dark of night:
Activity's field when I do wake and see;
In sleep my dream. Oh, Life of Life, the light
Thou art to me of day, the dark of night.
Relieve me of my vice and virtue; make
My heart void, and this heart made empty fill
With thy entirety. Thy excelling take
And make me great with it. Enfold me still,
Within thee: cover me, Protector bright,
My light of day who art, and dark of night.

C. R. Das, 19th–20th century

I am thirsting for your love, my Beloved! 882
I shall make this body a lamp, and my tender heart shall be its wick;
I shall fill it with the scented oil of my young love and burn it night and day at Your shrine, O Beloved!
For Your love I shall sacrifice all the wealth of my youth;
Your name shall be the crown of my head.
I am longing for You, O my Lord: for the season of the sowing has come; but You are not beside me.
Clouds gather on my brows and my eyes shed heavy showers.
My parents gave me to You, I have become Yours for ever; who but You can be my Lord?
This separation troubles my breast; make me Your own; make me perfect like You, O Lord of Perfection!

Mirabai, 16th century

Quiet the trees; quiet the creepers all. 883
In the sky's tranquil lap burns the sun's ray.
In my heart's temple doth the silence fall,
Worshipping Thee, Thou, Silent Majestic. Thou
Replenishest this tranquil heart. O Thou
Eternal, Absolute, with silence fill
Me and with song, in secret, silent, still.

C. R. Das, 19th–20th century

884 My spirit is sore grieved in Thy absence; come to me, O my Beloved!
I am ashamed in my inmost being when people say I am Thy bride, for have I touched Thy heart with mine?
Vain is my life! I have no taste for food: my eyes get no slumber.
I am restless within doors and without.
As water to the thirsty, so is the sight of the Lover to the bride:
Who will tell my Beloved that I am wasting away in His absence, I am pining for the assurance that He is mine?
I am dying for sight of my Lord!

Kabir, 14th century

Six prayers from Tukaram, an Indian peasant mystic, 1608–49

885 THE SENSE OF SIN

Lord, I have abandoned all for Thee,
Yet evermore desire riseth in my heart,
And maketh me forget Thy love:

Ah, save me, save me,
Save me by Thyself:

As thus I bow before Thee, Lord,
Come dwell within,
Live Thou Thy secret life in me,
And save me by Thyself.

886 MAN'S NEED OF GRACE

As a fish that is dragged from the water
Gaspeth,
So gaspeth my soul:

As one who hath buried his treasure,
And now cannot find the place,
So is my mind distraught:

As a child that hath lost his mother,
So am I troubled, my heart is seared with sore anguish:

O merciful God,
Thou knowest my need,
Come, save me, and show me Thy love.

GOD'S LOVE AND CARE 887

Of what avail this restless, hurrying activity?
This heavy weight of earthly duties?

God's purposes stand firm,
And thou, His little one,
Needest one thing alone,
Trust in His power, and will, to meet Thy need:

Thy burden resteth safe on Him,
And thou, His little one,
Mayest play securely at His side:

This is the sum and substance of it all—
God is,
God loveth thee,
God beareth all thy care.

GOD'S LIFE WITHIN 888

Take Lord, unto Thyself,
My sense of self: and let it vanish utterly:

Take, Lord, my life,
Live Thou Thy life through me:

I live no longer, Lord,
But in me now
Thou livest:

Aye, between Thee and me, my God,
There is no longer room for 'I' and 'mine'.

LOVE FOR GOD 889

Ah, Lord, the torment of this task that Thou hast laid on me
To tell the splendour of Thy love!

I sing, and sing,
Yet all the while the truth evadeth telling:

No words there are, no words,
To show Thee as Thou art:
These songs of mine are chaff,
No spark of living truth hath ever lit my lips:

Ah Lord, the torment of this task that Thou hast laid on me!

890 No deeds I've done nor thoughts I've thought;
Save as Thy servant, I am nought.

Guard me, O God, and O, control
The tumult of my restless soul.

Ah, do not, do not cast on me
The guilt of mine iniquity.

My countless sins, I Tuka, say,
Upon Thy loving heart I lay.

891 Round Thy lotus feet, O let my love be wrapt; and it matters naught where my body lie,
In city residence or forest hermitage, in rags of poverty, robes of wealth:
Teach me but to be faithful unto Thee.
Like the serpent of his gem deprived, so am I in agony without a vision of Thee, O Lord.
Let me not by praise or blame be moved: within the depths of my soul let me enshrine Thee:
And Thou wilt hold me dear, my Lord! Tulsidas, 16th century

892 There are three different paths to reach the Highest:
The path of I, the path of Thou and the path of Thou and I.
According to the first, all that is, was, or ever shall be
is I, my higher Self. In other words, I am, I was, and I
shall be for ever in Eternity.
According to the second, Thou art, O Lord, and all is Thine.
And according to the third, Thou art the Lord, and I am Thy
servant, or Thy son. Ramakrishna 1834–86

Seven prayers by Rabindranath Tagore, 1861–1941

893 This is my prayer to thee, my lord—strike, strike at the root of penury in my heart.
Give me the strength lightly to bear my joys and sorrows.
Give me the strength to make my love fruitful in service.
Give me the strength never to disown the poor or bend my knees before insolent might.
Give me the strength to raise my mind high above daily trifles.
And give me the strength to surrender my strength to thy will with love.

Where the mind is without fear and the head is held high; 894
Where knowledge is free;
Where the world has not been broken up into fragments by narrow domestic walls;
Where words come out from the depth of truth;
Where tireless striving stretches its arms towards perfection;
Where the clear stream of reason has not lost its way into the dreary desert sand of dead habit;
Where the mind is led forward by Thee into ever-widening thought and action—
Into that heaven of freedom, my Father, let my country awake.

Not for me is the love that knows no restraint, but like the foaming wine that, having burst its vessel in a moment, would run to waste. 895
Send me the love which is cool and pure, like your rain that blesses the thirsty earth and fills the homely earthen jars.
Send me the love that would soak down into the centre of being, and from there would spread like the unseen sap through the branching tree of life, giving birth to fruits and flowers.
Send me the love that keeps the heart still with the fullness of peace.

That I want thee, only thee—let my heart repeat without end. All desires that distract me, day and night, are false and empty to the core. 896
As the night keeps hidden in its gloom the petition for light, even thus in the depth of my unconsciousness rings the cry—I want thee, only thee.
As the storm still seeks its end in peace when it strikes against peace with all its might, even thus my rebellion strikes against thy love and still its cry is—I want thee, only thee.

When the heart is hard and parched up, come upon me with a shower of mercy. 897
When grace is lost from life, come with a burst of song.
When tumultuous work raises its din on all sides shutting me out from beyond, come to me, my lord of silence, with thy peace and rest.
When my beggarly heart sits crouched, shut up in a corner, break open the door, my king, and come with the ceremony of a king.
When desire blinds the mind with delusion and dust, O thou holy one, thou wakeful, come with thy light and thy thunder.

898 In the night of weariness let me give myself up to sleep without struggle, resting my trust upon thee.

Let me not force my flagging spirit into a poor preparation for thy worship.

It is thou who drawest the veil of night upon the tired eyes of the day to renew its sight in a fresher gladness of awakening.

899 Day after day, O Lord of my life, shall I stand before thee face to face? With folded hands, O Lord of all worlds, shall I stand before thee face to face?

Under thy great sky in solitude and silence, with humble heart shall I stand before thee face to face?

In this laborious world of thine, tumultuous with toil and struggle, among hurrying crowds shall I stand before thee face to face?

And when my work shall be done in this world, O King of kings, alone and speechless shall I stand before thee face to face?

900 My Lord God, my All in all, Life of my life, and Spirit of my spirit, look in mercy upon me and so fill me with thy Holy Spirit that my heart shall have no room for love of aught but thee.

I seek from thee no other gift but thyself, who art the giver of life and all its blessings. From thee I ask not for the world or its treasures, nor yet for heaven even make request, but thee alone do I desire and long for, and where thou art, there is heaven. The hunger and the thirst of this heart of mine can be satisfied only with thee who has given birth.

O Creator mine! Thou hast created my heart for thyself alone, and not for another, therefore this my heart can find no rest or ease save in thee; in thee who hast both created it and set in it this very longing for rest. Take away then from my heart all that is opposed to thee, and enter and abide and rule for ever. Amen.

Sadhu Sundar Singh, 1889–*c.* 1929

901 O Thou
who hast given me eyes
to see the light
that fills my room,
give me the inward vision
to behold thee in this place.

INDIAN

O Thou
who hast made me to feel
the morning wind upon my limbs,
help me to feel thy Presence
as I bow in worship of thee.

Chandra Devanesen, 20th century

O Hidden Life, vibrant in every atom, 902
O Hidden Light, shining in every creature,
O Hidden Love, embracing all in Oneness,
May each who feels himself as one with Thee
Know he is therefore one with every other.

Annie Besant, 1847–1933

Hear again my Word Supreme, the deepest secret of silence. 903
Because I love thee well I will speak to thee words of salvation.
Give thy mind to me, and give me thy heart and thy sacrifice, and thy adoration.
This is my Word of promise: thou shalt in truth come to me, for thou art dear to me.
Leave all things behind and come to me for thy salvation.
I will make thee free from bondage of pains. Fear no more.

Spoken by the Hindu representative at a
Commonwealth Day Observance in Westminster Abbey

Lord, make this world to last as long as possible. 904

Prayer of an 11-year-old child
on hearing of Sino-Indian border fighting

If I ask him for a gift, he will give it to me, and then I shall have to go away. But I don't want to go away. Give me no gift—give me thyself. I want to be with thee, my beloved. 905

Ascribed to the oral tradition of a hill tribe in Northern Bengal

Like an ant on a stick both ends of which are burning, I go to and fro without knowing what to do and in great despair. Like the inescapable shadow which follows me, the dead weight of sin haunts me. Graciously look upon me. Thy love is my refuge. 906

Source unknown

907 As thou hast set the moon in the sky to be the poor man's lantern, so let thy Light shine in my dark life and lighten my path; as the rice is sown in the water and brings forth grain in great abundance, so let thy word be sown in our midst that the harvest may be great; and as the banyan sends forth its branches to take root in the soil, so let thy Life take root in our lives.

Source unknown

908 O God, help me to victory over myself, for difficult to conquer is oneself, though when that is conquered, all is conquered.

Jain Scriptures

909 I have made my mind my temple,
My body I have dressed in a pilgrim's garb,
In my heart are the holy waters in which I bathe.
His Word to me is the very breath of life
I'll be born no more, ended is my strife.

My mind is engrossed in the Merciful Lord, O Mother.
Who can know of my heart's sorrow.
Except my Lord, I think of no other.

You Who are beyond reach, beyond description, beyond knowledge,

You Who are limitless,
Think of us!

You are spread over the water
And across the land.
In the spaces between the heavens and the earth
Are You,
In every heart burns bright Your light.

All teachings, all understanding, all comprehension
As You ordain all this is.

You are the shade in which we rest
And the mansions we raise.
None other beside You will I ever know, O Master,
Forever shall I sing in praise of You.

Men and beasts, all Your shelter seek,
You have to look after everyone.
This is Nanak's one prayer and only request
That he look on Your Will as the best.

via Harmindar Singh

Buddhist Spirituality

The Pāli Canon of Theravāda scriptures dates from the 6th century to the 3rd century BC, when, traditionally, the Canon was closed. Mahāyāna scriptures date from *circa* the 2nd century BC onwards.

Theravāda Buddhism

HOMAGE TO THE THREE GEMS 910

I pay homage to the Blessed One, who has attained to truth, the utterly pure, the perfectly enlightened;
Perfect in wisdom and virtue, the well-gone, the knower of the worlds;
The unequalled trainer of the open-hearted, teacher of gods and men, awakened, skilled in teaching Dhamma;
Who brought wisdom to this world, with its gods and lesser spiritual beings.
To this generation, with its thoughtful ones, rulers and people, he brought wisdom, penetrated and understood.
He brought the Dhamma, lovely at the beginning, lovely in the middle, lovely at the end.
He explained the holy life in its deepest meaning, complete and perfect, of surpassing purity.
The Blessed One I worship most highly,
To the Blessed One my head I bow down.

I pay homage to the Dhamma of the Blessed One,
Well expounded, visible to all, timeless, inviting one to come and see,
Leading onward, to be seen by each wise one for himself.
The Dhamma I worship most highly,
To the Dhamma my head I bow down.

I pay homage to the Sangha of the Blessed One's disciples,
To those who have practised well and reached the goal:
The community of saints, the well-gone,
Worthy of reverence, an incomparable field of merit for the world.
The Sangha I worship most highly,
To the Sangha my head I bow down.

911 **THE THREE REFUGES**

I take refuge in the Buddha, the perfectly enlightened one, the shower of the way.

I take refuge in the Dhamma, the teaching of the Buddha, which leads from darkness to light.

I take refuge in the Sangha, the fellowship of the Buddha's disciples, that inspires and guides.

912 **OFFERINGS TO THE BUDDHA**

Reverencing the Buddha, we offer flowers:
Flowers that today are fresh and sweetly blooming,
Flowers that tomorrow are faded and fallen.
Our bodies too, like flowers, will pass away.

Reverencing the Buddha, we offer candles.
To Him who is the Light, we offer light.
From His greater lamp a lesser lamp we light within us,
The lamp of wisdom shining within our hearts.

Reverencing the Buddha, we offer incense,
Incense whose fragrance pervades the air,
The fragrance of the perfect life, sweeter than incense,
Spreads in all directions throughout the world.

913 **TRANSFERENCE OF MERIT**

May the merit of any good deed I may have done be transferred to my virtuous Preceptors; to the teachers who so greatly benefit me; to my beloved parents and relatives; to human beings and spiritual beings; to friends and those who do not know me, or who dislike me, and may I win happiness and extricate myself from evil.

May the merits of any good deed I may have done be radiated all around with joyful ease. May craving and grasping be severed from me; may my inborn stains be purified until I am worthy of emancipation. On perishing, wherever I may be re-born, may I with upright mind, awareness, insight and vigour, lead a good life. May evil find no entrance to my heart.

The Buddha is my unexampled Teacher.
The Dhamma is my saviour unsurpassed.
The Sangha is my refuge excellent.

PANSIL (The Five Precepts) 914

I undertake the rule of training to refrain from killing or harming living beings.
I undertake the rule of training to refrain from taking what is not given.
I undertake the rule of training to refrain from licentiousness in sensual pleasures.
I undertake the rule of training to refrain from falsehood and all wrong speech.
I undertake the rule of training to refrain from drink or drugs which dull the mind.

THE TEN PERFECTIONS 915

I shall seek to develop the perfection of generosity, virtue, doing without, wisdom, energy, forbearance, truthfulness, resolution, love, serenity.

REFLECTIONS ON THE DHAMMA 916

The Dhamma-teaching, incomparably profound and minutely subtle
Is hardly met with, even in many aeons.
We can now see it, listen to it, accept and hold it.
May we completely understand the Buddha's true meaning.

The Dhamma is a teaching, profound, difficult to realize, hard to understand, tranquillizing, sweet, not to be grasped by mere logic, subtle, comprehensible only to the wise, which the Tathāgata, having realized it himself, and seen it face to face, has set forth.

The Blessed One said: 'Who sees the Dhamma sees me: who sees me sees the Dhamma.'

REFLECTIONS ON LOVE 917

The Blessed One said: 'Whatever grounds there be for good works done in this world, all of them are not worth one-sixteenth part of that love which is the heart's release. Love alone, which is the heart's release, shines and burns and flashes forth in surpassing them.'

Itivuttaka, I. 3, 7, Pāli Canon

THE ARAHANT'S [ENLIGHTENED BEING'S] MEDITATION ON LOVE 918

He beholds himself purified of all unskilled states, He beholds himself freed. When he beholds himself freed, delight is born . . . Being joyful, the mind is concentrated. He dwells suffusing one direction with a mind of loving-kindness, likewise the second direction, likewise the third, likewise the fourth: Just so, above, below, around. He dwells having suffused the world everywhere with a mind of loving-kindness, that is far-reaching, widespread, immeasurable.

Majjhima Nikāya, I. 283 Pāli Canon

919 THE PARABLE OF THE SAW

The Blessed One said: 'Though robbers or highwaymen might carve you limb from limb with a double-handed saw, yet even then whoever gives way to hatred is not a follower of my teaching. You should train yourselves like this: "Our minds will not become deranged, we will not utter evil speech, we will remain with a friendly heart, devoid of hatred: and, beginning with these people, we will develop the thought of loving-kindness."'

Majjhima Nikāya, I. 129, Pāli Canon

920 REFLECTIONS ON THE PARABLE OF THE SAW

The Blessed One said: 'There are five ways of speaking which others might use in addressing you. They might speak at a right time, or at a wrong time; according to fact, or not according to fact; gently or harshly; on what is connected with the goal, or on what is not connected with the goal; with a mind of friendliness, or with a mind full of hatred.

But if you were to reflect repeatedly on the parable of the saw, would you see any way of speech, subtle or gross, that you could not endure?'

Majjhima Nikāya, I. 129, Pāli Canon

921 MEDITATION ON LOVING ONE'S ENEMY

I will now develop the thought of loving-kindness towards the Three Noble Persons:

an admired person: I extend loving-kindess towards him.
a neutral person: I extend loving-kindness towards him.
an enemy: I extend loving-kindness towards him.

When I have ended this meditation, should I still feel resentment against my enemy, then I will rebuke myself, saying: 'Fie upon you, ruthless one! Has not the Blessed One said—' and I will repeat the parable of the saw.

Should I find that in spite of all my exertions I am not yet able to subdue my resentment, I will call to mind noble qualities in my enemy and reflect on them.

But should I still not be able to master my feelings, I will remember the words of the Buddha, 'that this person too is the owner and heir of his deeds; that he is sprung from them, and that he will have his wholesome and unwholesome deeds as his inheritance'. In this way I will overcome hatred and feel compassion.

The Venerable Nyānatiloka, Buddhist Monk, 20th century

MEDITATIONS ON THE DEFILEMENTS OF THE HEART 922

And what then are the defilements of the heart? Greed and covetousness, malevolence, anger, malice, hypocrisy, spite, envy, stinginess, deceit, treachery, obstinacy, empty-headed excitement, arrogance, pride, conceit, indolence. If a man thinks and knows that these are defilements of the heart, and strives to get rid of them, he becomes confident in the Buddha.

Majjhima Nikāya, I. 36, Pāli Canon

The purpose of the holy life does not consist in acquiring support, 923
honour or fame; nor in gaining virtue, concentration, or the eye of knowledge. But that unshakeable deliverance of the heart—that indeed is the object of the holy life: that is its essence, that is its goal.

Majjhima Nikāya, I. 204, Pāli Canon

MEDITATION ON THE PATH 924

And he strives with might and main along that path, searches it out, accustoms himself thoroughly to it; to that end does he remain steadfast in love towards all beings in all the worlds; and still to that does he direct his mind again and again until, gone far beyond the transitory, he gains the real.

Milinda's Questions, vol. 2, 1st century AD

I see the pure and the transcendent, without defect, 925
By seeing is man's salvation.

Sutta Nipāta, 788–9, Pāli Canon

THE SONG OF BLESSING 926

Not to serve the foolish, but to serve the wise,
To honour those worthy of honour—this is the highest blessing.

Much insight and education, self-control and pleasant speech,
And whatever word be well-spoken—this is the highest blessing.

Service to mother and father, the company of wife and child,
And peaceful pursuits—this is the highest blessing.

Almsgiving and righteousness, the company of kinsfolk,
Blameless works—this is the highest blessing.

To dwell in a pleasant land, with right desire in the heart,
To bear remembrance of good deeds—this is the highest blessing.

Reverence and humility, cheerfulness and gratitude, listening in due season to the Dhamma—this is the highest blessing.

Self-control and virtue, vision of the Noble Truths,
And winning to Nirvana—this is the highest blessing.

Beneath the stroke of life's changes, the mind that does not shake
But abides without grief or passion—this is the highest blessing.

On every side invincible are they who do thus,
They come to salvation—theirs is the highest blessing.

Sutta Nipāta, 258, Pāli Canon

Psalms of the Brethren

927 The burdened earth is sprinkled by the rain,
The winds blow cool, the lightnings roam on high.
Eased and allayed th' obessions of the mind,
And in my heart the spirit's mastery.

Theragāthā, Psalm 50, Pāli Canon

928 He, the great hero, counselled me, whose mind
Hath all transcended that our minds may know.
And I, hearing the Word, held close to him,
In loving pupillage and piety.
The threefold wisdom have I made my own
And all the Buddha's ordinance is done.

Theragāthā, Psalm 66, Pāli Canon

929 Aye with the good consort, with them
Who know, who understand, who see the Good.
Great is the Good, and deep and hard to see,
Subtle and delicately fine, to which
The wise and brave do penetrate, e'en they
Who strenuous live and lofty vision gain.

Theragāthā, Psalm 4, Pāli Canon

Crags where clear waters lie, a rocky world, 930
Haunted by black-faced apes and timid deer,
Where 'neath bright blossoms run the silver streams:
Such are the braes wherein my soul feels joy.
For that which brings me exquisite delight
Is not the strains of string and pipe and drum,
But when, with intellect well poised, intent,
I gain the perfect vision of the truth.

Theragāthā, Psalm 261, Pāli Canon

Psalms of the Sisters

Though I be suffering and weak, and all 931
My youthful spring be gone, yet have I come
Leaning upon my staff, and clambered up
The mountain peak.
My cloak thrown off,
My little bowl o'erturned, so sit I here
Upon the rock. And o'er my spirit sweeps
The breath of liberty! 'Tis won, 'tis won,
The Triple Lore! The Buddha's will is done!

Theragāthā, Psalm 24, Pāli Canon

Coming from noon-day rest on Vulture's Peak, 932
I saw an elephant, his bathing done,
Forth from the river issue. And a man,
Taking his goad, bade the great creature stretch
His foot: 'Give me thy foot.' The elephant
Obeyed, and to his neck the driver sprang.
I saw the untamed tamed, I saw him bent
To his master's will: and marking inwardly
I passed into the forest depths, and there
I' faith I trained and ordered all my heart.

Theragāthā, Psalm 32, Pāli Canon

What should the woman's nature signify 933
When consciousness is high and firmly set.
When knowledge rolleth ever on, when she
By insight rightly comprehends the truth?

To one for whom the question does arise:
Am I a woman [in these matters] or
Am I a man? Or what not am I then?
To such a one is Folly fit to speak. *Samyutta Nikāya*, I. 162, Pāli Canon

934 ON THE CULTIVATION OF THE HEART

Creating a thousand hands, with weapons armed, was Mara [Satan] seated on a trumpeting ferocious elephant. Him, together with his army, did the Lord of Sages subdue by means of his magnanimity.

By means of this virtue may joyous victory of heart be ours.

More violent than Mara was the indocile, obstinate demon Alavaka, who battled with the Buddha throughout the whole night. Him did the Lord of Sages subdue by means of his patience and self-control.

By means of this virtue may joyous victory of heart be ours.

Nalagiri, the mighty elephant, highly intoxicated, was raging like a forest-fire, terrible as a thunderbolt. Sprinkling him with the waters of loving-kindness, this ferocious beast did the Lord of Sages subdue.

By means of this virtue may joyous victory of heart be ours.

With uplifted sword, for a distance of three leagues, did wicked Angulimala run. Him did the Lord of Sages subdue by deep contemplation.

By means of this virtue may joyous victory of heart be ours.

Haughty Saccaka, who ignored truth, was like a banner in controversy, his vision blinded by his own disputations. Lighting the lamp of insight, him did the Lord of Sages subdue.

By means of this virtue may joyous victory of heart be ours.

The pure, radiant, majestic Baka, whose hand was bitten by the snake of tenacious opinions—him did the Lord of Sages cure with his medicine of wisdom.

By means of this virtue may joyous victory of heart be ours.

Jayamangala Gāthā

935 A BUDDHIST LITANY FOR PEACE

As we are together, praying for Peace, let us be truly with each other.

Silence

Let us pay attention to our breathing.

Silence

Let us be relaxed in our bodies and our minds.

Silence

Let us be at peace with our bodies and our minds.

Silence

Let us return to ourselves and become wholly ourselves. Let us maintain a half-smile on our faces.

Silence

Let us be aware of the source of being common to us all and to all living things.

Silence

Evoking the presence of the Great Compassion, let us fill our hearts with our own compassion—towards ourselves and towards all living beings.

Silence

Let us pray that all living beings realize that they are all brothers and sisters, all nourished from the same source of life.

Silence

Let us pray that we ourselves cease to be the cause of suffering to each other.

Silence

Let us plead with ourselves to live in a way which will not deprive other living beings of air, water, food, shelter, or the chance to live.

Silence

With humility, with awareness of the existence of life, and of the sufferings that are going on around us, let us pray for the establishment of peace in our hearts and on earth.

Amen.

The Venerable Thich Nhat Hahn in 1976

Indian Mahāyāna Buddhism

THE VOW OF THE BODHISATTVA 936

Living beings are without number: I vow to row them to the other shore. Defilements are without number: I vow to remove them from myself. The teachings are immeasurable: I vow to study and practise them. The way is very long: I vow to arrive at the end.

The Tathāgata [the One who has found the Truth] possesses abundant 937
Buddha-powers, and is able to set forth to all beings the doctrine of the knowledge of the Omniscient.
Even in this way, Sariputra, the Tathāgata by use of his knowledge and spiritual powers, teaches the Great Vehicle (the Mahāyāna).
There are those who are desirous of the Great Vehicle, and they are called Bodhisattvas (Great Beings). from the *Sutra of the Lotus of the Good Law*

938 He who clings to the Void
And neglects Compassion
Does not reach the highest stage.
But he who practises only Compassion
Does not gain release from the bondage of rebirth.
He, however, who is strong in the practice of both
He truly is the Bodhisattva. from Saraha's *Dohākosha*

939 Homage to the Perfection of Wisdom, the lovely, the holy! Avalokitesvara, the holy Lord and Bodhisattva, was moving in the deep course of the wisdom which has gone beyond.
He said . . .
'O Sariputra, a Bodhisattva, having relied on the Perfection of Wisdom, is not barricaded within his mind. Since the mind is no obstacle, he does not tremble, he has overcome what can overset, and in the end he attains Nirvana. All those who appear as Buddhas in the three periods of time wake up fully to the utmost, right and perfect enlightenment, because they have relied on the Perfection of Wisdom. Therefore, one should know the Perfection of Wisdom as the holy utterance, the great utterance, the utmost, unequalled allayer of suffering in truth: for what could go wrong? From the Perfection of Wisdom has this holy utterance come forth. It runs like this:
Gone, gone, gone beyond, gone altogether beyond.
O what an awakening, all-hail!' from the *Heart Sutra*

940 May the Buddhas deign to notice me
With minds full of pity and compassion;
Established in the ten quarters of space,
May they take away my transgression.
The sin that has been done by me
Through despising mother and father,
Through not understanding the Buddhas,
And through not understanding the good;

The sin of deed, word and thought
The threefold wickedness that I have done
All that will I confess
Standing before the Buddhas.

And those that dwell in the Rose-apple land [India],
And those in other world regions
Who do good actions,
May they approve all this. from *The Golden Splendour Sutra*

O ye sons of the Buddha! the radiant body of the Tathāgata in innumerable ways bestows benefits upon all beings. 941

It benefits us with its universal illumination which vanquishes the darkness of ignorance harboured in all beings.

It benefits us through its great compassionate heart, which saves and protects all beings.

It benefits us through its great loving heart, which delivers all beings from the misery of birth and death.

It benefits us by giving us a firm belief in the truth which cleanses all our spiritual impurities.

The innumerable rays of the light of intelligence emanate everlastingly from the spiritual body of the Tathāgata.

Whoever sees this light obtains the purest eye of the Dharma.

from *The Avatamsaka Sutra*

Five prayers from The Path of Light *by Santideva* c. AD 700

May I become a medicine for the sick and their physician, their support until sickness come not again. 942

May I become an unfailing store for the wretched, and be first to supply them with their needs.

My own self and my pleasures, my righteousness past, present and future, may I sacrifice without regard, in order to achieve the welfare of beings.

With clasped hand I entreat the perfectly 943
Enlightened Ones who stand in all the regions,
That they kindle the lamp of the Law for them
Who in their blindness fall into sorrow.

Death considers not what works be done or undone, and strikes us through our ease; 944
A sudden thunderbolt, unsure alike for the healthy and the sick.

For the sake of things unloved and things loved have I sinned these many times,
And never have I thought that I must surrender everything and depart.

Whence shall I find a kinsman, whence a friend, to protect me when the Death-god's messenger seizes me?
Righteousness alone can save me then, and for that I have not sought.

I come for refuge to the mighty Lords of the world [the Tathāgatas], the Conquerors, eager for the world's protection, who allay all fear.
To the Law [Dharma] learned by them I come with all my heart for refuge,
And to the congregation of the sons of enlightenment [the Bodhisattvas].

May my Lords take my transgression as it is:

Never more will I do this unholy work.

945 All the Buddhas in all the regions, I entreat with my hands folded;
May they light the lamp of Dharma, for those lost in suffering's wastes.

With folded hands I now petition the spiritual beings who are ready for Nirvana [the Bodhisattvas]
To stay here still for many ages, so that the world may not be struck with blindness.

Heedless of body, heedless of goods, of the merit I have gained and will gain still,
I surrender my all to promote the welfare of others.

946 He who wishes to follow the training should carefully guard his mind: he cannot follow the training if the fickle mind is unguarded.

The Truthfinder [the Buddha] has proclaimed that all dangers and fears, and the innumerable sufferings, arise only from the mind.
Wishing to move or speak, one should first consider in one's mind, and then act with skill and energy.

But if the mind is conceited, derisive, arrogant, sarcastic, insincere, deceitful, inclined to self-praise, to blaming, despising or insulting others—

then one should be like a piece of wood.

If one notices that the mind is defiled by passions, or intent on vain pursuits, one should like a valiant man curb it vigorously at all times.

If one like me, still not free from the defilements, should propose to set free from the defilements the beings extending through the ten directions of space, I would speak like a madman, ignorant of my own limitations.

Hence, without turning back, I shall always fight the defilements.

Thus resolving, I shall put forth effort to follow the training as it was proclaimed.

Tibetan Mahāyāna Buddhism

This uncreate mind of my wretched self is the brilliant Lotus-Body of the precious three in Unity . . . 947
Salutation to the Lotus-Body of blazing light, which is free from origination, destruction and change, perfect in activity, saving all living beings by means of self-existent compassion, and raining down perfections like wish-granting gems.

from *Tibetan Ceremonies*

O Avalokitesvara [Bodhisattva] of Great Compassion, whose form is 948
white and emits rays of light, for you are untouched by the defect of any imperfection: You have one face and show a smiling countenance, for you are filled with love for all beings: your eyes look downward with tranquillity, for you feel equal compassion for all . . . To Avalokitesvara, salutations and praise.

from *Tibetan Ceremonies*

Nothing save mind is conceivable. 949
Mind, when uninhibited, conceives all that comes into existence.
That which comes into existence is like the wave of an ocean.
The state of mind transcendent over all dualities brings Liberation.
Mind is beyond nature, but is experienced in bodily forms.
The realization of the One Mind constitutes the All-Deliverance.
Although sentient beings are of the Buddha-essence itself, not until they realize this can they attain Nirvana.
Seek, therefore, thine own Wisdom within thee.
It is the vast Deep.

from *The Tibetan Book of the Great Liberation*

O noble son, on this sixth day [of the Bardo, the after-death state] the 950
rays of light of the Four Wisdoms, extremely clear and fine, like the rays of the sun spun into threads, will come and shine upon thee, and strike against thy heart. O noble son, all those are the radiances of thine own intellectual faculties come to shine. They have not come from any other place. Be not attracted towards them; be not weak; be not terrified; but abide in the mode of not forming thought. In that state all the radiances will merge into thee, and Buddhahood will be obtained . . .

But, O noble son, along with the radiances of Wisdom, the impure lights of the six spheres of re-birth will also come to shine. Whereupon, be not afraid, nor be attracted to any of them: but rest in the condition of not forming thought. For if thou art one who hath not obtained the deep words of the teaching, thou wilt fear the pure radiances of Wisdom, and be attracted towards the impure objects of mortality. Act not so. Frame thy mind to think 'The compassionate radiances of Wisdom and of the Five Orders of Buddhas have come to take hold of me out of compassion. I take refuge in them.'

from *The Tibetan Book of the Dead*

Chinese Mahāyāna

951 The Perfect Way is only difficult for those who pick and choose.
Do not like, do not dislike: all will then be clear.
Make a hairbreadth of difference, and Heaven and Earth are set apart.
If you want truth to stand clear before you, never be for or against.
The struggle between 'like' and 'dislike' is the mind's worst disease.
While the deep meaning is misunderstood, it is useless to meditate on tranquility.
The Buddha-nature is featureless as space: it has no 'too little' or 'too much'.
Only because we take and reject does it seem to us not to be so . . .

from Sengts'an, The Third Patriarch 'On Trust in the Heart', AD 606

952 Every species of life has its own way of salvation,
They will not be antagonistic to one another.
If we leave our own path and seek for another way
Of salvation, we shall never find it.
If one wishes to find the true way
Right action will lead him to it directly.
He who treads the Path in earnest
Sees not the mistakes of the world.
If we find fault with others,
We ourselves are also in the wrong.
When other people are in the wrong we should ignore it:
It is wrong to find fault with others . . .
This world is the Buddha-world
Within which enlightenment may be sought.
To seek enlightenment by separating from this world
Is as foolish as to search for a rabbit's horn.

Right views are called 'transcendental',
Erroneous views are called 'worldly',
But when all views, both right and erroneous, are discarded,
Then the essence of wisdom manifests itself.

from *The Sutra of the Sixth Patriarch*, AD 668–770

Wherever I went I met words and did not understand them. 953
A lump of doubt inside the mind was like a willow-basket.
For three years, residing in the woods by the stream, I was altogether unhappy.
When unexpectedly I happened to meet the Dharmaraja [Ch'an Master] sitting on a rug.
I advanced towards him, earnestly desiring him to dissolve my doubt.
The master rose from the rug on which he sat deeply absorbed in meditation:
Then, baring his arm, he gave me a blow with his fist on my chest.
This all of a sudden exploded my lump of doubt completely in pieces.
Raising my head, I perceived for the first time that the sun was circular.
Since then I have been the happiest man in the world, with no fears, no worries.
Day in day out I pass my time in a most lively way.
Only I notice my inside filled with a sense of fullness and satisfaction.
I do not go out any longer, hither and thither, with my begging bowl for food.

Lohan Hoshang of Shōshu

Have mercy on me, O Beneficent One, I was angered for I had no shoes: 954
Then I met a man who had no feet.

Chinese saying

Japanese Mahāyāna

The Moon's the same old moon 955
The flowers exactly as they were
Yet I've become the thingness
Of all the things I see.

Satori poem by Bunan, 17th century

956 I moved across the Dharma-nature
The earth was buoyant, marvellous,
That very night, whipping its iron horse,
The void galloped into Cloud Street.

Satori poem by Getsudo, 13th century

957 Last year in a lovely temple in Hirosawa
This year among the rocks of Nikko
All's the same to me;
Clapping hands, the peaks roar at the blue.

Satori poem by Hakugai, 13th century

958 Many times the mountains have turned from green to yellow—
So much for the capricious earth!
Dust in your eyes, the triple world is narrow;
Nothing on your mind, your chair is wide enough.

from Muso, 13th century

959 Never ask your teachers to explain. But when your activity of mind is exhausted and your capacity for feeling comes to a dead end, if something should take place not unlike the cat springing upon the mouse, or the mother hen hatching her eggs, then a great flash of livingness surges up. This is the moment when the phoenix escapes from the golden net and when the crane breaks the bars of its cage.

from Hakuin, 18th century

960 Students, make your heart dwell in great loving-kindness, and whatever you may have of merit from your Zazen, offer it to all sentient beings. Avoid having personal pride, especially if you have more or better knowledge than others. Other teachings fail because each student believes only in his particular teaching. Just do Zazen innocently, without any aiming. This is the best Zazen.

from Keizan Zenji, 14th century

961 Therefore, let us work, let us develop all our possibilities; not for ourselves, but for our fellow-creatures. Let us be enlightened in our efforts, let us strive after the general welfare of humanity and indeed of all

creation. We are born here to do certain things. Life may be misery or not; it concerns us not; let us do what we have to do. We are not here wholly alone . . . we cannot save ourselves unless others are saved. We cannot advance unless the general progress is assured. We must help one another, we must abandon our vulgar egocentric ideas, we must expand ourselves so that the whole universe is identified with us, and so that our interests are those of humanity. The attainment of Nirvana and the manifestation of the Buddhist life is possible only through the denial of self-hood and through the united labour of all our brother creatures.

from Soyen Shaku, 19th century

Zazen is not a difficult task. Just free yourself from all incoming thoughts 962
and hold your mind against them like a great iron wall. Think of your own room as the whole world, and that all sentient beings are sitting there with you, as one . . .

from Soyen Shaku, 19th century

Chinese

Taoist Liturgy

The word 'Tao' is often translated as the Way, or Order of Nature, God immanent within the world. 'Tao' also means to speak, and so is sometimes translated as the *logos* or Word. Taoists, however, express their worship and aspiration more in liturgical movement and ritual than in worded prayers. The burning of incense is a central feature of Taoist worship, often preceded by purification rites and confession of sins. The high priest presides, attended by acolytes, musicians and singers. The reading of scripture, lighting of lamps, and sprinkling of charm water also form part of the worship. The following 'prayers' illustrate the spirit of Tao worship.

A DISCIPLE'S PRAYER 963

Great Absolute Hierarch, the Heavenly Master a *lu* [register] of this and this rank, connected with this and this particular divine office taking the oath to practise religion on behalf of Heaven, to assist humanity and benefit the universe. For this, today, has been set up a happy *Tsiao* for

Transmission [of the Tao], Salvation and Ordination in the Divine Office of the *Ling-pai* [Marvellous Jewel] as an offering to the High Absolute.

Seeking the protection of the Tao, sincerely trembling with great apprehension, humbly saluting, [the said disciple], having fasted and bathed, brings forward this memorial from his heart, and with a hundred salutes puts it before the jade throne of the Supreme Worthy of the Golden Hall in the Ultimate Vast Heavens to cast . . . a glance at this vulgar community and see the upright intention of his tiny servant, and bestow good fortune on his priestly work.

His servant, with the lowly sentiments of great gratefulness and utmost thankfulness, sincerely puts forward this petition.

964 A PRAYER OF WORSHIP TO SHANG TI

Thou Lord vouchsafed, O Ti, to hear us, for Thou regardest us as our Father. I, Thy child, dull and unenlightened, am unable to show forth my feelings. I thank Thee that Thou hast accepted the intimation, Honourable is Thy great name. With reverence we spread out these precious stones and silk, and, as swallows rejoicing in the spring, praise Thy abundant love.

(Prayer offered in AD 1538 by the then Emperor of the Ming dynasty, accompanied by the offering of a sceptre of blue jade, precious silks and stones, and the sacrifice of a bullock)

Later, at a second drink offering, the prayer continues:

965 All the numerous tribes of animated beings are indebted to Thy favour from the beginning. Man and creatures are emparadised, O Ti, in Thy love. All living things are indebted to Thy goodness, but who knows whence his blessings come to him. It is Thou alone, O Lord, who art the true parent of all things.

When the various offerings have been removed, the emperor continues:

966 The service of song is completed, but our poor sincerity cannot be fully expressed. Thy sovereign goodness is infinite. As a potter thou hast made all living things. Great and small are contained round [by Thee from harm]. Engraven on the heart of Thy poor servant is the sense of Thy goodness, but my feelings cannot be fully displayed. With great kindness Thou dost bear with us, and, notwithstanding our demerits, dost grant us life and prosperity.

Another prayer of the priest at his incense burning:

This day, burning incense, I seek refuge in the treasures of the Tao so that having obtained it I may gain eternal life, in perfect union with it. Now let us sing, in company with our merciful Father, as closely knit as flesh and bone . . . 967

There follows the hymn which begins: 'I rejoice in the law [of the Tao] as if it were my lover.'

Lastly comes the prayer at the *fu lu* (return to the incense burner):

O Official Envoys of the incense, Lords of the Dragon and Tiger to the left and right, Golden Girls and Boys attending upon the fragrance, and all Divine Beings, cause that at this place where I have today conducted an audience that the divine mushroom of immortality, cinnabar and jade green, may spontaneously grow from out of the golden liquor, and that the host of Perfected Immortals may meet in unity at this ardent incense-burner. May the Immortal Youths and Jade Girls of the Ten Directions attend upon and protect this incense, and transfer swiftly all that I have said before the heavenly throne of the Supremely Honoured . . . Jade Emperor Above. 968

A PRAYER SUMMONING THE EMPERORS OF THE FIVE DIRECTIONS FOR AID IN THE WAR AGAINST EVIL

Respectfully on high we invite 969
The Green Emperor of the East
Wood official who dissolves impurities;
Lord messengers, nine men.
The Red Emperor of the South,
Fire official, dissolver of impurities;
Lord messengers, three men.
The White Emperor of the West,
Metal official, dissolver of impurities;
Lord messengers, seven men.
Black Emperor of the North,
Water official, dissolver of impurities;
Lord messengers, five men.
Yellow Emperor of the Centre,
Earth official, dissolver of impurities;
Lord messengers, twelve men.

Ye who bear on high the talisman
That dissolves impurities, Lord messengers;
Ye who carry below the talisman
That dissolves impurities, Lord messengers;
Ye who this year, this month,
This day, this moment bear the talismans
To dissolve impurities, messenger troops,
Young men, Jade girls, one hundred and twenty in all,
Altogether, come down to this sacred *T'an*.

At the lighting of the new fire, the High Priest begins:

970 The Void Transcendent Mysterious Tao,
In the beginning gave birth to the One.
The One, it is primordial breath's beginning!
Therefore let us light one lamp before *Yüan-shih* [Heavenly Worthy]
To illumine the first green ancestral primordial breath's
Coming forth!

After the lighting of the lamp, he intones:

971 The Tao gave birth to the One Breath,
The One gave birth to the Two;
The Two, it is the second of the Primordial Breaths;
Therefore let us light a second lamp
In front of the Primordial Emperor [Ling-pao Heavenly Worthy],
Thereby illuminating the beginning of the
Shih-huan 'Tao' primordial breath.

Finally, after a long hymn in praise of the Heavenly Worthy, the high priest further intones:

972 The One gives birth to the Two;
The Two gives birth to the Three;
The Three, it is next in the 'series' of Primordial breaths;
Therefore let us in third place light a lamp
In front of the Primordial 'Old' One [Lao-tzu]
Thereby illuminating Primordial Old-One's coming forth.

973 SOME TAOIST BELIEFS AND WARNINGS

Vast and deep are the Nine Heavens,
Shining and wonderful the Most High;
Mysterious and ineffable the shining light of the gods.
Shining and clear is the pure Void;
Blessed is he who ascends to the regions of silence:
Eternal life comes to him who does not lose heart.
Tao is attained by the man of unconquerable will.
By stilling the emotions a man achieves perfection,
He who inhibits the life force degrades his body,
But he who holds to his essential being will flourish to old age.
With the strength of rock and the brightness of gold,
Thou wilt hide thy shadow and thy body will take its place among the immortals.
Thou wilt call upon the gods who surround thee on every side,
With the help of the Creator of heavens thou wilt quicken the divine energies;
Thou wilt fly through the Void,
And disguise thy form;
Long life and eternal youth will be thine
And thy brightness will be like that of the Heavens.
If thou breakest thine oath and betrayest these mysteries,
Ill fortune will visit all thy family.
Let each take heed not to bring these disasters upon himself.
I beg leave to sound this warning, O disciples of Tao! . . .
Mysterious and silent is the shining of the gods;
Happy is he who ascends to the Void.
By supreme meditation Tao is attained.
In order to have celestial radiance and awaken the essence;
Thy hair will recover its blackness, and thou wilt preserve thy youth.
I transmit these talismans every forty thousand years
And give thee power to transmit them every forty years.
If thou depart from them and divulge them,
If thou risest against the saints of heaven,
Thou wilt surely be plunged into the darkness of Hell!
Beware lest thou bring these evils upon thy head!
I make bold to give these warnings, O disciple.

Zoroastrian

Zarathustra or Zoroaster was a Persian prophet who lived in the late 7th and early 6th centuries BC about the same time as some of the great Hebrew prophets. He worshipped Ahura Mazda, the Supreme Being and Creator, and believed that man was made in the image of God. To him human history and personal life were a never-ending struggle between good and evil. The prayers in this section are modern prayers and show a deep love for Ahura Mazda and highly developed ethical principles. The Zoroastrians, generally known as Parsees, are a small community today, living mainly in North-West India. Some Jewish scholars think that Cyrus was a Zoroastrian.

974 A HYMN OF ZARATHUSTRA

Singing the holy hymns of Thy praise, my Lord,
Singing in the fullness of my heart,
With hands outstretched, I shall encompass Thee, O Mazda!
Kneeling in humble prayer, with Truth and the Good Mind by my side,
I shall verily reach Thy Presence, O Mazda.

975 IN PRAISE OF AHURA MAZDA

I address myself to Thee, Ahura Mazda, to Whom all worship is due. With outstretched arms and open mind and my whole heart, I greet Thee in spirit. Turn Thy countenance towards me, dear Lord, and make my face happy and radiant.

My heart yearns for Thee with a yearning which is never stilled. Thou art my most precious possession, greater and grander, lovelier and dearer by far than the life of my body and the life of my spirit. My joy is in Thee, my refuge is in Thee, my peace is in Thee. Let me live before Thee and with Thee and in Thy sight, I humbly pray.

Thou, dear Ahura Mazda, art the Master Planner, the Lord of all Creation, the Essence of Boundless Time and the very Spirit of Truth and Goodness. Thou art All-Wise and All-Knowing. Not a leaf falls but Thou knowest it. Thou tellest the number of trees and the leaves upon them. Thou knowest the number of particles of sand on any seashore and the number of stars overhead. Thou knowest me better than I know myself. Help me, then, dear Ahura Mazda, from day unto day, if it but be a little better to know Thee and understand Thee and comprehend Thee.

Thou art the Father and Lord of creation, of this corporeal world and the spritual, of all that breathes and breathes not. Thou dost dwell upon the vast expanse of the earth and Thou dost abide in the hearts of men. Thou art all-pervading, all seeing and all-knowing. Help me, Father Eternal, to feel Thy presence and influence within me and all around me during all the moments of my life.

Everything that my eyes rest upon reveals Thy glory. Thy name is written in every bit of Thy immense creation and in every human heart. I will glorify and magnify Thy name and remember Thee by day and by night. I will begin each day and retire to rest each night with Thy Name on my lips and with love for Thee in my heart. I will cultivate intimate friendship with Thy Divine Spark within me, listen to its wise counsel, and through it, endeavour to attain oneness with Thee.

FOR THE SPIRIT OF PRAYER 976

Help me, Ahura Mazda, to cultivate the habit of prayer. Enable me to know Thy will. I pray that I may conform my impulses to its demands. I will pray with concentration of my mind and I will pray with all my soul. I will pray to Thee in words of devotion with all my heart and I will pray to Thee aloud and I will pray to Thee in silence, for Thou dost hear my prayers even in thought. Thou dost read my thoughts and measure my feelings and know my aspirations. I will pray, Ahura Mazda, that prayer may lift me to Thee and make me Thine.

TRUE GREATNESS 977

Dear Ahura Mazda, men in this world claim greatness for many a varied reason but the truly great man in Thine eyes is the one who is wholly righteous, who has acquired an insight into Thy Law of Righteousness and who guides and helps others along its path. Thy gift of Divine Wisdom is vouchsafed unto them who serve Thy cause and purpose in life. The very strength and power are reserved for those who succour the poor and lowly. For righteousness is the highest blessing which Thou, Ahura Mazda, hast bestowed upon man.

IN THY IMAGE 978

In thy image let me pattern my life, O Ahura Mazda,
Let me awake with Thy name on my lips
In my eyes let me ever carry thy image
To enable me to perceive Thee,
And Thee alone, in every one else.

979 **A PRAYER OF PENITENCE**

I have sinned against Thee, Ahura Mazda, in thought and word and deed. I have denied Thee. Intolerable is the burden of my misdoings. I have been tempted to sins and iniquities. I confess my sins to Thee, I acknowledge my sins. I humble myself before Thee. Kneeling at Thy feet, I repent. I prostrate myself before Thee to do due penance for my sins. I am fallen. Thou alone can raise me and take me by the hand.

As a penitent supplicant I come back to Thee. Forgive me for what I have done amiss. Absolve me from my sins. I approach Thee with a contrite heart, for to none else can I go but Thee.

980 **TO BE A WORTHY WORKER IN THY KINGDOM**

Help me, Ahura Mazda, to be one of the righteous ones of all time. Strengthen me to work for the active propagation of righteousness and to wage a relentless and successful war against wickedness, that I may prove a worthy worker in the inauguration of Thy Kingdom of Righteousness.

981 **EACH DAY**

Dear Ahura Mazda, I begin this day with Thy holy Name. Help me to spend it usefully.

982 **AT THE CLOSE OF EACH DAY**

My thanks to Thee, dear Ahura Mazda, for a full and fruitful day.

983 **GRACE AT MEAL TIMES**

For these and all Thy blessings so kindly bestowed upon us, our most sincere thanks, dear Ahura Mazda.

984 **AT THE NEW YEAR**

As we start another year, we look back with gratitude, Ahura Mazda, for all Thy help and guidance in the year just passed. We fully appreciate that whatever we have done, achieved or acquired in the past is the outcome of Thy kindness and love, and we earnestly pray, All-wise Lord, that you continue to be with us along life's journey and show us the correct path to follow. Grant us the necessary power and strength of body, mind and spirit to overcome any obstacles on the way.

A PRAYER FOR STRENGTH 985

Grant me, dear Ahura Mazda, physical and moral strength to be Thy valiant and worthy soldier unto the end. Give me wisdom, O Wise Lord, to know and discern the truth and give me the courage to stand by truth and goodness, unfettered and undeterred by fear. Let Thy guiding hand lead me in life.

PRAYER OF HUSBAND AND WIFE AT THEIR MARRIAGE 986

We pray, dear Ahura Mazda, with our hearts full of gratitude, that you bless us, help us and guide us as we start our lives together, and always be with us and with all those whom we love and cherish.

PRAYER AT THE INVESTITURE OF A CHILD WITH THE SACRED TUNIC AND GIRDLE 987

With the investiture of this tunic and girdle, we consign this child, dear Ahura Mazda, to thy love and care. Open his eyes, dear Lord, to his daily duties and help him in their loyal performance. Fill his mind with Thy thoughts and ideals, help him to live up to them and lead him from day unto day to be near their realization, O Divine Guide of all.

Bless this child on this auspicious day of his life, dear Ahura Mazda, with Thy guidance, help and love, and give him a healthy body, a pure mind and a wide and noble outlook on life. Bless his parents, relatives and friends also with Thy kindness and love so that they can contribute substantially in moulding this child and making him a good Zoroastrian and a good citizen of the world. Let this child, his parents and all those who are with and around him in life live in goodwill, understanding and mutual love throughout their tenure on earth.

ON A BIRTHDAY 988

Every passing year makes my life shorter and time that is gone can never be recalled. Assist me, Ahura Mazda, to be wise from the experiences of the past and to move into the future with joy and hope. Guide me to make the best use of each day and each opportunity as they come so that I may glorify the name of my ancestors, my religion, my community and my country. Grant me Thy clear and pure mind, I pray, and devotion to Thee in everything I say or do. May the heavenly sun light my way for many a year to come and may Thy love and blessings always be with me in life. May I always remain worthy of Thy love!

989 **IN MEMORY OF ZARATHUSTRA**

On this sacred day of our Prophet's birth/death, our hearts go out to Thee, Ahura Mazda, in prayer and gratitude for the gift of Thy messenger, and for the truths and sublime mysteries revealed through him to us and to mankind. Countless years have passed since our holy Prophet lived and died but his message and teachings prevail, and will influence the destinies of men throughout history, as they are both divine and eternal. They are the revelations to us human beings of the purpose of Thy creation and of Thy requirements in this world.

Bless his soul, Ahura Mazda, in eternity with Thy highest blessings and let his message spread and sanctify the four corners of the earth. Help us, his faithful adherents, to emulate him in our lives and endeavour to bring his message of love and righteousness to all people. May his holy spirit guide and sustain us till the end.

990 **PRAYER AT A FUNERAL**

Today we stand before Thee, dear Ahura Mazda, with the earthly remains of . . . whom Thou hast called back to Thee. Nothing can bring warmth to this body. The light will never return to its eyes, the pulse will never throb anew and the heart will not resume its beating. None can breathe the breath of life back into it. It is now a lifeless piece of clay. The body is dead and the dead is dust.

Death has freed . . . from his material bondage. He has shed his frail earthly mansion and departed this life to live hereafter in the realm of the spirit. His earthly work is done and he has laid down his burden. From the din and dust of life's struggle, he has gone to the deathless world of peace and rest where light fades not and happiness fails not. Our beloved has died in body to live in spirit a life higher and nobler than our thoughts can measure and minds can conceive. Let him rest in everlasting peace and joy with Thee, Ahura Mazda.

991 **A FINAL ASCRIPTION**

Everything that is, that will be, the most majestic, the best, the most sublime—all, all come from Ahura of Zarathustra.

Greek and Roman Civilization

Most glorious of immortals, Zeus 992
the many-named, almighty evermore,
nature's great sovereign, ruling all by law—
hail to thee. On thee 'tis meet and right
that mortals everywhere should call.
From thee was our beginning; ours alone
of all that live and move upon the earth
the lot to bear God's likeness,
thee will I ever chant, thy power praise.
For thee this whole vast cosmos, wheeling round
the earth, obeys, and where thou leadest
it follows, ruled willingly by thee.
In thy unconquerable hands thou holdest fast,
ready prepared, that two-tiered flaming blast,
the ever-living thunderbolt:
nature's own stroke brings all things to their end.
By it thou guidest aright the sense instinct
which spreads through all things, mingled even
with stars in heaven, the great and the small—
who art King supreme for evermore.
Nought upon earth is wrought in thy despite, O God,
nor in the ethereal sphere aloft which ever winds
about its pole, nor in the sea—save only what
the wicked work, in their strange madness.
Yet even so thou knowest to make the crooked straight,
prune all excess, give order to the orderless;
for unto thee the unloved still is lovely—
and thus in one all things are harmonized,
the evil with the good, that so one Word
should be in all things everlastingly.
One word—which evermore the wicked flee.
Ill-fated, hungering to possess the good,
they have no vision of God's universal law,
nor will they hear; though if obedient in mind
they might obtain a noble life, true wealth.
Instead, they rush unthinking after ill:
some with a shameless zeal for fame,
others pursuing gain, disorderly;
still others folly, or pleasures of the flesh.

But evils are their lot, and other times
bring other harvests, all unsought—
for all their great desire, its opposite.
But Zeus, thou giver of every gift,
who dwellest within the dark clouds, wielding still
the flashing stroke of lightning, save, we pray,
thy children from this boundless misery.
Scatter, O Father, the darkness from their souls,
grant them to find true understanding—
on which relying thou justly rulest all—
while we, thus honoured, in turn will honour thee,
hymning thy works forever, as is meet
for mortals, while no greater right
belongs even to the gods than evermore
justly to praise the universal law.

Cleanthes (*c.* 330–*c.* 231 BC), Hymn to Zeus

993 Do with me henceforth as thou wilt. I am of one mind with thee, I am thine. I decline nothing that seems good to thee. Send me whither thou wilt. Clothe me as thou wilt. Will thou that I take office or live a private life, remain at home or go into exile, be poor or rich, I will defend thy purpose with me in respect of all these.

Epictetus, *c.* AD 60–140

994 Hear me, ye Gods, who hold firmly the tiller of sacred wisdom, ye who kindle within men's souls a fire that flames upward and draws them toward heavenly things, when they have abandoned their dark caves and have cleansed themselves by your holy mysteries. Hear me, ye Saviours, ye great ones, and from holy scriptures may the sacred light shine forth upon me and scatter the shadows, so that I may rightly understand both the eternal God and mortal men; so that no daemon may harm me, and drag my soul downward beneath the stream of forgetfulness, and thus ever hold me back, remote from the blessed ones—my soul, tossed about by the vast horrifying waves of Becoming, threatening ever to sweep it down to unplumbed depths of destruction—and let no torturing pain entangle me in the deceitful snares of life. Hear me then, ye Gods, who are leaders of enlightened wisdom, and while I toil up the path that leads on high reveal to me the hidden truth contained in the sacred words.

Proclus, *c.* AD 411–85

Arise, shine, thou greatest of the gods, thou blessed one, 995
crowned with flame,
Image of God, the begetter of all, thou guiding star of souls.
Hear me, and cleanse me from all the defilements of sin.
Accept my bitter tears and pleading. The horrid stain
remove from me, and keep far from me the penalty I deserve,
and make mild the stern eye of all-seeing Diké.

Proclus (*c.* AD 411–85), Hymn to Helios

From the confusing tumult of a Becoming, do thou lead me steadily, upward and onward, a wandering soul, to the holy light. 996

Proclus (*c.* AD 411–85), Hymn to the Muses

PRAYER TO RE-HAR-AKHTI 997

Do not punish me for my numerous sins, for I am one who knows not his own self, I am a man without sense. I spend the day following after my own mouth, like a cow after grass.

Holy is God, the Father of all, 998
Holy is God, whose will is accomplished by his own powers,
Holy is God, who wills to be known and is known by his own,
Holy art thou, who by Logos has constituted all existing things,
Holy art thou, of whom all nature was born as the image,
Holy art thou, whom nature has not formed,
Holy art thou, who art more mighty than all power,
Holy art thou, who art greater than all eminence,
Holy art thou, who art superior to all praises.

from the Hermetic Corpus,
a collection of prayers covering 1st to 3rd centuries AD

May I be no man's enemy, and may I be the friend of that which is eternal and abides. May I never quarrel with those nearest to me; and if I do, may I be reconciled quickly. May I never devise evil against any man; if any devise evil against me, may I escape uninjured and without the need of hurting him. May I love, seek, and attain only that which is good. May I wish for all men's happiness and envy none. May I never rejoice in the ill-fortune of one who has wronged me . . . When I have done or said what is wrong, may I never wait for the rebuke of others, but always rebuke myself until I make amends . . . May I win no victory that harms 999 either me or my opponent . . . May I reconcile friends who are wroth with one another. May I, to the extent of my power, give all needful help to my friends and to all who are in want. May I never fail a friend in danger. When visiting those in grief may I be able by gentle and healing words to soften their pain . . . May I respect myself . . . May I always keep tame that which rages within me . . . May I accustom myself to be gentle, and never be angry with people because of circumstances. May I never discuss who is wicked and what wicked things he has done, but know good men and follow in their footsteps.

Eusebius, a late Ionic Platonist

1000 Demeter, thou who feedest all my thought,
grant me but worthiness to worship thee.

Aristophanes, *c.* 448–*c.* 380 BC

1001 O beloved Pan, and all the other deities of this place, grant that I may become beautiful in my soul within, and that all my external possessions may be in harmony with my inner man. May I consider the wise man to be rich, and may I have such riches as only a man of self-restraint can bear or endure.

Plato (*c.* 427–348 BC), Socrates' prayer at the end of the *Phaedrus*

1002 O blessed queen of heaven . . . thou who illumines all the cities of earth with your feminine light, thou who nourishes all the seeds of the world with your damp heat, giving your changing light according to the wanderings, near or far, of the sun: by whatever name or form it is right to call upon you, I pray that you end my great labour and misery, raise up my fallen hopes, and deliver me from the wretched fortune which for long has pursued me. Grant peace and rest, if so it please you, to my adversities . . .

Apuleius, *fl. c.* AD 155

1003 Bestow, O God, this grace on us, that in the school of suffering we should learn self-conquest, and through sorrow, even if it be against our will, learn self-control.

Aeschylus, 525–456 BC

1004 Lord of Lords, grant us the good whether we pray for it or not, but evil keep from us, even though we pray for it.

Plato (*c.* 427–348 BC), Alcibiades

O God, grant that no word may fall from us, against our will, unfit for the present need. 1005

Pericles, *c.* 500–429 BC

O God, our sins are many; strip us of them like a garment. 1006

A Sumerian poet, *c.* 2000 BC

Open my eyes, O God, to behold true beauty, divine beauty, pure and unalloyed, not clogged with the pollutions of mortality and the vanities of human life. So beholding beauty with the eyes of the mind I shall be enabled to bring forth, not images of beauty but realities, and nourishing true virtue may become thy friend and attain to immortality, O God of truth and beauty. 1007

based on a passage from Plato's *Symposium*

Muslim

PRAISES AND PRAYERS FROM THE QUR'ĀN

In the Name of God, the merciful Lord of mercy. 1008
Praise be to God, the Lord of all being,
the merciful Lord of mercy,
Master of the day of judgement.
You alone we serve: to You alone we come for aid.
Guide us in the straight path,
the path of those whom You have blessed,
not of those against whom there is displeasure,
nor of those who go astray.

Surah 1: The Fātihah, or Opener

Our Lord, we have wronged our own souls. If you forgive us not and withhold Your mercy from us, we are altogether lost. 1009

Surah 7. 23

O my Lord, let security and truth precede and follow me wherever You lead me. Let authority and succour from Your presence be with me. 1010

Surah 17. 80: prayer given to Muhammad

1011 Our Lord, do not lay it to our charge when we forget and are at fault. Our Lord, do not have us bear as You did our predecessors. Our Lord, what would be more than we could carry do not lay upon us. Rather, grant us pardon, forgive us and have mercy on us. For You are our Sovereign. Be our aid against those who hold You in contempt.

Surah 2. 286: prayer commended to Muslims

1012 Our Lord, give us mercy from Your presence and let a right wisdom order the situation in which we find ourselves.

Surah 18. 10: prayer of the Seven Sleepers of Ephesus

1013 In God's Name be the course and the mooring: let us embark.

Surah 11. 41: prayer of Noah

1014 He called upon his Lord, saying: Things overwhelm me: come to my help.

Surah 54. 10: prayer of Noah

1015 Our Lord, in You we have trusted. To you we have turned in penitence. Yours is our final destiny. Lord, ever mighty and wise, let us give no occasion to the enemies of truth, but forgive us.

Surah 60. 4–5: prayer of Abraham and his father

1016 O my Lord, enlarge my heart and facilitate the task I face. Take the stammer from my speech that they may understand what I tell them.

Surah 20. 25–8: prayer of Moses

1017 Our Lord, we have believed. Forgive us and have mercy on us. Yours is the utmost mercy.

Surah 23. 109

1018 Our Lord, forgive us and our brethren who in the faith came on ahead of us. Let there be in our hearts no rancour against believers. Our Lord, surely You are gentle and merciful.

Surah 50. 10: prayer of emigrants to Medina coming from Mecca

MUSLIM

O my Lord, make me minded to thankfulness for Your grace towards me 1019
and my parents, and to deeds of righteousness acceptable to You. Make me, in turn, blessed in my children. To You have I come in penitence. Here I am as one of the surrendered.

Surah 46. 15

Grant us, O Lord, in our wives and in our offspring the joy of our eyes. 1020
Make us patterns of reverence for all who would revere You.

Surah 25. 74

PRAYER DURING THE DAYS OF THE ISLAMIC FAST OF RAMADĀN 1021

O my God, the petitioners stand before Thy gate, and the needy seek refuge in Thy courts. The ship of the wretched stands on the shore of the ocean of Thy grace and goodness, seeking passage into the presence of Thy mercy and compassion. O my God, if in this blessed month Thou forgivest only those whose fasting and performance is right, who will take the part of the transgressor who defaults, when he perishes in the sea of his sins and transgression? O my God, if Thou art merciful only towards the obedient, who will take the part of the rebellious? If Thou receivest only those who have done well, then what of those who have fallen short?

O my God, those who fast have surely gained, the faithful doers have victory and the sincere are delivered. But we, Thy guilty servants, have mercy upon us out of Thy compassion. Liberate us from damnation by Thy pardon; forgive us our trespasses with the rest of the believers, men and women, through Thy mercy, O Thou most faithful.

from Mukhtasar Ad'iyat Ramadān

Whatever share of this world Thou dost bestow on me, bestow it on 1022
Thine enemies, and whatever share of the next world Thou dost give me, give it to Thy friends. Thou art enough for me!

Rābi'ah of Basra

O Lord, grant us to love Thee: 1023
grant that we may love those that love Thee;
grant that we may do the deeds that win Thy love.

Muhammad

1024 **FROM THE PRAYERS OF MUSLIMS TO MECCA**

O God, truly Thou hast said in Thy descended Book: 'Call unto Me and I will answer you.' We have called unto Thee, O Lord. So forgive us in accordance with Thy command. For Thou dost not break Thy promise. Our Lord, truly we have heard the caller calling us to faith: 'Believe in your Lord.' And, O Lord, we have believed. Then forgive us our trespasses and rid of us of our iniquities. Let us be called hence with the righteous.

O our Lord, bring us what Thou hast promised by Thy messenger. Let us not be confounded on the day of resurrection. Verily Thou dost not break promise.

O our Lord, in Thee have we trusted, to Thee have we returned. Thine is the ordering. Forgive us, O Lord, and our brethren who have preceded us in the faith. Let there be no rancour towards those who have believed. For Thou art kindly and merciful. O Lord, make our light complete and forgive us. Thou art powerful over all things.

O God, I take refuge with Thee from unbelief and poverty. I take refuge with Thy good pleasure from Thine anger and with Thy pardoning grace from Thy retribution. I take refuge with Thee from Thee. I do not withhold the praise of Thee. Thou art as Thine own praise sayeth.

from Manāsik al-Hajj wa Ad'iyat al-Tawāf

1025 O God, I ask of Thee a perfect faith, a sincere assurance, a reverent heart, a remembering tongue, a good conduct of commendation, and a true repentance, repentance before death, rest at death, and forgiveness and mercy after death, clemency at the reckoning, victory in paradise and escape from the fire, by thy mercy, O mighty One, O Forgiver, Lord increase me in knowledge and join me unto good.

Prayer used in the 7th circuit of the Ka'bah in Mecca

1026 Doubly at thy service, O God.
Amen. Lord.

Another prayer used by the pilgrim at Mecca

1027 It is glory enough for me
That I should be Your servant
It is grace enough for me
That You should be my Lord.

Arabic prayer

MUSLIM

All that we ought to have thought and have not thought, 1028
All that we ought to have said, and have not said,
All that we ought to have done, and have not done;

All that we ought not to have thought, and yet have thought,
All that we ought not to have spoken, and yet have spoken,
All that we ought not to have done, and yet have done;
For thoughts, words and works, pray we, O God, for forgiveness.

from an ancient Persian prayer

Intention is a vital part of each statutory act of Muslim obligation, whether confession of faith, worship, almsgiving, fasting or pilgrimage. The intention must be affirmed as a prelude to the action and a focus of sincerity. Here is part of the 'Intention' of the Great Pilgrimage. 1029

O God, I wish to perform the pilgrimage. Make it a ready thing to me and accept it from me. I have intended the pilgrimage: I have consecrated myself for it unto the Most High. To Him be strength and majesty.

Here am I before Thee, O Lord, here before Thee. Before Thee who hast no partner with Thyself. Here at Thy service, praise and grace are Thine, and power.

There is no partner with Thee.

O God I consecrate to Thee my [shaven] hair, my body and all my members . . . Thereby I seek Thy gracious countenance, O Thou Lord of the worlds.

from Manāsik al-Hajj wa Ad'iyat al-Tawāf

O Lord, I beseech Thee, make me thankful for the grace Thou hast bestowed upon me . . . And these Thy servants who are gathered to slay me, in zeal for Thy religion and in desire to win Thy favour, pardon them and have mercy upon them. For verily if Thou hadst revealed to them what Thou hast revealed to me, they would not have done what they have done. If Thou hadst hidden from me what Thou hast hidden from them, I should not have suffered this tribulation. Glory to Thee in whatsoever Thou doest and glory to Thee in all that Thou willest. 1030

Prayer of Al-Hallāj al-Mansūr, one of the greatest of the Sufi mystics, crucified for 'heresy' in 922 by his fellow Muslims in Baghdad

O my God, let my transgressions be hidden in the overshadowing of Your mercy and all my blemishes under the cover of Your tender compassion. 1031

O my God, has the fugitive slave any to whom he may return save his Lord? For who but He will protect him from his Master's anger?

O my God, if grief for wrongdoing be repentance then truly, by Your might I swear, I am among the penitent. If seeking forgiveness for sin be like laying down a load, then such a seeker am I.

O my God, by Your power that rules me, forgive me indeed and pardon me in Your condescension toward me. You who know me through and through, befriend me. For it is You, Lord, who have opened a door of pardon for Your Servants—penitence is its name. You have said: 'Repent before God in sincerity.' What excuse shall be his who neglects to enter that door when You have opened it? O my God, shameful though Your servant's evil be, the pardon which is Yours will make it good.

O my God, I am not the first to transgress and find Your pardon nor to resist Your good purpose and yet to experience Your gracious dealing. 'Tis You who respond to the cry of the distressful, unveiling the source of their distress, knowing every secret thing. Great is Your righteousness. Relying on Your goodness and grace, I have sought Your mercy: for Your loving mercies' sake I have made my plea. Hear my cry. Let me not be disappointed of my hope in You. Accept my penitence and put away my sin, O Lord of the uttermost mercy.

Zain al-'Àbidin, great-grandson of the Prophet Muhammad

1032 O my God, only Your kindness and compassion can restore my brokenness. My poverty nothing can enrich but Your gentleness and goodness. Only grace from You can calm my agitation. My frailty Your power alone can strengthen. My longings nothing but Your bounty will ever satisfy. My destitution will be made good by Your wealth alone. My need of You none other can fulfil. Only Your mercy can gladden my distress. My sorrow of heart only Your compassion will relieve. My thirst will not be slaked unless You reach to me, nor my fearing soul be set at rest except I find You.

Only the sight of Your countenance of grace can meet my deepest yearning. It is only in drawing near to You that rest is truly mine. Your Spirit only will restore my broken heart: my sickness only Your medicine will heal. It is only when You are near that my grief is lifted. Only Your pardon laves my wound. The stain in my heart only Your forgiveness can take away. It is Your command alone that stills the whispering in my bosom.

For You are the utmost hope of the hopeful, the goal of the quest of the questioners, the ultimate that petitioners seek, the crown of all that men desire. You are the guardian of the well-doers, the security of the timorous, the treasure of the deprived, the wealth of the destitute, the succour of those who cry for help, the satisfier of the needs of the poor and the wretched. On You I call, O most merciful and gracious. I humble myself before You and make my plea. My cry and my yearning are that You would refresh me with Your kindly Spirit and continue to me Your good pleasure.

For here am I standing at the door of Your goodness, setting myself in the way of Your righteousness to breathe upon me, and taking firm hold of the strong rope—the sure grasp of one who clings to You. O my God, do mercy to Your unworthy servant, whose word is faint, whose deed is scant. In Your rich forbearance do well to him. Shelter him under Your shade, You who are Lord of all the merciful, kingly, glorious and mighty.

Munājāt Zain al-'Àbidìn

Praise be to God, ever unmatched in power and greatness, from and to 1033
eternity. His is the glory that excels, He is the One, the only, the ever living, the all sufficient, the disposer who brings into being and makes to pass away, the arbiter of will who decrees and decides and determines, in whose power resides all lapsing and receding and approaching in the world of things.

He is the listener, the observer, who hides us in His grace, who surveys all that we conceal or that we disclose, the King who bestows and withholds, who brings together and who puts apart, who enriches and makes poor. He is the One who speaks the eternal word from of old which never perishes and never fades.

from Tahārat al-Qulūb

O Thou who hast clothed my heart with love as a robe of honour, mortal 1034
time shall never wear that garment thin. Journeying and staying, Thou art ever my recompense, following after me whenever my grasp loses hold of the rope of faith.

O my God, wilt Thou destroy with fire the face that worshipped Thee, the tongue that has spoken thanks to Thee, the heart that knew Thee? I fear, after Thou hast guided my steps and preserved me with Thy grace and ample patience, lest Thou shouldest divest my heart of the robe of Thy protection and even take from me what I was minded to expect from Thee.

O my God, how wilt Thou cut off from Thy service one who has found his perfect satisfaction in the grace of Thy presence.

Joy art Thou of the hearts that have Thee as their one goal, Thou who art all desired, all forbearing.

Renew our fear toward Thee, if it has grown weak and feeble.

from Tahārat al-Qulūb

1035 O Lord God, truly we worship Thee of our ready will. It is against our will that we transgress. We fear Thee in that Thou art great: we hope in Thee because Thou art God. We fear Thee because we are Thy servants. Our love is Thine: our fears are ours. Have mercy upon us for the sake of the grace of Thy Kingliness and the frailty of us Thy subjects.

O my God, how wilt Thou requite our transgressions, poor as we are and cast upon Thee? At Thy door we have waited, kneeling. Incline toward us with all who are loved of Thee.

It suffices us for strength that we should be Your servants. It suffices us for honour that Thou shouldest be our Lord.

O my God, in that Thou lovest Thou art ours: in that Thou art loved make us Thine.

O my God, all joy outside Thee flees away: all pre-occupation save with Thee is vain. To be happy in Thee is to be happy indeed: to be happy apart from Thee is delusion.

O my God, my whole plea is my need: my whole case is my lack of one.

from Tahārat al-Qulūb

1036 O God, I fear Thee not because
I dread the wrath to come: for how
can such affright, when never was
A Friend more excellent than Thou?

Thou knowest well the heart's design,
The secret purpose of the mind,
And I adore Thee, light divine,
Lest lesser lights should make me blind.

Abū-l-Husain al-Nūrī

1037 Liturgical, or ritual, prayer in Islam (known as *Salāt*) follows a prescribed pattern of word and action. The bodily postures express in a 'sacramental' way the sense of the praise and prayer that accompany them. There are slight variations according to the time of day but the language of a single *rak'ah*, or sequence, within the prayer rite is as follows:

God is greater. Glory be to Thee, O God, and praise. Blessed is Thy Name and transcendent Thy majesty. There is no god but Thee.

I turn my face to Him who gave being to the heavens and the earth in true devotion. Not for me the fellowship of false worship. Truly my worship and my oblation, my living and my dying, are God's alone, the Lord of all being. For there is no god beside Him. So is it laid upon me as one who is surrendered.

O God, King Thou art, there is no god beside Thee. Thou art my Lord and I am Thy servant. I have been in the wrong: my ill-doing I acknowledge. Forgive me all my transgressions. For only from Thee is there forgiveness for evil done. Guide me as only Thou art able into the finest quality of living and by the power that is Thine alone turn me right away from evil ways.

I seek refuge with God from the Satan we repudiate.

God is greater. Glory to my Lord the great.

(Here follows the Fātihah, or Opening Surah of the Qur'ān: see Qur'ān prayers, p. 329.)

God listens to him who praises. Our Lord, to Thee be the praise. God is greater. Glory to my Lord, the most high.

Forgive me, O God, and have mercy on me, guide me and restore me, nourish, refresh and stablish me. God is greater.

To God are due acts of praise and liturgies of worship and deeds of good.

O Prophet, peace be on you and the mercy of God and His blessing, and on us and on all true servants of God be peace.

My witness is that there is no god but God and that Muhammad is His servant and messenger.

Peace be on you [*plural*] and God's mercy. (Said twice, turning the head first to right and then to left in salutation on the faith-community.)

Some of the richest treasures of Islamic piety are to be found in the manuals of prayer, known as *Awrād wa Ahzāb*, of the great Orders of Sufi mystics. These 'Prayer Books' were collections of the famous founders and masters bequeathed to the generations of their disciples and circulating in endless reprints through the bazaars and markets, as well as the mosque precincts, of Islam. One of the most famous is that of Ahmad al-Tijānī. 1038

O my God, my unworthiness is clear enough to You. The state I'm in is not concealed from You. My request is that I might draw near to You, that I might have Your directive. Guide me then to Yourself by Your own light. Make me to stand in the truth of servanthood within Your hands.

My prayer to You is through the hiddenness of Your gentleness, the gentleness of Your way of dealing, through the very beauty of Your elusiveness, through the greatness of Your might and the utter secret of Your power, by all that is untold in Your transcendence.

I have taken Your Name for my citadel and pleaded the intercession of Your messenger Muhammad—the blessing and peace of God be upon him.

O my God, draw me to Yourself, You my Lord, my Master. Nurture me, that I may pass away from myself into You. Let me not be ambushed in myself, hindered and held in the world of sense. Make me pure in word and deed.

O God, You who clothe the hearts of those who understand in the light that is divine where angels cannot lift their heads, so overwhelming is the omnipotent glory, You have said in the decree of Your mighty Book and in Your words from eternity: 'Call upon Me and I will hear you and answer.' O God, answer us, for what we have remembered and what we have forgotten. Hear our cry of Your grace. Amen, Amen, Amen, You who say to anything: 'Be' and it is.

from Ahmad al-Tijānī

'God is the light of the heavens and the earth. The likeness of His light is as a niche where a lamp burns—the lamp in a glass and the glass, as it were, a star for brilliance. The lamp is kindled from a blessed tree, an olive neither of the east nor the west, the oil of which is almost incandescent of itself without the touch of fire. Light upon light. God guides to His light whom He wills.'

Qur'ān, Surah 24. 35

1039 'Alī, cousin and son-in-law of Muhammad, and the fourth Caliph of Islam, is second only to the Prophet in the veneration of Shī'ah Muslims. There are many prayers attributed to him in tradition.

O God, I seek refuge with Thee, lest I be like a servant who repented before Thee unworthily, though he had knowledge of Thy mysteries, and returned back to his transgression and his sin. Make this my penitence such that I do not need after it yet another penitence, again to put away its sequel and to abide securely.

O my God, I acknowledge my ignorance before Thee and have nought but my ill-doing wherewith to come before Thee. In Thy patience take me into the shelter of Thy mercy and hide me graciously in the curtain of Thy pardon.

O my God, I repent before Thee of all that is in the thoughts of my heart, the sight of my eyes, the words of my tongue, that contravenes Thy will or falls away from Thy love . . .

O God, have mercy upon me, lonely as I am. Under Thy hand and in awe of Thee, my heart is anguished and for very fear of Thee my frame is troubled. My transgressions, O God, have brought me near to requital in the loss of Thee. Were I to keep silent none would speak for me and were I to try to intercede I have no leave or means . . .

Spread Thy mercy to take me wholly in and hide me in the glory of Thy veil. Do with me as greatness would with a worthless servant who cried and was granted mercy or as one rich in wealth who heard a poor man's plea and refreshed him. For, O my God, I have no defender from Thee: let Thy might be my defence and let Thy goodness be my intercessor. My sins have made me afraid: let Thy pardon set me at rest.

translated from a written Arabic text

Rahmān Bāba was a Pathan poet and saint who lived in the Peshawar Valley in the seventeenth century. He wrote exquisite Pashto verses and ghazals in the tradition of the great Muslim Persian poet, Hāfiz of Shiraz. Among them is the following with the translater's title 'Credo'. 1040

What a marvellous creator is my Lord:
All authority is subject to my Lord.

All the holy ones of old you may recall,
Unsurpassed in excellence is still my Lord.

Nothing does He need or want from anyone,
Seeking favours none should reckon with my Lord.

Out of nothing He created everything,
He sustains and nourishes it all, my Lord.

Like an artist He perfectly formed all things.
Yet He hearkens to all that man would speak, my Lord.

Of the unimagined in this time and space
Very essence, very fragrance is my Lord.

Of all structures in this world and in the next
Peerless architect and builder is my Lord.

All the pages not yet written He has read,
Perfect knowledge of all secrets has my Lord.

Be it hidden, manifest, or half obscured,
Cognizant of any matter is my Lord . . .

Lest His oneness be considered poverty
In His unity abundant is my Lord.

Fellowship with anyone they do not need
Who have found a lasting friendship with my Lord.

Why should I go anywhere in search of Him?
Right beside me in my cottage is my Lord.

He is never liable to change, Rahmān,
In eternity remains unchanged my Lord.

Rahmān Bāba

1041 God made this universe from love
For Him to be the Father of.
There cannot be
Another such as He.

What duty more exquisite is
Than loving with a love like His?
A better task
No one could ever ask.

Rahmān Bāba

1042 No matter where I turn my head
In village or in desert
Deep silence has engulfed the dead
And they have left no message.

Which way they disappeared, God knows,
And what has them befallen,
For I can find no news of those
Who from the cliff have fallen.

From here where do you go to stay?
What kind of dwelling is it?
Tell me, O travellers who pay
To this serai a visit.

O you who in God's favour stand
And hold the key to worship,
O blessed teachers, take my hand
And lead me to God's doorstep.

I know there is account with God
For all, that now is hidden,
Rahmān is trembling at the thought
Of what may there be written.

Rahmān Bāba

1043 Constantly revolving
Worldly things and norms
Ever are dissolving
Into other forms.

All too many troubles
Has a life so brief,
If impatience doubles
Triple will your grief.

People, when they bargain
Can, if they so like,
Cut the profit margin
Make it give and take.

Though the world so many
Beauties can present
Saw Rahmān not any
Beauty like his friend.

Rahmān Bāba

O God, whose mercies are unnumbered, whose command none can resist, whose light is never extinguished and whose compassion cannot be hid, Thou who for Moses opened up the waters and for Jesus raised the dead to life (peace be on each of them) and for Abraham cooled the fire and preserved him safe, send down blessing upon our master Muhammad and give me joy of my business and a safe issue. 1044

O God, in the shining light of the splendour of the veils of Thy throne, I repair me from my enemies and take my shelter in the strength of Thy power from all who would deceive me.

from Al-Fuyūdāt al-Rabbāniyyah, of Muhammad Sa'id al-Qādiri

O God, let our tongues be refreshed with the remembrance of Thee, our souls obedient to Thy command, our hearts filled with the knowledge of Thee, our spirits sanctified with the vision of Thee, and our secret selves graced by nearness to Thee. 1045

In this world of Thine provide for us in simple austerity that in Thy presence the fullness may be ours. For all authority is Thine.

O God, no heart is at rest except close to Thee, no servant lives except by Thy gentleness and kindly grace. There is no continuing to be unless Thy decree be so. O Thou who in tenderness hast graced the righteous and the blessed in their access to Thy presence so that salvation is theirs and the knowledge of Thy mysteries, O my Lord, what door shall I seek out unless it be Thine? to whose court shall I repair if not to Thine?

from Al-Fuyūdāt al-Rabbāniyyah

Reflective prayer in the poetry of Jalāl al-Dīn Rūmī most famous of Persian mystical poets and spiritual masters in the thirteenth century. 1046

Do you seek no more of Him than to name His Name?

We are the flute: our music is all Thine.

The sun of the soul sets not and has no yesterday.

Love is the astrolabe of God's mysteries.

If the sun that illumines the world were to draw nearer,
The world would be consumed.

God has chosen me to be His house.

If thou takest umbrage at every rub
How wilt thou become a polished mirror?

O God, show us all things in this house of deception:
Show them all as they really are.

Through love the stake becomes a throne,
Through love the king becomes a slave.
Our soul, the breath of our praise, steals away
Little by little from the prison of this world . . .
Our breaths soar up with choice words, as a gift from us
To the abode of everlastingness.
Then comes to us the recompense of our praise,
A recompense manifold from God the merciful.
Then He causes us to seek more good words, so that
His servant may win more of His mercy.
Verily the source of our delight in prayer
Is the divine Love which without rest
Draws the soul home.

from the Mathnawī of Jalāl al-Dīn Rūmī

1047 Muhammad Iqbāl (1875–1938), jurist, philosopher and poet, was one of the most influential minds in this century in Islam. He is held in high honour in Pakistan as its most creative leader, though he died nine years before it came into being. The following is from *The Secrets of the Self*, his most celebrated poem.

O Thou that art as the soul in the body of the universe,
Thou art our soul, and art ever fleeing from us.
Thou breathest music into life's flute:
Life envies death, when death is for Thy sake.
Once more bring comfort to our sad hearts:
Once more dwell in our breasts:
Once more demand from us the sacrifice of name and fame.
Strengthen our weak love,
We are often complaining of destiny.
Thou art of great price and we have nought.
Hide not Thy fair face from the empty-handed . . .
Give us the sleepless eye and the passionate heart.

Muhammad Kāmil Husain of Cairo (1902–77) published in 1954 a remarkable study of the arrest and suffering of Jesus and what he saw as the significance of Good Friday for the Muslim. Translated in 1959 into English (*City of Wrong*), it studies the dilemma of Jesus' disciples after Gethsemane and the chapter concerned ends as follows: 1048

They called upon God in these words:

O God, Thou hast been gracious unto men and hast bestowed conscience upon them. It is a spirit from Thee. What it enjoins and what it prohibits are alike Thine. Whoever obeys it obeys Thee: he who flouts it flouts Thee. Thou hast left to us the obeying of it. Keep our doings within the bounds of conscience.

O God, do not let us be so encumbered with the things of this world that we transgress the bounds of conscience.

O God, so inspire men that they follow no other guidance. Teach them not to override it for any alternative however impressive and to set up no idols to be worshipped or esteemed as good, to its exclusion . . .

O God, guide those who preside over human affairs that they establish no order that will oblige men to transgress conscience and that they do not inflict on others wrongs that are immediate and concrete for the sake of something supposedly and ultimately good for society. For this is the origin of man's tragic trouble and the source of the evil within him.

O God, Thou hast endowed conscience with no material force to compel men's reluctant obedience. So give them inwardly a spiritual compulsion in which they will follow it out of choice and delight. This will eliminate wrong: the wiping out of evil and injustice will strengthen the faith of men and will guide them into the right path.

O God, give me light in my heart and light in my tongue and light in my hearing and light in my sight and light in my feeling and light in all my body and light before me and light behind me. Give me, I pray Thee, light on my right hand and light on my left hand and light above me and light beneath me, O Lord, increase light within me and give me light and illuminate me. 1049

ascribed to Muhammad

Our Father in heaven, may Your name be sanctified; Your commandment stretches over heaven and earth, may Your compassion come upon earth as it is in heaven. Forgive us our sin and wrongdoings, You the Lord of all good things; cause Your mercy to descend upon us, Your healing upon this sickness, and it will be healed. 1050

Hadith al-Ruqya

1051 I thank You Lord for knowing
me better than I know myself,
And for letting me know myself
better than others know me.
Make me, I ask You then, better
than they suppose,
And forgive me for what they
do not know.

Abū Bakr—the father-in-law of Muhammad

1052 O Lord, may the end of my life be the best of it; may my closing acts be my best acts, and may the best of my days be the day when I shall meet Thee.

A closing Muslim prayer

Bahá'í

The Bahá'í faith began in 1844 when a young Persian by the name of the Báb (the Gate) proclaimed that the Lord of the Age was soon to appear and that his own mission was to prepare the world for his coming. In 1863 Bahá'u'lláh (the Glory of God) declared himself to be the 'Promised One' foretold by the Báb. In the Bahá'í faith there is no priesthood or clergy and, although devotional gatherings form an essential feature of community life, prayer is individual rather than congregational and there is no liturgy. Among the many prayers revealed by Bahá'u'lláh are three alternative obligatory prayers to be recited daily, from which the believer is free to choose. The shortest one consists of a single verse which is to be recited at midday. The medium is to be recited three times a day, in the morning, at noon, and in the evening. The long prayer is to be recited once in every twenty-four hours. The believer is free to choose any one of those three prayers, but is under the obligation to recite one of them, and in accordance with any specific directions with which each is accompanied. The long prayer, selected for this anthology, is characteristic of Bahá'í faith and devotion.

1053 (To be recited once in twenty-four hours)

Whoso wisheth to recite this prayer, let him stand up and turn unto God, and, as he standeth in his place, let him gaze to the right and to the left, as if awaiting the mercy of his Lord, the Most Merciful, the Compassionate. Then let him say:

O Thou Who art the Lord of all names and the Maker of the Heavens! I beseech Thee by them Who are the Day-Springs of Thine invisible Essence, the Most Exalted, the All-Glorious, to make of my prayer a fire that will burn away the veils which have shut me out from Thy beauty, and a light that will lead me unto the ocean of Thy Presence.

Raising his hands in supplication towards God:

O Thou the Desire of the world and the Beloved of the nations! Thou seest me turning toward Thee, and rid of all attachment to any one save Thee, and clinging to Thy cord, through whose movement the whole creation hath been stirred up. I am Thy servant, O my Lord, and the son of Thy servant. Behold me standing ready to do Thy will and Thy desire, and wishing naught else except Thy good pleasure. I implore Thee by the Ocean of Thy mercy and the Day-Star of Thy grace to do with Thy servant as Thou willest and pleasest . . . By Thy Most Great Name, O Thou Lord of all nations! I have desired only what Thou didst desire, and love only what Thou dost love.

Kneeling, and bowing the forehead to the ground:

Exalted art Thou above the description of any one save Thyself, and the comprehension of aught else except Thee.

Then standing:

Make my prayer, O my Lord, a fountain of living waters whereby I may live as long as Thy sovereignty endureth, and may make mention of Thee in every world of Thy worlds.

Let him again raise his hands in supplication, and say:

O Thou in separation from Whom hearts and souls have melted, and by the fire of Whose love the whole world hath been set aflame! I implore Thee by Thy Name through which Thou hast subdued the whole creation, not to withhold from me that which is with Thee, O Thou Who rulest over all men! . . . Thine is the authority to command whatsoever Thou willest. I bear witness that Thou art to be praised in Thy doings, and to be obeyed in Thy behests, and to remain unconstrained in Thy bidding.

Raising the hands, and repeating three times the Greatest Name, All-Glorious, then bending down with hands resting on the knees:

Thou seest, O my God, how my spirit hath been stirred up within my limbs and members, in its longing to worship Thee, and in its yearning to remember Thee and extol Thee; how it testifieth to that whereunto the Tongue of Thy Commandment hath testified in the kingdom of Thine utterance and the heaven of Thy knowledge. I love, in this state, O my Lord, to beg of Thee all that is with Thee, that I may demonstrate my poverty, and magnify Thy bounty and Thy riches, and may declare my powerlessness, and manifest Thy power and Thy might.

Standing and raising the hands twice in supplication:

There is no God but Thee, the Almighty, the All-Bountiful. There is no God but Thee, the Ordainer, both in the beginning and in the end. O God, my God! Thy forgiveness hath emboldened me, and Thy call hath awakened me, and Thy grace hath raised me up and led me unto Thee . . . Thine is the command at all times, O Thou Who art the Lord of all names; and mine is resignation and willing submission to Thy will, O Creator of the heavens!

Let him then raise his hands thrice, and say:

GREATER is God than every great one!

Kneeling and bowing the forehead to the ground:

Too high art Thou for the praise of those who are nigh unto Thee to ascend unto the heaven of Thy nearness, or for the birds of the hearts of them who are devoted to Thee to attain to the door of Thy gate. I testify that Thou hast been sanctified above all attributes and holy above all names. No God is there but Thee, the Most Exalted, the All-Glorious.

Then sitting:

I testify unto that whereunto have testified all created things, and the Concourse on high, and those who dwell in the all-highest Paradise, and beyond them the Tongue of Grandeur itself from the all-glorious Horizon, that Thou art God, that there is no God but Thee, and that He Who hath been manifested is the Hidden Mystery. . . . I testify that it is He Whose name hath been set down by the Pen of the Most High, and Who hath been mentioned in the Books of God, the Lord of the Throne on high and of earth below.

Standing erect:

O Lord of all being and Possessor of all things visible and invisible! Thou dost perceive my tears and the sighs I utter, and hearest my groaning, and my wailing, and the lamentation of my heart. By Thy might! My trespasses have kept me back from drawing nigh unto Thee; and my sins have held me far from the court of Thy holiness. Thy love, O my Lord, hath enriched me, and separation from Thee hath destroyed me, and remoteness from Thee hath consumed me. I entreat Thee by Thy footsteps in this wilderness, and by the words 'Here am I, Here am I', which Thy chosen ones have uttered in this immensity, and by the breaths of Thy Revelation, and the gentle winds of the Dawn of Thy Manifestation, to ordain that I may gaze on Thy beauty and observe whatsoever is in Thy book.

Repeating the Greatest Name thrice, and bending down with hands resting on the knees:

Praise be to Thee, O my God, that Thou hast aided me to remember Thee and to praise Thee, and hast made known unto me Him Who is the Day-Spring of Thy signs, and hast caused me to bow down before Thy Lordship, and humble myself before Thy Godhead, and to acknowledge that which hath been uttered by the Tongue of Thy grandeur.

Rising:

O God, my God! My back is bowed by the burden of my sins, and my heedlessness hath destroyed me. Whenever I ponder my evil doings and Thy benevolence, my heart melteth within me, and my blood boileth in my veins. By Thy Beauty, O Thou the Desire of the World! I blush to lift up my face to Thee, and my longing hands are ashamed to stretch forth toward the heaven of Thy bounty . . . O Lord of all being, O King of the seen and the unseen!

Repeating the Greatest Name thrice, and kneeling with forehead to the ground:

Praise be unto Thee, O our God, that Thou hast sent down unto us that which draweth us nigh unto Thee, and supplieth us with every good thing sent down by Thee in Thy Books and Thy Scriptures. Protect us, we beseech Thee, O my Lord, from the hosts of idle fancies and vain imaginations. Thou, in truth, art the Mighty, the All-Knowing.

Raising the head and sitting:

I testify, O my God, to that whereunto Thy chosen Ones have testified, and acknowledge that which those who dwell in the all-highest Paradise and those who have circled round Thy mighty Throne have acknowledged. The kingdoms of earth and heaven are Thine, O Lord of the worlds.

PRAYERS FROM OTHER TRADITIONS OF FAITH

Primal

Prayers of African Religions

1054 **GOD THE CREATOR**

In the time when God created all things, he created the sun.
And the sun is born and dies and comes again.
He created the moon,
And the moon is born and dies and comes again.
He created the stars,
And the stars are born and die and come again.
He created man.
And man is born and dies and comes not again.

Dinka, Sudan

1055 **AT THE NEW MOON**

May you be for us a moon of joy and happiness. Let the young become strong and the grown man maintain his strength, the pregnant woman be delivered and the woman who has given birth suckle her child. Let the stranger come to the end of his journey and those who remain at home dwell safely in their houses. Let the flocks that go to feed in the pastures return happily. May you be a moon of harvest and of calves. May you be a moon of restoration and of good health.

Meusa, Ethiopia

1056 **AT A SACRIFICE FOR RAIN**

We make this sacrifice in order to have rain.
If thou hearest our prayer, grant us rain.
Thou art our Father, everyone is here to ask rain of thee.
We are wrong-doers.
If one of us engages in strife today,
If one of us sheds blood, we will not have rain.
Thou art our Father. Grant us rain.
The earth is dry, our families are ruined.
Thou art our Father. Grant us rain.

Giur, Sudan

PRAYER FOR CHILDREN 1057

You elders, Okango, Olapa [and other names],
Today we give you your food,
Give us health and wealth,
Let all bad things go with the setting sun,
Let them go afar.
Spirits, our homestead is now silent:
Give our women children,
We like to hear the cries of children.

Adhola, Uganda

Lord, why have you given me a body which does not function like that of other women? Why have you made me a curse among my kindred? Who shall look after me in my old age? Who shall bury me when I am dead? Shall my name be forgotten after I am buried and my compound be turned into a desolate waste? These are the questions that worry me Lord; but in my anxiety I have forgotten the good things you have done for me. Thank you Lord for the gift of a healthy body, for a good and sympathetic husband; and above all thank you for making me a Christian. In my need for a child, my friends have tempted me, my relations have tempted me—either to turn to pagan worship or to break your law of purity—not because they want to lead me astray, but because they love me and would like to see me with an issue of my own. In my difficult moment do not permit me to fall into sin or to lose my faith, for my soul is more important to you than ten sons. 1058

Christian prayer of a childless African woman

DEDICATING A BABY 1059

To thee, the Creator, to thee, the Powerful,
I offer this fresh bud,
New fruit of the ancient tree.
Thou art the master, we thy children.
To thee, the Creator, to thee, the Powerful,
Khmvoum [God], Khmvoum,
I offer this new plant.

Pygmies, Zaire

LITANY FOR A SICK CHILD 1060

Mother: O spirits of the past, this little one I hold is my child: she is your child also, therefore be gracious unto her.

Women (*chanting*): She has come into a world of trouble; sickness is in the world, and cold and pain: the pain you knew: the sickness with which you were familiar.

Mother: Let her sleep in peace, for there is healing in sleep: let none among you be angry with me or with my child.

Women: Let her grow: let her become strong: let her become full-grown: then will she offer such a sacrifice to you that will delight your hearts.

Aro, Sierra Leone

1061 BLESSING A NEW HOUSE

May the person who is going to live in this house have many children, may he be rich; may he be honest to people and good to the poor; may he not suffer from disease or any other kind of trouble; may he be safe all these years.

Nyola, Kenya

1062 PRAYER OF A HUNGRY MAN

God of our fathers, I lie down without food,
I lie down hungry,
Although others have eaten and lie down full.
Even if it be but a polecat, or a little rock rabbit,
Give me and I shall be grateful!
I cry to God, Father of my ancestors.

Baralong, S. Africa

1063 INCANTATION OVER A NEW SWORD

If the owner of this meets with an enemy, may you go straight and kill your adversary; but if you are launched at one who has no evil in his heart, may you miss him and pass on either side without entering his body.

S. Africa

1064 A BUSHMAN'S PRAYER

Father-Creator, Provider-from-of-old, Ancient-of-days—fresh-born from the womb of night are we. In the first dawning of the new day draw we nigh unto thee. Forlorn are the eyes till they've seen the Chief.

S. Africa

EVENING PRAYER 1065

Now that evening has fallen,
To God, the Creator, I will turn in prayer,
Knowing that he will help me.
I know the Father will help me.

Dinka, Sudan

PRAYER TO THE LIVING DEAD 1066

O good and innocent dead, hear us: hear us, you guiding, all-knowing ancestors, you are neither blind nor deaf to this life we live: you did yourselves once share it. Help us therefore for the sake of our devotion, and for our good.

Mende, Sierra Leone

READINESS TO DO GOD'S WILL 1067

O my Father, Great Elder,
I have no words to thank you,
But with your deep wisdom
I am sure that you can see
How I value your glorious gifts.
O my Father, when I look upon your greatness,
I am confounded with awe.
O Great Elder,
Ruler of all things earthly and heavenly,
I am your warrior,
Ready to act in accordance with your will.

Kikuyu, Kenya

Grandfather, 1068
Look at our brokenness.
We know that in all creation
Only the human family
Has strayed from the Sacred Way.
We know that we are the ones
who are divided
And we are the ones
Who must come back together
To walk in the Sacred Way.

Grandfather,
Sacred One,
Teach us love, compassion, and honour
That we may heal the earth
And heal each other.

Ojibway people of Canada

1069 THREE SIOUX INDIAN PRAYERS

Ho! Great Spirit, Grandfather, you have made everything and are in everything. You sustain everything, guide everything, provide everything and protect everything because everything belongs to you. I am weak, poor and lowly, nevertheless help me to care in appreciation and gratitude to you and for everything. I love the stars, the sun and the moon and I thank you for our beautiful mother the earth whose many breasts nourish the fish, the fowls and the animals too. May I never deceive mother earth, may I never deceive other people, may I never deceive myself, and above all may I never deceive you.

Bishop Vine Deloria

1070 Great Spirit! You did reveal your loving concern to our forefathers so that they called you the Great, Holy and Mysterious One—Wakantanka, the Creator and Sustainer of all.

In your Love, you gave us Mother Earth; the wonders of Heaven and the beauty of Nature for our enjoyment, where all men could live in Peace, as brothers of your Creation!

For centuries our people walked in beauty before you! For this rich Heritage, help us to be eternally grateful!

Because you are ever a Great, Eternal and Living Spirit, in due time, you chose to send your Son among us that all people might know your continued love and concern.

Guide us in our days, help each of us as your Children to be proud of our Great Heritage, to know and to be who we are, and to share with others, becoming one humanity within your Everlasting Love, as the many colours come together to form the rainbow in the sky.

Finally, Gracious Father, give us new visions of your Will and help each one of us to have a share in each other's accomplishments.

All this, we ask through Him
Who came not to destroy but to make all things new,
Your Son, our Lord. Amen.

Bishop Harold Stephen Jones

Oh Great Spirit, help me never to judge another until I have walked two weeks in his moccasins. 1071

CHORDS OF PRAISE 1072

I shall sing a song of praise to God:
Strike the chords upon the drum.
God who gives us all good things—
Strike the chords upon the drum—
Wives, and wealth, and wisdom.
Strike the chords upon the drum.

Baluba, Zaire

Japanese

A PRAYER FOR THE PROTECTION OF THE DEITIES WHICH GUARD THE GATES OF THE IMPERIAL PALACE 1073

I humbly speak your names:
Kusi-iha-mato,
Toyo-iha-mato-no-mikoto,
Because you dwell massively embedded like sacred massed rocks
In the inner and outer gates of the four quarters,
Because if from the four quarters and the four corners
There should come the unfriendly and unruly deity called Ame-no-maga-tu-hi,
You are not bewitched and do not speak consent to his evil words—
If he goes from above,
You guard above,
If he goes from below,
You guard below,
And lie in wait to protect
And to drive away
And to repulse him with words;
Because you open the gates in the morning
And close the gates in the evening;
You enquire and know the names
Of those who go in and those who go out;
And if there be any fault or error,
In the manner of Kamu-naho-bi and Oho-naho-bi [the rectifying deities]
You behold it rectified and hear it rectified,
And cause [the court attendants] to serve tranquilly and peacefully.

Therefore [I speak] your names:
Toyo-iha-mato-no-mikoto and
Kusi-iha-mato-no-mikoto
And fulfil your praises. Thus I humbly speak.

1074 A PRAYER OF THE HIGH PRIEST OF THE GRAND SHRINE OF ISE

All of you *kamu-nusi-be*[1] and *mono-imi*,[2] hear the heavenly ritual, the solemn ritual words
Which I humbly speak in the solemn presence of
Ama-terasi-masu-sume-oho-mi-kami,[3]
Whose praises are fulfilled,
With the great shrine-posts firmly rooted
And the cross-beams of the roof soaring high towards the High Heavenly Plain,
On the upper reaches of the Isuzu river
At Udi in Waterahi. Thus I speak.
By the solemn command of the Emperor,
[I pray] that you make his life a long life,
Prospering [his reign] as an abundant reign,
Eternal and unmoving as the sacred massed rocks,
That you favour also the princes which are born,
That you [protect] long and tranquilly
The various officials,
As well as even the common people of the lands of the four quarters of the kingdom,
And that you cause to flourish in abundance
The five grains which they harvest.
With this prayer [I offer]
The tribute threads habitually presented by the people of the Kamube[4]
Established in the three counties and in the various lands and various places,
And the great wine and the great first fruits prepared in ritual purity,
Placing these in abundance like a long mountain range.
I, the great Nakatomi,[5] abiding concealed behind the solemn *tama-gusi*[6]

[1] Persons responsible for performing the ceremony of worship.
[2] Virgins serving the Sun Goddess at Ise.
[3] The Sun Goddess worshipped at the Grand Shrine.
[4] Groups of peasantry attached to certain lands the income of which was devoted to the support of a shrine.
[5] The member of the family who officiated at the ritual functions.
[6] A sacred implement held by the officiant.

On the seventeenth day of the sixth month of this year,
Do humbly speak your praises as the morning sun rises in effulgent glory.
Hear me, all of you *kamu-nusi-be* and *mono-imi*. Thus I speak.

These two Shinto prayers are taken from *Norito*, a collection of Ancient Japanese ritual prayers, compiled by Donald Philippi

With gratitude and hope we recognize 1075
That all the sacred Shinto shrines we prize
Are but reflections of Celestial Light
Bestowed on humble earth by Heavenly skies.

Ittoen—The Garden of One Light

Have us born anew and let us possess our being through the Providence of Light. 1076
Teach us to respect the essence of all religions, and lead us to learn the One Ultimate Truth.
Have us perform our duties out of penitence, and do all our work out of gratitude.
Enable us to perfect the way of our living by completely submitting to the Laws of Nature.
Grant that we may return to the land of 'perfumed nook of heavenly flowers' [Nirvana] and so tread in the Paradise of Light.

Odoru Shukyo—Dancing Religion

Almighty God of the Universe, source of deities, 1077
Peace of the whole world, peace of the whole world,
When all the people comply with the will of God,
Give us a Heavenly Kingdom, which is pleasant to live in.

Tenrikyo—Religion of Heavenly Wisdom

Sweep away all evils and save us, O God our parent! 1078

Sekaikyusei Kyo—Religion of World Messianity

Hallelujah, hallelujah, the welcome time of the descent and appearance of God the Messiah has come . . . 1079
What a transport of joy there is to meet the voice of the Great Messiah, as he descends from the clouds of glory.

1080 Miroku, the Great God, comes forth . . .
Miroku, the Great God, from of old has planted the heaven upon earth,
Miroku, the Great God, even as comes a thief, has secretly been born below.
Leaving behind the highly exalted throne, to bring salvation
Miroku has been born below.

Three Shinto Prayers

1081 A MORNING PRAYER

I reverently speak in the presence of the Great Parent God: I pray that this day, the whole day, as a child of God, I may not be taken hold of by my own desire, but show forth the divine glory by living a life of creativeness, which shows forth the true individual.

1082 AN EVENING PRAYER

I reverently speak in the presence of the Great Parent God: I give Thee grateful thanks that Thou hast enabled me to live this day, the whole day, in obedience to the excellent spirit of Thy ways.

1083 A PRAYER FOR REPENTANCE

I reverently speak in the presence of the Great Parent God: Grant Thy grace that in the matter of this egotism (. . .) receiving Thy regulation, no matter what it may be, I may ever keep and perform it and effect a change of mind.

1084 ADVICE TO MONKS

Those who enter the gate of Buddhism should first of all cherish a firm faith in the dignity and respectability of monkhood, for it is the path leading them away from poverty and humbleness. Its dignity is that of the sonship of the Dharmaraja of the triple world; no princely dignity which extends only over a limited area of the earth compares with it. Its respectability is that of the fatherhood of all sentient beings; no parental respectability belonging only to the head of a little family group equals it. When the monk finds himself in this position of dignity and respectability, living in the rock-cave of the Dharma where he enjoys the greatest happiness of a spiritual life, under the blissful protection of all the guardian gods of the Triple Treasure, is there any form of happiness that can surpass his?

The shaven head and the dyed garment are the noble symbols of

Bodhisattvahood; the temple-buildings with all their ornamental fixtures are the honorific emblems of Buddhist virtue. They have nothing to do with mere decorative effects.

That the monk, now taking on himself these forms of dignity and respectability, is the recipient of all kinds of offerings from his followers; that he is quietly allowed to pursue his study of the Truth, not troubling himself with worldly labours and occupations—this is indeed due to the loving thoughts of Buddhas and Fathers. If the monk fails in this life to cross the stream of birth-and-death, when does he expect to requite all the kindly feelings bestowed upon him by his predecessors? We are ever liable as time goes on to miss opportunities; let the monk, therefore, be always on the watch not to pass his days idly.

The one path leading up to the highest peak is the mysterious orthodox line of transmission established by Buddhas and Fathers, and to walk along this road is the essence of appreciating what they have done for us. When the monk fails to discipline himself along this road, he thereby departs from the dignity and respectability of monkhood, laying himself down in the slums of poverty and misery. As I grow older I feel this to be my greatest regret, and, O monks, I have never been tired day and night of giving you strong admonitions on this point. Now, on the eve of my departure, my heart lingers with you, and my sincerest prayer is that you are never found lacking in the virtue of the monkish dignity and respectability, and that you ever be mindful of what properly belongs to monkhood. Pray, pray, be mindful of this, O monks!

The last words of the monk Dai-o Kokushi, from the translation of Dr D. T. Suzuki, the great authority on Zen

THE FOUR GREAT VOWS OF ZEN BUDDHISTS IN JAPAN 1085

However innumerable beings are, I vow to save them;
However inexhaustible the passions are, I vow to extinguish them;
However immeasurable the Dharmas are, I vow to master them;
However incomparable the Buddha-truth is, I vow to attain it.

Recited in the Zen sect after every meditation

THE ETERNAL MYSTERY 1086

O Supreme Eternal Reality, Pure Being beyond all subject and object, beyond all cerebral thinking, Unconceptualizable and Unverbalizable, dwelling in silence, I long to experience the nameless, incomprehensible being, as Moses did at the Burning Bush, burning and never consumed, a higher consciousness, before which I can only bow in silence and reverence, glimpsing indescribable suchness and eternal mystery.

Anon. A Christian tries to pray in Zen terms

VII

PRAYERS TOWARDS THE UNITY OF MANKIND

The last section of the anthology includes prayers from all sources, reflecting a common concern for the sorrows and hopes of mankind, the movement towards human unity, and the consummation beyond this life, the completion of creation planned by the Creator God, both for the individual and the whole universe.

Great art thou, O Lord, and greatly to be praised. Great is thy power and thy wisdom is infinite. And thee would man praise, man but a particle of thy creation, man that bears about him his mortality, the witness of his sin, that thou resistest the proud. Yet would man praise thee, he but a particle of thy creation. Thou awakenest us to delight in thy praise. For thou madest us for thyself and our heart is restless until it rest in thee. Grant me, Lord, to know and understand which is first—to call on thee or to praise thee? And again, to know thee or to call on thee? For who can call on thee, not knowing thee? For he that knoweth thee not may call on thee as other than thou art. Or is it better that we call on thee that we may know thee? 1087

St Augustine, 354–430

What can I say to you, my God? Shall I collect together all the words that praise your holy Name? Shall I give you all the names of this world, you, the Unnameable? Shall I call you 'God of my life, meaning of my existence, hallowing of my acts, my journey's end, bitterness of my bitter hours, home of my loneliness, you my most treasured happiness'? Shall I say: Creator, Sustainer, Pardoner, Near One, Distant One, Incomprehensible One, God both of flowers and stars, God of the gentle wind and of terrible battles, Wisdom, Power, Loyalty and Truthfulness, Eternity and Infinity, you the All-merciful, you the Just One, you Love itself? 1088

Karl Rahner, 1904–84

Thou, O Lord, by thine operations didst bring to light the everlasting fabric of the universe, and didst create the world of men. From generation to generation thou art faithful, righteous in judgement, wondrous in might and majesty. Wisely hast thou created, prudently hast 1089 thou established, all things that are. To look around is to see thy goodness; to trust in thee is to know thy loving kindness. O most Merciful, O most Pitiful, absolve us from our sins and offences, from our errors and our shortcomings. Lay not every sin of thy servants and handmaidens to their charge, but make us clean with the cleansing of thy truth. Direct thou our goings, till we walk in holiness of heart and our works are good and pleasing in thy sight and in the sight of our rulers. Yea, Lord, show the light of thy countenance in peace upon us for our good; and so shall we be sheltered by thy mighty hand, and saved from all wrongdoing by thine outstretched arm. Deliver us from such as hate us without a cause; to us and all mankind grant peace and concord, even as thou didst to our forefathers when they called devoutly upon thee in faith and truth; and make us to be obedient both to thine own almighty and glorious Name and to all who have the rule and governance over us upon earth.

St Clement of Rome, *c.* 100

1090 O Thou Source of all spiritual truth and treasure! O Thou Fountainhead of love and grace! Thou Nameless One of many Names, sought for in many religions: what treasures we shall have when we tell one another of what we have found! Infinite in the mystery of thy Being, unfathomable in the depths of thy wisdom, perfect in thy Goodness, untraceable in thy Eternity, wonderful in thy created universe, active within the spirit of man, transfiguring the lives of sages, prophets, saints, humble loving souls, near at hand in presence, immediate in call, working out thy loving purpose in human history! How shall I speak of Thee, Thou All of Truth, Goodness, Love and Peace, Thou Heart of Compassion and Tenderness, Thou Goal of every seeker—O Thou! O That! O All!

G.A.

1091 Praise be to him who alone is to be praised. Praise him for his grace and favour. Praise him for his power and goodness. Praise him whose knowledge encompasses all things.

O God, grant me light in my heart and light in my tomb, light in my hearing and light in my seeing, light in my flesh, light in my blood and light in my bones.

Light before me, light behind me, light to right of me, light to left of me, light above me, light beneath me.

O God, increase my light and give me the greatest light of all. Of thy mercy grant me light, O thou most merciful.

Abu Hamid Al-Ghazali, 450–505

O God, 1092
Let us be united;
Let us speak in harmony;
Let our minds apprehend alike.
Common be our prayer;
Common be the end of our assembly;
Common be our resolution;
Common be our deliberations.
Alike be our feelings;
Unified be our hearts;
Common be our intentions;
Perfect be our unity.

Hindu Scriptures (*Rig-Veda*)

O most high, almighty, good Lord God, to Thee belong praise, glory, honour and all blessing. 1093

Praised be my Lord God with all his creatures, and especially our brother the sun, who brings us the day and who brings us the light; fair is he and shines with a great splendour; O Lord, he signifies to us Thee.

Praised be my Lord for our sister the moon, and for the stars, the which he has set clear and lovely in the heaven.

Praised be my Lord for our sister water, who is very serviceable unto us and humble and precious and clean.

Praised be my Lord for our brother fire, through whom Thou givest us light in the darkness; and he is bright and pleasant and very mighty and strong.

Praised be my Lord for our mother the earth, the which doth sustain us and keep us, and bringeth forth divers fruit, and flowers of many colours, and grass.

Praised be my Lord for all those who pardon one another for his love's sake, and who endure weakness and tribulation; blessed are they who peaceably shall endure, for Thou, O most Highest, shalt give them a crown.

Praised be my Lord for our sister the death of the body.

Blessed are they who are found walking by thy most holy will.

Praise ye and bless ye the Lord, and give thanks unto him, and serve him with great humility.

St Francis of Assisi, 1181–1226

1094 O God, I praise Thee for the universe which Thou hast evolved over unending centuries, vitalizing matter with energy, bringing forth man as the peak of thy creating wisdom, working to unify mankind, initiating a process of spiritualizing. O Creator God, let me be a willing partner in building the universe of thy will and in divinizing man, in unity with Thee permeating thy creation with love and incorporating souls into the eternal.

G.A., based on Teilhard de Chardin

1095 How easy, Lord, it is for me to live with you.
How easy it is for me to believe in you.
When my understanding is perplexed by doubts
or on the point of giving up,
when the most intelligent men see no further
than the coming evening, and know not
what they shall do tomorrow,
you send me a clear assurance
that you are there and that you will ensure
that not all the roads of goodness are barred.

From the heights of earthly fame I look back
in wonder at the road that led
through hopelessness
to this place whence I can send
mankind a reflection of your radiance.
And whatever I in this life may yet reflect,
that you will give me;
And whatever I shall not attain,
that, plainly, you have purposed for others.

Alexander Solzhenitsyn

1096 O God, I call upon thee by thy great truth, by the truth of the light of thy gracious countenance, the truth of thy mighty throne, by that greatness and majesty, beauty and splendour, power and authority of thine that uphold thy throne, and by the reality of thy Names, hidden and concealed, which none of thy creatures has pondered.

O God, I call upon thee by the Name that thou hast set upon the night that it became dark, and upon the day that it became light, upon the heavens that they spread forth, and upon the earth that it came to rest, upon the mountains that they stood, and upon the seas and valleys that they flow, upon the fountains that they rise and the clouds that they give rain.

from *Prayers of the Naqshabandi Order*, 14th century

I would pray, O Lord, not only for myself but for all the household to which I belong, for all my friends and all my fellow workers, beseeching Thee to include them all in thy fatherly regard. I pray also— 1097

for all who will today be faced by any great decision:

for all who will today be engaged in settling affairs of moment in the lives of men and nations:

for all who are moulding public opinion in our time:

for all who write what other people read:

for all who are holding aloft the lamp of truth in a world of ignorance and sin:

for all whose hands are worn with too much toil, and for the unemployed whose hands today fall idle.

Let me now go forth, O Lord my God, to the work of another day, still surrounded by thy wonderful lovingkindnesses, still pledged to thy loyal service, still standing in thy strength and not my own.

John Baillie 1886–1960

The sins of the world, 1098
such dreadful sins.
not just the personal sins
but the solidarity of sin
greater than the total
of individual sins,
nuclear evil in endless fission,
O Lamb of God.

The sin of racial pride
that sees not the faith
that all men are divinely made
nor the riches of pigment
in portrait faces,
the same psychology
and religious search,
that each is the sibling
for whom Christ died.

The burgeoning greed
that never heeds the needs of others
involved in a merciless system,
looking only at profit and dividend,
the last of possessions
that cannot accompany us
at our last migration:

Take away these sins,
O Lamb of God.

The massive sin of war,
millions of lives impersonally destroyed,
billions of pounds wasted
on weapons, bombs,
truth enslaved,
the hungry still unfed,
grief stalking unnumbered homes:
Weep over us,
O Lamb of God.

The sin of the world,
alienation from thee
not just weakness
but evil intention,
organized and unrestrained
with its own momentum
leading to death:
O Lamb of God,
take away this sin.

Begin with me,
O Lamb of God,
forgive my sins,
cleanse my heart,
disarm my will
and let me fight
armed with thy truth, righteousness and love
with thy cross of love
incised upon my heart,
O Lamb of God.

G.A.

1099 O God of earth and altar,
Bow down and hear our cry;
Our earthly rulers falter,
Our people drift and die;
The walls of gold entomb us,
The swords of scorn divide,
Take not thy thunder from us,
But take away our pride.

From all that terror teaches,
From lies of tongue and pen,
From all the easy speeches
That comfort cruel men,
From sale and profanation
Of honour and the sword,
From sleep and from damnation,
Deliver us, good Lord!

G. K. Chesterton, 1874–1936

Cure thy children's warring madness, 1100
Bend our pride to thy control;
Shame our wanton selfish gladness,
Rich in goods and poor in soul.
Grant us wisdom, grant us courage,
Lest we miss thy Kingdom's goal.
Lest we miss thy Kingdom's goal.

Harry Emerson Fosdick, 1878–1969

Almighty God, from whom all thoughts of truth and peace proceed: 1101
Kindle, we pray thee, in the hearts of all men the true love of peace; and guide with thy pure and peaceable wisdom those who take counsel for the nations of the earth; that in tranquillity thy kingdom may go forward, till the earth is filled with the knowledge of thy love; through Jesus Christ our Lord.

Bishop Francis Paget, 1851–1911

May the memory of two world wars strengthen our efforts for peace, 1102
May the memory of those who died inspire our service to the living,
May the memory of past destruction move us to build for the future,
O God of peace,
O Father of souls,
O Builder of the Kingdom of Love.

G.A.

Lead me from death 1103
to Life, from falsehood to Truth
Lead me from despair
to Hope, from fear to Trust

Lead me from hate
to Love, from war to Peace

Let Peace fill our heart,
our world, our universe.

Written by Satish Kumar, a member of the Jain community, and adopted by the Prayer for Peace movement, 1981

1104 Prosper the labours of all Churches bearing the name of Christ and striving to further righteousness and faith in Him. Help us to place thy truth above our conception of it and joyfully to recognize the presence of thy Holy Spirit wherever he may choose to dwell among men. Teach us wherein we are sectarian in our intentions, and give us grace humbly to confess our fault to those whom in past days our Communion has driven from its fellowship by ecclesiastical tyranny, spiritual barrenness or moral inefficiency, that we may become worthy and competent to bind up in the Church the wounds of which we are guilty, and hasten the day when there shall be one fold under one Shepherd, Jesus Christ our Lord.

Bishop Brent of the USA, 1862–1929

1105 Lord of the nations, Creator, Redeemer and Father of all men, we thank thee for the vision of thy purpose to gather all nations into a commonwealth of justice, peace and brotherhood. We thank thee for the United Nations Organization with its aim to avoid war, with its service in production of food, its promotion of education and health, its care of refugees and children. Guide all the nations and their leaders, we pray thee, into deeper unity, greater efforts for peace, more generous contributions to human welfare, that men may live free from fear and free from want, and help thee to build the universe of thy love.

G.A.

1106 O God, who hast made of one blood all nations of men for to dwell on the face of the earth, and didst send thy blessed Son, Jesus Christ, to preach peace to them that are afar off, and to them that are nigh: Grant that all the peoples of the world may feel after thee and find thee; and hasten, O heavenly Father, the fulfilment of thy promise to pour out thy Spirit upon all flesh; through Jesus Christ our Saviour.

Bishop George Cotton, 1813–66

PRAYERS TOWARDS THE UNITY OF MANKIND

O God of many names, 1107
Lover of all nations,
We pray for peace
  in our hearts,
  in our homes,
  in our nations,
  in our world,
the peace of your will,
the peace of our need.

G.A.

We beseech thee, O God, the God of truth, 1108
That what we know not of things we ought to know
  Thou wilt teach us.

That what we know of truth
  Thou wilt keep us therein.

That what we are mistaken in, as men must be,
  Thou wilt correct.

That at whatsoever things we stumble
  Thou wilt yet establish us.

And from all things that are false
And from all knowledge that would be hurtful,
  Thou wilt evermore defend us,
    Through Jesus Christ, our Lord.

Bishop Brooke Foss Westcott, 1825–1901

O bless this people, Lord, who seek their own face 1109
under the mask and can hardly recognize it . . .

O bless this people that breaks its bond . . .

And with them, all the peoples of Europe,
All the peoples of Asia,
All the peoples of Africa,
All the peoples of America,
Who sweat blood and sufferings.

And see, in the midst of these millions of waves
The sea swell of the heads of my people.
And grant to their warm hands that they may clasp
The earth in a girdle of brotherly hands,
Beneath the rainbow of thy peace.

Leopold Sedar Senghor

1110 Here, Lord, before you tonight are the bodies of sleeping men:
The pure body of the tiny child,
The soiled body of the prostitute,
The vigorous body of the athlete,
The exhausted body of the factory worker,
The soft body of the playboy,
The surfeited body of the rich man,
The starved body of the poor man,
The paralysed body of the cripple,
All bodies, Lord, of all ages.

I offer them all to you, Lord, and ask you to bless them,
While they lie in silence, wrapped in your night . . .

May these bodies be developed, purified, transfigured,
By those who dwell in them.

Michel Quoist

1111 O thou Source of Love and Compassion
in the sufferings of all thy children,
we offer our compassion also
for the hungry, and the sick in body, mind or heart,
the depressed and the lonely,
all living in fear and under stress,
all stricken in grief,
the unemployed and the rejected,
and those burning with hatred.
Strengthen us to work for their healing
and inspire us to build with thee
the Kingdom of love
where none shall cause suffering to others
and all be caring, loving children of thine,
Our Compassionate, all-embracing Father,
everpresent, everloving,
never failing.

G.A.

1112 We offer our thanks to thee
for sending thy only Son to die for us all
In a world divided by colour bars,
how sweet a thing it is to know
that in thee we all belong to one family.

There are times when we
unprivileged people,
weep tears that are not loud but deep,
when we think of the suffering we experience.
We come to thee, our only hope and refuge.
Help us, O God, to refuse to be embittered
against those who handle us with harshness.
We are grateful to thee
for the gift of laughter at all times.
Save us from hatred of those who oppress us.
May we follow the spirit of thy Son Jesus Christ.

A Bantu pastor

O Eternal Word, 1113
who from the beginning hast revealed
glimpses of truth and righteousness
through prophets of many faiths:
We praise Thee
that all that is of value
is found fulfilled and perfected in Thee,
and all that is mistaken
finds its correction
in Thee.
Do Thou draw all seekers of truth and righteousness
to thyself,
and vouchsafe to them the unsearchable riches
that we have found in Thee, dear Lord.

G.A.

Gather us in, Thou love that fillest all; 1114
Gather our rival faiths within thy fold.
Rend each man's temple-veil and bid it fall,
That we may know that Thou hast been of old;
Gather us in.

Gather us in: we worship only Thee;
In varied names we stretch a common hand;
In diverse forms a common soul we see;
In many ships we seek one spirit-land;
Gather us in.

Each sees one colour of thy rainbow-light,
Each looks upon one tint and calls it heaven;
Thou art the fullness of our partial sight;
We are not perfect till we find the seven;
Gather us in.

G. D. Matheson, 1842–1906

1115 O Christ, my Way
to the God of all salvation,
Men of other faiths
believe they have their own salvation faith.
Be with them, dear Lord,
to encourage them on their way
to their own Jerusalem
so that we all find ourselves
with the spirits of just men made perfect
with the saints of every age and faith
in the presence of the Eternal God
the God of many names,
Creator, Lover, Saviour of us all.

G.A.

1116 A great crowd
that no man can number
out of every race and tongue,
Simple souls who want to be
what you want them to be
and to do what you want done
and to bear
all that is your will,
living by the truth they know,
eager for more,
forgetting themselves
but never forgetting you,
perfect simplicity
with regard to themselves,
perfect contentment
with all that comes their way,
perfect peace of mind
in utter self-forgetfulness,

realizing only
  the greatness
  and goodness,
  the all-ness
  of you,
    O King of saints.

G.A.

God be merciful unto us, and bless us: and show us the light of his countenance, and be merciful unto us; 1117
That thy way may be known upon earth: thy saving health among all nations.
Let the people praise thee, O God: yea, let all the people praise thee.
O let the nations rejoice and be glad: for thou shalt judge the folk righteously, and govern the nations upon earth.
Let the people praise thee, O God: let all the people praise thee.
Then shall the earth bring forth her increase: and God, even our own God, shall give us his blessing.
God shall bless us: and all the ends of the world shall fear him.

Psalm 67

Now may every living thing, young or old, weak or strong, living near or far, known or unknown, living or departed or yet unborn, may every living thing be full of bliss. 1118

The Buddha

Eternal God, whose image lies in the hearts of all people, 1119
We live among peoples whose ways are different from ours,
  whose faiths are foreign to us,
  whose tongues are unintelligible to us.
Help us to remember that you love all people with your great love,
  that all religion is an attempt to respond to you,
  that the yearnings of other hearts are much like our own and are known to you.
Help us to recognize you in the words of truth, the things of beauty, the actions of love about us.
We pray through Christ, who is a stranger to no one land more than another, and to every land no less than to another.

World Council of Churches, Vancouver Assembly, 1983

1120 Prayer, the Church's banquet, Angels' age,
God's breath in man returning to his birth,
The soul in paraphrase, heart in pilgrimage,
The Christian plummet, sounding heaven and earth;
Engine against the Almighty, sinner's tower,
Reversed thunder, Christ-side-piercing spear,
The six-days' world transposing in an hour,
A kind of tune, which all things hear and fear;
Softness, and peace, and joy, and love, and bliss,
Exalted manna, gladness of the best,
Heaven in ordinary, man well drest,
The milky way, the bird of Paradise,
Church-bells beyond the stars heard, the soul's blood,
The land of spices; something understood.

George Herbert, 1593–1633

1121 O Praise God in his holiness: praise him in the firmament of his power.
Praise him in his noble acts: praise him according to his excellent greatness.
Praise him in the sound of the trumpet: praise him upon the lute and harp.
Praise him in the cymbals and dances: praise him upon the strings and pipe.
Praise him upon the well-tuned cymbals: praise him upon the loud cymbals.
Let everything that hath breath: praise the Lord.

Psalm 150

Appendix

Notes on the Development of Eucharistic Prayers

(i) THE ANAPHORA OF ST BASIL

The eucharistic prayer ascribed to St Basil of Caesarea may well be the work of that great bishop and theologian, conforming the traditional prayer of his church in Cappadocia to the mature understanding of God as Trinity to whose formulation in the late fourth century he so largely contributed. For many centuries it was the prayer most often used in the Byzantine Church, until it was displaced by the shorter anaphora of St John Chrysostom. It is used now on twelve days in the Orthodox liturgical year. Like all eastern anaphoras it is a fixed prayer. It begins with praise to the Father, who has revealed himself in Jesus Christ, through whom the Holy Spirit has been manifested. Enabled by that Spirit, all creation praises the triune God in the words of the Sanctus. After the Benedictus the prayer resumes with lengthy praise of God for his mighty works in creation and redemption; above all for the coming of the Son into the world. This part of the prayer closely follows the Creed in its recital of the Son's incarnate life, his death and resurrection, and leads into the narrative of institution. The commemoration of Christ's saving deeds, including his second coming, is followed by the offering of the gifts and the invocation of the Holy Spirit to manifest them as the body and blood of Christ, so that those who receive them may be united in the communion of the Holy Spirit. The intercession concludes the prayer. The fourth eucharistic prayer in the modern Roman Missal follows the anaphora of St Basil in containing an extended account of the mystery of salvation.

(ii) THE ANAPHORA OF THE LITURGY OF ST JOHN CHRYSOSTOM

This is the normal eucharistic prayer of the Orthodox churches. The possibility certainly cannot be excluded that it is the work of the great Archbishop of Constantinople himself. It reflects the pattern and content of the eastern prayer as it had come to be by the end of the fourth century. By contrast with the Latin canon, which had a number of variable prefaces leading up to the Sanctus, it is a fixed prayer. It begins with thanksgiving to God for his own being, leading into the song of the angels. There follows thanksgiving for the redeeming work of Christ in his incarnate life, to which is attached the narrative of the institution. The commemoration of the death and resurrection of Christ and the offering of the gifts of bread and wine is followed by the invocation of the Holy Spirit to consecrate them and to impart to the communicants the fruits of salvation. The prayer concludes with an intercession.

(iii) THE OLD ROMAN CANON

The canon of the old Roman mass goes back to at least the fourth century. Once its use had spread throughout the western part of the Church, it remained the only eucharistic prayer in the Roman rite until the reforms instituted by the Second Vatican Council. The Roman eucharistic prayer normally gave brief thanks to God, amplified on feast days and other special occasions by the insertion of proper prefaces—not introductory passages, as their name might suggest, but proclamations of God's mighty works in redemption. The thanksgiving culminated in the Sanctus. The term canon came in time to be restricted to the sequence of prayers following the Benedictus. These prayers began by asking God to accept and bless the gifts of bread and wine being offered. There followed a commemoration of the living and of the saints. A further petition for the acceptance of the gifts led into the narrative of institution, containing the Lord's words which by the late Middle Ages were considered the formula of consecration. Two subsequent paragraphs reflected a far earlier understanding of consecration, going back perhaps to the second century, in which God was asked to accept the gifts and command them to be carried to his heavenly altar. Commemorations of the departed and of the saints preceded the final doxology.

(iv) THE FOURTH EUCHARISTIC PRAYER OF THE NEW ROMAN MISSAL

This prayer reflects the influence of the eastern tradition on the renewed Roman Catholic eucharist. Like the eastern prayers, it is fixed, and so is distinguished from the other three prayers, for which variable prefaces are provided. Praise of God for his own being leads into the Sanctus, which is followed by a recital of God's dealing with man from the Creation to Pentecost. It leads naturally into the first invocation of the Holy Spirit, praying for the consecration of the bread and wine. The narrative of the institution provides the ground upon which this request is made. It is followed by a characteristic feature of all the new Roman prayers: an acclamation said by the people, of the kind found in some eastern liturgies. The commemoration of the death and resurrection of Christ and the offering of the gifts is followed by a second invocation of the Holy Spirit, asking for the fruits of communion. Brief intercessions conclude the prayer, which is a rich synthesis of the biblical and patristic presentation of God's saving work.

(v) THE FIRST EUCHARISTIC PRAYER OF THE HOLY EUCHARIST, RITE I, OF THE EPISCOPAL CHURCH IN THE USA

This prayer represents a significant stage in the development of Anglican eucharistic worship. It came into the first American Prayer Book of 1790 from the Scottish Liturgy of 1764. That service embodied the aspirations of those more catholic-minded Anglicans who found the communion service of the English Book of Common Prayer of 1662 too little in accord with the eucharistic worship of the early church and of the eastern church which they believed had preserved the earliest tradition. Over a century before, the Scottish Prayer Book of 1637 had in its communion service leaned more towards the first English Prayer Book of 1549 than to the apparently more drastic revision of 1552, to which the 1662 Book largely adhered. The eucharistic prayer of 1549 had retained outwardly the basic shape of the Roman canon, though its content had been significantly altered. In the 1552 Book its component parts were rearranged in order to express more clearly a reformed understanding of the communion service. In particular what later came to be called the Prayer of Oblation was detached from the institution narrative and placed after the reception of communion. The Scottish Book of 1637 replaced it after the Prayer of Consecration, and included in it a commemoration of the passion, resurrection and ascension of Christ. To this prayer the authors of the Scottish Liturgy of 1764 added two elements: an offering to God of the bread and wine, deliberately omitted in 1549; and a petition that God would bless the gifts with his word and Holy Spirit. This prayer, found in the 1549 Book before the narrative of institution, was placed in the 1764 service after both it and the commemoration of Christ's saving deeds, in the eastern position, though not eastern in content. Liturgical revision, based on traditional Anglican material, has produced similar eucharistic prayers in other churches of the Anglican Communion.

(vi) THE THIRD EUCHARISTIC PRAYER OF RITE A, FROM THE ALTERNATIVE SERVICE BOOK OF THE CHURCH OF ENGLAND

Like the second eucharistic prayer in the Roman Missal, this prayer draws its inspiration from the eucharistic prayer found in the 'Apostolic Tradition' of Hippolytus of Rome, usually believed to represent a tradition of the early third century. It reflects both the return of western churches to early sources, and the growing convergence of Roman Catholic and Anglican traditions. It begins with thanksgiving, largely for the saving work of Christ, concluded by the Sanctus. An invocation of the Holy Spirit leads into the narrative of the institution, followed, as in the Roman prayers, by an acclamation of the people. The commemoration of the death and resurrection of Christ is followed by a thanksgiving for the royal priesthood of the Church, a very early feature of the prayer of Hippolytus. Having asked God to accept the Church's worship, the prayer concludes with a petition, again inspired by an ancient source, that the Spirit may gather all who share in the eucharist into the unity of God's Kingdom.

THE CHURCH OF SCOTLAND

The Church of Scotland, presbyterian in its ministry and in its succession, has in its *Book of Common Order* (1940) a liturgy which is close to the new liturgies, indeed anticipating them in some details, and authorizing alternative services of Holy Communion. It includes an order 'which may be used at a second table', when the communicants receive 'the elements already consecrated' at an earlier service. It also provides 'a short order, for use after an ordinary service, a marriage service, or when sickness or other circumstances make it desirable to use a shortened form'.

In many churches 'the sacrament of the Lord's Supper or Holy Communion' is not frequently celebrated. But emphasis is placed on preparation for the sacrament, and there is provided a service of preparation nearly as long as the actual celebration. Prayer no. 698 indicates its devotional character.

In all these services the words of administration 'in giving the bread and giving the cup' are:

> Take ye, eat ye; this is the body of Christ which is broken for you: this do in remembrance of Him.

and

> This cup is the new covenant in the blood of Christ, which is shed for many unto remission of sins: drink ye all of it.

In addition, the *Book of Common Order* provides a substantial service of thanksgiving 'for the Sacrament' which includes a prayer of remembrance, for 'all thy saints who have entered into rest, especially those with whom we have had communion here' (see no. 746).

EUCHARISTIC PRAYERS IN THE FREE CHURCHES

Historically Baptists, Congregationalists, Methodists, and Presbyterians have valued the freedom of permitting biblically instructed ministers in a loose relationship with their congregations pastorally to pray as moved by the Holy Spirit. Recently, however, the liturgical committees of these denominations in both Britain and the United States have produced service books in which eucharistic prayers serve increasingly as models for ministers to use.

Such service books appear to have based their eucharistic prayers upon five principles. The first is the need for a biblical warrant in the communion service and for a genuinely Christian content. This is exemplified by the anamnesis or memorial reference to the inauguration of the Lord's Supper by Our Lord himself, the repetition of the prophetic manual acts of fraction and libation, the use of the Lord's Prayer, and eucharistia or thanksgiving for the gift of God in creation as also in redemption.

The second principle is the importance of claiming the ecumenical inheritance of Christianity in all its fullness. This means that eucharistic prayers include the western structure of the canon together with the eastern form of consecration in the *epiklesis*. Most prayers include the salutation, the *Sursum corda*, the seasonal Preface, the *Tersanctus*, the *Benedictus qui venit*, and a concluding oblation. Thus increasingly services which were often memorialist in character, are more often virtualist theologically, and they not infrequently express a belief in the real presence of the risen Lord.

A third principle in designing eucharistic prayers is to allow for the firm order of a liturgy, to which are added free prayers and silent prayer.

In the fourth place, following the most recent practice in Roman Catholic and Anglican liturgies, there is the provision of several alternative eucharistic prayers to provide variety and flexibility within order, and to allow the use of eucharistic prayers from other traditions, especially in ecumenical interchanges.

The fifth and final principle is a desire to include both classical and contemporary prayers in these service books, which give equal emphasis to the Liturgy of the Word and the Liturgy of the Lord's Supper.

The 1980 *A Book of Services* of the British United Reformed Church gives an excellent summary of the aims of the eucharistic prayers of all the Free Churches:

> The basic elements and order of the eucharistic prayer are:
> the recital of the mighty acts of God in creation and redemption, often with special thanksgiving according to the season of the year;
> the commemoration with bread and wine of the sacrificial death and resurrection of Christ 'until he come';
> invocation of the Holy Spirit, praying that what we do in obedience to Christ may be united to his perfect sacrifice and that we may be made one in him and receive the benefits of his passion and victory.

In conclusion it is noted that the eucharistic prayers of the Free Churches are not ecclesiastically binding. Ministers are free to use them as printed or to adapt them or even disregard them. Moreover, the eucharist is rarely held on every Lord's Day, but more commonly at monthly intervals. However, the attendance on communion Sundays is usually a high proportion of the local congregation.

The Methodist Church

The United Methodist Church in the USA produced in 1972 a Communion Service Book entitled 'At the Lord's Table', with no less than 22 forms of the Great Thanksgiving or Eucharistic Prayer. These are all the same in structure and in most of the wording, but include what is called in other Churches a special preface for the great festivals of the year or for such occasions as harvest, weddings, funerals and memorial services, thus making it easy for the minister to use.

All these services are close to the revised liturgies now being used in other Churches, showing that there has been consultation among the revising bodies. The liturgical revisions show great similarity in structure, content and wording, and also in devotional faith and worship which could pave the way to mutual recognition of our most sacred forms of eucharistic worship.

John Wesley intended that the Methodist people would conform to the usages of the Book of Common Prayer, and for America he issued an abridgement known as the Sunday Service. The changes are not very radical though some of them correspond to what the Puritans had desired at the Savoy Conference. The Absolution is in the lay form, and there are certain emendations which make the service somewhat less penitential. Many Wesleyans in this country much preferred the 1662 Book of Common Prayer rather than 'our venerable Father's abridgement'. The Wesleyans and, from 1932, the Methodist Church were very much governed in their liturgical practice by the 1662 Book, and for some churches the order of morning prayer was mandatory in their trust deeds. The various Methodist sects who proliferated in the nineteenth century preferred freer forms of service, and did not authorize office books like the Wesleyans; but they did provide books of eucharistic orders and prayers, not necessarily in the hands of their people, but for the guidance of ministers. The orders tended to be more of the Free Church type, with the sacrament carried round the seated people, but there was material from the Book of Common Prayer.

Acknowledgements

The editor and publisher gratefully acknowledge permission to reproduce copyright material in this anthology.

Wherever possible the following list is arranged alphabetically by the ascription given at the foot of each prayer. Where no suitable author or title appears in the text the prayers are listed separately under the section in which they occur (e.g. Prayers of Adoration, Prayers of the Church etc.). The references are to the numbers of the prayers.

All rights in respect of the Authorized King James Version of the Holy Bible and the Book of Common Prayer 1662 are vested in the Crown in the United Kingdom and controlled by Royal Letters Patent. (1; 73–99; 133; 567; 577–8; 585–6; 591; 593; 597; 599; 602; 606; 609; 618; 627; 629; 634; 652; 655; 663; 673; 682; 687; 691; 695–6; 700; 709–13; 716–19; 722; 740; 743; 747; 749–50; 761; 773; 780; 781; 784)

Extracts from the Revised Standard Version of the Bible, are copyright 1946, 1952, 1971 by the Division of Christian Education of the National Council of the Churches of Christ in the USA. Used by permission. (37; 39; 40–72; 100–32; 149; 154; 160; 167; 177; 181; 191; 194; 236; 269; 270; 294; 341; 389; 391; 401; 416; 430; 470; 489; 528; 561; 562; 793–808; 1117)

Prayers from the 1928 Prayer Book and prayers and material from The Alternative Service Book 1980 are © Central Board of Finance of the Church of England and are reproduced with permission. (134, 603, 701, 711, 715, 727, 734, 745, 752, 768, 769)

The English translation of the *Exsultet* (657), the Blessing of Water (689), the prayers for the Preparation of the Altar and the Gifts (725), Eucharistic Prayer IV (732), and the Lamb of God (735) from *The Roman Missal* © 1973, International Committee on English in the Liturgy, Inc. All rights reserved.

Prayers of Adoration

Tao: from *Operation Redemption* by Sir George Trevelyan (1981). Used by permission of Thorsons Publishing Group Ltd. (29). Brahman: ibid. (30).

Prayers of Christians: Personal and Occasional

Dependence (140); Affirmation (155); Daily (330–1); Penitence (347; 355); Right Living (377; 382; 392; 398); Protection (419; 420; 426; 432; 435); Suffering (440; 442; 449); Devotion (485) and Gifts of the Spirit (512): all from *Morning, Noon and Night* edited by the Revd John Carden. Reprinted by permission of The Church Missionary Society.

Penitence: 'O Lord, remember not only the men and women of good will . . .', quoted in *Blessings*, edited by Mary Craig, © 1979 by Mary Craig and published by Hodder & Stoughton Ltd. (367)

Prayers of the Church

Orthodox: from *Festal Menaion: The Service Book of the Orthodox Church*, translated by Mother Mary and Archimandrite Kallistos Ware (614; 621; 632;

647; 775; 779): and from *The Lenten Triodion*, translated from the original Greek by Mother Mary and Archimandrite Kallistos Ware. (628; 633; 642; 648; 653–4; 766; 768; 782) All reprinted by permission of Faber & Faber Ltd.

Prayers from Other Traditions of Faith

Jewish: from *Forms of Prayer for Jewish Worship: Daily, Sabbath and Occasional Prayers* (1977). Used by permission of The Reform Synagogue of Great Britain. (836–45; 848; 850)

Indian: from *The Vedic Experience* by R. Panniker, published and copyrighted by Darton, Longman & Todd Ltd., London. Used by permission. (853–863)

from *Morning, Noon and Night*, edited by the Revd John Carden. Used by permission of the Church Missionary Society. (905)

Buddhist Spirituality: pp. 439–46. Translation copyrighted by the Pali Text Society. Used by permission. (916–20; 922–4; 927–33)

Chinese: Taoist Liturgy

from *Chinese Religions* by D. Howard Smith. Used by permission of Weidenfeld & Nicolson Ltd. (963–66)

from *Science and Civilisation in China*, vol. 5, by Joseph Needham. Used by permission of Cambridge University Press. (967–8)

from *Taoism and the Rite of Cosmic Renewal*, by Michael Saso. Used by permission of the translator. (969–72)

Muslim

from the Qur'ān, (1008–20) translated by Kenneth Cragg. Used by permission.
from Mukhtasar Ad'iyat Ramadān, translated by Kenneth Cragg in *The Muslim World Quarterly*, vol. 47.3, July 1957, pp. 210–23. Used by permission. (1021)

Prayers used in the 7th circuit of the K'abah in Mecca: translated by Kenneth Cragg in *The Muslim World Quarterly*, vol. 45.3, July 1955, pp. 269–80. Used with permission. (1025–6)

Primal

from *Prayers of African Religion* by Professor John Mbiti. Used by permission of The Society for Promoting Christian Knowledge. (1054–7; 1059–67; 1072)

Japanese

from *Norito: A New Translation of the Ancient Japanese Ritual Prayers*, by Donald L. Philippi (The Institute for Japanese Culture and Classics, Kokugaku-in University, Tokyo, 1959). Used by permission of the author. (1073–5; 1079–80)

Aeschylus: from *An Anthology of Prayers*. By permission of A. Stanley T. Fisher. (1003)

An African Canticle: from *Morning, Noon and Night*, edited by the Revd John Carden. Used by permission of the Church Missionary Society. (34)

from *Ahmad al Tijani*, translated by Kenneth Cragg. Used by permission. (1038)

ACKNOWLEDGEMENTS

Alcuin: from *More Latin Lyrics* by Helen Waddell, edited by Sr Felicitas Corrigan. Used by permission. (242; 274; 340; 424; 479)

Angilbert: from ibid. (463)

Anon., 3rd–6th Century: from *Early Christian Prayers* by A. Hamman (Longman, 1961). (7)

Saint Anselm: from 'Proslogion' from *The Prayers and Meditations of Saint Anselm*, trans. Benedicta Ward (Penguin Classics 1973) p. 266. Copyright © Benedicta Ward, 1973. Reprinted by permission of Penguin Books Ltd. (183)

George Appleton: from *In His Name* (rev. ed. 1978) (18); and from *Daily Prayer and Praise* (457), by permission of Lutterworth Press; from *Journey for a Soul*, (Collins) used by permission of the author (208); from *Jerusalem Prayers for the World Today* (238; 452; 1102), from *One Man's Prayers* (241; 282; 287; 460; 498; 501; 533; 534; 1111; 1113; 1115), from *Acts of Devotion* (514; 559), and from *The Word is the Seed* (1098; 1116). Reprinted by permission of The Society for Promoting Christian Knowledge.

Apuleius: from *The Golden Ass*, trans. W. Adlington, revised by S. Gaselee. Loeb Classical Library (Harvard University Press: William Heinemann Ltd.). By permission. (1002)

St Augustine: from *The Confessions of St Augustine*, trans. F. J. Sheed and published by Sheed & Ward Ltd, London. Used by permission. (173; 175)

Authorized Daily Prayer Book, reprinted by permission of Singer's Prayer-Book Publication Committee. (22; 830)

Avatamsaka Sutra: from *The World of the Buddha*, edited by Lucien Stryk. By permission of Grove Press, Inc. (941)

Rahmān Bāba: from *Selections from Rahmān Bāba* (Poul Kristensen, 1977), translated by Jens Enevoldsen and used with his permission. (1040–3)

Bahá'í Prayers: reprinted by permission of the Bahá'í Publishing Trust. (35; 1053)

John Baillie: from *A Diary of Private Prayer* (1936). By permission of Oxford University Press. (220; 312; 352; 396; 414; 456; 1097)

Bede: from *More Latin Lyrics* by Helen Waddell, edited by Sr Felicitas Corrigan. Used by permission. (421)

Bernard, SSF: Used by permission of the author. (193)

Joseph L. Bernardin: from *The Journalist's Prayer Book*, edited by Alfred P. Klausler and John De Mott. Copyright © 1982 Augsburg Publishing House. Used by permission. (406)

Boethius: from *More Latin Lyrics* by Helen Waddell, edited by Sr Felicitas Corrigan. Used by permission. (14)

Bunan: from *The World of the Buddha*, edited by Lucien Stryk. By permission of Grove Press, Inc. (955)

Canadian Prayer Book: excerpts from the Book of Common Prayer of the Anglican Church of Canada, © The General Synod of the Anglican Church of Canada, 1962. Printed with permission. (776; 782)

Carmina Gadelica: edited by Alexander Carmichael. Used by permission of the Scottish Academic Press Ltd. (264; 548)

Teilhard de Chardin: from *La Messe Sur Le Monde* (12; 525) and from *Le Milieu Divin*. (182; 369; 450)

G. K. Chesterton: Used by permission of Oxford University Press. (1099)

ACKNOWLEDGEMENTS

Cleanthes, *Hymn to Zeus*; from *Hellenistic Religions*, edited by Frederick C. Grant. Copyright © 1953 by Macmillan Publishing Company, renewed 1981 by the Estate of Frederick Clifton Grant. Reprinted by permission of Macmillan Publishing Company. (992)

Clement of Rome: from *Early Christian Writings*, translated by Maxwell Staniforth (Penguin Classics 1968). Copyright © Maxwell Staniforth, 1968. Reprinted by permission of Penguin Books Ltd. (1089)

Father Edmund Colledge: translations from *The Way*. Used by permission. (473; 521; 551–2)

David B. Collins: from *The Journalist's Prayer Book*, edited by Alfred P. Klausler and John De Mott. Copyright © 1982 Augsburg Publishing House. Used by permission. (214)

Consecration of a Bishop, Chaldean Rite: from *Early Christian Prayers* by A. Hamman (Longman, 1961). (703)

Contemporary Prayers for Public Worship: edited by Caryl Micklem (1967). Reprinted by permission of SCM Press Ltd. (published in the USA by William B. Eerdmans Publ. Co., Michigan). (235; 356; 454; 526)

J. L. Cowie: from *Worship Now*, published by The Saint Andrew Press, Edinburgh 1972. Reproduced with permission. (405)

Margaret Cropper: from *New Life: A Book of Prayers* (Longman, 1942). Used by permission of Mrs Anne Hopkinson, Literary Executor. (293)

Margaret Cropper: from *Draw Near*. Used by permission of The Society for Promoting Christian Knowledge. (146; 156; 333; 461; 481)

Dante: from *Paradiso*, Canto XXIII, trans. by Dorothy Sayers, 11, 52–4, 67, 70, 72 (Penguin Books). Used by permission of David Higham Associates Ltd. (812)

Hans Denck: from *Mutual Irradiation: A Quaker View of Ecumenism*, by Douglas V. Steere (1971). Reprinted by permission of Pendle Hill Publications, Wallingford, PA 19086, USA. (190)

Chandra Devanesen: from *Morning, Noon and Night*, edited by the Revd John Carden. Used by permission of the Church Missionary Society. (901)

St Dimitrii of Rostov: from *The Orthodox Way*, by Bishop Kallistos Ware. Used by permission of Mowbray & Co., Ltd. (5)

Eusebius: from *Five Stages of Greek Religion*, by Gilbert Murray (1925). Used by permission of Oxford University Press. (999)

Forms of Prayer (Jewish): from *Forms of Prayer for Jewish Worship: Daily, Sabbath and Occasional Prayer* (1977). Used by permission of The Reform Synagogue of Great Britain. (23–4)

Harry Emerson Fosdick: Used by permission of Dr Elinor Downs. (1100)

Charles de Foucauld: from *In Search of the Beyond*, by Carlo Carretto published and copyrighted 1975 by Darton, Longman and Todd Ltd., London and used by permission. (245)

St Francis of Assisi: from *St Francis of Assisi Omnibus of Sources: Early Writings and Early Biographies*, edited by Marion A. Habig OFM. Copyright © 1973 Franciscan Herald Press, 1434 W. 51st Street, Chicago, IL 60609. Used with permission. (170; 217; 550; 1093)

Getsudo: from *The World of the Buddha*, edited by Lucien Stryk. Used by permission of Grove Press Inc. (956)

ACKNOWLEDGEMENTS

Ann Griffiths: from *Homage to Ann Griffiths*. Used by permission of Church in Wales Publications. (397)

Gabrielle Hadingham: Used with permission. (268)

Hakugai: from *The World of the Buddha*, edited by Lucien Stryk. Used by permission of Grove Press, Inc. (957)

Hakuin: from *The Zen Koan*, by Isshu Miura and Ruth Fuller Sasaki. Copyright © 1965 by Ruth Fuller Sasaki. Used by permission of Harcourt Brace Jovanovich, Inc. (959)

Dag Hammarskjold: from *Markings*, translated by Leif Sjoberg and W. H. Auden. Copyright © 1964 by Alfred A. Knopf Inc. and Faber & Faber Ltd. Used by permission of the publishers. (248; 257; 329; 817)

Heart Sutra: from *Buddhist Wisdom Books*, translated by Edward Conze. Used by permission of Unwin Hyman Ltd. (939)

Hermetic Corpus: from *Gnosticism: An Anthology* (edited by R. N. Grant, Collins, 1961). (998)

Hildebert: from *More Latin Lyrics*, by Helen Waddell, edited by Sr Felicitas Corrigan. Used by permission. (509)

Hindu Scriptures (*Rig-Veda*): from *Prayers for the Future of Mankind* (ed. Solomons, Wolfe Publishing Ltd., 1975). (1092)

Michael Hollings and Etta Gullick: from *You Must Be Joking Lord* (163); from *As Was His Custom: Prayers and Readings for Each Day of the Year* (297; 488); from *It's Me O Lord* (510; 304); from *The One Who Listens* (438) and from *The Shade of His Hand* (480). All reprinted by permission of the publisher Mayhew McCrimmon Ltd., 10–12 High Street, Great Wakering, Essex. All rights reserved.

S. C. Hughson: from *With Christ In God* (1948). Used by permission of The Society for Promoting Christian Knowledge. (275)

Cecil Hunt: from *Uncommon Prayers*. First published 1948. Used by permission of Hodder & Stoughton Ltd. (370)

Kamil Husain: from *City of Wrong*, translated by Kenneth Cragg (Djambatan Publishers, 1959). Used by permission of the translator. (1048; 1097)

Martin Israel: from *The Pain That Heals*. © 1981 by Martin Israel. Used by permission of Hodder & Stoughton Ltd. and The Crossroad Publishing Co. (247)

Pope John XXIII: from *Journal of a Soul*, translated by Dorothy White. Reprinted by permission of Geoffrey Chapman, a division of Cassell Publ. Ltd., Artillery House, Artillery Row, London SW1P 1RT, and Doubleday & Co., Inc. (226)

St John Chrysostom: from *Manual of Eastern Orthodox Prayers*. Used by permission of The Society for Promoting Christian Knowledge. (524)

St John of the Cross: from *Complete Works*, translated by E. Allison Peers (Burns & Oates, 1963). (471–2)

Julian of Norwich: from *Revelations of Divine Love*, edited by Dom Roger Hudleston OSB (Burns & Oates, 1952). Used by permission of Search Press Ltd. (791; 814)

Keizan Zenji: from *Zen Mind, Beginner's Mind* by Sunryu Suzuki. Used by permission of John Weatherhill Inc. (960)

Søren Kierkegaard: from *The Prayers of Kierkegaard* by P. F. Lefevre. Copyright 1956 The University of Chicago. Used with permission. (192; 230; 310; 496)

ACKNOWLEDGEMENTS

From *The Journals of Kierkegaard 1834–1854*, translated by Alexander Dru (Collins/Fontana, 1958). (790)

Kontakion for Love: from *Manual of Eastern Orthodox Prayers*. Used by permission of The Society for Promoting Christian Knowledge. (276–7)

Lohan Hoshang of Shōshu: from *On Indian Mahayana Buddhism* by D. T. Suzuki. Used by permission of Unwin Hyman Ltd. (953)

The Lutheran Book of Worship: Copyright © 1978. Used by permission of Augsburg Publishing House. (714)

F. B. Macnutt: from *The Prayer Manual* (Mowbray & Co., Ltd., 1951). Used with permission. (273)

from Manāsik al-Haji wa Ad' iyat al-Tawāf, translated by Kenneth Cragg in *The Muslim World Quarterly*, Vol. 45.3, July 1955, pp. 269–80. Used by permission. (1024; 1029)

W. R. Matthews: from *Seven Words*. First published 1933. Used by permission of Hodder & Stoughton Ltd. (434; 546)

Edward Maycock: Previously unpublished prayer. Used by permission of Dr James Maycock. (240)

Metropolitan Philaret of Moscow: from *Manual of Eastern Orthodox Prayers*. Used by permission of The Society for Promoting Christian Knowledge. (299)

Eric Milner-White: from *My God My Glory* (3; 145; 198; 311; 354; 404; 504; 516; 535) and from *Procession of Passion Prayers* (303; 346; 484). Used by permission of The Society for Promoting Christian Knowledge.

Eric Milner-White and G. W. Briggs: from *Daily Prayer* (1941). By permission of Oxford University Press. (515)

Muso: from *The World of the Buddha*, edited by Lucien Stryk. Used by permission of Grove Press, Inc. (958)

National Pastoral Congress, Liverpool: Used by permission of the Archbishop of Liverpool. (278)

Nicolas of Cusa: from *The Golden Sequence* by Evelyn Underhill. Used by permission of Methuen & Co. (4)

Reinhold Niebuhr: from *Justice and Mercy*, ed. Ursula Niebuhr (Harper & Row, 1974), epigraph written in 1943 (301), pp. 11, 12 and 13 (393; 394; 543): from *Hymns of Worship*, ed. Ursula Niebuhr (Association Press, New York, 1939) p. 224 (201). All reprinted by permission of Ursula M. Niebuhr, D.D., Literary Executor.

Origen: from *Early Christian Prayers* by A. Hamman (Longman, 1961). (342)

St Paulinus of Aquileia: from *More Latin Lyrics* by Helen Waddell, edited by Sr Felicitas Corrigan. Used by permission. (427)

Pericles: from *An Anthology of Prayers*. Used by permission of A. Stanley T. Fisher. (1005)

Plato: from *An Anthology of Prayers*. Used by permission of A. Stanley T. Fisher. (1004)

from *Prayers of the Naqshabandi Order*: translated by Kenneth Cragg in *Alive to God* (OUP, 1970). Used with permission. (1096)

Proclus: from *Hellenistic Religions*, edited by Frederick C. Grant, Copyright © 1953 by Macmillan Publishing Company, renewed 1981 by the Estate of

Frederick Clifton Grant. Reprinted by permission of Macmillan Publishing Company. (994–996)

Prudentius: from *More Latin Lyrics* by Helen Waddell, edited by Sr Felicitas Corrigan. Used with permission. (522)

A Pygmy Hymn: from *Prayers of African Religion* by Professor John Mbiti. Used by permission of The Society for Promoting Christian Knowledge. (33)

Michel Quoist: from *Prayers of Life* (1965). Used by permission of Gill & Macmillan Ltd., Dublin and of Sheed & Ward, 115 E. Armour Blvd., Kansas City, MO. (222; 357; 1110)

Karl Rahner: from *Prayers for Meditation*, translated by R. Brennan (Burns & Oates Ltd 1977). (1088)

Yves Raquin, SJ: from *Paths to Contemplation*, translated by P. Barrett. Used by permission of Anthony Clarke Books. (6)

Bishop Basil Roberts: Used by permission of The United Society for the Propagation of the Gospel. (253)

The Roman Missal: Used by permission of Burns & Oates Ltd. (630; 656–7; 724; 736; 789)

Sister Ruth, SLG: Used with permission. (17; 474; 500)

Sue Ryder and Leonard Cheshire: from *Blessings*, edited by Mary Craig (Hodder & Stoughton, 1979). Used by permission of the authors. (446)

Santideva: from *The Path of Light*, translated by L. D. Barrett. Used by permission of John Murray (Publishers) Ltd. (942–5); and from *The Heart of Buddhist Meditation*, translated by Nyanoponika Thera. Used by permission of Century Hutchinson Ltd. (946)

Saraha: from *Buddhist Texts Through the Ages*, edited by Edward Conze. Used by permission of Bruno Cassirer (Publishers) Ltd. (938)

Scottish Book of Common Prayer: Used by permission of the Publications Committee of the Scottish Episcopal Church. (221; 620; 646; 678)

Léopold Sédar Senghor: 'Prayer for Peace', Part V, Abridged, from *Selected Poems of Léopold Sédar Senghor*, translated John Reed and Clive Wake. Copyright Editions du Seuil 1948. Translation © OUP 1964. Used by permission of Editions du Seuil, Georges Borchardt Inc. and Oxford University Press. (1109)

Sengts'an, The Third Patriarch: from *Buddhist Texts Through the Ages*, edited by Edward Conze. Used by permission of Bruno Cassirer (Publishers) Ltd. (951)

Bishop Serapion: from *Early Christian Prayers* by A. Hamman (Longman, 1961). (172)

Gilbert Shaw: from *The Face of Love: Meditations on the Way of the Cross* (rev. ed., 1977, SLG Press). Copyright The Sisters of the Love of God. Used with permission. (16; 261; 353; 453)

Alexander Solzhenitsyn: World © by Alexander Solzhenitsyn, translated by Alwyn and Dermot McKay by permission of Claude Durand. (1095)

Soyen Shaku: from *Zen for Americans* (D. T. Suzuki, trs.). Published by The Open Court Publishing Company, La Salle, Illinois. (961–2)

Jan Struther: from *Enlarged Songs of Praise*. Used by permission of Oxford University Press. (375)

ACKNOWLEDGEMENTS

Sadhu Sundar Singh: from *Morning Noon and Night*, edited by the Revd John Carden. Used by permission of the Church Missionary Society. (900)

A Sumerian Poet: from *An Anthology of Prayers*. Used by permission of A. Stanley T. Fisher. (1006)

from *The Sutra of the Sixth Patriarch*: in *A Buddhist Bible* edited by Dwight Goddard. Copyright 1938, 1966 by E. P. Dutton. Reprinted by permission of the Publisher, E. P. Dutton, a division of NAL Penguin Inc.

St Symeon, The New Theologian: from *The Orthodox Way* by Bishop Kallistos Ware. Used by permission of Mowbray & Co., Ltd. (579)

Rabindranath Tagore: from *Gitanjali* (892–4; 896–9) and from *Fruit Gathering* (895), in *Collected Poems and Plays*. Copyright 1916 by Macmillan Publishing Co., Inc., renewed 1944 by Rabindranath Tagore. Used by permission of Macmillan, London & Basingstoke, and Macmillan Publishing Co., Inc.

from *Tahárat al-Qulúb*: translated by Kenneth Cragg. Used with permission. (1033–5)

John Taylor, Bishop of Winchester: Used by permission of the author. (210)

William Temple: from *Readings in St John's Gospel* (prayer commencing 'Worship is the submission . . .', and 144; 572); prayers 213 and 539 were taken from *The Prayer Manual* (ed. F. B. McNutt, Mowbray 1951). All used by permission of Macmillan, London & Basingstoke.

from *The Tibetan Book of the Dead*, by W. Y. Evans-Wentz (3/e., 1956) (950) and from *The Tibetan Book of the Great Liberation* by W. Y. Evans-Wentz (1968) (949). Used by permission of Oxford University Press.

Tibetan Ceremonies: in *Buddhist Himalaya* by D. L. Snellgrove. Used by permission of Bruno Cassirer (Publishers) Ltd. (947–8)

Tukaram: from *An Indian Peasant Mystic*, ed. J. S. Hoyland (Prinit Press, Dublin, USA). Used with permission. (885–90)

The United Society for the Propagation of the Gospel. Used with permission. (415; 425; 436; 441)

Vespers of Pentecost: from *The Orthodox Way* by Bishop Kallistos Ware. Used by permission of Mowbray & Co., Ltd. (671)

Vespers of Ascension: from *Byzantine Daily Worship*, by the Most Revd Joseph Raya and Baron Jose de Vinck. Used by permission of Alleluia Press, New Jersey. (669)

The Way: excerpts used by permission of the Editor. (13; 136; 161; 343–4; 363; 495)

Simone Weil: from *Waiting on God* (Collins/Fontana, 1951). (792; 818)

Zoroastrian: from *Let Us Pray to Ahura Mazda* by Noshir H. Vajifdar. Used with permission. (974–91)

ADDENDA

Book of Common Order: reproduced by kind permission of The Saint Andrew Press on behalf of the Church of Scotland's Panel of Worship. (698; 746)

St Hildegarde: trs. Charles Williams, originally published in *The House of the Octopus* by Charles Williams (London: Edinburgh House Press, 1945), reprinted in his *Collected Plays* (OUP, 1963). (508)

ACKNOWLEDGEMENTS

Gerard Manley Hopkins: extracts from 'Jesu Dulcis Memoria' and 'S. Thomae Aquinatis' from *The Poems of Gerard Manley Hopkins* (4th ed. 1967) ed. W. H. Gardner and N. H. Mackenzie. © The Society of Jesus 1967. (465; 520). Reprinted by permission of Oxford University Press on behalf of The Society of Jesus.

Blaise Pascal: reprinted from Pascal: *Pensées*, trs. A. J. Krailsheimer (Penguin Classics, 1966). Copyright © A. J. Krailsheimer, 1966. Used by permission of Penguin Books Ltd. (815)

Evelyn Underhill: from *Meditations and Prayers* (privately printed). (407)

Although every effort has been made to trace and contact copyright holders in a few instances this has not been possible. If notified the publishers will be pleased to rectify any omission in future editions.

Index of Authors and Sources

Numbers refer to prayers. More detailed sources for some of the prayers may be found in the Acknowledgements.

INDEX OF AUTHORS AND SOURCES

INDEX OF AUTHORS AND SOURCES

INDEX OF AUTHORS AND SOURCES

INDEX OF AUTHORS AND SOURCES

Subject Index

Numbers refer to prayers

SUBJECT INDEX